PERSISTENT ILLUSIONS

PERSISTENT ILLUSIONS

VISUAL CULTURE AND HISTORICAL MEMORY IN INTERWAR HUNGARY

NÓRA VESZPRÉMI

CORNELL UNIVERSITY PRESS

Ithaca and London

This book is part of a project that has received funding from the European Research Council (ERC) under the European Union's Horizon 2020 research and innovation programme (Continuity/Rupture: Art and Architecture in Central Europe 1918–1939 [CRAACE], grant agreement No 786314).

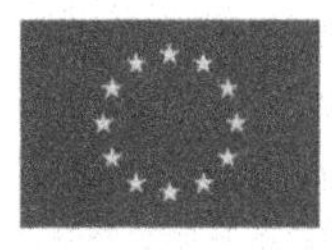
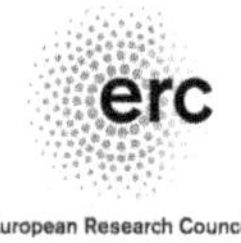

European Research Council
Established by the European Commission

First published 2025 by Cornell University Press

Librarians: A CIP catalog record for this book is available from the Library of Congress.

ISBN 9781501782299 (hardcover)
ISBN 9781501782305 (paperback)
ISBN 9781501782312 (epub)
ISBN 9781501782329 (pdf)

CONTENTS

List of Illustrations   vi

Acknowledgments   ix

Introduction   1

1. Spectacles of Renewal   29

2. Irredentist Spacetime   69

3. History into Landscape   102

4. The Archive and the Ruin   136

5. Heroes and Rebels   169

    Epilogue   204

Notes   219

Bibliography   253

Index   279

ILLUSTRATIONS

0.1. View of Freedom Square, Budapest, with the
Irredentist Sculpture Group in 1943. — 2

1.1. Decorations for 1 May 1919 in Budapest with busts of
Lenin and Karl Liebknecht. — 35

1.2. Page from the 22 November 1919 issue of the magazine
Képes Krónika with scenes from Horthy's procession on
16 November 1919. — 37

1.3. Andor Dudits, *Oath in the Vérmező*, sketch, 1920,
Hungarian National Gallery, Budapest. — 40

1.4. Mihály Bíró, *In the Woods of Orgovány (Horthy V)*, 1920,
National Széchényi Library, Budapest. — 48

1.5. Mihály Bíró, *The Beasts (Horthy XVII)*, 1920,
National Széchényi Library, Budapest. — 49

1.6. Tibor Gönczi-Gebhardt, poster for the Saint Emeric
jubilee, 1930, National Széchényi Library, Budapest. — 55

1.7. Ferenc Sidló, *Saint Stephen*, Székesfehérvár, 1938. — 60

1.8. Sándor Légrády, stamp series for the Saint Stephen
jubilee, 1938. — 61

1.9. Noémi Ferenczy, *Saint Stephen tapestry*, 1940–1941,
Jósa András Museum, Nyíregyháza. — 65

2.1. János Pásztor, *East*, 1920, and Zsigmond Kisfaludi Strobl,
North, 1920. — 72

2.2. Ferenc Sidló, *West*, 1920, and István Szentgyörgyi, *South*, 1920. — 72

2.3. Cover of Ottó Légrády, ed., *Justice for Hungary: The Cruel
Errors of Trianon* (Budapest: Légrády Brothers, 1930). — 87

2.4. Postcard depicting the *Reliquary Country Flag*, c. 1929. — 91

2.5. Lajos Márton, series of irredentist stamps, c. 1928,
National Széchényi Library, Budapest. — 94

2.6. Irredentist memorial in the Maria Theresa barracks,
Budapest, 1927. — 95

2.7. Sándor Petten, *Hungarian for Hungarian*, series of stamps, 1939.   97

3.1. Nándor Lajos Varga, *Turkish Wars (Hungarian Past XXII)*,
early 1930s/1940.   103

3.2. Nándor Lajos Varga, *1919 (Hungarian Past XXXVIII)*,
early 1930s/1940.   104

3.3. Ernő Jeges, *The Castle of Beckó/Beckov*, illustration from
the volume *Vérző Magyarország*, ed. Dezső Kosztolányi
(Budapest: Pallas Nyomda, 1921), 81.   108

3.4. Nándor Lajos Varga, *The Miracle Stag (Hungarian Past I)*,
early 1930s/1940.   113

3.5. Jenő Haranghy, *The Unity of Hungary*, poster, 1919,
National Széchényi Library, Budapest.   117

3.6. Ferdiš Duša, *At the Black Váh* (from the series *Down the Váh*),
1930–1933, Slovenská národná galéria, Bratislava.   121

3.7. Ferdiš Duša, *Hričov* (from the series *Down the Váh*),
1930–1933, Slovenská národná galéria, Bratislava.   122

3.8. György (George) Buday, illustration from *Bátorligeti mesék*
(Tales from Bátorliget), 1937.   125

3.9. Imro Weiner-Král, *Devín* (from the series *Bratislava*), 1937,
Slovenská národná galéria, Bratislava.   131

3.10. Imro Weiner-Král, *City and People* (from the series *Bratislava*),
1937, Slovenská národná galéria, Bratislava.   133

4.1. Andor Dudits, *Antal Grassalkovich with András Mayerhoffer*,
mural in the National Archives of Hungary, Budapest,
1927–1928.   147

4.2. Andor Dudits, *The Golden Bull*, mural in the National
Archives of Hungary, Budapest, 1925–1926.   148

4.3. The Székesfehérvár Medieval Ruin Garden in 1938 with
Saint Stephen's Mausoleum in the background.   156

4.4. Vilmos Aba-Novák, *The History of the Holy Right Hand*,
1938, reconstruction early 1990s, Medieval Ruin Garden,
Székesfehérvár.   158

4.5. The interior of Saint Stephen's Mausoleum, c. 1940,
with Vilmos Aba-Novák's mural *The Mystery of
the Holy Crown*.   159

4.6. Vilmos Aba-Novák, *The Mystery of the Holy Crown*, detail.   159

4.7. Lili Sztehlo, two panels from the Saint Stephen window,
1938, reconstructed by Gábor Gonzales and Judit Fűri, 1997,
Medieval Ruin Garden, Székesfehérvár.   162

4.8. Lili Sztehlo's stained glass window with the Saint Stephen
sarcophagus, Medieval Ruin Garden, Székesfehérvár, 2022.   163

5.1. Gyula Derkovits, *Dózsa on the Throne of Fire (1514 IX)*,
1928–1929, Budapest History Museum—Museum Kiscelli,
Municipal Gallery, Budapest.   170

5.2. Unknown lithographer after László Hegedűs, *Matthias at
the Gates of Vienna*, teaching aid, 1913, Hungarian
National Museum Historical Picture Gallery.   172

5.3. János Horvay, Lajos Kossuth monument, 1911–1927,
Budapest, Kossuth Square.   176

5.4. Gyula Derkovits, *Clash (1514 VI)*, 1928–1929,
Budapest History Museum—Museum Kiscelli,
Municipal Gallery, Budapest.   182

5.5. Gyula Derkovits, *Dózsa on the Bastion (1514 V)*, 1928–1929,
Budapest History Museum—Museum Kiscelli,
Municipal Gallery, Budapest.   185

5.6. Gyula Derkovits, placard for workers' demonstration,
1930, Hungarian National Gallery, Budapest.   189

5.7. Nándor Lajos Varga, *Dózsa (Hungarian Past XVI)*,
early 1930s/1940.   193

5.8. The Gate of Heroes with Éva Lőte's statues and
Vilmos Aba-Novák's *Christ* and *Allegory of Action*, 1936.   195

5.9. Vilmos Aba-Novák, *Soldiers with Their Graves*,
detail from the Gate of Heroes, 1936.   197

5.10. Károly László Háy, *The Death of Zrínyi (Between Two
Pagans for One Homeland)*, 1941, Hungarian National
Gallery, Budapest.   200

5.11. Károly László Háy, *History*, sketch for a fresco, 1941.
Hungarian National Gallery, Budapest.   201

Acknowledgments

I am grateful for the support of many institutions and colleagues, without whom it would not have been possible to complete this book. First of all, I want to thank the European Research Council for funding my research for more than five years. From 2018 to 2024, I held a research fellowship that formed part of the ERC Advanced Grant project *Continuity/Rupture: Art and Architecture in Central Europe 1918–1939*. This funding not only provided me with invaluable research time and covered the costs of my work but also meant that I was part of a close-knit research team. The support, encouragement, and feedback I received from my colleagues over the years has been essential to this book and is present on every page. I am grateful to the principal investigator, Matthew Rampley, and to my colleagues Christian Drobe, Marta Filipová, and Julia Secklehner for all their advice, help, and friendship throughout the project. Special thanks are due to the project administrator, Jana Hájková, for her incredibly effective and patient support in all my administrative needs.

The project began at the University of Birmingham and subsequently moved to Masaryk University, Brno. I am grateful to both universities for the support they provided and to the Department of Art History, Curating, and Visual Studies at Birmingham and the Department of Art History in Brno for welcoming me. The University of Birmingham granted me an honorary fellowship after the project moved, helpfully providing me with a base in the United Kingdom. In 2023, I held a four-month visiting position at the Centre for Arts, Memory, and Communities at Coventry University, where I greatly benefitted from discussions with colleagues.

In the past almost six years, many colleagues and friends have supported me in numerous ways—by helping me access sources, providing me with information, discussing my ideas with me, giving me feedback on drafts, inviting me to present or publish my research. I am grateful for all the help I have received. In particular, I would like to thank Samuel Albert, Eszter Békefi, Elizabeth Benjamin, Katarína Beňová, Francesca Berry, Judit Boros, Wendy Bracewell, Barbara Büki, Lenka Bydzovská, Cornelia Cabuk, Orsolya

Danyi, Gábor Egry, Kati Evans, Robert Evans, Tim Haughton, Michaela Hojdysz, Claire Jones, Anna Kopócsy, Nazar Kozak, Janet Landay, Zsóka Leposa, Elizabeth L'Estrange, Walter Moberly, Radka Nokkala Miltová, Bernadett Piskolti, T. Csaba Reisz, Klaus Richter, Enikő Róka, Juliet Simpson, Camilla Smith, Anita Szarka, László Százados, Erika Szívós, György Szücs, Robert Waterhouse, and András Zwickl.

I am grateful for the editorial support I received from Bethany Wasik at Cornell University Press and to all who contributed to the publishing process. I also want to thank the two anonymous peer reviewers for their insightful comments, which have been extremely helpful.

It would not have been possible to sustain this long project without the support and companionship of my friends, who were always there for me even when we were separated by thousands of kilometers and COVID lockdowns. As always, I am grateful to my family, Tamás Veszprémi, Zsuzsanna Németh, Ágnes Veszprémi, and Éva Veszprémi, for the countless ways in which they have unfailingly supported and encouraged me in these long, and often difficult, years.

PERSISTENT ILLUSIONS

Introduction

Memorials usually commemorate events or people. In Budapest, in 1921, a new memorial commemorated space (fig. 0.1). The previous year, the Treaty of Trianon signed in Versailles had codified Hungary's new borders, awarding two-thirds of the country's former territory to neighboring states. Inaugurated in January 1921 in Freedom Square (Szabadság tér) in the city center, the *Irredentist Sculpture Group* consisted of four sculptures, each representing a direction on the compass and a corresponding former region of Hungary. In the allegorical figures, the "lost" lands materialized in an urban square in the center of the capital, marking out a space where crowds could gather to commemorate the country's territorial loss. Freedom Square had previously been associated with the memory of the 1848 revolution. From the moment of its inauguration, the *Irredentist Sculpture Group* overwrote these old meanings with a new message that would profoundly shape Hungarian politics and culture in the next two decades.

As individual works of art, the irredentist sculptures followed nineteenth-century models. Stylistically, they could hardly be seen as innovative. Nevertheless, their conflation of spiritual and material space and their reinterpretation of an urban square through their mere presence were definitely unsettlingly modern. Analyzing identity and ritual in Italian Fascism, Mabel Berezin has described how Fascism "colonized" time and the everyday by inscribing its ideology into patterns of daily life through recurring events and

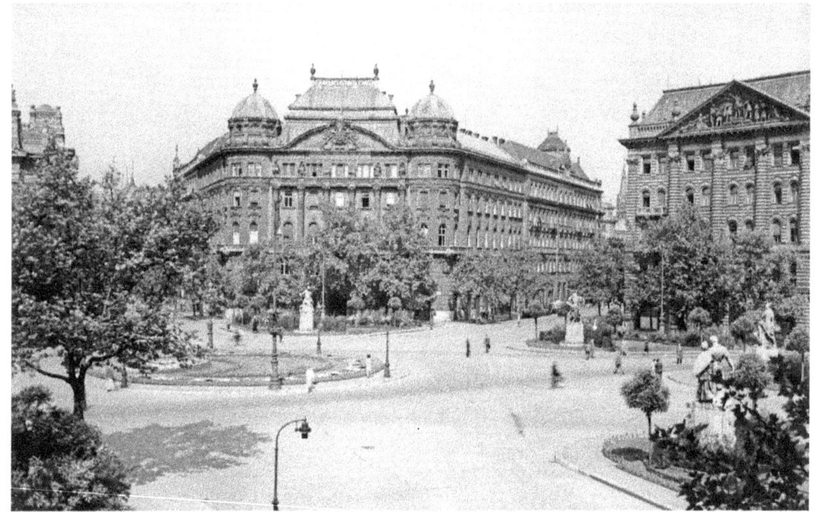

FIGURE 0.1.   Carl Lutz, View of Freedom Square, Budapest, with the *Irredentist Sculpture Group* in 1943.
Photo: Archiv für Zeitgeschichte ETH Zürich / Agnes Hirschi / fortepan.hu

commemorations.[1] Almost two years before Benito Mussolini took power in Italy, the irredentist sculptures similarly appropriated central Budapest to inscribe a spiritual vision of the former "Greater Hungary" into the fabric of the city and the daily routines of its inhabitants. They proclaimed that understanding national territory as a transcendent, indivisible whole was an essential element of Hungarian national identity, a principle to live by in every moment. Miniature versions and images of the sculptures cropped up everywhere in Hungarian public life—in pubs, in shops, on postage stamps— to disseminate this message. The sculptures were old-fashioned in a formal sense. Nevertheless, intended to reshape broader understandings of historical time and space rather than just conveying a certain interpretation of a specific event, they were at the forefront of developments in their own time and were powerful vessels of meaning that foreshadowed the ideological trajectory of interwar Europe.

This book explores how visual representations of the historical past in interwar Hungary helped reframe cultural memory by saturating various aspects of modern life and wide sections of public discourse. I argue that modernity and modernism played a crucial role in the culture of the conservative regime headed by Admiral Miklós Horthy (1868–1957), influencing the visual representation of history in the service of the regime's memory politics. Furthermore, I trace a variety of ways in which modernist artists tackled historical subject matter, whether expressing viewpoints that supported, complicated, challenged, or rejected official ideologies. My approach is unconventional for two reasons: First, images of history are rarely considered central to early twentieth-century modern culture; in fact, modernists around the turn of the century often defined themselves and their art in opposition to the "historicism" of the previous period. Second, the official culture of the Horthy regime in Hungary is rarely characterized as modern. Before 1989, the artistic production of the regime was routinely described as "historicist" and contrasted with modernism, as exemplified by the comprehensive handbook on Hungarian art between 1919 and 1945 published by the Hungarian Academy of Sciences in 1985, which discussed most official art under the heading *Historicism and Academicism*.[2] From the 1980s onward, an increasing number of studies have complicated this simplified picture by examining right-wing modernist movements, modern official commissions, the broad appeal and political diversity of neoclassicism in interwar art, and artistic interactions that crossed the political spectrum.[3] Research has highlighted the strong opposition between "national" and "modern"—the latter conceptualized as "alien"—that informed the ideology of nationalism in early twentieth-century Hungary and the ensuing quest for an "acceptable" national modern art.[4] There has, however, been no systematic attempt to analyze the modernity of the Horthy regime—one that would account for stylistically conservative yet ideologically innovative works such as the *Irredentist Sculpture Group* as well as for the more clearly modernist formal idioms of official art.

Interwar right-wing movements often rejected modernist art, but they also drew on it in their self-representation. In exploring the modernity of the Horthy regime, this book draws on international scholarship that has, in the past decades, analyzed the ambivalent relationship between modernism and right-wing politics with much nuance. In *Modernism and Fascism*, Roger Griffin described Fascism as an alternative modernism that offered new answers to the tensions of modernity.[5] As he noted in the book, many of the most innovative modern artists offered their services to right-wing regimes, even in Nazi Germany, where products of modern art were famously branded as "entartete Kunst" (degenerate art). In Fascist Italy, where art was not restricted stylistically, many official commissions took on an impeccably modern, often radically avant-garde form.[6] Elsewhere, too, modernist art was often married with right-wing or conservative politics, and art historians have explored examples of this, as well as of "moderate" and classicist modernisms, from Poland to France.[7]

Horthy's regime in Hungary was a right-wing authoritarian system.[8] It was built on resentment against the Versailles peace treaties and hence on belligerence against neighboring countries. Its inherent antisemitism manifested not only in exclusionary rhetoric but also in anti-Jewish legislation and culminated in the Hungarian Holocaust. Its suppression of left-wing activism affected many modernist and avant-garde artists, who emigrated around the time of its inception and could only return—if they chose to—in the late 1920s. Many government ideologues and right-wing critics voiced their hostility to modern art in terms resembling the Nazi rhetoric of "entartete Kunst"; the idea that modernism was "foreign" and alien to the national spirit had been deeply rooted in Hungarian nationalism since the late nineteenth century.[9] Nevertheless, although its political and cultural elites sought to build close contacts with Mussolini's Italy, Horthy's Hungary was not a Fascist state. Its governance allowed for some political competition, and it was not ruled by one man alone. Despite borrowing some of the aesthetics of Fascism, it lacked the revolutionary zeal of the Italian movement and was much more conservative. Nevertheless, it did not ban modern art for formal or stylistic reasons; works directly criticizing the regime faced censorship, but the art world was otherwise not restricted by the state. Indeed, modernism played an important role in some of the regime's prestige projects, and in such cases, the political as well as the artistic fault lines became blurred. At the Hungarian pavilion of the 1937 Paris World's Fair, one contributor was the Gobelin artist Noémi Ferenczy (1890–1957), a lifelong Communist whose art was celebrated as a key achievement of Hungarian modernism by prominent progressive critics (see chap. 1). Despite her political convictions and artistic approach, Ferenczy participated in the 1937 pavilion and gained a major commission in connection with the 1938 Saint Stephen jubilee, the regime's most extensive and lavish representation of its ideology as it entered its final, destructive phase.

Illuminating these blurred areas is an important aim of this book, but there is more at stake than adding one more example, one more country and regime, to the panorama of right-wing modernisms already discussed in literature. Focusing on the relationship between visual culture, historical memory, and modernity, this book explores how great ruptures in the present can change understandings of the past, and how the visual imagery of these new interpretations becomes structurally embedded in the modern world. In the aftermath of the First World War, Europe struggled to make sense of the devastation and the ensuing seismic shifts that reshaped the continent. Empires disappeared, new countries were born, national borders were moved. Communism erupted onto the world stage as a movement with immense international resonance. Industrialization seemed to be speeding up. As Walter Benjamin so poetically put it: "A generation that had gone to school on a horse-drawn streetcar now stood under the open sky in a countryside in which nothing remained unchanged but the clouds, and beneath these clouds, in a field of force of destructive torrents and explosions, was the tiny, fragile human body."[10] According to Benjamin, the forceful, rapid modernization brought about by the war had extinguished the last sparks of a dying tradition—that of storytelling based on memory. The memory of the time before the war was no longer organic; it was dislocated from a present that no longer understood. In the fundamentally transformed context of postwar Europe, the past had to be narrated and visualized in new ways. Even if the stories and images seemed old, they were no longer the same. This book examines these transformations and their continued resonance in twenty-first-century cultural memory through the example of Hungary.

The Treaty of Trianon, which drastically reduced the country's territory, was the core event that defined Hungarian politics in the next decades. The conceptualization of this loss as a decisive national catastrophe formed a cornerstone of the ideology of the Horthy regime, and the drive to win back territories fueled right-wing nationalist movements. Resentment over Trianon stretched across the political spectrum and played a role in Social Democratic and Communist activism, too.[11] Although often fashioned in Hungarian commentary as a unique catastrophe that concluded a long line of national catastrophes, Trianon was not one of its kind; it was the Hungarian version of the enormous shifts affecting countries across Europe after the Great War. Several other countries had lost territories in the peace treaties or had expected to gain more—so much so, in fact, that "revisionism," the idea that the treaties should be revised, can be investigated comparatively as a Europe-wide, consistent ideology.[12] Changes in countries' borders meant that concepts of nation, history, culture, and national territory were also reshaped. German culture provides many examples of this from the 1920s—not all of them associated with the Nazis—stretching across a broad political spectrum.[13] Even in countries that had benefitted territorially from the peace treaties, historical memory needed to be reframed. Some of these countries, such as Czechoslovakia, were brand-new, and history was indispensable for creating and shaping national identities and loyalties.[14]

How did these profound geographical and political shifts change the popular perception of national history? How were these changes related to constructions of national identity? An examination of the representation of history in interwar Hungarian political culture offers intriguing lessons in this regard. Bringing this together with the question of modernity and modernism takes this line of inquiry further. In the early twentieth century, modern technology was transforming culture and its consumption. Understandings of nation, of identity, of the role of one's nation in the world, and of national and world history were disseminated in brand-new ways. In modern culture, the imagery of nation, country, and history could envelop the public like never before, suffusing the everyday and reshaping people's mental maps with a previously unseen force. Art and visual culture engaged people through new modes of expression, whether through the formal innovations of modernism or through traditional imagery that employed the features of modernity to colonize the mental and physical spaces of everyday life.

Today, perhaps, we are in a particularly salient moment to assess these developments. The Russian invasion of Ukraine has called the world's attention to how conceptions of history, disseminated through the latest technology and tailored to today's society, can serve to construct and impose "a revised understanding of patriotism, of the meaning of Russianness and even of truth itself."[15] It is timely to discuss how such constructs are formed and disseminated and how old and new technologies and traditional and modern forms of expression can simultaneously participate in these processes. This book explores how historical memory is formed through political agency but also how some of its imagery lives on as political interests change. In today's Hungary, irredentist imagery is still present: invoking "a historical trauma, it . . . speaks to current feelings of loss and disenfranchisement, offering symbolic compensation through the transference of historical glory, pride, and self-esteem within a mythological framework."[16] Many images and notions discussed in this book possess a continued allure.

This is why the modernity of the *Irredentist Sculpture Group* matters. Interpretations of history formed in the interwar period are often long-lived and resistant. We still inhabit the modern culture in which they were created, and the answers they offer to the ambiguities and crises of modernity seem familiar. This book explores products of modern visual culture and the mental frameworks they reflected and shaped. By analyzing examples from Hungary, I aim to offer a more general lens for examining the ideological shifts in Europe after the First World War and the role of visual culture in making ideas and identities feel tangibly real.

Locating Memory

Emphasizing the locations where past events had taken place was an important element in making historical narratives tangible; hence, the question of memory and space meanders through this book. The connection between the two is an essential aspect of the crisis in memory and identity reverberating across Europe after the First World War. The remembrance of Trianon in Hungary was a manifestation of this broader crisis, even if it was exploited by political propaganda to such an extent that this has become hard to see. Trianon certainly was—and is—a "site of memory," a "node" in the nation's collective memory that has a symbolic function in conceptualizations of national identity.[17] In the interwar period, however, it was more than that; it was a central driver, an encompassing framework for the remembrance of the past. This was due to its immediate political significance and continuous exploitation by various political actors but also to how it expressed broader anxieties about nation and identity. These two aspects are almost impossible to disentangle. With its major territorial losses, Hungary was a new country. Historical memory had to be reframed to fit this new geopolitical reality. What did it mean to be Hungarian? Did Hungarian history equal the history of the Hungarian state? How could the important locations of Hungarian history be remembered if those locations now lay outside the borders? Throughout the book, and especially in chapters 2 and 3, I argue that the spatial dimension of history gained increased importance in interwar Hungary, and much of the visual culture expressing historical memory gave material form to these issues. As chapter 5 demonstrates, this was not restricted to products of official culture but also surfaced in the midst of its most strident opposition.

In recent historiography, interest has shifted from the purely political toward the cultural and social implications of post-1918 border changes in Central Europe.[18] The "cartographical imaginary" has received attention in studies exploring the power of mental maps in political decision-making or the relationship between geographical research and nationalism.[19] Originating from cognitive psychology, the concept of mental maps describes how we assign values to specific locations in our mental images of our spatial surroundings.[20] Their historical study explores how "collective representations of an—experienced or imagined—spatial environment . . . affect processes of cultural group formation."[21] Drawing on this line of inquiry, I employ the concept of mental mapping to investigate how the meanings of historically significant locations shifted after 1918. Throughout the chapters, a variety of examples—monuments, posters, book illustrations, stained glass windows—show how Trianon recalibrated the mental maps of interwar Hungarians. Meanings shifted, and the "detached lands" turned into one unified site of memory, while "Dismembered Hungary" was a site of disappointment but also one that stood in for the entirety of Greater Hungary. Works of art and visual culture expressed this in a wide variety of ways.[22]

One iconic image—that of Greater Hungary with the new borders dissecting it—performed a large share of the memory work to reshape interwar Hungarian mental maps and would become ubiquitous in the interwar period in a wide variety of incarnations. There were, however, many other ways to invoke spatiality in commemoration. The memorial described earlier, the *Irredentist Sculpture Group*, is a case in point. In some way, monuments always connect space and time—they mark a location for commemorating events from the past. Literature on monuments tends to assume that until the late twentieth century, monuments did this in a simple and uniform way. The "state-sponsored monument's traditional function as self-aggrandizing locus for national memory," as James E. Young put it, was expressed in a large-scale, monumental object, permanently placed in a public space, that "shouldered the memory work" for its viewers by promoting the preferred interpretation of the past as unquestionable truth.[23] There is no doubt the *Irredentist Sculpture Group* has such a function, and chapter 2 describes how it molded the public remembrance of Trianon into a preferred narrative that remained influential for decades to come. Yet, in other ways, the irredentist sculptures differed from the model I have just described. Made of artificial stone, they were not intended as permanent. Although their figures were life-size, their ensemble was not monumental in the vein of public monuments that dominate the urban space around them; as figure 0.1 shows, they were dispersed under the trees, making them more reminiscent of the decorative sculptures of gardens than an imposing public monument. This was because the real monumentality of the *Irredentist Sculpture Group* lay in the empty space they marked out in front of them—a space for crowds and rituals. The monuments created an absence that had to be filled, a gesture particularly apt for commemorating the loss of territories.

As I explain in chapter 2, the rituals performed by various activist groups near the *Irredentist Sculpture Group* connected Trianon to other events of Hungarian history and even to the religious calendar. In this way, the sculptures defined national territory as a central lens through which to view historical time. A host of subsequent representations of territorial loss shaped Trianon into a framework for understanding Hungarian history and national identity. In the memory politics of the Horthy regime, previous "national tragedies" became prefigurations of Trianon. The tragic narrative forged in this process is a striking example of what Ann Rigney has called the "scarcity of memory."[24] This phenomenon, where "certain narratives provide a cultural framework for other stories [and l]ater events are superimposed on earlier ones to form memorial layers," explains how interwar interpretations of history fit into older narratives and how this ensured their resilience.[25] The metaphor of "layering" is itself spatial, and the example of Trianon in interwar Hungarian cultural memory shows how chronological narratives can merge with their spatial dimensions in national cultural memory as they historicize, and hence naturalize, concepts of national territory—the true shape of the country.[26]

This brings me to another reason why the spatiality of memory is central to my investigation. The lands Hungary lost in 1920 were multiethnic. Incorporated into Czechoslovakia, Romania, the Kingdom of Serbs, Croats, and Slovenes (later Yugoslavia), and Austria, the regions were home to speakers of Slovak, Romanian, German, Ruthenian, Yiddish, and Hungarian. From the nineteenth century, the national movements of different groups had created their own narratives, attaching their interpretations of history to places in the contested lands. The mental maps of different nationalisms overlapped and their narratives intertwined, necessitating a transcultural approach to memory.[27] In examining the politics of memory in visual culture, I highlight how the Hungarian government's concepts of history and place clashed with other interpretations. Populations in the "lost" territories were, of course, important targets for Hungarian memory politics, which aimed to convey that Hungarian speakers—and the lands they inhabited—naturally formed part of the Hungarian nation, while other ethnic groups were also better off under the guidance of the Hungarian nation. Minorities in the contested territories were caught in the "triadic nexus" described by Rogers Brubaker—between the "nationalizing" nationalism of the state they lived in and the "homeland" nationalism of Hungary.[28] The overlaps and contrasts between the models of history promoted by the Hungarian government, the government of the "nationalizing" state, as well as of the various nationalities living together in the territories in question are wonderfully visualized in artworks that depict historical memory in geographical space. In chapter 3, I examine a range of historical landscapes that depict places in Slovakia and reveal kin-state Hungarian, minority Hungarian, Slovak, and Czechoslovak perspectives. In the ethnically diverse space of Central Europe, dissected by new borders and reshaped by new identity politics, it is always important to keep in mind this multiplicity of perspectives that opens up transnational vistas even in a book that largely focuses on Hungary itself.

By highlighting the reach of the historical narratives of the Hungarian state beyond its post-1920 borders, I have veered into a new topic: the memory politics of the Horthy regime. To introduce some of the themes examined in this book, I provide an introductory overview of the regime itself and the ideological uses of the past in its politics.

The Horthy Regime and Its Politics of Memory

The terms *cultural memory*, *collective memory*, *social memory*, and *historical memory* are often used interchangeably, with slight nuances in meaning, to denote common understandings of the past accepted by smaller or larger social groups. I have chosen historical memory as the central concept in this book to express that my focus is on events from the (often distant) past that belong to broader narratives of national history and receive attention from scholars of history as well as from the wider public. Nevertheless, I also employ the other terms when appropriate. Whether historical, cultural, or collective, these concepts of memory encompass not only the narratives societies construct about their past but also the practices and institutions that preserve these interpretations. Such narratives are fundamental to group identities, but they are always in flux, constantly reiterated and reshaped by memory practices. In this book, I do not treat historical memory as an entity that exists independently from the actions that shape it. The field of memory studies emphasizes that memory is a process rather than a fixed entity.[29] The shaping and mediation of collective memory involves ongoing work, while the canons and interpretations of memory sites are subject to constant revision in line with the political and cultural aims of different groups.[30] To highlight the role of political will in shaping historical memory, I often refer to the "politics of memory."[31]

The Horthy regime cultivated an elaborate politics of memory in support of its political goals. Its opponents promoted their own alternative narratives, although with more limited means. At a time of crisis and insecurity, narratives that highlighted the continuous history of the nation, its ancient origins, and its justified claims to territories outside the borders had heightened appeal. This, again, was not unique to Hungary; such narratives—and with them, debates about the historical primacy and territorial rights of different groups—tend to resurface with greater ferocity in periods of national "identity soul-searching."[32] In many countries in East-Central Europe, the interwar period produced (often mythicized) narratives about national history that live on to this day.[33] This book examines artworks promoting some of these narratives and interpretations. It is therefore useful to provide an overview of the most important themes in the regime's memory politics.

A central aim was to fit the chaotic events around the end of the First World War into a narrative that presented Horthy's regime as the purveyor of hope. Assigning blame for Trianon to opponents was crucial. The regime defined itself in opposition to the two revolutionary regimes that had arisen, in quick succession, in the immediate aftermath of the war. As the Habsburg

Empire disintegrated, in October 1918, the Hungarian government declared the end of the union with Austria. On 31 October, the so-called Aster Revolution elevated the liberal Count Mihály Károlyi (1875–1955), a prominent pro-independence politician, to lead the country as prime minister. Having formed a government of liberals and Social Democrats, on 16 November, Károlyi proclaimed the Hungarian People's Republic. Governing a war-torn country while desperately trying to fend off attacks from Czech, Serb, and Romanian armies aiming to enforce their territorial claims, the People's Republic could not hold. On 21 March 1919, the Social Democratic Party merged with the Hungarian Communist Party, a Bolshevik organization led by Béla Kun (1886–1938), and the Hungarian Soviet Republic was born. In existence for just 133 days, the Soviet Republic never truly consolidated itself and remained a chaotic conglomerate of various ideologies and ambitions. It comprised progressive ideas and a quest for positive change, which drew in some of the best minds of the time, but these coexisted with the brutality and die-hard dogmatism that ignited the Red Terror, the politically motivated murder of three to four hundred people across the country.[34] Faced with the Romanian invasion, a hostile Entente, and growing counterrevolutionary activity, the Revolutionary Council of Governance finally resigned. On 16 November 1919, Horthy, a central figure of the growing counterrevolutionary movement, triumphantly rode into Budapest on a white horse, leading his army and being celebrated by sympathizers.

Horthy's march into Budapest was an iconic event, conceived as a symbolic recapture of the city. It was designed to overwrite the public events the Soviet Republic had held in the city just months before, especially the grandiose celebrations organized on 1 May. Chapter 1 examines these public spectacles and how they shaped memory and space in the city. Here, I am more concerned with how Horthy's procession and its subsequent memorialization expressed the overall narrative that was beginning to form. The country's territorial loss—only codified on 4 June 1920 by the Treaty of Trianon but in effect since late 1918, when Czech, Romanian, and Serbian forces swiftly occupied parts of what was still officially Hungary—was interpreted as a national catastrophe unfairly imposed on the country by hostile outsiders, the negotiators of the Entente. Internal enemies were, however, also blamed. Although the Soviet Republic had attempted to fight off Czech and Romanian armies using its depleted means and tried in vain to gain a place at the negotiating table at Versailles, this was quickly forgotten, and the Communist government came to be seen as facilitating Trianon. Together with Károlyi's preceding revolutionary liberal government, the Soviet Republic was conceptualized as an anomaly in Hungarian history.[35] The stereotyping of the Communist leaders as "alien" and Jewish fanned the flames of the increasing antisemitism of the postwar years.[36] The self-representation of Horthy and his regime was centered around the idea that the regent would be able to "resurrect" Hungary and lead its trajectory back to its natural course, which would eventually include regaining the lost territories.

Where that natural course lay, however, was not always clear. In the nineteenth century, the main driving force in Hungarian politics had been liberal nationalism. Until 1867, Hungary had been one of many constituent lands of the Habsburg Empire, with limited political power. Dissatisfaction with this status quo and with antiquated feudal structures ignited a revolution and the War of Independence in 1848. Although imperial forces finally defeated the Hungarian army in 1849, the ensuing period of direct rule from Vienna could not be sustained for long. Weakened by external wars, the Austrian government opted to resolve long-standing tensions by signing the 1867 Austro-Hungarian Compromise, which awarded Hungary with the autonomy of a nation state within the imperial framework, allowing it to form its own government and direct its own internal affairs. The subsequent decades were marked by a liberal political elite that aimed to build up a centralized administration largely modelled on France. Budapest developed into a modern metropolis, with ring roads, factories, museums, theaters, hospitals, and an opera house. The ideology of the Horthy regime embraced the nationalist aspects of these developments but was wary of the liberalism of the revolution and the period after the Compromise, creating an ambivalence around the memory of the nineteenth century and its most important political figures. Instead of just overwriting the memory of the Soviet Republic, the regime sought to overwrite the memory of the liberal period while still paying lip service to the aims and achievements of nineteenth-century nationalism.

In 1913, a young historian named Gyula Szekfű (1883–1955) published *The Exiled Rákóczi*, which presented Francis II Rákóczi (1676–1735), prince of Transylvania and leader of an uprising against Habsburg rule, as a seriously flawed human being rather than a national hero.[37] The book's irreverent critique of an icon of the independence movement created a huge scandal that reached beyond the confines of academia into the popular press. A few years later, however, Szekfű emerged as the foremost ideologue of the new right-wing regime with his 1920 book, *Three Generations*.[38] Rethinking the history of the previous century, Szekfű blamed the liberal politicians of the period from 1848, including the leaders of the revolution, for Hungary's decline and hence for Trianon. Their policies of Magyarization had unnecessarily antagonized minorities, while their philosemitism and support for capitalism had allowed recently immigrated Jews to direct the economy. Szekfű's book contained much of the ideology of the early Horthy regime in seminal form: the centering of Trianon, antiliberalism, antisemitism, and a conflicted relationship to the legacy of 1848.

The antiliberalism of the Horthy regime was not unique in Europe and, in fact, mirrored wider developments. After the First World War, the economic optimism and liberalism of the prewar years became suspect and resulted in a widespread trend of deglobalization and nativism, not just in the lands of the former Habsburg Empire but across the world.[39] In many places, this was expressed as strong opposition to the prewar liberal model of nation building. In Italy, opposition to the liberal governments of the decades that had followed the unification of the country was essential to the proto-Fascist movements from which Mussolini would arise. The "faceless" liberal Italy and its "incomplete" Risorgimento became the most important central images of Fascist propaganda that thoroughly shaped the Fascist historic imaginary.[40] Developments in Hungary—Horthy's ride into Budapest and the reinterpretation of history that followed—exemplified wider trends, and therefore, the way the regime employed memory in its politics has broader implications.

After the fall of the Soviet Republic, the new Hungarian Parliament voted to restore the monarchy. This was why Horthy, as head of state, held the title of regent. Although he claimed to accept the Habsburgs' right to succession, Horthy successfully repelled Charles IV's attempts to return as king of Hungary. This was in line with the Paris Peace Conference, which required the dismantling of Habsburg rule. In his self-representation, Horthy often fashioned himself as a constitutional monarch, even though he did not hold the title.[41]

The dawn of the Horthy regime was marked by violence. As the aforementioned events unfolded, groups led by officers of Horthy's army roamed the land committing atrocities motivated by anti-Communism and antisemitism. They abducted and tortured thousands suspected of Communist sympathies or simply of Jewish descent, murdering over a thousand people. As he consolidated his power, Horthy sought to distance himself from these events, which came to be known as the White Terror.[42] The violent antisemitism of the regime's inception was subsequently channeled into its ideology of "Christian nationalism."[43] In 1920, the Hungarian Parliament passed one of the first anti-Jewish laws of interwar Europe, the so-called *numerus clausus*, which limited the number of students from minority backgrounds at universities.

In the consolidation of the Horthy regime after its violent inception, one man played an essential role. István Bethlen (1874–1946), an emblematic opponent of the Károlyi government and the Soviet Republic, became prime minister in April 1921. Realizing that tensions needed to be deescalated to keep the country running, Bethlen signed an agreement with the Social Democrats that legalized the party and allowed it to take part in elections but limited the number of seats it could gain and its right to organize protests. The Communist Party remained outlawed, but Bethlen also sought to disempower (with only temporary success) the extreme right, both within and outside his party.[44] In 1928, his government withdrew the most clearly discriminatory passages of the numerus clausus. Bethlen's foreign policy was led by the conviction that Hungary's borders should be modified through legal rather than military means. While waiting for the revision of Trianon, Hungarians needed to concentrate their efforts on nurturing culture and education in the remaining land in order to prove their cultural superiority.

Bethlen's stabilization of the regime was largely successful, as it enabled the system to function without full authoritarianism, allowing a level of cultural openness and limited political opposition while relying on censorship and legislation that banned "offending the Regent" (*lèse-regent*) to maintain overall ideological control.[45] Bethlen's foreign policy also bore fruit with a 1927 agreement of friendly alliance with Mussolini's Italy. He was an astute politician, but some events were outside of his control. As he reached the peak of his career, the Great Depression hit Hungary. Bethlen had no good answers for the growing financial crisis and ensuing dissatisfaction. In 1932, he was forced to resign, making way for more radical right-wing administrations.

Gyula Gömbös (1886–1936), prime minister from 1932 to 1936, had been an early ally of Horthy and a prominent figure of the far right since the counterrevolution. Sidelined by Bethlen, he reemerged as the crisis deepened. Open about his Fascist sympathies, Gömbös strengthened ties with Italy, aimed for friendly ties with Austria, and sought relations with Hitler's Germany. Following his death, subsequent governments continued along similar lines. In 1938, this politics bore fruit: orchestrated by Germany after the partitioning of Czechoslovakia in the Munich Agreement, the First Vienna Award granted parts of Slovakia to Hungary. In 1940, it was followed by the Second Vienna Award, which transferred Northern Transylvania from Romania to Hungary. By this time, Hungary had joined the German-Japanese alliance, left the League of Nations, and enacted two anti-Jewish laws, which would be followed by two more in 1941 and 1942. In June 1941, Hungary attacked the Soviet Union, thereby fully joining the war on the German side.

As this short overview demonstrates, the Horthy regime was not a monolith; its politics were shaped by a number of strong personalities as well as by external factors. As we see later in this book, the radicalization of the 1930s was accompanied by shifts in the politics of memory and in artistic style. Nevertheless, some characteristics spanned across the entire period. The regime reinterpreted figures and events from Hungarian history to support a broader narrative that relied on a few cornerstones: the idea that former Hungary ("Greater Hungary") was an integral, natural whole; the loss of territories as a national catastrophe; the history of Hungary as a tragic narrative shaped by a succession of similar catastrophes; Christianity as integral to Hungarian national identity; and Horthy as redeemer and the hope of "national resurrection." To a certain extent, this was rooted in narratives formed and promoted in the nineteenth century.

One of the central features of the Horthy regime's ideology was its "Christian nationalism"—the idea of "Christian Hungary."[46] On one level, *Christian* was often employed to simply mean not Jewish or not Communist; it was a marker of the regime's identity in opposition to its counter concepts. More broadly, however, Christian (Catholic) symbolism infused the regime's rhetoric and self-representation to such an extent that it amounted to a political religion. This is another point of difference between the Horthy regime and Italian Fascism: while Mussolini sought to triumph over the Catholic Church and actively promoted the ancient Roman Empire as an alternative reference point for Italian national identity, Horthy worked with the church and sought to merge its power with that of the state. Due to the salience of Christianity in the regime's political culture, religious themes were prominent in official commissions and—as examples in this book show—they often overlapped with the representation of history. Religious holidays and rites, jubilee years of royal saints, provided occasions for visualizing the past hand in hand with the politics of the present.

One of the most important historical figures celebrated by the Horthy regime was King Stephen I (c. 975–1038), or Saint Stephen, Hungary's first king, who had converted the kingdom to Christianity. Stephen was employed as a symbol of revisionism; the land he had ruled over, "Saint Stephen's Hungary," was seen as the country's original, natural state. He was, however, also a historical figure in whom state and church, politics and religion were united in a way that suited the Horthy regime. The Saint Stephen Jubilee Year of 1938 was the greatest and most spectacular event of the regime's memory politics.

In the late nineteenth century, Saint Stephen as a political symbol had been favored by liberal supporters of the Compromise who advocated tolerance toward ethnic minorities. Although his propagation of Christianity was far from bloodless, Stephen was remembered as a king who had united and pacified the country. Ethnonationalists, by contrast, celebrated Árpád (c. 845–907), the ancient Magyar leader who had led the Conquest of the territory of Hungary in the late ninth century.[47] This cult was more militant; it referred to the subjugation of the previous inhabitants of the land by Magyars by force. Hence, it justified present-day Hungarian hegemony with the Magyars' military prowess and warned minorities to accept their inferior position.

In 1896, countrywide festivities were organized to celebrate the thousandth anniversary of the Conquest. The most important monuments centered Árpád and his Magyars: the Millennium Monument in Heroes' Square in Budapest (which also featured statues of Hungary's most important kings and queens behind the central column celebrating Árpád) and seven further millennium monuments erected across the country (on these, see chap. 2). Although the Horthy regime reelevated Stephen into the position of most important founder of the nation, the cult of Árpád and the ancient tribes also lived on. Canonized as a saint in 1083, Stephen was most cherished by the Catholic Church. The public celebration of the Catholic holiday of 20 August, Saint Stephen's Day, had been mandated by Empress Maria Theresa. Pagan Árpád was a more secular figure and hence more relatable to Protestants.[48] Catholic and Protestant narratives of Hungarian history diverged in the nineteenth century; Catholic histories tended to be more favorable to the Habsburgs, while Protestant ones emphasized Hungarian struggles for autonomy.[49] Calvinists, especially, saw their religion, oppressed for centuries by the Catholic Empire and its Hungarian Catholic elites, as the true Hungarian one.[50] These tensions continued into the interwar period.

Another movement that focused on ancient Magyars and the Conquest was Turanism, a mixture of scholarship, dilettantism, politics, and a vivid historical imagination.[51] Turanists rejected the Finno-Ugric origins of the Hungarian language and instead claimed that Hungarians originated from Central Asia and were related to "Turanic" (Turkic) peoples. The influence of the movement is demonstrated by the fact that almost all interwar Hungarian prime ministers belonged to the Turan Society, including, for instance, the geographer and politician Pál Teleki (1879–1941), who served as prime minister from 1920 to 1921 and again from 1939 to 1941 and as president of the Turan Society from its foundation in 1910 to 1916.[52] Not untypically, Teleki's interest in Turanism, geography, and eugenics was intertwined.[53] Turanism motivated a diverse range of preoccupations, from an ethnographic interest in "related" peoples to cultural diplomacy and imperialist ambitions in Turkey and Central Asia as well as the racialization of true Hungarianness as "Turanic"—an idea that, as we see in chapters 1 and 4, surfaced in the artistic representation of historical scenes by the late 1930s.

In addition to Saint Stephen, other historical personalities and events were also invoked by the regime. The 1526 Battle of Mohács, when Hungarians suffered a devastating defeat by the Ottoman Turks, was an important one. Following this defeat, the Ottomans invaded part of the Kingdom of Hungary, which was subsequently tripartitioned into Ottoman and Habsburg territories and the Principality of Transylvania. Hence, Mohács as a "national catastrophe" with territorial loss appeared as a prefiguration of Trianon in interwar narratives.[54] Hungarian history was commonly viewed as a series of tragedies in the nineteenth century, when defeat in the revolution and the War of Independence was also added to the sequence. This narrative of victimhood, sacrifice, and future resurrection gained new traction after Trianon.

Closely related to the narrative of victimhood was the narrative that emphasized struggles for national independence as the main thread in Hungarian history, often projecting modern definitions of the nation onto the more distant past. As mentioned earlier, this form of storytelling was seminal to Protestant narratives of history. In the official politics of memory of the Horthy regime, its position was ambiguous. Rákóczi and his followers, the *kuruc* rebels, were disparaged by Szekfű, but the prince nevertheless featured in Horthy's self-representation as one of the regent's historical precedents, and his equestrian statue was set up next to the Parliament building in 1937.[55] Attitudes toward the revolution and War of Independence of 1848–1849 and its leader Lajos Kossuth (1802–1894) were similarly ambivalent in a regime that defined itself as counterrevolutionary. I discuss examples of this in the next chapters.

The Horthy regime maintained a strong—although not total—hold over public life. The Communist Party was banned; the Social Democratic Party could delegate representatives to the parliament, but only a limited number. Direct critiques of the regent and the regime faced censorship in the press. At the same time, the government was able to use a wide range of public institutions to disseminate its message, supported by ostensibly independent charities furthering revisionism, political Christianity, and anti-Communism. Case studies in this book show how these channels helped images of history permeate the everyday in thoroughly modern ways. By contrast, the opposition's options were limited. Nevertheless, as I argue in chapter 5, opponents of the regime aimed to exploit the ambivalent points, the vulnerabilities, of official memory politics to influence the national historical imaginary.

I return to many of these points in the following chapters, where the memory politics of the Horthy regime and its opponents inform the analysis of individual artworks. For now, this brief summary should suffice. The aim of this book is not just to explore the politics of memory but to understand the role of modernity and visual culture in its power. I provide a range of examples; to round off this introduction, it is useful to discuss how they were chosen.

Modernity and Visual Culture: The Scope of This Book

There are concepts that have been defined so many times, in so many ways, on thousands of printed pages, that providing a succinct explanation for the purposes of one's own study feels daunting. Modernity and modernism are two of these concepts. The best I can do here is to briefly set out the working definitions I have used, which have proved useful in understanding the official and unofficial visual culture of interwar Hungary and in placing it into a wider European context.

The main problem with the word *modern* and its cognates is their dual meaning: *modern* originally meant new, up-to-date, improved, but it has also come to signify a specific period and artistic movement(s). These two interpretations still live on. By *modern age*, we usually mean a period, starting in the late eighteenth century but perhaps earlier or later, when life became profoundly altered by the effects of *modernization*—technological, industrial, social, and political changes seen as forces of renewal that drove society *forward*. The Industrial Revolution, capitalism, embourgeoisement, the revolutions of the eighteenth and nineteenth centuries, the emergence of nationalism and the nation state, urbanization, the expansion of the press, and the development of the *modern* public sphere are all phenomena of modernization. They decisively reshaped the societies where they exerted their power. How people communicated with each other and the state, how they saw their own position within wider communities, how they related to tradition and the past, how they worked, relaxed, and raised their families, and by which characteristics they identified themselves all changed fundamentally. By the first half of the twentieth century, modernity included photography, film, mass events, advertising, cars, the idea of national self-determination, Communism, Fascism, the extension of the right to vote, charities and activist groups, and the experience of the first mass-industrialized war. It is in this sense that I discuss the modernity of the Horthy regime.

Modernism is a different term. In art history, the term *modern art* does not merely indicate when the art was produced, nor does it simply express whether it was new in its own time. Instead, modern art encompasses specific artistic trends. Modern art can date from the work of Gustave Courbet (1819–1877) or Édouard Manet (1832–1883), but it can refer more narrowly to developments from the late nineteenth century into the early twentieth, also described as *modernism*. By way of "selective appropriation," only certain examples of the modern are included, which then serve to represent artistic modernity as a whole.[56] Modern art rejected the academic traditions of previous centuries and consciously aimed for something new. In painting, this meant treating the pictorial plane as an autonomous system rather than a window onto a three-dimensional world. Many modernists renounced nineteenth-century historicism, which led to an undoubted decline in historical subject matter.

Modernism can be seen as a fruit of modernity, but this does not mean that the relationship between the two is without conflict. Indeed, one definition, which extends the term from art to culture and politics, suggests that modernism was an antagonistic reaction to modernity: it sought to remedy the supposed destruction, decay, and alienation that characterized the new, modern world.[57] In this way, modernism encompassed "paradoxical if not opposed trends towards revolutionary and reactionary positions, fear of the new and delight at the disappearance of the old, nihilism and fanatical enthusiasm, creativity and despair."[58] Griffin built on these definitions when defining Fascism as a modernist movement focused on the *palingenesis*—rebirth—of the nation.[59] The Horthy regime may not have been Fascist, but its ideology was definitely centered around rebirth or, to use their preferred phrasing, resurrection. Their central project was to remedy the damage caused by Trianon—itself undoubtedly a phenomenon of modernity. This definition has proved very useful when tracing the modernist aspects of interwar Hungarian culture. The idea of regeneration, a feature of early twentieth-century avant-gardes in both art and politics, and from left to right, surfaces in the art of interwar Hungary again and again, as several case studies in this book show.[60]

Hence, while many of the examples discussed in this book were not works of modern art in a strict sense, they engaged with aspects of modernity and modernism. Then again, some *were* works of modern art. Artworks such as *1514* by Gyula Derkovits (1894–1934) show that historical subject matter was not at odds with modern art, nor with left-wing activism. Other examples, such as the work of Nándor Lajos Varga (1895–1978) or Vilmos Aba-Novák (1894–1941), show that a modern style and approach could encompass images of not only history but also right-wing ideology. By employing broader definitions of modernism and focusing on the relationship with modernity, we can discuss artworks from across the political spectrum without trying to match artistic styles with political views—a practice that has often pervaded the discussion of these artworks. In this way, it is possible to position the "conservative modernism" that often served as a positive reference point in right-wing discourse compared to the "degenerate" avant-garde into the broader context of modernist artistic production. In Hungary, an example was the so-called School of Rome, a loose group of artists supported by a government scholarship set up to create a modern, monumental style for official commissions.[61] According to its mastermind, the art historian Tibor Gerevich (1882–1954), this scheme would produce an art that would relate to the tradition of the Italian Old Masters through the lens of its own age, leaving behind "decrepit" academicism.[62] The sense of renewal was central to these trends, too, and exploring their relationship to official and unofficial narratives of regeneration is a fruitful line of inquiry.

This book avoids identifying modernism or modern art with "progressive" politics and highlights how modern trends surfaced in official art. However, it also goes further. Modernism is a specific phenomenon, but modernity is more diverse. My topic is not historical imagery in modernism; it is historical imagery in the modern world of interwar Hungary. I examine how it filtered through society along networks of activism, entertainment, politics, industry, and scholarship, treating the modern world as a medium in itself. This also means that instead of limiting its inquiry to the traditional subjects of art history—painting, sculpture, prints, and drawings—this book traces the representation of the past in various other media, such as magazines, posters, stamps, and public processions. Consequently, the subject of the book is visual culture rather than solely art. Instead of observing its subject from the perspectives of artists or the art world, it focuses on the imagery that everyday people, albeit from different walks of life, encountered when navigating the increasingly fraught public sphere of interwar Hungary.

When analyzing interwar modernity and modernism and their embeddedness in society, it is of course useful to look at contemporary definitions of modernity. One of these, which offers an encompassing model of society and culture, has been especially influential. Writing in the early 1940s, the sociologist Ferenc Erdei (1910–1971) described Hungarian society as divided into "modern" and "traditional" groups.[63] *Modern* encompassed urbanity, industrialization, internationalism, and left-wing and liberal politics, while *traditional* meant the countryside, nationalism, vernacular culture, conservatism, and religion. Erdei's work became influential in late twentieth-century history writing, but it was just one of many similar formulations. In fact, Erdei himself never published this essay, which only appeared in 1976, after his death. Strong oppositions between modern and traditional or "populist" and "urban" cultural trends predated its publication. They existed in the interwar period, went on to shape public and underground cultural life under Communism, and still surface in history writing as well as in journalism. Indeed, it seems that postulating the existence of decisive dual divides within society and culture is a particularly pervasive feature of sociological models in Hungary.[64]

Besides being overly simplified, the idea of the dual society is problematic for a more serious reason. Often implicitly, and sometimes explicitly, these models equate *modern* with Jewish and *traditional* with Christian or non-Jewish groups in society. Erdei himself openly posited this duality. As Gábor Gyáni has shown, Erdei's model reflected the ideas and debates of its own time—the early 1940s. Its focus on a dichotomy between *Jewish* and *Christian* is inseparable from the fervent antisemitism of a time when Hungary enacted four successive anti-Jewish laws.[65] With Gyáni's lead, the theory of dual society has been the subject of strong critique in recent historiography, but the debate is not settled.[66] The case studies in this book nevertheless demonstrate that drawing a strict line between modern and traditional obscures the complexity of the interwar period. Furthermore, identifying one or the other with Jewish and non-Jewish groups risks perpetuating an antisemitic cliché, even if the aim is to discuss modernization as a positive phenomenon.

Therefore, this book aims to cut across such constructed dichotomies. It examines, for instance, cases in which capitalist industry helped disseminate the nationalist message of the state, left-wing artists contributed to state projects, and artworks made for the Communist Party received praise in the right-wing press. It explores the activities of the "populist" movement (of which Erdei was a prominent member), which stretched across divisions between left and right, modern and traditional, in its own idiosyncratic ways. It holds that modernity took many forms and cannot be matched to religion, ethnicity, or even political preferences. Unless it is crucial to understanding their work, I do not dwell on the Jewish origins of individual artists. Culture produced by Jewish people was integral to Hungarian culture, and if these artists were separate or marginalized, this was a result of antisemitic policies and prejudices and not of inherent features of their work.

The goal of the politics of memory is to disseminate a political message by mobilizing the remembrance of the past. Tracing the channels through which this happens helps us understand how the process shapes identities beyond the formal public sphere.[67] Rituals of remembrance define, through participation and exclusion, those who are included in their narratives of the past and of the nation and those who are not.[68] In the case of Horthy's Hungary, the Christian and counterrevolutionary elements of the spectacle made clear who was excluded on a religious and political basis. The examples discussed in this book show how some further groups featured, or did not, in representations of the past. Peasants were, for instance, included in urban festivities as passive representatives of the regime's ideology—of national tradition contrasted with urban decadence (see chap. 1). Nevertheless, by the 1930s, the fact that the situation of the peasantry was in reality far from ideal became more salient in public discourse, and with the rise of the populist movement, they, too, emerged as agents of history. Through textbooks and so-called demonstrative images, schools were of course crucial channels of dissemination. The expansion of primary education under Bethlen's Minister of Religion and Education Kuno Klebelsberg (1875–1932) hence helped disseminate narratives of history to groups not previously included.

In addition to employing the politics of memory at home, Hungarian governments were keen to reach audiences abroad. Proving the worth of Hungarian culture to the world in order to justify revisionist claims was central to Klebelsberg's program. To this end, he founded a network of Hungarian institutes in cities abroad, which served the purposes of historical research and also played a role in cultural diplomacy.[69] Italy was a primary target for these efforts, and the School of Rome was a fruit of building international contacts in the arts in line with the higher goals of cultural diplomacy. Tourism was an important source of revenue but also served the self-representation of the state. Through spectacles such as those examined in chapter 1, foreign visitors to Hungary could become acquainted with promoted constructs of Hungarian identity and history.

In aiding cultural diplomacy and the work of the Hungarian institutes, Hungarians living abroad also played an important role.[70] This book focuses on events and artistic commissions in Hungary and hence cannot delve into the role of émigrés, but I highlight this aspect here because it constituted a channel through which artworks and narratives reached broader audiences, sometimes returning to Hungary itself. This was, perhaps, even more important to the left-wing opposition than to supporters of official politics. After the fall of the Hungarian Soviet Republic, many left-wing artists and intellectuals left the country and settled in places like Vienna, Berlin, Paris, Moscow, or the United States. The Communist Party itself operated in illegality in Hungary, steered from Vienna and Moscow. Channels for disseminating left-wing memory politics were limited in Hungary, but there was more scope to publish material abroad for international distribution. Because Hungarian modernist artists joined international networks and some of them achieved lasting international fame, émigré artists and the trends they represented are today usually better known to international audiences than the remaining art scene in Hungary.[71] For this reason, and in order not to overextend its scope, this book focuses on Hungary, giving particular attention to the official culture and the political context from which émigré artists had extracted themselves. Examples that include a series of prints by the Vienna émigré Mihály Bíró (1886–1948) nevertheless show that émigré networks provided developments in Hungary with a transnational dimension that can never be completely discounted.

There is another omission I want to address in more detail, because it is one I tried hard to avoid. The artists and other producers of visual culture discussed in this book are predominantly men. This might seem like a glaring oversight at first; even though the art world was highly patriarchal, there were many excellent women artists in interwar Hungary. Yet, historical subject matter seems to be relatively rare in their work. Of the New Group of the Association of Hungarian Women Artists, an organization of modernists with mostly conservative political views, only one painter, Anna Bartoniek (1896–1978), ventured to explore historical subject matter, probably motivated by a personal connection: her sister, Emma Bartoniek (1894–1957), was a historian and archivist at the National Széchényi Library who published extensively on sixteenth- and seventeenth-century Hungarian history.[72] Why is this? Academic institutions had traditionally discouraged women from more "serious" genres such as history, and when modernism devalued historical subject matter and increased appreciation for genres more often practiced by women artists—still lifes, portraits, landscapes—most women artists never looked back. The state itself was not only patriarchal but decidedly masculine in its ideology; hence, gaining large official commissions as a woman was an exceptional feat. Therefore, the relative lack of women artists in this book reflects the nature of the Horthy regime and of interwar Hungarian society more broadly; it is a feature, not a bug. Nevertheless, a number of women who made important contributions to the visual representation of the past do appear in the chapters, such as the Gobelin artist Ferenczy, the sculptor Éva Lőte (1906–1966), and the stained glass artist Lili Sztehlo (1897–1959). It is no coincidence that the majority were active in the applied arts, which were considered more feminine. It is important to note that while the regime was undoubtedly patriarchal, many women were active in public life and shaped the developments I discuss. From the staunchly right-wing lesbian writer Cécile Tormay (1875 / 1876–1937) to the "Pro Hungaria" Women's World Association, they, too, are important characters in this book.

Finally, a few words about what this book is not. It is not a comprehensive survey of the art or visual culture of interwar Hungary. Many otherwise important artists and artworks go without mention here simply due to their nonhistorical subject matter. This book deals more extensively with works representing the regime's ideology than with dissenting projects, but it is not an overview of official art either. Instead, it investigates a selection of themes that I found particularly revealing and fruitful. When selecting my case studies, I had to leave out, often with great regret, many further works that would have fit my argument. In general, I aimed for deeper discussion of fewer examples rather than for a panoramic overview.

My focus on specific issues also means that my points of emphasis and my protagonists differ markedly from standard art historical overviews of the period. For instance, despite the book's focus on modernity, the art historian and philosopher Lajos Fülep (1885–1970), an important and eloquent champion of modernism in Hungary, plays no significant role. This is because the book's subject is not the modernism of Fülep. Instead, it is the modernity of the academic painter Andor Dudits (1866–1944) watching film footage to recreate the reality of a day in 1920 without resorting to allegory or of Aba-Novák combining Byzantium with the avant-garde to create a mural celebrating Horthy. It is a different kind of modernity—but it is a story that needs to be told.

The Structure of the Book

This book consists of five chapters, each of which explores a separate theme through case studies. To begin, chapter 1 examines how the memory politics of the interwar period developed over time and demonstrates how different features of the modern world helped disseminate its messages. It focuses on mass celebrations through which governments showcased their ideology while demanding public participation. The first—highly spectacular—example was the festive procession on 1 May 1919 under the Hungarian Soviet Republic, with Budapest dressed up like a work of avant-garde art. Public ceremonies constructed frameworks for understanding the recent past, but they were also, in themselves, political acts shaping the present. Another striking case was Horthy's triumphal procession into Budapest on 16 November 1919, held on the anniversary of the proclamation of the Hungarian People's Republic. By overwriting the recent past, the procession became a foundational event that would itself be commemorated on its anniversaries in the 1930s. Instead of drawing on the art of the past, reports, paintings, films, and other media representing Horthy's rise to power drew on features of modernity to make the events appear real and timely, presenting them as the only possible reality. While parallels can be drawn with Mussolini's Fascist spectacles, especially given the alliance between Hungary and Italy from the late 1920s, Horthy's first spectacles predated Mussolini's rise to power. In contrast to Italian Fascism, the Horthy regime did not present itself as revolutionary; the imagery of total renewal was missing from its arsenal. Instead, it employed modernity in more banal ways that were equally efficient in making the ideology pervade everyday life. Through a discussion of the celebrations staged between 1919 and 1938, the chapter traces how the regime gradually subsumed the urban modernity it originally railed against into its visual rhetoric.

As a contrast to official representations of the recent past, chapter 1 also discusses a work that embodies counter memory: a series of prints depicting the White Terror by Bíró. Drawing on the great tradition of nineteenth-century artistic lithography, the prints combine hauntingly beautiful technical execution with extremely gruesome subject matter, to a shocking effect. They are captivating works of art, but did they ever stand a chance against the deluge of official imagery? The reality effect constructed by the latter relativized the testimony of artistic renditions such as Bíró's. Contemporary ideas about reality in artistic representation, also voiced by left-wing critics, positioned Bíró's efforts as outdated in the modern world.

Chapter 2 narrows its focus to examine a specific iconic product of interwar visual culture that embodied and disseminated a crucial component of the regime's ideology. The *Irredentist Sculpture Group* in Freedom Square in Budapest was swiftly removed in 1945. While in place, however, the sculptures promoted an influential framework for conceptualizing national history and territory as an indivisible whole. Referring to this framework as *irredentist spacetime*, the chapter explores how the monuments inscribed it into the fabric of the city, contributing to the symbolic reoccupation of "sinful" Budapest. Transcending the urban space it redefined, the imagery of the sculptures recurred in stamps, posters, and mass-produced miniatures displayed in unexpected places. Its ubiquity was a product of the modern world, not only because it was achieved with the help of techniques of mass production but also because the images were disseminated through an alignment between separate sectors of modern society: civil organizations, industry, small entrepreneurs, and the government. This helped the monuments persist even after they were physically long gone. The chapter ends with an exploration of how their imagery and message live on in today's Hungary.

Chapter 3 continues the theme of memory and space. In nineteenth-century Hungarian visual culture, mountainous landscapes and ruined castles had stood for the unknowability of history and the subtleties of a multiethnic past within the Habsburg Empire. After 1918, this visual tradition was instrumentalized in nationalist agitation in successor states. The chapter contrasts illustrations from Hungarian irredentist publications with examples from Czechoslovakia, demonstrating how the genre of the historical landscape came to visualize new, more exclusive twentieth-century concepts of national territory. Landscapes helped naturalize the idea that a certain area of land belonged to a nation by historical right, in line with nationalist mythologies that endowed certain rivers or hills with an inherent "national-ness" or saw them as marking a country's "natural" borders.

Historical landscapes combined elements of nature and culture; they showed human-made remnants of the past, such as ruined castles, within the thriving and often uncontrollable natural environment, hence bringing together historical and geological time. Artworks examined in this chapter often employed deliberate archaisms, in style and subject matter, to empha-size their connection to a past they invoked to legitimize territorial claims. To Hungarian irredentists, the castles of western Slovakia were not vessels of ancient legends but elements of national heritage in a modern sense that proved the continuity of Hungarian hegemony in the region. In other works, such as the *Bratislava* series by Imro/Imre Weiner-Kráľ (1901–1978), the cas-tle represented the multilayered nature of historical memory in a multieth-nic region. Central to the chapter is Varga's woodcut series *Hungarian Past*, which combined historical sources with fantasy in montage-like composi-tions, clearly drawing on the lessons of the avant-garde. Promoting a narra-tive of Hungarian history in line with official ideology, the series neverthe-less also posed questions about the reconstructability of the past.

These questions, as well as the issue of heritage, return in chapter 4, which examines the role of historical scholarship in shaping and disseminat-ing the Horthy regime's ideology. Historians in interwar Hungary produced research of undeniable quality and importance. As members of a modern academic establishment, they made use of cutting-edge institutions such as the newly built National Archives and employed up-to-date methodologies. Nevertheless, their research formed a crucial part of the regime's memory politics. The chapter explores case studies in which art, scholarship, and poli-tics worked together to endow official conceptions of Hungarian history with both visual appeal and academic gravitas. The interior decoration of the National Archives of Hungary in Budapest (1924–1929) and the Medieval Ruin Garden built to preserve the remains of the eleventh century Basilica of King Stephen I in Székesfehérvár (1938) are revealing examples. In both cases, the murals presented a narrative of Hungarian history that glorified the Horthy regime while incorporating the seemingly objective results of archival research and recent archaeological excavations. The chapter reveals not only how the images promoted a political ideology but also how the interpretation of historical facts was shaped by ideological concerns that continue to resonate after the Horthy regime's demise.

The National Archives were decorated under the close direction of Klebelsberg, while the Ruin Garden was opened under his more radical successor, Bálint Hóman (1885–1951). Besides demonstrating the shift in cultural politics, the comparison between the two projects also shows, yet again, that modernity and right-wing state ideology were not enemies. The painter decorating the archives was a member of the old guard. Educated at a nineteenth-century academy, Dudits insisted that his art had nothing to do with politics. His old-fashioned compositions aestheticized Klebelsberg's consolidatory politics and Szekfű's pro-Habsburg model of Hungarian history. By the time Aba-Novák painted his murals in the Székesfehérvár Ruin Garden, the racism, antisemitism, and belligerency of the regime were more overt; the year of the Saint Stephen jubilee also saw the first anti-Jewish law and the first Vienna Award. Artists were required to represent the supposed racial characteristics of Hungarians both in the physiognomies they painted and in their style, and Aba-Novák and Sztehlo conformed to this. Yet, Aba-Novák's visual language was much more modern than Dudits's. Modernity, right-wing radicalism, and attunement to historical scholarship cohabited in the decoration of the Ruin Garden.

If history was so crucial to the self-representation of the Horthy regime, how could oppositionary movements employ it to promote their own values? Chapter 5 explores this question by placing an emblematic work commissioned by the illegal Hungarian Communist Party, Derkovits's *1514* (1928–1929), into the context of official memory politics. Examining the representation of historical "heroes" in official visual culture through a variety of media, from images produced as teaching aids to public monuments, it argues that because of its ambivalent stance toward historical examples of rebellion, the Horthy regime could not build up a fully consistent interpretation of the past. Works like *1514* and other opposing projects aimed to exploit these weaknesses. The chapter examines affinities between artworks expressing left- and right-wing political ideas, demonstrating how they existed in a shared political and artistic culture. Following events up to the early 1940s, it traces how history and its imagery became a crucial battleground in a highly critical time.

By the end of the period covered in the book, the Hungarian government had led the country into an alliance with Nazi Germany. At the end of the Second World War, the regime fell, to be replaced a few years later by a Communist authoritarian regime. The epilogue traces the afterlives of artworks, images, and concepts discussed in the five chapters. It shows that, although the memory of the Horthy regime was strongly condemned under Communism and many of its visual reminders erased, the conceptualizations of history and nation constructed by these images lived on in Communist ideology and endure, albeit in different forms, to the present day. These afterlives reflect how political and social actors shape cultural memory over a longer period, drawing on precedents and adapting them to new circumstances.

This leads me to the title of the book. When I began this book, I planned to trace long-lived motifs in Hungarian cultural memory. I attributed their persistence to a continuous undercurrent of popular belief that preserved, and continues to preserve, these ideas across ruptures of regime change. As I progressed with the research, I increasingly questioned this assumption. Looking at historical imagery close-up reveals with particular clarity how many "persistent" motifs of cultural memory are in fact "persistent illusions," constructed and reconstructed by identifiable actors and political will rather than sustained by an eternal and immaterial collective memory. As the concept of invented traditions has taught us, often ideas that seem to be ancient are in fact not that old. At the same time, this does not mean that specific reiterations of historical motifs do not derive from precedents or build on existing beliefs or tropes. Balancing these aspects is an important task of any exploration of historical memory. This book investigates why and how certain motifs persist and how they help reshape conceptual frameworks in times of crisis, but it also asks whether their persistence itself is one of the illusions the politics of memory employs. More fundamentally, it speaks to why we are so attached to some of our illusions—ideas of duality, of distinct cultural trends, of a clear and easy difference between authoritarian officialdom and progressive resistance.

CHAPTER 1

Spectacles of Renewal

On 16 November 1919, Miklós Horthy rode into Budapest leading a triumphal procession. The admiral on his white horse subsequently became one of the most influential icons of interwar Hungarian culture.[1] The event took place exactly a year after Mihály Károlyi had proclaimed the Hungarian People's Republic. The procession route included locations around the city that had featured in the grandiose 1 May celebrations held during the Hungarian Soviet Republic, symbolically recapturing the city from Communists. An attribute of victorious military leaders since antiquity, the white horse had an additional meaning: it was associated with ancient Hungarians, their leader, Árpád, and their ninth-century conquest of the territory of Hungary.

Suffused with references to the recent and distant past, the procession was a seminal example of a spectacle of history in interwar Hungarian visual culture. Yet, as attested by contemporary photos, the event was rather low-key for a triumphal march. Horthy and his army wore their uniforms and marched along undecorated streets. There were no historicizing props, no elaborate stage settings, no spectacular costumes to place the event into a historical perspective. Instead, everything emphasized contemporariness. Its historical symbolism notwithstanding, the procession was not designed to represent the past but to be a historical event in its own right. Its goal was not to evoke but to make history.

"Fascism makes history, it does not write it." Taken from a speech Benito Mussolini made to the Senate in 1929, this was one of the most popular mottoes of Italian Fascism. As Claudio Fogu has argued, it encapsulated the essence of the collective imaginary formed by Fascist culture, which rejected the preoccupation with the *historical* past in favor of celebrating the *historic*, epoch-making agency of Fascists in the present.[2] History was only relevant insofar that it could be subsumed into the Fascist transformation of life. Three years after Horthy's procession, in the March on Rome, thirty thousand Blackshirts marched to the Eternal City and paraded on its streets, pressuring the king into handing power to Mussolini. Celebrated as the historic foundational event of Fascism, the march involved a greater degree of political action than Horthy's procession, which took place after the transfer of power had already happened. Nevertheless, in the next twenty years, both served as iconic moments—sites of memory, if you will—that expressed the transformational nature of Horthy's and Mussolini's respective regimes. Represented in text and image, restaged or reimagined at anniversaries, both of them captured the historic imaginary.

The official culture of the Horthy regime is often described as neobaroque—a designation most famously employed by Gyula Szekfű—or historicist, an empty revival of late nineteenth-century eclecticism.[3] The modernity of Mussolini's Fascist culture is, by contrast, rarely denied today. It is well known that modernist and avant-garde art that embraced such movements as futurism and rationalism was integral to Fascist cultural production, and the intricate ways in which the regime drew a wide spectrum of artists into its fold have been thoroughly explored in literature.[4] Moreover, as Roger Griffin has shown, this was not simply a practical strategy for dominating the public sphere but was inherent to Fascist culture, which was modernist in its own right; like other modernisms, it emerged as a regenerative reaction to how modernity had transformed the world.[5] In making history, Mussolini employed public spectacle and new visual technologies in highly modern ways.[6] As this chapter shows, all of these features were present in Horthy's Hungary too, even if sometimes dressed up in a historicist guise.

It is necessary to note here that interwar Hungary was not a Fascist state. Horthy's regime lacked the revolutionary fervor of Mussolini's movement and retained many conservative traits that distinguished it markedly from Italian Fascism. Nevertheless, Italy is a useful starting point for understanding the regime's modernity. This is partly because successive governments of interwar Hungary had aimed for friendly relations with Italy from the mid-1920s onward and targeted the Fascist country with their cultural as well as political diplomacy. This resulted in a thick web of cultural links and a strong trend of Italophilia in the art world. Beyond these direct contacts, however, lay even deeper affinities that related the Hungarian and Italian movements to a broader spectrum of new political cultures in interwar Europe. One parallel between Mussolini's and Horthy's ideologies was the idea of *regeneration*—whether after a supposedly flawed Risorgimento and victorious yet not sufficiently rewarded participation in the Great War or after liberal decline, a lost war, revolutions, and Trianon. This idea of making right what was ruined by modernity through a quest for cultural and spiritual renewal is crucial to the alternative modernism offered by Fascism.[7] It is, however, not unique to it. In response to the contradictions of the modern world, many political and cultural movements offered a spiritual regeneration encompassing all areas of life. Spanning the political spectrum from left to right, they included artistic avant-gardes, socialism, and Italian nationalism and Fascism, which Emilio Gentile has placed into the context of other regenerative modern movements.[8] The rhetoric of renewal connected modernism with "an antidemocratic, racist, and authoritarian agenda" in Romania, where ideas of rejuvenation suffused the culture of Corneliu Codreanu's Fascist movement, which profusely drew on Christian symbolism in the manner of Horthy's Hungary.[9] Fascism could incorporate some of the greatest canonical works of modernism; Le Corbusier's regenerative vision of the modern city garnered much interest among interwar French right-wing and Fascist movements.[10] Exploring similar dynamics in the Horthy regime and interpreting its quest for "resurrection" as a form of modernism helps us better connect its official culture to the broader political cultures of interwar Europe.

Such an approach also produces a new understanding of the regime's reaction to the Soviet Republic. In the regime's ideology, the Soviet Republic was the ultimate symbol of the decline and destruction that had to be rectified through "resurrection." The spectacular celebrations organized on 1 May 1919 in Budapest seemed to encapsulate all that went wrong, and the 16 November procession was designed as a counter performance in direct opposition to the previous event. Nevertheless, this chapter conceptualizes the relationship between the two as linear rather than oppositional. A profoundly modern, new political device—and, in a certain sense, artistic genre—was employed on 1 May: the mass public spectacle. And 16 November overrode its memory by turning many features into their exact opposite, signaling both an understanding of the new device and an ambition to adapt it to the new regime's needs. By 1930, the Hungarian government was organizing spectacular public celebrations on a larger scale.

Mass events like those analyzed in this chapter tapped into something fundamentally modern: an interest in the "crowd" as an agent and subject of politics. Driven by anxieties about industrialization, urbanization, and the social upheavals of the 1870s, the crowd became the subject of intense scientific interest in late nineteenth-century France. Social theorists investigated the crowd as an irrational organism that paralyzed the minds of individual participants. Fear of the crowd's unpredictability spurred an interest in developing techniques of control. Spectacle was such a technique. As one of the most influential theorists, Gustave Le Bon (1841–1931), argued: "Crowds being only capable of thinking in images are only to be impressed by images. It is only images that terrify or attract them and become motives of action."[11] He therefore encouraged leaders to adopt methods of theatricality.

Influenced by these ideas, Mussolini referred to the crowd as material to be molded by him, the artist.[12] Walter Benjamin called this the aestheticization of politics and warned that it could only "culminate in one thing: war."[13] According to Benjamin, Fascist politics preserved existing property structures and avoided giving the masses their rights, but it had to give them *something*; it replaced political action with symbolic mass events proclaiming a fake renewal. Rooted in the rise of the crowd, the aestheticization of politics was a thoroughly modern phenomenon.

In observing the anniversaries of recent and more distant historical events by organizing celebrations and commissioning artworks, the Horthy regime made its interpretation of history present, shaping a historic imaginary as in Italy. In doing so, it employed various devices of modernity—technologies that offered an increased reality effect, channels of dissemination that meandered through modern society, and various forms of modernist visual representation. This chapter examines some of the celebrations from 1919 to 1940, tracing how the regime grew increasingly confident in its modernism. In 1919, the aim of Horthy's procession was to symbolically subjugate Budapest and position its recent Communist turn—and with it the radical modernism of the 1 May celebrations—as a historical anomaly. By 1938, the modernity of Budapest was integral to the picture of past and present that the regime aimed to project, forming a historic imaginary in which the commemoration of the distant past became indistinguishable from present political action. To tell the story, however, I must start with the Soviet Republic.

The Crowd on a Stage

The Hungarian Soviet Republic was in power for less than five months, from 21 March to 1 August 1919. Its memory was, however, kept vividly alive in the next two decades as a counter concept that encapsulated all that Horthy and his supporters stood against. The image of Budapest decorated for the

May Day festivities—"dressed in red rags," as Horthy would put it—became a recurring trope in right-wing rhetoric designed to evoke revulsion toward the capital city and its liberal middle class.[14] It encapsulated the idea, often expressed in interwar commentary, that Communism—an ideology alien to the "Hungarian spirit"—had taken root in the capital due to its mixed population, in contrast to the countryside, where its Hungarian character had been preserved.[15]

The scale of the 1 May festivities is astonishing even today, especially given that they took place at a time of serious scarcity and ongoing war, as the Hungarian Red Army struggled to fight off Czechoslovak and Romanian forces.[16] Due to this, even left-wing sympathizers questioned whether it was appropriate to organize such a large event that seemed to serve as a smoke screen hiding the Soviet Republic's dire situation.[17] Nevertheless, the celebrations went ahead. The streets were filled with flags and placards, and ephemeral monuments were set up in all major squares, roads, and parks. The decorations included several large sculptures and painted *panneaux* prepared by a large group of artists at breakneck speed.[18] On the Buda side of the Danube, on the picturesque Gellért Hill, the statue of the eleventh-century priest Saint Gerard—an academic work erected in 1904—was enclosed in a giant yellow and red column. Beneath it, a large allegorical painting promoted the future Communist paradise. On the Pest side, along the grand avenue Kossuth Lajos Street, new statues commemorated heroes of the international workers' movement, such as Vladimir Lenin or Karl Liebknecht, while existing statues of historical figures were covered up with gigantic red spheres. On Kossuth Square, next to the Parliament building, a decorative pavilion named the House of Labor was constructed around the statue of Gyula Andrássy, Hungary's prime minister after the Compromise. Lenin and Liebknecht appeared in this location as well. The best-known part of the festive decorations is the transformation of the 1896 Millennium Monument, which was completely covered up, its central column turned into an obelisk decorated with a sculptural portrait of Marx.

The goal was to create a true spectacle. Well-known views of Budapest were transformed in a way bound to grab attention. The geometric shapes proclaimed a new beginning, a revolutionary renewal compared to the overall historicist appearance of the city. The ensemble was still somewhat eclectic: the House of Labor, for instance, was a neoclassical temple, while the portrait of Marx was the work of György Zala (1858–1937), the veteran historicist sculptor who had created the original statues of the Millennium Monument. Even the modernist artists of the Soviet Republic differed from each other in their approach; there was no unified model of modernity governing the appearance of the installation.[19] The simmering tension within early Communist culture between the abstract art championed by the revolutionary avant-garde and the requirement that art should be easily comprehensible to the proletariat left its mark on the decorations.[20] Nevertheless, it did not overshadow the radical modernity of the spectacle.

The decorations followed Soviet precedents and echoed Lenin's ideas on monumental propaganda, which envisioned decorating cities with large inscriptions, ephemeral and permanent statues, and red flags, while providing explanations to all images in order to educate the masses.[21] In this, Lenin had probably been influenced by Le Bon. The Budapest installation certainly applied the lessons of crowd psychology, as organizers aimed to astound and control the people by offering an immersive spectacle. Control was paramount, because the crowd was not just an audience but also part of the show. It was material to be shaped and directed. It is therefore no surprise that several of the main organizers, such as the stage designer Elek Falus (1883–1950) or the director László Márkus (1881–1948), were theater professionals. The way the masses spread out was an essential component of the overall meaning. Instead of being confined to one main route, the crowd was instructed to walk along several roads at the same time, hence expressing the main message: Budapest now belonged to the proletariat.[22]

Did this plan work in practice? It is difficult to reconstruct what people in the crowd really saw on 1 May 1919, as opposed to what they were supposed to see. Textual sources recount the experience in ways that fit broader narratives. The closest thing we have are amateur photographs that survived the tribulations of a century. Judging from these images, the decorations were spectacular, but they could not erase Budapest's historicist visage, formed under the Austro-Hungarian Monarchy. In one picture, two monumental decorative elements—austere arches topped by large spheres covering two nineteenth-century statues—can be seen with the Danube in the background (fig. 1.1). The revolutionary monuments are almost pathetically outsized by two late nineteenth-century apartment blocks, the Clotilde Palaces, which flank the similarly enormous arch of Elizabeth Bridge. Photographed from another angle, the backdrop to the monuments is the Paris Courtyard, a glamorous shopping arcade built less than a decade before, a tribute to capitalism.[23] This does not negate the immersive effect of the decorations, but it shows to what extent they relied on imaginative work on the part of their audience. They demanded focused attention and a suspension of perception regarding peripheral objects that did not fit into the event's narrative.

The idea of renewal, of a new start, was central to the May Day festivities. Visually, they expressed this by hiding the symbols of the prewar status quo,

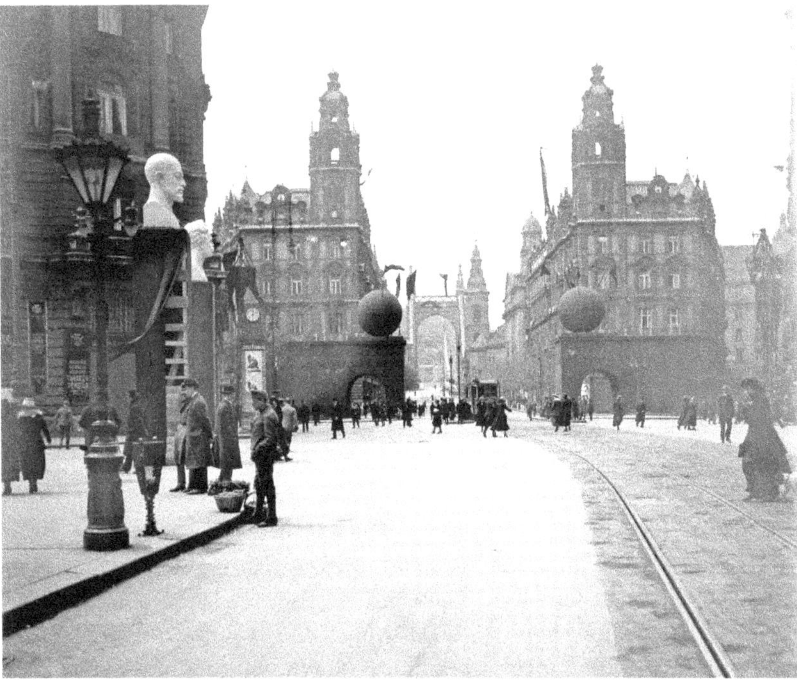

FIGURE 1.1.   Decorations for 1 May 1919 in Budapest with busts of Lenin and Karl Liebknecht. Photo: Frigyes Schoch / Fortepan

especially those that promoted the liberal nationalist political elite's narratives of national history, and by replacing these old symbols with new, left-wing heroes and a radically different, abstract art. History was to be remade, and by proceeding along the streets, all those who participated could contribute to its remaking. In this sense, it did not matter that the old face of Budapest was peeking out from behind the decorations, because the making of history was a work in progress. Furthermore, it was not just the city that was to be transformed but, more importantly, also its inhabitants. Public rituals shape political identities by leaving their mark on the spaces and cyclical times that frame people's daily lives—especially if they periodically recur.

May Day 1919 never recurred, at least not until the Communist turn of the late 1940s, and even then in a rather different form. Yet, the way it conceptualized history and its renewal continued to animate the public celebrations and rituals of the Horthy regime. Horthy's procession into Budapest on 16 November was designed as a historic act, but it was one whose primary purpose was to erase and rewrite. The choice of date, the white horse, and the route through the city all served a purpose.[24] Followed by his army, Horthy retraced some of the locations used on 1 May, treating Budapest as a land to conquer and subdue. He set up his headquarters in the art nouveau Gellért Hotel, by Gellért Hill, and it was in the square in front of the hotel that the mayor and other representatives of the municipality officially welcomed him. Saint Gerard was no longer covered up and was instead employed as a symbol; the mayor compared the saint's martyrdom to the martyrdom of Budapest under Communist rule. Horthy was not moved, however. He denounced Budapest, which had "trodden the Holy Crown and the national colors into the mud and dressed in red rags," and stated that forgiveness was not unconditional; first, the city would have to "return to its homeland."[25] Horthy and his army then continued across the city, symbolically recapturing its public spaces. The procession ended at the Parliament building, which now had completely new decoration. Where statues of Lenin and Liebknecht had stood a few months before, a green tent was now spread over an altar. Behind it, a giant golden cross proclaimed Christianity as the bulwark of the new regime.

Horthy's procession was a public spectacle with ritualistic elements, but it was not a ritual the crowd could participate in. While on 1 May, the crowd was positioned as the main actor, on 16 November, ordinary residents of Budapest were onlookers who watched Horthy and his army symbolically occupy the streets. Although the event was essentially a reconquest and helped build Horthy's subsequent image as "new Árpád," it is doubtful whether the march itself projected this historical frame of reference to onlookers. What spectators saw from the roadside was not a historical pageant but a contemporary military parade (fig. 1.2). This was, however, itself a form of historic representation; it emphasized that great, historic events were taking place right then, in that very moment. Like the May Day celebrations, the procession declared the advent of a better world. On May Day, this bright future was represented by abstract shapes—a new art. On 16 November, the idea of regeneration was expressed by Christian symbolism—something more traditional at first sight than giant spheres but radically appropriated and rethought by the Horthy cult.

The messianic cult of Horthy as redeemer unfolded flamboyantly in a speech by the conservative writer Cécile Tormay (1875–1937) given in front of the Parliament:

> It is dawn today! You have brought it—and we, women, like two thousand years ago, on the morning of the Holy Bible, at the foot of the Golgotha, have come to greet the resurrection! Your homecoming is a Hungarian dawn and a Christian resurrection after a terrible bloody Calvary,

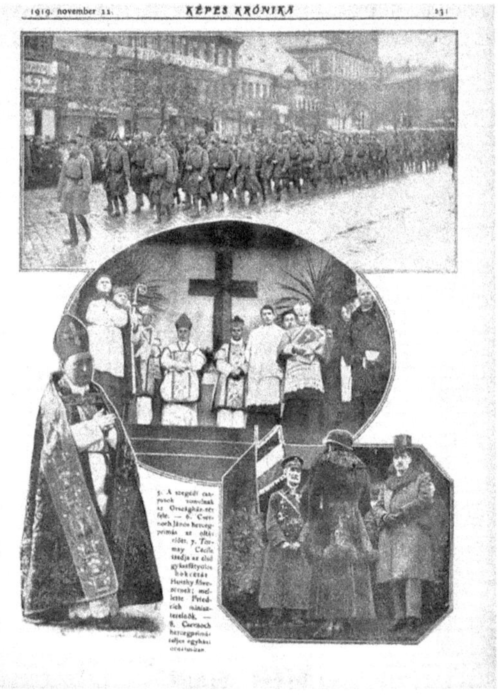

FIGURE 1.2. Page from the 22 November 1919 issue of the magazine *Képes Krónika* with scenes from Horthy's procession on 16 November 1919.

in which Károlyi, the Hungarian Iscariot, and his demonic collaborators betrayed, tortured, robbed and demeaned the Hungarian nation. It was the darkest night of our history, and now the morning is so promising, because you have come. For six months, the name of hope in Hungary has been Horthy.[26]

With its simple uniforms and religious props, its apparent sobriety, and its positioning of Horthy as redeemer, 16 November encompassed a strange duality that nevertheless formed a coherent whole. It is interesting to observe, for instance, the contrast between textual commentary, which often used religious language similar to Tormay's, and visual reportage, which was much more reserved. Instead of conjuring up historical or biblical parallels in their illustrations, magazines such as the *Képes Krónika* (*Illustrated Chronicle*) used photographs that emphasized the contemporariness of the event: the fact that it had taken place in the material reality of the present (fig. 1.2).

In one picture, Horthy's army marches along a street. The soldiers are wearing their military hats and coats, while the cobbled street glistens in the insistent November sleet. In another, Tormay herself is handing a bouquet to Horthy. She is seen from behind, her elegant fur coat dotted with snow; her hunched shoulders indicate she is cold. Opposite her, Horthy stands wearing his admiral's uniform, while Prime Minister István Friedrich (1883–1951) sports a top hat—certainly not conjuring up biblical times. Religious references only appear in pictures showing the ecclesiastical participants of the ceremony, but these, too, are simple portraits rather than images of a religious ceremony involving metaphysical transformation.

The texts and the images employed different strategies but ultimately constituted two sides of a coin. Adulatory texts promoted the desired interpretation, providing contemporary events with historical and metaphysical depth. The photographs, in turn, grounded them in everyday reality. The May Day celebration had offered abstract ideals, future utopias. The message of 16 November was that order would return. To gigantic spheres and obelisks, a simple procession in uniform offered the best antidote. In photographs of 1 May, the reality of Budapest seemed to awkwardly disrupt the message, while in Horthy's spectacle, it was the focus, a reality to be harnessed. We do not peddle utopias, the implication seems to be; we restore what the country truly *is*. Horthy's reconquest was a myth of monumental dimensions, but what made it graspable were the snowflakes on Tormay's fur coat.

Photography was central to the promotion of public rituals. After all, not everyone in the country could be present, but many more had access to illustrated magazines. Photography—a relatively new tool—helped turn the present into history and performed this transformation in real time. Control over the photographic image meant controlling the narrative. The leaders of the Soviet Republic had been aware of this and had commissioned official photographs of May Day to be disseminated in the press. Aiming to set up a museum of the Soviet Republic, they also called on amateurs to donate any pictures they may have taken.[27] Materials for the planned museum, including sculptures from the festivities, were stored in the Hungarian National Museum. After the fall of the Soviet Republic, a crowd the organizers could no longer control stormed the museum and destroyed most of the revolutionary collection.[28]

The Horthy regime had more time to disseminate its narratives through rituals and images and make them part of the everyday. Published in many magazines and accompanied by adulatory texts, the image of Horthy riding a white horse became ingrained in the historic imaginary as a symbol of the fall of the Soviet Republic and the dawn of a new era. Its apparent reality, graspable through photographs, was a prerequisite for its subsequent mythicization. The sense of the *historic* significance of 16 November 1919 suffused interwar culture through the many subsequent incarnations of this image as well as through celebrations and anniversaries remembering, referencing, or restaging this event. In the 1920s, under Prime Minister István Bethlen, anniversaries of the procession were subdued, but they expanded in the mid-1930s under hardline right-wing Prime Minister Gyula Gömbös.[29] By this time, organizers looked to Italy and incorporated parallels with Mussolini's March on Rome.[30] As noted earlier, Mussolini saw the crowd as material to be shaped, but nevertheless, as Mabel Berezin has pointed out, public access to Fascist celebrations was often strictly limited, with the "crowd" made up of official invitees.[31] Hence, Horthy's procession was not as different from these mass events as it would seem at first sight. Its subsequent reiterations, as well as the regime's other events, ritually colonized the calendar in a manner similar to the Fascist rituals of Italy. Drawing on newer technologies and the channels of public life, employing modern techniques of reshaping social identities and controlling the public sphere, the Horthy regime positioned itself as the primary maker and arbiter of history—the sole, real option in the present and the only true lens for viewing the past.

The Oath in the Vérmező: Illusions of Documentation

On 11 April 1920, a solemn ceremony took place in Budapest, in an area called the Vérmező, just beneath Castle Hill. The National Army—the troops that had helped Horthy to power—took an oath to uphold the constitution in the presence of the regent and other officials. The next month, the Union of Defensive Leagues (Védőligák Szövetsége), a nationalist organization formed to protest Hungary's territorial loss, announced a competition for a monumental painting depicting the ceremony. In August, they exhibited the submitted sketches at the Hungarian National Museum.

The Transylvanian-born Ferenc Márton (1884–1940) had entered a highly fanciful composition. Instead of representing the oath as it had actually been, he reimagined it as a twentieth-century version of the "blood oath," a mythical pact between the leaders of the seven Hungarian tribes in the ninth century that involved shedding blood from their arms into a shared chalice. From the nineteenth century, this event had symbolized the constitutionalism of the Hungarian nation. Márton's sketch is now lost, but, as described by the artist himself, it showed "leader Horthy" standing on a mound "above the ruins, projected onto the glimmering background of the gloomy sky, as if he had just arisen from the earth or descended from the sky." He is about to cut himself to shed his blood, while "from below a mass of hands raised up in oath reach toward him, with orders of shock troops and leaders behind them."[32]

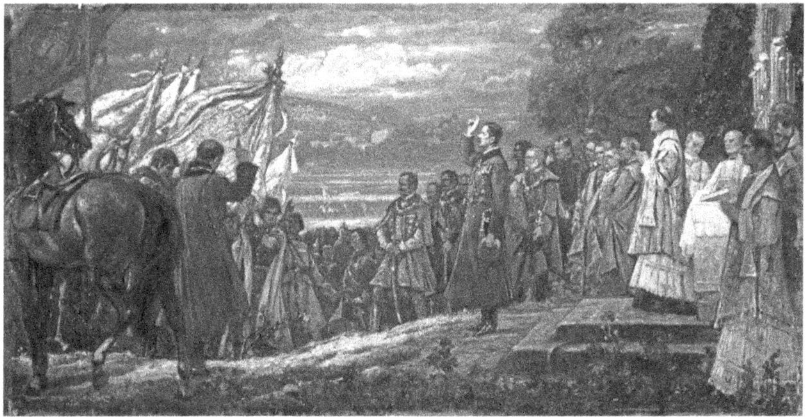

FIGURE 1.3.   Andor Dudits, *Oath in the Vérmező*, sketch, 1920, Hungarian National Gallery, Budapest.
Photo: Szépművészeti Múzeum / Museum of Fine Arts, 2025

Márton's sketch garnered much attention. The daily *Budapesti Hírlap* stated that it was "undoubtedly the best in terms of absolute artistic merit" thanks to "the originality of the idea, the unity of the structure, the momentum and genuine passion expressed in the compositional elements."[33] Yet, it did not win the competition. Instead, the first prize, and with it the commission for a monumental painting, went to the older painter Andor Dudits (1866–1944), who had—as the *Budapesti Hírlap* acknowledged—adhered more closely to the rules by submitting a conventional history painting rather than a symbolic composition (fig. 1.3).

In Dudits's picture, Horthy raised his hand in oath as he conducted the ceremony. He was surrounded by prominent contemporaries rigidly arranged into a group portrait. In the left-hand part of the composition, soldiers waved flags and raised their hands as they took the oath.[34]

Despite receiving a consolation prize, Márton felt insulted. Angrily, he kicked a hole into the painting—an act of iconoclasm widely reported by the excited press. In one of the reports, the still indignant Márton explained why his painting stood out: "I did not intend [the picture] as a portrait album of the participants, but as a compositive [*sic*], idealizing, symbolic artwork."[35] The mention of a portrait album was clearly a jab at the winning entry.

Márton was an eccentric artist with a bad temper who had submitted a bewilderingly bizarre composition, but his claim that the jury had been looking for a certain kind of quasi-documentary was correct. The official visual culture of the Horthy regime used a range of techniques to make its interpretation of the recent past appear not only true but also tangibly, relatably *present*. Events such as Horthy's procession or the oath in the Vérmező made it possible for members of the public to experience history in the making, and this experience was further disseminated by modern innovations such as photography and film. This did not mean, however, that traditional art forms no longer had a role. Dudits's *Oath in the Vérmező* demonstrates how painting could incorporate new forms of visual culture to monumentalize the Horthy regime's transformed present.

As in the case of the triumphal procession, the date and place of the oath had a symbolic relevance. This time, the ceremony sought to appropriate and overwrite a Hungarian revolutionary narrative that stretched back in time beyond the Soviet Republic. The eleventh of April marked the anniversary of the so-called April Laws of 1848, a key event of the revolution in which the Hungarian Parliament introduced liberal legislation with the grudging approval of the Habsburg imperial government. The symbolism of the location reached back even further, to the eighteenth century. Vérmező is today a public park, but in the nineteenth and early twentieth centuries, it served as a military training field. It gained its gruesome name—*Vérmező* means "field of blood"—after participants of the Hungarian Jacobin conspiracy were executed there by imperial authorities in 1795. Unsurprisingly, it served as one of the main locations in the May Day celebrations of 1919, when a giant sarcophagus was constructed there as a memorial to the executed Jacobins. While the memory of 1848 was something the Horthy regime sought to appropriate and reinterpret, the Jacobin tradition—an important reference point for left-wingers since the late nineteenth century—was one to be extinguished.[36] Throughout its existence, the regime regularly used the Vérmező for official festivities involving military parades in order to provide the space with new meanings. These included commemorating the formation of Horthy's army in Szeged, celebrating the anniversary of the fall of the Soviet Republic, and, in 1934, observing the fifteenth anniversary of Horthy's victorious ride into Budapest. The oath of the National Army was the first of these events.

Although the oath recalled multiple events from the historical past simply by virtue of its date and location, the ceremony did not explicitly reference these. Photos published of the event show it was rather low-key, lacking historicizing props. According to press reports, Horthy arrived on horseback and inspected his soldiers from the back of his steed.[37] At the actual ceremony, he stood on the ground listening to the mass before the oath.[38] It was this religious component that most articles and photos focused on, instead of references to history. A photo of soldiers taking the oath shows the temporary altar in the background with a group of ecclesiastical figures wearing ceremonial robes.[39] There is a randomness to the photos that works against historical allusions. In the picture of Horthy at the mass, the regent's lone figure separated from the group gives him an air of importance, but any expression of majesty is undercut by the undisciplined nature of the larger group, whose members adopt different poses; some are looking away, and two men on the left seem to be chatting to each other. The reality effect created by these unruly details was more important in reportage than references to the past, which could have been conveyed through other types of visual material, such as drawings. Indeed, the right-wing extremist *Képes Krónika*, which was unable to photograph the event (and true to form blamed this on a Jewish plot), opted to eschew pictures altogether rather than replace photos with artists' impressions.[40]

That "presentness" was key to how the event was to be remembered is demonstrated by the Union of Defensive Leagues' decision to reward Dudits's painting over Márton's. In its emphasis on the group portrait element, the winning composition centered documentary value much like the photographs published in the press. When it announced its competition, the union had organized a cinema screening of all footage of the event for painters interested in participating. It had even issued a call to amateur filmmakers/photographers to hand in copies of any images they had captured.[41]

This quest for the historical accuracy of details was not new; nineteenth-century history painters had often used primary sources such as old paintings and prints or surviving items of clothing or weapons to make their compositions historically "faithful." This was especially true of late nineteenth-century ceremonious, official commissions—the nearest precedents to Dudits's picture. The status of photography and film as evidence was, however, radically different from that of a sixteenth-century portrait. In the 1920s, newspapers often reported on the efficacy of photography as documentation.[42] By contrast, the ability of painting to accurately reflect reality was increasingly questioned in art criticism. To cite an example as remote as possible from Dudits's aesthetics, even the doyen of the Hungarian avant-garde, Lajos Kassák (1887–1967), penned an essay on painting and photography emphasizing the latter's superior documentative qualities.[43] The flip side of Kassák's—and many others'—argument was that while photography was a useful technological invention, it was not an art.

By encouraging painters to build on film and photography, the Union of Defensive Leagues made clear it expected a painting of the oath that not only had documentary value but also would be perceived as possessing the modern quality of presentness. At the same time, the intention was to infuse the event with the gravitas of history, hence connecting it to a larger narrative. Dudits's painting achieved this by adding a host of details that deviated from the "reality" of the scene captured in the photographs. For instance, in his painting, Horthy stands on a mound rather than at the same level as the soldiers on the ground—a compositional device that elevated the regent's importance. As the *Budapesti Hirlap* explained when the finished painting was unveiled in 1923, the arrangement belonged among the artistic rather than the political aspects of the picture. Many entrants to the competition had struggled with "grouping the parading army around the figure of the regent in a way that makes the imposing monumentality of the picture palpable for the viewer," and Dudits had solved this by elevating Horthy and arranging the group behind him.[44] The paper justified minor changes to the composition with artistic requirements, glossing over the political implications. Dudits had, however, made some more important changes, too, and these concerned the group portrait itself—the part that was supposed to create the reality effect.

The original competition had been for a painting depicting the oath of the *army*. Yet, the winning entry (as well as Márton's version) focused on Horthy, rather than the army, taking the oath. This reflected an important early shift in Horthy's image, transforming him from a powerful military leader into an upholder of Hungary's laws in peacetime. The military character of the army is subdued in the painting; Horthy is not represented at its helm but is overlooking it as its protector, himself bound by higher laws to which he swears allegiance. This should not be understood as a gesture of humility; the closest analogy was the oath taken by Hungarian kings as part of the coronation ceremony. In the first months after his march into Budapest, Horthy's self-representation was that of a military autocrat, but after the declaration of the regency, he increasingly appeared as a constitutional monarch.[45]

With Horthy taking the place of the Habsburg ruling family, it is notable that—according to contemporary descriptions—the painting included two Habsburgs, princes Joseph and Joseph Francis, in Horthy's entourage.[46] The painting spoke to a particular historical moment and its complex politics. When Horthy assumed power, the return of the Habsburgs was still a realistic possibility, and support for the idea—legitimism—was a strong political movement. Just weeks before the oath, on 27 March, Charles IV had entered Hungary and requested that Horthy hand over power to him. Horthy had previously tried to placate legitimists, but now he had to take a stand; he refused the king's request and banished him from the country. In October, Charles returned with military force and was defeated in the brief Battle of Budaörs. The oath represented the moment when Horthy broke with legitimism and took the place of Hungary's ruler.[47] The inclusion of Habsburgs, as well as legitimist politicians, in the composition highlighted that they, too, had witnessed the ceremony. For this to be confirmed, their presence had to be solid and realistic; a fantasy composition with the blood oath would not do. This had to be an image of unity that depicted Horthy's ascension as indisputable. Dudits, the artist, lent his eyes and hand to the purpose of making it real.

The figures standing behind Horthy were recognizable to contemporaries. According to the *Pesti Napló* (*Pest Journal*), the group included the Habsburg princes, the legitimist politician Andrássy, the right-wing radical Gömbös, Nándor Urmánczy (1868–1940), president of the Union of Defensive Leagues, previous and future prime ministers Albert Apponyi, Friedrich, and Bethlen, Budapest Mayor Jenő Sipőcz, and the writer Jenő Rákosi. Among the priests, an important figure of the counterrevolution, the Franciscan friar and military bishop István Zadravecz (1884–1965), could be recognized alongside Ottokár Prohászka, bishop of Székesfehérvár, and Primate János Csernoch.[48] The painting hence provided a full tableau of the regime's political elite in 1920.

Zadravecz gave a speech at the festive unveiling of the painting on 13 May 1923 and publicly praised it on other occasions.[49] Privately, however, he also expressed criticism. In his diary, he not only pointed out the iconographical shift from the oath of the army to that of Horthy but also complained how the painting diminished his own crucial role in the ceremony. "The mass had been performed by me, helped by one or two military priests, but Dudits . . . had also included Primate Csernoch, Nuncio Schioppa, Prohászka, protestant superintendents such as Raffay, Józan and Petrik, as well as civilian notabilities who had not even been present."[50] Zadravecz hinted that the changes had been motivated by a quest for "parity": the painting was to encompass a broad range of political and religious (Christian) persuasions within Hungary's ruling elite. Painters had been urged to employ film footage, but ultimately this was a call for *realism*, not *reality*. The apparent objectivity of the group portrait served to endow a constructed image with an illusion of documentary value.

In the years up until 1945, when it mysteriously disappeared, the propagandistic potential of the painting was fully exploited by the regime. The picture was displayed at various events before being moved to the Hungarian National Museum, from where it was permanently loaned to the Officers' Casino. Moreover, Dudits authorized the Archduke Joseph Sanatorium Association, a charity operating tuberculosis sanatoria across the country, to print color reproductions and sell them to benefit the organization. Governmental and local authorities encouraged their institutions to buy and distribute the reproductions.[51] This mode of dissemination was characteristic of the way official and private institutions intertwined in Horthy's Hungary and of how the regime employed these entanglements to transmit its message.

On 22 February 1924, the minister of religion and education ordered all primary and secondary schools to raise funds for the Sanatorium Association; in return, they would receive reproductions of Dudits's painting.[52]

In this way, the *Oath in the Vérmező* became one of many "demonstrative images" used in education, joining reproductions of nineteenth-century history paintings depicting seminal events from the distant past. The oath was presented as having equal importance. Dudits signaled this by elevating Horthy onto the mound and by staging the scene in front of a stormy sky, artistic gestures that endowed the composition with sublimity. In the end, this appearance of greatness, of making history, was the most important aim of all. In May 1923, when Dudits gifted a preliminary study of the painting to the regent, Horthy thanked him for this depiction "of the most significant scene from recent times in Hungarian history."[53]

The Art of Dissent: Mihály Bíró's Horthy and the Reality of Suffering

The interpretation of the events of 1919–1920, the circumstances in which Horthy rose to power, was a crucial element of interwar memory politics around which everything else revolved. As the example of the *Oath in the Vérmező* has shown, proponents of the government's preferred interpretation had access to a range of channels to disseminate their view across society. Room for alternatives was, by contrast, severely limited by strict legislation against "offending the regent."[54] For dissenters, it was virtually impossible to disrupt the way the official narrative had suffused the public sphere. Such interventions were only possible abroad, and this is what left-wing émigrés attempted in 1930, on the tenth anniversary of Horthy's regency. On 27 February 1930, the Austrian left-wing newspaper *Der Abend* printed, under the title "Zehn Jahre Horthy," six images showing Horthy's participation in the postrevolutionary White Terror.[55] The history of these images demonstrates not only the immense difference between possibilities to promote the official and alternative interpretations of history but also the significance of the "reality effect" in successful propaganda in the interwar period. The images printed in *Der Abend* were, by then, ten years old. Like Dudits's picture, *Horthy*, the series of lithographs by Mihály Bíró (1886–1948), employed realism—and, unlike Dudits's work, even naturalism—to make a claim for objectivity. The artistic means they employed were, however, limited by the circumstances and by the artist's character. In fact, I argue that the prints as means of visual persuasion were *less* modern than Horthyite propaganda, questioning the usual view that equates political and artistic conservatism.

Best known for his political posters, especially the emblematic *Man with the Red Hammer*, Bíró was a longtime Social Democrat who had created the famous image for the party in 1912.[56] During the Soviet Republic, he took on a role in cultural politics and was one of the organizers of May Day. After the fall of the Communist regime, he emigrated to Vienna and remained active in the Social Democratic movement. His *Horthy* series formed part of his activism. Originally produced in 1920 as a portfolio of lithographs, *Horthy* depicted episodes from the White Terror, emphasizing Horthy's personal responsibility and not shying away from the most gruesome details. In Hungary, it was strictly banned; any copies discovered were immediately confiscated and destroyed.[57] Bíró and his comrades focused on disseminating the series abroad to raise international awareness, and hence the lithographs were captioned in four languages (Hungarian, English, French, and German). The publisher was the Anzensgruber Verlag owned by Philipp Suschitzky, who often worked for the Austrian Social Democratic Party.[58] Therefore, *Horthy* may have been produced under the party's auspices, to be distributed through its international networks. Initially issued on large sheets, the prints were also reproduced as cheap postcards distributed as far away as the United States.[59]

Due to the terrors of the recent Great War and its aftermath as well as to the emergence of photography and film, the representation of extreme violence was a timely topic in art criticism in the 1920s. The Hungarian art critic Ernő Kállai (1890–1954), a left-winger who had been involved in Kassák's avant-garde group and had emigrated to Berlin after the fall of the Soviet Republic, made his own contribution to the debate in 1927. Kállai began by critiquing *The Trench* by the German artist Otto Dix (1891–1969), a work that depicted the devastation of war and took the "materialistic representation of reality to such brutal extremes" that it could not be compared to any other product of modern painting.[60] According to Kállai, all art that depicted something realistically in order to reject it contained an inner contradiction: realistic representation required identification on part of the artist, leading to a situation where it became impossible to determine whether Dix, for instance, had been "led by repulsion or pleasure" in his work.[61] There was, Kállai continued, an "optical device of modern technology" much better suited to representing violent events: photography. To Kállai, photography was not art, but as a means of documentation, it was eminently superior to anything a human hand could produce:

> Because they do not offer art, which reevaluates things in a formal sense and therefore inherently contains an essential mood different from real life, photographs strike us vehemently as fragments of another, hor-

rible reality. . . . Their inconsolably grey, emotionless objectivity points out, with an almost unbearable, record-like faithfulness, all details of the terrible mechanism of war one by one, and within this it shows the human being, defenselessly exposed to all terrors.[62]

Seen from our present, Kállai's argument resonates with discussions about the ethics of war reportage or the representation of atrocities such as the Holocaust. The difference is that we no longer believe in the objectivity of photography and film and, in fact, consider them chief culprits in presenting suffering as an object of viewing pleasure. This was, however, less clear in the 1920s, and we have to take this into account to understand Bíró's Horthy.

The *Horthy* series can be seen as an example of the issues raised by Kállai. It depicts the most gruesome scenes using an artistic technique—the colored lithograph—that inevitably recalled classic precedents from the nineteenth century, thereby softening the viewer's confrontation with the subject matter. Bíró was an immensely skilled lithographer, and many of the details are hauntingly beautiful: the greenish-brown hues of the gently drawn foliage in Sheet V, *In the Woods of Orgovány*, or the way the streetlight illuminates the dark night in Sheet X, *Pay or Die* (fig. 1.4). The former image, however, shows a scene of mass murder, with paramilitaries plundering the bodies of their Jewish victims, while in the latter sheet, they rob a man who obviously has no recourse to justice. The contrast between this and the beauty of the technique is profoundly unsettling.

Would Bíró's goals have been better served by photographs? Visual documentation of some of the events of the White Terror certainly did exist. The Entente had welcomed Horthy's emergence, the fall of the Soviet Republic, and the (hoped for) stabilization of Hungary, but by 1920, rumors of extreme violence caused international concern. In the British Parliament, Colonel Josiah Wedgwood, a Labour Party Member of Parliament, repeatedly inquired whether the government had any knowledge about issues such as "the approximate number of persons suspected of socialism and communism now interned or imprisoned in Hungary."[63] Dissatisfied with the information received, the Labour Party and the Trade Union Congress set up an investigative committee under Wedgwood's leadership in early 1920 to gain insight on the ground. Committee members travelled to Hungary and examined photographic evidence of the events in addition to interviewing survivors of counterrevolutionary violence as well as Hungarian officials. The resulting report was dire; it listed cases of torture, murder, imprisonment without due process, and other atrocities against individuals while also documenting the Hungarian government's suppression of trade unionism and other left-wing activities.[64]

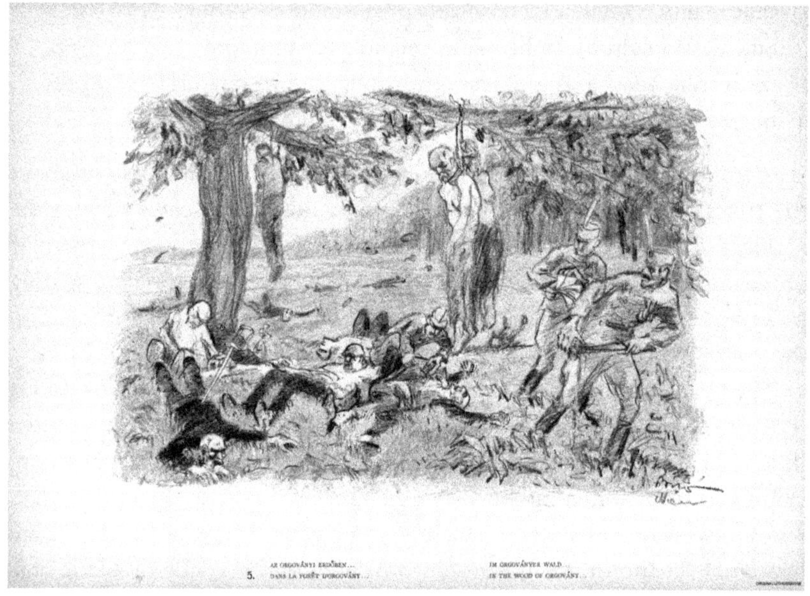

Figure 1.4.   Mihály Bíró, *In the Woods of Orgovány (Horthy V)*, 1920, National Széchényi Library, Budapest, Map, Poster, and Small Print Collection.
Photo: National Széchényi Library

Several images in Bíró's series correspond to the report.[65] One heinous case appearing in both had been recounted to the committee by "Mrs. Hamburger," the sister-in-law of Communist People's Commissar Jenő Hamburger, whose first name has unfortunately been lost to history.[66] Hamburger, whose husband had fled to Vienna with his more prominent brother, had been imprisoned without due process along with Béla Neumann, a family friend. There, she was raped and tortured by militiamen for weeks. Their captors, who included one of the main militia leaders Iván Héjjas, instructed Neumann to rape Hamburger and punished him with emasculation after he refused multiple times. Neumann did not survive the ordeal, and his body was thrown into the Danube. Bíró's Sheet XVII, *The Beasts*, shows Neumann's tragic fate and militiamen assaulting Hamburger in the background (fig. 1.5). Following her eventual release from captivity, Hamburger fled to Vienna, where she reported her experiences to the committee.

In his prints, Bíró filtered the brutality of the White Terror through art historical tradition. *The Beasts* clearly recalls *Ya No Hay Tiempo* (c. 1810–1814), a sheet from Francisco Goya's (1746–1828) *The Disasters of War*, which depicts the imminent torture of an unconscious man by a soldier pointing a sword to his groin as other soldiers are about to rape the female members of the fam-

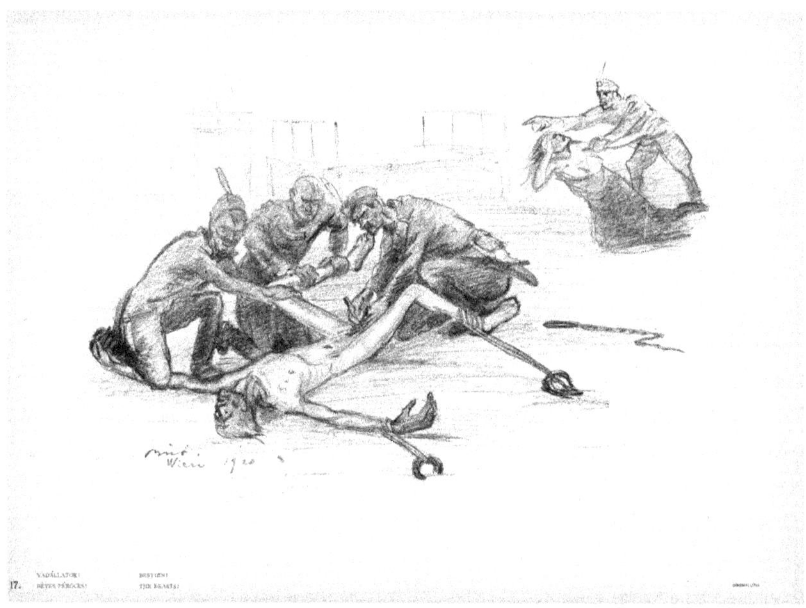

FIGURE 1.5. Mihály Bíró, *The Beasts (Horthy XVII)*, 1920, National Széchényi Library, Budapest, Map, Poster, and Small Print Collection.
Photo: National Széchényi Library

ily. However, while the comparison highlights Bíró's artistic depiction of violence—something Kállai would have frowned on—it also reveals his intention to document, rather than mythicize, the atrocities. In Goya's series, visual drama is created by subtle effects of light and shadow enveloping the main scenes and by fine lines that soften the contours and create ambiguity. By contrast, Bíró's images are more naturalistic. They lack the softness of Goya's shadows and leave no question about what is going on. However dainty the lithographed lines, they delineate the details as clearly as the Wedgwood report itself.

A similar approach can be observed in how Bíró employed the language of satire. To Kállai, satire was a problematic art form; it aimed for social critique but could only draw in viewers by making the subject of its critique visually appealing. A main offender was the nineteenth-century lithographer Honoré Daumier (1808–1879), undoubtedly one of Bíró's models. Daumier, wrote Kállai, created romantic visions that elevated their derided subject matter to a sublimity it did not deserve.[67] "All artistically significant dissent," he continued, "exposes the object of its caricature to such fundamental depths that, in its shadow, terrible or ridiculous facts build up to a closed world order. And once this order is in place it produces a kind of justification, a certain perverted glorification of its details."[68]

Was Bíró guilty of this? The prints can be seen as avoiding such pitfalls. In his political posters, Bíró often employed the satirical language of visual hyperbole that amounted to romantic visions. In *Horthy*, however, he refrained from hyperbole, even though he employed satire in many of the titles of sheets (for instance, in Sheet II, *The Governor Has a Good Time*, Horthy and his men dine while observing the torture of a prisoner). All figures are life-sized within the pictorial world and exist in the same reality. The images suggest that while their violence is outrageous and hard to believe, it does indeed reflect the terrible reality of postrevolutionary Hungary.

Despite these efforts, there remains an inherent contradiction between the visually appealing artistic techniques of *Horthy* and its violent subject matter. The contradiction is not resolved; it cannot be resolved. Yet, the endeavor works: the visual beauty of artistic skill draws our eyes to scenes we would rather not look at. Ultimately, this was Bíró's aim: to force the world to look. The extreme naturalism of the compositions is extraordinary in the context of late nineteenth- and early twentieth-century lithography and shockingly thwarts the viewer's expectations. Through this shock, the prints deny their own status as art and claim for themselves the accuracy of photographic documentation.

Large lithographs were too expensive and bulky to be widely distributed, so Bíró's images were almost immediately reproduced as postcards. In this version, the beauty of lithographed lines is no longer present, and stark naturalism comes fully to the fore. When *Der Abend* reprinted some of the images in 1930 for the Horthy anniversary, all color and beauty were gone. Occupying a whole page in a paper, the prints fully assumed the role of photographic reportage. Ironically, however, the newspaper had to verbally explain that each of the scenes was a depiction of reality rather than a figment of the artist's imagination.[69] Without the reality effect provided by snowflakes and furs, the testimony of the prints was incomplete. Despite their immensely poignant employment of naturalism, they no longer stood on their own as historical documentary.

In Hungary, official institutions and the regime-friendly press all celebrated Admiral Horthy on his anniversary in 1930. The only flies in the soup were the "diatribes" that had appeared in the international left-wing press, for which Hungarian papers blamed the "Socialist Second Internationale" and its "anti-Horthy press campaign."[70] On the publication of Bíró's prints in Vienna, the Hungarian government took action. Following its complaints, the editors of *Der Abend* were charged with obscenity and received a suspended one-month prison sentence.[71] Ultimately, those who wielded power had more room to shape narratives about recent history. Indeed, Bíró's lithographs and postcards were eliminated so successfully by interwar authorities that few copies are accessible today. The regime, meanwhile, continued to use mass events to mold cultural memory into its preferred narrative.

The Present into History: The Anniversary of the Battle of Mohács

Commemorating events such as the oath in the Vérmező was an important part of memory politics but ultimately was ineffective if it did not also reshape national history as a whole. Recent events such as Trianon or the revolutions had to be placed into a broader context in which the disappointments, chaos, and violence made sense. When the oath was staged on 11 April, the parallel with 1848 helped construct a narrative in which Horthy's ascent fit into the history of Hungarian constitutionalism. In a similar way, a host of other events and personalities from the past came to be employed as reference points. Rather than just involving historicist spectacle, their anniversaries merged old and modern to make history and the present appear as one.

In 1926, the Hungarian state commemorated the four hundredth anniversary of the Battle of Mohács, one of the most seminal Hungarian sites of memory. On 29 August 1526, the Hungarian army had suffered a devastating defeat by the Ottoman Turks. The young King Louis II died in the battle, and within two decades, the Kingdom of Hungary was tripartitioned into a Habsburg-ruled Kingdom, Ottoman-occupied territories, and the Principality of Transylvania. Hungary's existence as a major independent state in Europe was over. Although it was one of many early sixteenth-century battles against the Ottomans, the romantic imagination of the nineteenth century stylized Mohács into *the* great national tragedy.[72] In this narrative, the defeat of the War of Independence in 1849 appeared as a new Mohács. After 1920, Trianon could also be added to the storyline. The Hungarian-Turkish wars held great significance in interwar right-wing memory; the Hungarians were viewed as the bulwarks of Christian Europe, with the Ottomans cast as historical prefigurations of twentieth-century Communists, enemies of Horthy's "Christian Hungary."[73] The Mohács–Trianon parallel was especially pertinent because both events were connected to territorial loss.[74] Hence, it is no surprise that the commemorations held in 1926 referenced Trianon.

The parallel between Mohács and Trianon became ingrained as an interpretative framework almost immediately after the treaty was signed. In 1922, two theaters in Budapest premiered two different plays about Mohács—one by Géza Voinovich (1877–1952), a writer and literary historian, at the National Theater, and the other by Dezső Szomory (1869–1944), an art nouveau author, at the Magyar (Hungarian) Theater. Reviewing Voinovich's play *Mohács*, the magazine *Színházi Élet* (*Theater Life*) noted that "a new version of the terrible disaster of Mohács is playing out in front of our eyes right now."[75] Voinovich was a conservative in his art and his politics, but the production of his play was a modern one. It was staged by Sándor Hevesi (1873–1939), perhaps the greatest interwar Hungarian theater director, who embraced the modernism of artists such as Edward Gordon Craig. As evidenced by photos in *Színházi Élet*, the costumes evoked the sixteenth century but sifted through a twentieth-century aesthetic.[76] This was in contrast to the other play, *Louis II*, which had been directed by Márkus, a director partly responsible for the festivities of 1 May 1919. His revolutionary sympathies did not stop Márkus from creating a full historical spectacle; the costumes were detailed and lavish, and so were the stage sets, which he designed himself.[77] The photos and descriptions in *Színházi Élet* emphasized that the performance was a feast for the eyes. This time, the actors were photographed with sets in the background, gesturing forcefully with dramatic facial expressions. A photo of the actress Lili Darvas in the role of the widowed queen shows her kneeling in a chapel, dressed in black, her heavy velvet robe and the light effects reminiscent of a nineteenth-century history painting.[78] The Budapest theater world was very much part of the liberal urban culture ideologues the Horthy regime wished to eradicate. Szomory, the writer of *Louis II*, would die in the Budapest ghetto in 1944. But when it came to historicist spectacle, nobody did it better than the theaters of Budapest.

The official festivities of 1926 were different. The main events took place in Mohács, near the southern border of Hungary, handily moving the focus away from sinful Budapest. In fact, one of the most important events was a pilgrimage to Mohács in which participants sailed down the Danube, away from Budapest, toward a more deserving part of the country. Once there, pilgrims could view a large exhibition of industrial products from Mohács and the nearby larger city of Pécs. Some events focused on economy and industry (a National Industrial Producers' Congress; a Beekeepers' Day), others on the Catholic religion (a Catholic Day; an Assembly of Catholic Schoolteachers), creating a curious medley. Commemorating an old, lost battle with an industrial exhibition might seem random, but the texts accompanying the program made the reasoning crystal clear. Mohács was located close to the Yugoslav border. Its county, Baranya, had been considerably larger before Trianon but had been dissected by the new borders. Hence, as one festive guidebook, published by the right-wing irredentist paper *Magyarság*, explained, Baranya was "a miniature mirror of the former, happy Greater Hungary." It had "everything in a smaller version that we used to have at a larger scale": mountains, valleys, forests, agriculture, mines, factories, a multiethnic population.[79] The industrial-cultural exhibitions in Mohács and Pécs served as reminders of the former greatness of the country but also of its progress in present times toward the future. In 1526, according to the guidebook, the Greater Hungary of the time died. "Hungarians who know that resurrection eventually happened make a pilgrimage to Mohács for this year's anniversary with their hearts filled with piety, to strengthen their faith in resurrection after Trianon at this site of mourning."[80] Ongoing industrial production was a sign of hope.

Few photographs of the official festivities in Mohács are available today, a fact that suggests that visual spectacle was not a central issue. The illustrated supplement of the *Pesti Napló* published photographs of the one-time battlefield and of monuments in Mohács. A double spread included pictures of priests and young local women dressed in traditional garb above unrelated images of crowded beaches in England.[81] A five-minute newsreel showed Horthy and other notables making speeches, soldiers marching in twentieth-century uniforms, and current views of the historical location; all of it focused on the here and now.[82] Unlike at the theaters of Budapest, reviving the sixteenth century was not the goal; it was the present that had to be emphasized.

One of the most modern ecclesiastical buildings of interwar Hungary was occasioned by the Mohács anniversary, even though it was only realized years later. The foundation stone for a new memorial church was ceremoniously laid during the 1926 festivities. The architect Aladár Árkay (1868–1932) had won a competition to design it in 1924, but construction only began in 1929. After Árkay's death, his son, Bertalan (1901–1971), took over the commission.[83] By then, the younger Árkay had designed a scandalously modern church in the Városmajor area of Budapest. In a similar vein, he turned his father's original design for the Mohács building, a Byzantine-inspired centralized church with the Hungarian Holy Crown as its dome, into a solemn, simple structure with rounded and cubic forms and unadorned walls. In this way, his work embraced the present and future rather than the past.

With its unassuming industrial exhibitions and lack of large-scale demonstrative events, the Mohács anniversary hardly recalls Fascist Italy, but Mussolini's comment about making rather than writing history is nonetheless relevant. By focusing on the contemporary and the everyday, the anniversary rejected the idea of history as a linear narrative and instead merged the present with the past. Mohács was important solely because it helped explain the present and conceptualize the historic developments, the resurrection of Hungary, that would surely soon unfold before the interwar public's eyes.

History into the Present: The Saint Emeric Jubilee

The next major jubilee took place just four years after the Mohács anniversary, but it merged historical scenery and modern spectacle in completely different—and certainly more lavish—ways. The past years had been eventful. In 1927, the commissioners of the League of Nations, stationed in Hungary to oversee the implementation of the peace treaty, left the country. This opened new possibilities for official campaigning against Trianon. The government's revisionist politics picked up steam, thanks to support from various sources abroad, including, most importantly, Italy.[84] A treaty signed between the two countries in 1927 cemented Italy as Hungary's major ally. Prime Minister Bethlen's consolidatory politics bore fruit and solidified his position—but only briefly. Soon afterward, the Great Depression hit Hungary, causing instability that eventually led to Bethlen's resignation in 1932.

Hence, 1930 was a crucial moment for the regime to assert itself, and it did so by victoriously promoting a pillar of its ideology: the notion of "Christian Hungary." This was occasioned by the nine hundredth anniversary of the death of Saint Emeric (c. 1007–1031), son of King Stephen I (Saint Stephen), first king of Hungary. As the ruler who had unified and Christianized the kingdom, Stephen was a central figure in the memory politics of the regime; he came to symbolize Hungary's independence and historical right to the lost territories. The nine hundredth anniversary of his death in 1938 was marked by large-scale celebrations coinciding with an International Eucharistic Congress held in Budapest. The jubilee of his only son, celebrated eight years earlier, is less discussed today but equally illuminates the regime's ideological hold on society.

Emeric had died before his father and had played no significant political role. His main claim to sainthood was that he had, according to legend, pledged to remain a virgin and kept his pledge even after his marriage. Due to this, the jubilee was less overtly concerned with current politics and instead focused on the moral education of young people, transposing memory politics into the everyday and the most intimate private sphere. The overall aesthetic of the jubilee, markedly different from that of the Mohács anniversary, was shaped by this characteristic. This time, historicist elements were more prominent. Their role was to adapt the past to twentieth-century modernity to explain how Saint Emeric's legacy could be relevant to modern life. The poster promoting the central event encapsulated this perfectly (fig. 1.6).

"The Triumphal Journey of Christ the King along the Danube" was a grandiose procession of ships, one of them carrying the Eucharist.[85] In the poster, the youthful prince stands on a ship sailing up the river. Wearing a dainty crown and a short, colorful tunic and calmly holding a sword pointed

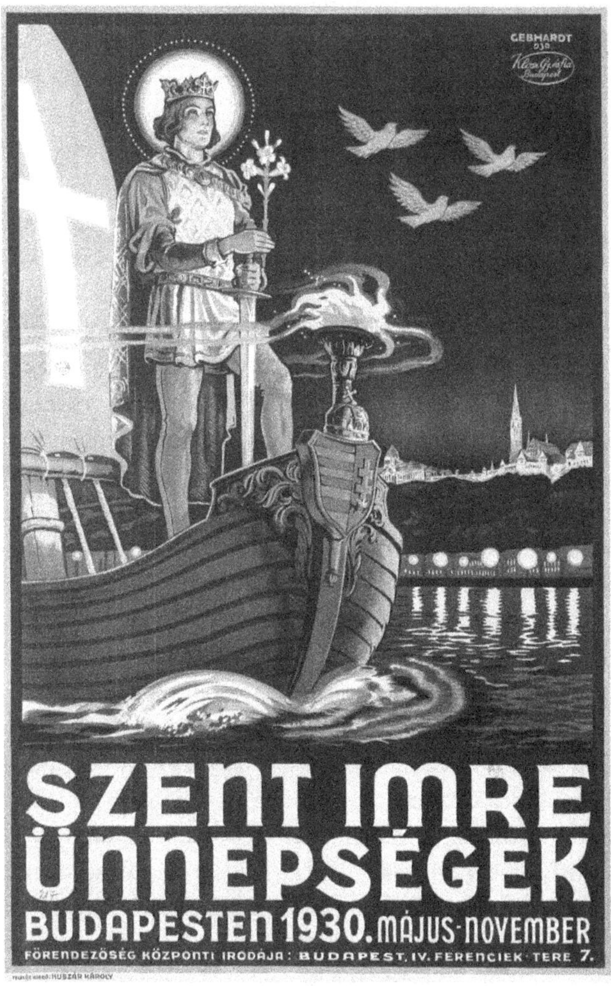

FIGURE 1.6.   Tibor Gönczi-Gebhardt, poster for the Saint Emeric jubilee, 1930, National Széchényi Library, Budapest, Map, Poster, and Small Print Collection.
Photo: National Széchényi Library. Tibor Gönczi-Gebhardt © OOA-S 2024

downward, he is a medievalist fantasy—Prince Charming himself, but with a halo. Behind him, in the background, the outlines of Budapest's castle area appear, with domes, spires, old houses. Yet, below castle hill, the scene is illuminated by electric lights. They cast colorful reflections on the surface of the river, competing with the flame of the torch at the bow of the prince's ship. It is the capital, Budapest—as the poster shows—that welcomes the prince, and the lights are reminders that he is sailing through a bustling metropolis. Designed by the prolific graphic artist Tibor Gönczi-Gebhardt (1902–1994), the poster was one of many that promoted Budapest as a tourist destination by fitting its historical visage into an art deco mold. The ubiquity of this approach helped mask the ideological message on the Saint Emeric poster.

While the most important architectural commission for the Mohács jubilee evolved into a modernist church, the architecture of the Saint Emeric jubilee was characterized by revivalism. Budapest, the "sinful city," was now central to the celebrations, which provided an occasion for its reshaping and hence self-redemption. In southern Buda, near the trajectory of Horthy's 1919 procession, where a main road had been renamed Miklós Horthy Road, the Cistercian order constructed an enormous new building for its secondary school. Completed in 1929 for the jubilee, it was joined by an adjacent church built between 1936 and 1938.[86] This part of the city was renamed Szentimreváros (Saint Emeric's Town). That a school was one of the most important products of the jubilee reflected the event's focus on youth. The school and the church, both the work of Gyula Wälder (1884–1944), are examples of the 1930s baroque revival. Critics of the Horthy regime often described its culture as neobaroque, an epithet first employed by Gyula Szekfű, who had transformed from the regime's ideologue into its critic by the mid-1930s.[87] Wälder's church and school provided evidence for this verdict. The baroque was, however, not the only historical style conjured up at the jubilee. The statue of Saint Emeric festively erected in the center of Saint Emeric's Town, in the round junction predictably called Miklós Horthy Circus, evoked the same late medieval chivalric atmosphere as Gebhardt's poster. Notably donated by the Habsburg Archduchess Isabella, the sculpture was the work of Zsigmond Kisfaludi Strobl (1884–1975), a favorite for official commissions.[88]

The renewal of ecclesiastical art was a much discussed—and contested—issue of great political relevance. In 1928, Kuno Klebelsberg, the minister of religion and education, launched the Rome Scholarship so young artists could be trained and then fulfill monumental commissions for state and church alike. As the art historian Tibor Gerevich explained, the aim was to create a modern art rooted in tradition.[89] This was an ambition shared with Italy; around the same time, the Mussolini regime organized several international exhibitions of ecclesiastical art, which Hungarian artists were encouraged to participate in.[90] The images of Saint Emeric produced for the jubilee have to be understood in this context.[91] When the painter György Kákay-Szabó (1903–1964), a recipient of the Rome Scholarship, depicted the prince on horseback in a medievalesque panel painting with a golden background but employed the modern formal language of New Objectivity, he sought renewal, not revival.[92]

The imagery of youth was, of course, central to myths of national regeneration in the early twentieth century.[93] Italian Fascism had emerged from modernist protest movements that presented themselves as youthful, healthy, and future-oriented in contrast to the "declining" liberal ruling class. In Romania, Codreanu called his "idealistic, youthful, voluntary movement" the Legion of the Archangel Michael, invoking religious imagery and emphasizing the "purity" of youth in a way comparable to the Saint Emeric jubilee.[94] Nevertheless, there were also differences. Compared, for instance, with the muscular figures of legionnaires produced by artists affiliated with Codreanu's movement, images of youth emerging from the Saint Emeric jubilee are dainty and serene.[95] The Horthy regime's inherent conservatism and the consolidatory politics of the Bethlen government did not accommodate images of raw power and revolutionary radicalism. Instead, the Saint Stephen jubilee promoted a regeneration based on piety, patriotism, and obedience. The cleansing of sinful Budapest could be achieved by constructing a leafy new suburb with historicizing buildings promoting the Catholic faith.

Unlike the Mohács jubilee, the Saint Emeric jubilee foregrounded historical imagery and historicizing styles. Nevertheless, it still emphatically centered the present. It is notable that none of the most important artistic commissions recalled the early eleventh century, Emeric's own time. Even those that were medievalist referred to the late medieval period. Instead of focusing on Saint Emeric himself, they evoked his worship over the years. It was not the historical figure of Emeric they commemorated, but his memory—the way his figure had, throughout the centuries, connected national history with Catholic ritual, embodying a narrative that demonstrated the longevity of the idea of Christian Hungary. Moreover, the focus on virginity helped expand the notion from the realm of politics into private life. The jubilee hailed Emeric as a myth adaptable to contemporary times, but most of all, it celebrated the present as the master of the past.

Research and Ideology: The Saint Stephen Jubilee

The largest, most influential, and most discussed jubilee celebrated in interwar Hungary was the nine hundredth anniversary of the death of Saint Stephen in 1938. By then, Hungary was on a steady course of right-wing radicalization. The longest-serving prime minister of the 1930s was Gömbös (1886–1936, in office 1932–1936), a leading figure of the interwar radical right and open Fascist sympathizer. In 1938, the government was headed by Béla Imrédy (1891–1946, in office 1938–1939), a determined antisemite who sought to reduce the powers of Parliament and establish himself as an autocratic leader. Although his attempts were thwarted by other members of the government, his antisemitic politics faced much less pushback. In May

1938, Parliament approved the first anti-Jewish law, and at the end of the year, Imrédy proposed the second; it would be accepted a few months later, by which time he had been forced to resign. Before that happened, however, Imrédy had achieved enormous diplomatic success. November 1938 saw the so-called First Vienna Award, in which Italy and Germany agreed to rejoin part of Slovakia to Hungary.

Hence, 1938 was a year when the politics of the Horthy regime culminated and a new phase began, from where a straight line led to the war and the Holocaust. The Saint Stephen jubilee hallmarked this moment; it celebrated a historical figure who served as an essential symbol of the regime. Stephen I, Hungary's first king and the founder of the kingdom, had held great significance since the nineteenth century as a symbol of the legitimacy and continuity of the Hungarian state. In the interwar period, this symbolism also extended to the "territorial integrity" of the state: the often-used phrase "the Kingdom of Saint Stephen" referred to the country as it was before 1918. Suffused with Christian—more precisely, Catholic—imagery but always putting religion in the service of the political message, the Saint Stephen jubilee was the ultimate manifestation of the Horthy regime's Christian nationalism, a "political religion" with a set of symbols, myths, and values that "all patriots must revere for the sake of the nation's good and the social order."[96] In terms of combining modern and historical, religious and political, the celebrations continued along the path set by the Saint Emeric jubilee, developing many of the previous event's characteristics in a more magnificent form. This time, however, the dainty virgin prince was replaced by a powerful ruler embodying strength and virility.

The marriage of church and state is clear from the timeline. From 25 to 29 May 1938, the International Eucharistic Congress took place in Budapest. Catholic archbishops, bishops, and around fifty thousand pilgrims arrived from all over the world to participate in the grandiose ceremonies, with thousands of people taking the Eucharist. The day after the congress ended, the Saint Stephen jubilee year began with yet another Roman Catholic ceremony: a mass in Kossuth Square, next to the Parliament building, and a procession carrying the Holy Right Hand, a relic of Saint Stephen, to Heroes' Square.[97] From here, the government took over. The Parliament ceremoniously debated draft legislation enshrining respect for Saint Stephen into law. Then, it festively approved the law at an external session held in Székesfehérvár, a town founded by Stephen. In the next weeks, numerous events took place across the country. Highlights included the unveiling of a statue of Saint Stephen and the opening of the new Medieval Ruin Garden in Székesfehérvár, the unveiling of the restored ruins of Stephen's royal palace and basilica in Esztergom, the exhibition of the Hungarian Royal Crown (the "Holy Crown") in Buda Palace, and finally the ceremonious "country-wide sightseeing" of the Holy Right Hand, which travelled across Hungary on a "Golden Train" to be venerated by the population. All events were well attended by political leaders, who made sure to remain protagonists throughout.

As the prominent showcasing of archaeological sites demonstrates, historical research played a central role in the Saint Stephen jubilee. The minister of culture, Bálint Hóman (1885–1951), was a historian and former director of the Hungarian National Museum as well as a politician of the hard right. The works of visual art commissioned under his direction promoted an image of history that was explicitly politicized according to contemporary concerns while also shown to be supported by scholarship. I return to the relationship between politics and historiography in chapter 4. The remainder of this chapter covers how the different elements of the jubilee coalesced into a consciously modern display of the regime's ideology at a time when "resurrection" seemed to be in progress and history seemed to be made.

The extensive volume published in 1940 to document the achievements of the jubilee often quotes positive press reactions to the commissioned artworks. These texts almost invariably cite the combination of history and modernity as the most laudable feature of the works. One of the main artworks was the bronze equestrian statue of King Stephen by Ferenc Sidló (1882–1954) unveiled in the Székesfehérvár main square on 18 August 1938 (fig. 1.7). The *Pester Lloyd* praised Sidló's sculpture for uniting originality and historical imagination, for representing a true "Turan Hungarian" type, and for "bringing historical realism in harmony with contemporary stylization" while employing Byzantine and Romanesque motifs.[98] The 1940 volume then went on to discuss the "modern" murals of the Ruin Garden, painted by Vilmos Aba-Novák (1894–1941), a former recipient of the Rome Scholarship. His mural designs for the Székesfehérvár Ruin Garden had won the Saint Stephen painting competition of the ministry; a main requirement was strict adherence to historical research.[99] Aba-Novák respected this while carrying out the commission in his characteristic Byzantinesque yet modern style.

An art form that was able to disseminate the visual culture of the jubilee into daily life was the postage stamp. Issued by the state and distributed widely in the country and abroad, stamps "are socio-political statements and tools for nation-building and molding of public's collective memory. . . . [They] serve the construction of an 'imagined community' . . . by guaranteeing the visibility of the patria in quotidian landscapes and preventing its citizens from forgetting who they are (or are expected to be) and where they (are expected to) belong."[100] Through depictions of Saint Stephen, stamps promoted notions of the temporal and spatial dimensions of Hungary and Hun-

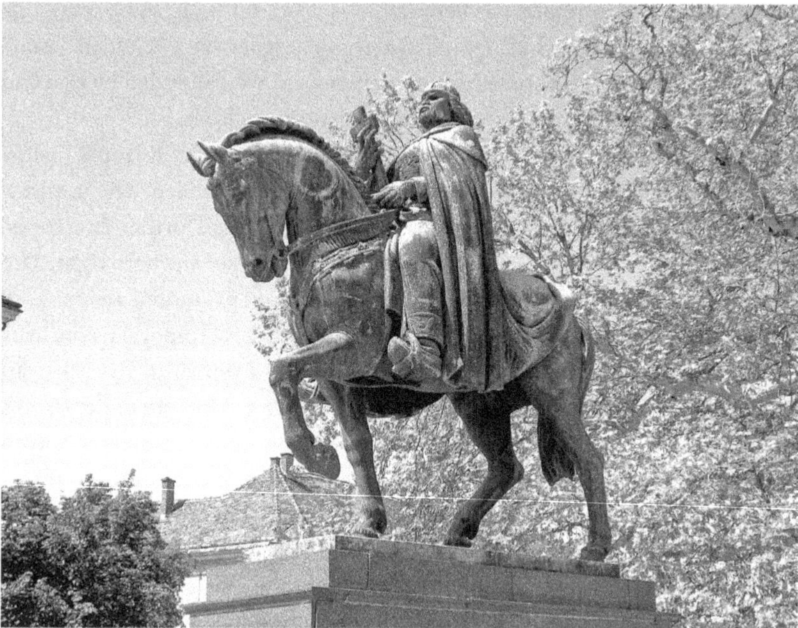

FIGURE 1.7.   Ferenc Sidló, *Saint Stephen*, Székesfehérvár, 1938.
Photo: Globetrotter19 / Wikimedia Commons, CC BY-SA 3.0

garianness. In issuing stamps for the jubilee, Hungarian authorities followed the internationally established practice of publishing commemorative stamps for occasions such as anniversaries or world's fairs—that is, events that held special significance in promoting concepts of national identity. In the United States, "commemoratives served as a powerful tool for disseminating federally sanctioned episodes of American history" while also providing revenue for the events.[101] There, as well as in the countless other countries that began printing commemorative stamps by the 1920s and 1930s, stamps could serve as miniature memorials; like their monumental counterparts, they offered "one vision of the past," devoid of other perspectives.[102]

The organizers commissioned two sets of stamps for the jubilee. The announcement for the first design competition referred artists to the National Commission for Monuments for advice on the correct representation of historic towns.[103] Entries had to include at least three scenes: a "stylized" representation of King Stephen, Abbot Astric receiving the crown from the pope, and Stephen contemplating a cross in the sky. The competition also suggested further scenes, but artists were free to include their own ideas. The winner was Sándor Légrády (1906–1987), by then an experienced stamp designer. The art historian Elemér Czakó analyzed the stamps at length in the far-right

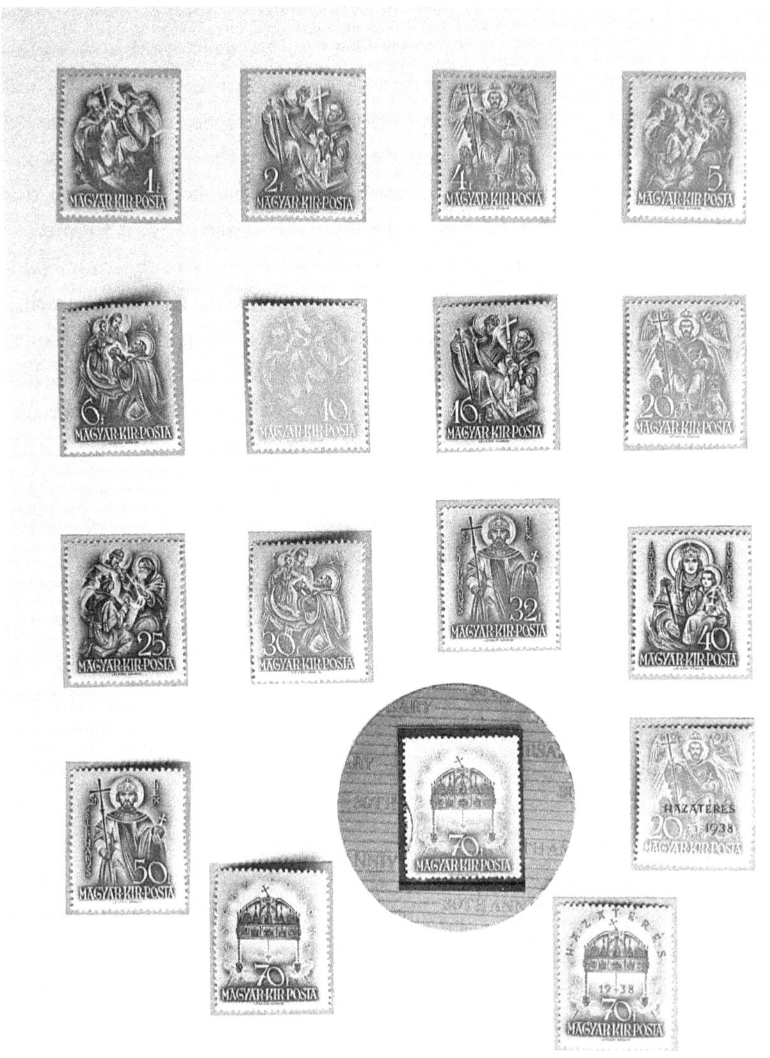

FIGURE 1.8.   Sándor Légrády, stamp series for the Saint Stephen jubilee, 1938, private collection. Photo by author. Sándor Légrády © OOA-S 2024

newspaper *Új Nemzedék* (*New Generation*), praising Légrády for his thorough knowledge of printing techniques, which allowed him to treat the perforated edges of the stamps as decorative motifs.[104]

What stands out in Légrády's designs is a specific kind of dynamism. In the swirling compositions, double curves such as the figures' halos lead the eye (fig. 1.8). Most of the compositions are dynamic, with one figure positioned higher than the other and connections between them forged by forceful gestures and strong eye contact. In *Saint Stephen Founding the Cathedral of Székesfehérvár* (2 fillér), the model of the cathedral seems to tumble forward out of the picture. The most static composition is *Saint Stephen on the Throne* (32 fillér), but even here, the king's powerful gaze provides the image with a forcefulness rarely found in such representative compositions. As Czakó noted, this was in line with how recent research had revised the image of Saint Stephen.[105] While medieval chronicles had emphasized the saintly piety of the king, historians of the interwar period described him as a forceful and strong personality in line with the political leadership cults of the 1930s. In the form of stamps, this new interpretation could reach people across the country and abroad. The single-figure images of the enthroned monarch and the Virgin Mary were easily accessible in their iconicity, while the busy compositions of the other scenes required careful scrutiny and immersion from philatelists.

The image of the strong and forceful Saint Stephen was disseminated in the miniature in other ways. The famous Herend porcelain factory created small versions of Sidló's equestrian statue for commercial distribution. Although not everyone was fond of these colorfully glazed figures—Kállai described the translation of the bronze statue into porcelain as a "bad mistake"[106]—they reiterated the overall message of the jubilee in yet another medium, making it even more pervasive. Colorful porcelain statuettes usually embody "sweetness," but in this case, the decorative object preserved the hardness of the king's face and gaze, in some versions even emphasizing his Asian (that is, ancient Hungarian "Turanic") features and his frown.

All of these examples suggest that the commemoration of Saint Stephen in the 1930s was centrally shaped by the state, with the help of the Catholic Church, and that the jubilee represented the culmination of these authoritative efforts. This is, however, a one-sided picture. The essential—and thoroughly modern—feature of the remembrance of Saint Stephen in the interwar period was precisely how commercialized it was and how it was upheld and shaped by industrial production, advertising, and tourism. Stamps were not the first small printed objects that transmitted the cult of Saint Stephen into people's homes. As an iconic figure, Saint Stephen had given his name in the 1920s and 1930s to Szent István beer, Szent István chocolate, Szent István cognac cherries, and countless other products, all produced by one company that owned Saint Stephen's name as a brand.[107] By indicating the Hungarian origin of these products to consumers, Stephen functioned as a marker of national identity. Sometimes, these products displayed an image of the king on their labels, but the name was often enough; indeed, instead of Stephen's stern, powerful face, advertisements for Szent István malt coffee usually featured a naked, plump baby comically spilling the drink from an overly large jug. "Banal nationalism" cannot get more banal than this.[108]

The power of the Saint Stephen jubilee lay in how it harnessed the consumer culture of modernity. The jubilee was able to bring back historical spectacle and yet remain focused on the present by incorporating the needs of tourism. The 1938 events were preceded by smaller, yearly celebrations of Saint Stephen, which were seen as increasingly important in promoting Budapest as a holiday destination. From 1924, 20 August, Saint Stephen's Day, occasioned weeklong—and from 1928, two-week-long—festivities in Budapest, combined with a harvest festival. Promoting the "nationalization" of Budapest by giving its spaces over to participants from the "pure" countryside, these events aimed to turn the originally Catholic holiday into a secular celebration of Hungarian nationalism.[109] More and more elaborate as the years passed, Saint Stephen festivities embraced historical spectacle. In 1928, a procession along the grand Stefánia Avenue evoked scenes from Hungarian history in forty *tableaux vivants* on carriages, from ancient times to Trianon. Featuring colorful, dazzling costumes and emotional compositions, the procession had been designed by a familiar figure: Márkus, then chief director of the Opera House.[110]

Following this established path, the 1938 jubilee featured events resembling the colorful historical pageants of the nineteenth century. These spectacles dominated press reports. Journalists reveled in describing the lavish decorations of the parliamentary session held in Székesfehérvár—the purple draperies, the flags, the gilded double cross. Discussing ceremonial processions, they admired the pomp of colorful "purple, green and violet" Hungarian ceremonial costumes, the "díszmagyar."[111] The Holy Right Hand procession included a parade of guilds—a late medieval concept still alive in interwar Hungary. Indeed, none of these events claimed to revive the past. They were not conceptualized as roleplay but as showcases of the present—more precisely, perhaps, of how the present still vividly incorporated traditions of the past.

However, the most pervasive visual trope that permeated press reports was the one in the poster for the Saint Emeric jubilee eight years earlier: the spectacle of illuminations at nighttime. The fireworks of 20 August appeared in many photos but, as in the Saint Emeric poster, electric lighting was an even more central feature. A photo of the fireworks also showed the illuminated Chain Bridge. Another nocturnal image showed the Danube naval procession of the Eucharistic Congress, with rays of light emanating from Gellért Hill toward the sky.[112] The dazzling, electrified metropolis united past and present, captured through the modern medium of photography.

In the 1930s, promoting Budapest as a tourist destination became increasingly important in how the Hungarian state presented itself abroad.[113] This often involved incorporating history into celebrations of the city. At the 1937 Paris World's Fair, for instance, one of the attractions was the large-scale terracotta relief *The Queen of the Danube* by ceramicist Margit Kovács (1902–1977), which told the history of Budapest in ten colorful scenes evoking the atmosphere of folktales and medieval illuminated manuscripts as part of a room promoting the city and its rich spa culture.[114] In a similar vein, the Saint Stephen weeks increasingly focused on tourists, foregrounding the expectations of consumerism and the tourist industry. The electrification of Budapest was considered a major allure. In a thoughtful exploration of these developments, Alexander Vari observed that "in the process of taking over Budapest and nationalizing the city . . . by Horthy's supporters, by the 1930s it was rather the capital city and its interregional interests that were urbanizing nationalism."[115] On my part, I would describe this as an opposite process: it was the representative politics of the interwar regime that subsumed the modernity embodied by Budapest, hence neutralizing it as a threat. Whichever way we look at it, however, one thing is clear: by the 1938 Saint Stephen jubilee, the modernity of Budapest and the historic spectacle of the Horthy regime became one.

Modernity Incorporated

The success of the 1938 Saint Stephen jubilee was so enormous and its budget so oversized that artistic commissions continued after the year ended. Between 1939 and 1942, the Executive Committee of the Saint Stephen Memorial Year sponsored a project to decorate town halls across the country with tapestries showing scenes from the king's life.[116] One of the artists commissioned was the prominent Gobelin maker Noémi Ferenczy (1890–1957). The daughter of one of the most respected modern painters, Károly Ferenczy (1862–1917), Noémi had studied her craft in France and developed a unique style inspired by folk art and medieval tapestries. Simple yet thoughtfully composed, monumental yet decorative, her art was celebrated as the pinnacle of Hungarian modernism by liberal critics—a rare honor awarded to a woman artist.[117] Ferenczy was known for working alone, at her own pace, and for her uncompromising artistic personality. She was a committed Communist who had taken part in the Soviet Republic and been active in the underground movement ever since. Yet, in 1937, she participated in the Hungarian pavilion at the Paris World's Fair, and two years later, she accepted the commission to design and weave a Saint Stephen tapestry for

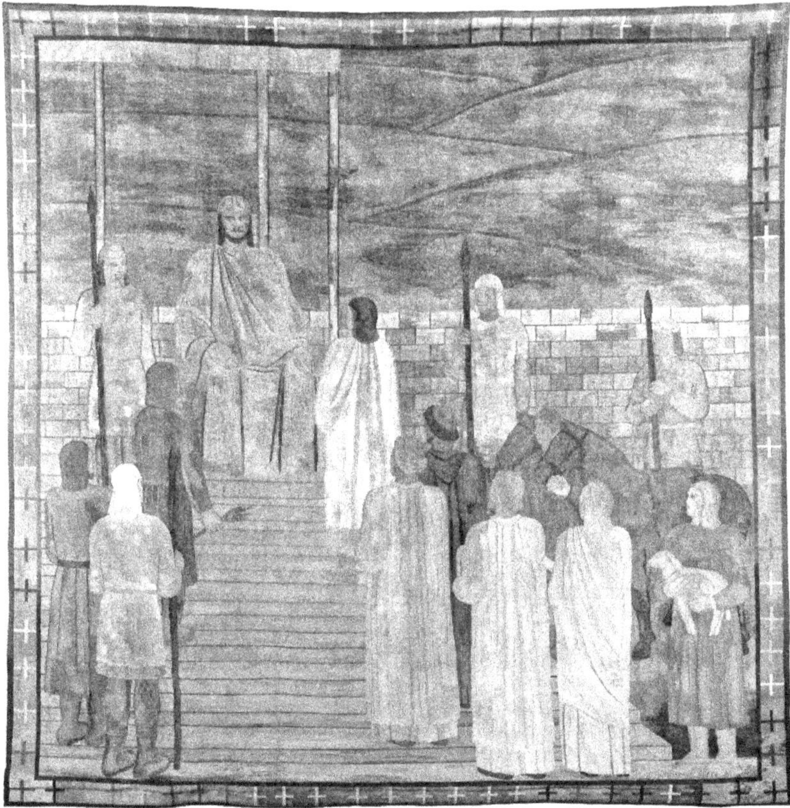

FIGURE 1.9. Noémi Ferenczy, *Saint Stephen Tapestry*, 1940–1941, wool, tapestry woven with the Gobelin technique, 300 x 300 cm, Jósa András Museum, Nyíregyháza, inv. no. 68.1.1. Noémi Ferenczy © OOA-S 2024

the Nyíregyháza town hall.[118] The chosen subject was *Foreigners and Hungarians in the Court of the King* (fig. 1.9).

This scene was based on King Stephen's *Admonitions*, a treatise written for Prince Emeric by a court cleric and traditionally attributed to the king himself. The relevant passage stated that "the unilingual and unicultural country is weak and perishable. Therefore, I order you, my son, to benevolently protect and respect the newcomers so they would rather stay with you than elsewhere."[119] Based on these words, Saint Stephen can be—and has been—held up as a symbol of openness and internationalism as well as of nation building. Indeed, in nineteenth-century culture, he had represented a liberal nationalism, the idea of a multiethnic state, as opposed to the ethnic nationalism symbolized by Árpád.[120] Nevertheless, there was no doubt the tapestry would ultimately serve state ideology. When it was inaugurated on

17 November 1941 as part of the festivities marking the departure of the Nyíregyháza hussar regiment to the Soviet front, it was described as "radiating the ancient Hungarian imperial idea; Saint Stephen's idea, which is destined to rule the Danube Basin."[121]

We can only speculate why Ferenczy accepted this commission. Due to her meticulous work process, Ferenczy had always found it hard to make a living from her art. State commissions must have provided her with income and visibility. Throughout the successive authoritarianisms of twentieth-century Hungary, artists have navigated the murky area between collaboration and autonomy. Their desire to continue creating art for a wider audience often led to questionable ethical choices. Like all clever authoritarianisms, the Horthy regime aimed to incorporate its own critics. Here, I am less interested in how that happened to Ferenczy, the person, than in how her uncompromising modernism—described as such by progressive contemporaries—became a vehicle of official representation.

For this to happen, Ferenczy grudgingly had to make concessions to the ministry. In her first designs, Stephen was not perched on a throne but standing in the doorway of the castle at the same level as the visitors.[122] In another early design, some visitors carried bags on their shoulders—attributes of the wanderer. After Ferenczy presented her designs, "diplomatic relations lapsed," as she herself put it, between her and the Saint Stephen Memorial Year Committee. According to Ferenczy, among other modifications, they made her remove the wanderers, whom they described as "beggars."[123] Her altered designs were accepted in February 1940, and she finished the tapestry—nine square meters in size—in March 1941. It showed King Stephen sitting on a throne above a set of stairs, under a canopy, in front of a brick wall. He is being approached by figures wearing robes of different colors and styles—one a monk with a tonsure, one carrying a lamb. The committee adjusted Ferenczy's design to the guiding principles of the jubilee: Stephen had to be a strong, stern ruler, rather than a humble saint welcoming his guests as an equal, and his guests had to be dignitaries, not lowly beggars. What the committee did not reject, however, was Ferenczy's formal language. Her figures are just as solid and blocklike, her scenery just as abstract as in her other work—characteristics that, to her modernist friends, related her work to Giotto's. It was not the modernism but the little details potentially evoking contemporary society and its inequalities—the beggars—that the committee could not abide.

From Horthy's entrance in 1919 to the Saint Stephen jubilee in 1938, the Horthy regime exploited various components of modernity to disseminate its politics of memory. Early ceremonies, like the triumphal procession or the oath in the Vérmező, did not require historicist staging or props. Even though they recalled events of the past, the emphasis was on their contemporariness, their monumental historical significance in the present. By the 1930s, the strategy shifted. Constructing new formal idioms to represent the past through the modernization of historical styles became a central aim in cultural politics.

Throughout these shifts, the state employed history to gain and retain ideological control over society and, more immediately, over the crowds that attended the spectacles. History was not to be relived but rather put to the service of the present; an aim consistently reflected in the aesthetic choices made by organizers. Events such as Horthy's 1919 procession or the oath in the Vérmező were staged at a time of direct confrontation. They referenced events of the past but *made history* in the present, helping participants enact the new regime's us-versus-them narrative. Artworks such as Dudits's painting disseminated the ideology by eschewing historical allegory for photographic realism, hence grounding the regime's message in the present. But that grounding could not have happened had it not been for the various channels meandering across society—charities, educational institutions, health-care providers—through which the image could be distributed for all to see. Opponents of the regime had no access to equivalent routes, so works such as Bíró's *Horthy* had no comparable audience. Church, industry, national and local government, schools, the press, and civil associations all cooperated in constructing a coherent vision of history and its relevance in the present, as exemplified by the Mohács anniversary.

The Saint Emeric anniversary shifted the spotlight onto one of these actors: the Catholic Church. It was the first of two great jubilees where the symbiosis between the state and the church became central. The neobaroque buildings of Saint Emeric's Town were among the jubilee's main products, but the promotion of the event emphasized its presentness by, for instance, foregrounding the electric illumination of Budapest in the official poster. The us-versus-them narrative was still fundamental to the regime; the notion of Christian Hungary was based on the exclusion of those who did not fit into this model of Hungarian identity. Nevertheless, by involving the previously "sinful" Budapest, this jubilee signaled the intention of incorporating the modern metropolis and its culture—as long as it did not resist. In the Saint Stephen jubilee, this design was in full bloom. The regime promoted its interpretations of history through its own version of modern art, employing all the trappings of modernity and subsuming the metropolis itself. As in Italy, the regime was able to integrate competing models of modernity to promote its ideas of national regeneration.[124] Official culture was confident enough to invite modernists under its protective shade, regardless of their ideological persuasions. Once under its umbrella, they must have felt as if it were everywhere. Those who did remain outside would soon feel the land slipping from under their feet.

CHAPTER 2

Irredentist Spacetime

On 16 January 1921, a new group of monuments were unveiled in Freedom Square (Szabadság tér) in Budapest (figs. 2.1–2.2). Commissioned by the Union of Defensive Leagues, the four sculptures represented regions in the north, east, south, and west that had been awarded to neighboring countries in 1920. In his speech at the inauguration, István Zadravecz solemnly stated that those present would not rest until reunification. According to Nándor Urmánczy, union president, the sculptures demanded justice. The place where they stood would be "a place of pilgrimage for the nation"; it was a "furnace of hatred and revenge."[1]

The Trianon Treaty had allocated two-thirds of the former lands of Hungary to other states. Millions of people were affected, often traumatically. Many who identified as Hungarians had to relocate to the new, smaller Hungary from areas outside the borders and became "Trianon refugees"; others, on both sides of the borders, were cut off from family and friends, and still others had to find new livelihoods due to the disruption of long-standing economic and trade circuits. In the next two decades, political elites and activists successfully channeled these diverse feelings of loss and confusion into a radical nationalist politics.[2] The two forms of anti-Trianon activism—more diplomatic *revisionism* and more militant *irredentism*—were prominent in interwar Hungarian culture, from elite politics to the everyday.[3] The monuments in Freedom Square—known as the *Irredentist Sculpture Group*—stood at the beginning of this process. They helped mold personal experience and memory into a broader narrative in line with political expectations. Describing the "end of a tradition of memory" in modern times, Pierre Nora wrote about the institutions, ceremonies, and objects (e.g., museums, anniversaries, or monuments) that produce and "maintain by artifice" the *lieux de mémoire* that would have been preserved organically in collective memory before the historical age.[4] In James E. Young's apt formulation: "In shouldering the memory-work monuments may relieve viewers of their memory-burden."[5] The Union of Defensive Leagues was keen to shoulder the burden and offer up its own interpretation of the events for broad swathes of society to consume. In doing so, it made a significant contribution to turning Trianon into the site of memory it is today, at a time when the ink on the treaty had barely dried.

Hungary was not the only country in Europe with territorial grievances after the end of the First World War. The revision of the borders defined at the Versailles peace conference was central to the politics of several states in Central and East Central Europe. Driving not just foreign and military policies but also policies on welfare and education, revisionism assumed the features of a comprehensive ideology.[6] The vision of an ideal homeland was central to nationalist and Fascist movements and their quest for regeneration. These visions often encompassed territories that lay outside the country's legal borders. To irredentists, in any country, the spiritual unity of the nation with "its" land made the determinations of negotiations and peace treaties irrelevant. This way of thinking reached back to the nineteenth century; the term *irredentism* originated from Risorgimento Italy, where desired territories were referred to as "Italia irredenta," unredeemed Italy. In the interwar period, irredentism and its twin movement, revisionism, developed into international ideological frameworks. One new aspect was the foregrounding and solidification of historical arguments, the elaboration of an ideal—sometimes mythical—past that justified the territorial demands of this "historic irredentism."[7] As a result, national space and historical time became interdependent in irredentist thought, forming a mental framework that I call *irredentist spacetime*.

This chapter explores the *Irredentist Sculpture Group* and other monuments in Freedom Square as expressive examples of a way of thinking that proliferated in interwar Europe. In the Hungarian context, the sculptures visualized a range of ideas that were to become solid features of Trianon as a site of memory and disseminated them in a variety of ways, including by marking out a space for commemoration within the city and creating effective and recognizable imagery that could be transferred into new contexts. These monuments were more than just static objects occupying a certain space in the city. An examination of their versatility can extend past the Hungarian circumstances and lead to more general insights about the territory of the nation as historical memory.

Shaping Space

The idea of the irredentist monuments was first pitched by the architect K. Róbert Kertész (1876–1951), then head of the Department of Construction Work at the Ministry of Religion and Education. It was subsequently picked up by the Union of Defensive Leagues, the same organization that had commissioned Dudits's *Oath in the Vérmező*.[8] Erected in the immediate aftermath of Trianon, the *Irredentist Sculpture Group* was an example of large-scale, overt campaigning that would remain unmatched until the late 1920s. The Versailles treaties had imposed a strict ban on public agitation against their provisions. After coming to power in April 1921, Prime Minister Bethlen toned down irredentist campaigning and outsourced propaganda activities to ostensibly nongovernmental organizations, which he drew under strict oversight.[9] The irredentist sculptures were set up before Bethlen's time, but the symbiosis between the government and nongovernmental campaign groups is observable here too. While the union took full responsibility for the project, it entrusted its artistic direction to Minister of Religion and Education István Haller (1880–1964). The four artists commissioned to model *East*, *North*, *South*, and *West*, János Pásztor (1881–1945), Zsigmond Kisfaludi Strobl (1884–1975), István Szentgyörgyi (1881–1938), and Ferenc Sidló, as well as the architect of the pediments, Jenő Lechner (1878–1962), had been recommended by Kertész (figs 2.1 and 2.2). Middle-aged sculptors trained in the academic tradition—partly in Budapest but also in Paris (Pásztor), Vienna (Kisfaludi Strobl), Brussels (Szentgyörgyi), and Munich (Sidló)—they had all achieved some success through public commissions by 1920. By the standards of the right-wing regime, some of them had spotty pasts. During the 1919 Hungarian Soviet Republic, Kisfaludi Strobl had been a member of the Artists' Welfare Committee, while Sidló had been deputy chair of the artists' union.[10] Nevertheless, this was easily forgotten. Following their contribution to the irredentist monument, all four sculptors were favored by authorities up until the regime's demise. Sidló would go on to produce the emblematic equestrian statue of Stephen I for the Saint Stephen jubilee in 1938.

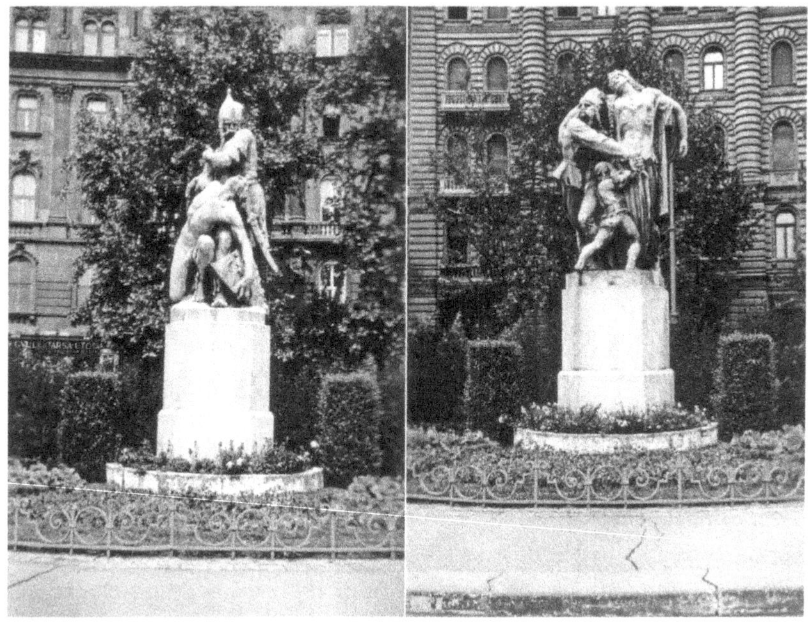

Figure 2.1. Left: János Pásztor, *East*, 1920; Right: Zsigmond Kisfaludi Strobl, *North*, 1920.
Photos: Kristóf Kelecsényi / Fortepan

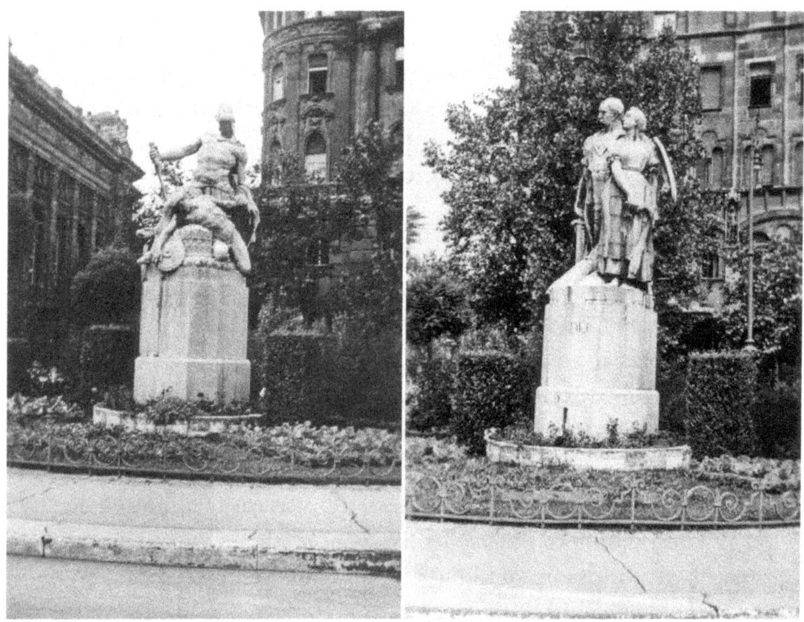

Figure 2.2. Left: Ferenc Sidló, *West*, 1920; Right: István Szentgyörgyi, *South*, 1920.
Photos: Kristóf Kelecsényi / Fortepan

The sculptures personified the respective regions through specific historical references that I discuss later. First, it is best to take a bird's-eye view to understand how the sculptures, as an ensemble, conceptualized space. This was, after all, their raison d'être. Unlike most monuments, they did not commemorate events or people, but places. They reminded their viewers of the past, and in that sense, they were memorials, but the events they evoked—including Trianon itself—were relevant only because they related to geography, to space, to the idea of national territory and its abrupt change. Time and space became one.

In representing the four directions of the compass, the four irredentist sculptures conjured up four specific regions detached from Hungary and allocated to Austria, Czechoslovakia, Romania, and the Kingdom of Serbs, Croats, and Slovenes (later Yugoslavia). Together, they evoked the totality of the lost territories and did so in an arrangement seemingly at odds with the subject matter of the individual sculptures. Instead of following the compass, the sculptures stood in a semicircle at the northern edge of Freedom Square (fig. 0.1). There is certainly a practical explanation for this. Freedom Square was to become a location for commemorating Trianon, and this was the best way to create a large, open-ended space for crowds to gather. The arrangement also had a symbolic function: it helped create the fusion of materiality and spirituality characteristic of the irredentist concept of national space. Those standing in front of the monuments would experience a moment of disorientation while realizing that the four sculptures representing the four directions did not, in fact, indicate those directions. That patch of land in central Budapest would hence gain a different, transcendent spatiality, impossible to integrate into a prosaic map grid. As a space carved out for commemoration, it would be separated from the rest of the city and elevated far above the everyday. Originally planned in the late nineteenth century, Freedom Square was shaped like a basilica, with a rectangular southern end and a semicircular apse in the north. The sculptures stood along the outline of this apse, imbuing its sacred form with a new message—the one most sacred to irredentists.

The sublimation of actual geographical space into a spiritual idea of Hungary turned the "lost lands" into a unified site of memory marked by longing, romanticized and conceptually separated from the remaining lands. This attitude, prevalent in interwar Hungarian irredentism, lives on to this day, not just in contemporary irredentist speech but in seemingly apolitical throwaway comments about "territories outside the borders." It is precisely this descent into "banal nationalism" that shows the power of Trianon as a site of memory, shaped, in its earliest years, by iconic representations such as the irredentist sculptures.[11]

It is here worthwhile to compare the irredentist sculptures to a group of monuments erected in 1896 as part of the millennium celebrations. For the increasingly ethnonationalist Hungarian state, the millennium provided an occasion to promote the idea of Hungarian hegemony over other ethnic groups. One project involved the construction of seven monuments across the country to commemorate key events of the Conquest. Most of the statues stood in the borderlands or in areas inhabited by ethnic minorities, sending an explicit warning to these groups.[12] Depicting victorious Hungarian warriors on imposing columns, they outlined the vast spatiality of the conquered land by marking out its extent in real space. One monument, for instance, stood in Dévény/Devín, near present Bratislava, commonly regarded as the westernmost point ancient Magyars had reached. Marking the border, the statue sent a message to local Slovak and German speakers as well as to Austria. Another monument stood near Munkács/Mukachevo, in Subcarpathian Ruthenia, where the Magyars had entered from the east. By defining locations across Hungary through the historical events that had happened there, the millennium monuments played a role similar to that of the irredentist sculptures decades later. There was, however, a notable difference: some of the millennium monuments were set up in central locations that would remain part of "Dismembered Hungary," while the sculptures only commemorated the desired lost borderlands.

In a certain sense, the irredentist sculptures of Freedom Square can be seen as inversions of the millennium monuments. In 1896, the sculptures took possession of actual spaces, their ensemble stretching across the Hungarian lands in all directions. By 1921, many of those spaces belonged to new countries. Therefore, the new sculptures were mere representations of places that they symbolically brought together in one small space in central Budapest. In 1896, the borderlands and the heart of the country had belonged together structurally. In 1921, the revered but lost borderlands could only be commemorated in the remaining central land, now devalued in irredentist eyes. Their spiritual transposition into the capital through the monuments signaled a fundamentally new approach, a radical change to the status and meaning of these lands in Hungarian cultural memory. More broadly, it exemplified a new way of connecting place and history in defining the nation.

Merging Space and Time

Irredentism conceptualized the relationship between geographical space and historical time in a particular way, expressed not only in the irredentist sculptures but in countless other products of interwar Hungarian culture.

This powerful ideological framework, referred to in this book as *irredentist spacetime*, guided the reinterpretation of the past in the new geopolitical reality and connected it to future political and territorial aspirations. But what, exactly, was—or is—irredentist spacetime? An example might serve as the best explanation. In Hungary, 6 October marks the anniversary of the 1849 execution of thirteen generals of the 1848–1849 Hungarian Revolution and War of Independence, called the "Arad martyrs" after the town where their execution had taken place. Located in Transylvania, Arad became part of Romania in 1920. The town's nineteenth-century monument commemorating the Arad martyrs was seen as an emblem of Hungarian domination and removed by the new authorities. On 6 October 1937, the conservative daily *Pesti Hirlap* (*Pest Newspaper*) dedicated its editorial to this "invisible monument":

> From the dismembered country, from the regions that have been torn off, from all parts of the world where Hungarians live, sighs of remembrance drift on this dreary October day toward Arad. Thoughts and sighs fly freely across the borders between countries, like birds; today the thoughts and sighs of millions and millions of Hungarians flutter and circle around the Arad bastion, hitting their wings into the wooden planks, behind which is hidden the monument dedicated to the martyrs.[13]

The invisible monument then grew into a more encompassing metaphor:

> The monument to the Arad thirteen has hence disappeared. But it has only disappeared from in front of our eyes, because to feel its presence eternally and everywhere no monument is necessary for us, and today it is not just the covered statue, but also the wooden fence that surrounds it, that sends an ever-powerful alert and reminder to the Hungarian nation.
>
> We have, after all, seen that it only takes a pencil stroke to cede territories that had belonged to one country, one nation, for a thousand years, to the neighbor lying in wait, it only takes one handwave from the new authority for a monument to disappear because it was an uncomfortable reminder of the past thousand years; but does a pencil stroke, a handwave suffice to destroy, together with the national border and the monument, the ancestral, emotional, spiritual, historical bonds of which borders and monuments alike are often only symbols?
>
> . . .
>
> For, what has happened? The blissful and greater Hungary had, on this day, mourned heroes and martyrs; heroes and martyrs from whose

lives the bliss and greatness of their descendants had grown. The sorrowful and dismembered Hungary no longer only mourns the heroes and martyrs, but also the soil in which they are buried and the land for which they, the heroes and martyrs, had sacrificed their lives.[14]

A perception of borders as formed by uncontestable historical forces, and hence as eternal, but at the same time, paradoxically, also as artificial and flimsy; a simultaneous understanding of Greater Hungary as a spiritual entity and a well definable geographical area; a heightened sense, in historical consciousness, of *where* events had taken place and how these locations are consequently connected to each other by historical chains of events; the idea that any commemoration of events and personalities now necessarily means the commemoration of places, of "Hungarian soil": these are some of the elements of irredentist spacetime.

Through irredentist spacetime, the ideology of revisionism and irredentism affected how people understood their nation's—and hence their own—position within Europe and within history. A powerful and vivid concept, irredentist spacetime was everywhere in Hungary, reflected in diverse aspects of culture. It lay behind some of the public ceremonies discussed in the previous chapter. The Mohács anniversary, for instance, conflated the southern Hungarian town's historical significance as the site of a sixteenth-century devastating military defeat with the fact that it was now located at the country's border due to the loss of territories to its south. Those making a pilgrimage to Mohács for the 1926 anniversary had the opportunity to commemorate this dual meaning as one singular site of memory. The ceremonies and processions allowed the contemporary crowd to enact irredentist spacetime through participation.

Hungary was far from alone in justifying its territorial claims through historical precedents. "Historical irredentism" as a way of thinking underpinned nationalist movements throughout interwar Europe.[15] In Germany, the main points of reference were the Holy Roman Empire, embodied most importantly in Frederick I Barbarossa, as well the eastern conquests of the Teutonic knights.[16] Greek irredentists invoked the Byzantine Empire, Bulgarians the great Bulgarian Kingdom of medieval times.[17] In Italy, Mussolini's concept of *romanità* recalled the empire of ancient Rome. The commemorative gestures associated with these ideas often combined space and time in a way reminiscent of the *Irredentist Sculpture Group*. In Italy, for instance, the emphasis on Trieste's ancient monuments and their connections to Rome helped embed the newly acquired city into the national territory of Italy in mental maps.[18] A range of monuments in Trieste commemorated the successful "redemption" of Istria, bringing the peninsula to the largest nearby city in a gesture similar to the Freedom Square monuments, but in celebration instead of mourning. In Germany in 1925, the fiftieth anniversary of the inauguration of the monument to Chief Hermann (Arminius) in Detmold was celebrated with a "star run"—sixteen races starting from different borderlands of the country, all ending at the monument on the same day, while smaller races took place across Germany. Having defeated the Romans in AD 9, Hermann was remembered as a unifier of German tribes, and in 1925, this unity was expressed in a commemorative ritual that merged territorial and temporal unity—a "national synchronicity," as Martin H. Geyer has described it.[19] In Lithuania, whose capital, Vilnius, had been awarded to Poland in 1918, the city of Kaunas became a substitute capital. Here, monuments were erected commemorating Vilnius, while national institutions were designed to be temporary, until the "redemption" of the lost capital.

The concept of irredentist spacetime helps us understand the mental framework created by these types of commemorations and hence how ideal visions of the country's territorial extent could become integral to national identities. Erected to commemorate "Hungarian soil," the irredentist sculptures were *par excellence* representatives of irredentist spacetime. Their mission was to represent the history and territory of Hungary as one spiritual entity. Laying out an accurate geography and chronology was not important. The sculptures connected the lands they evoked into a historical continuity, but they merged history and myth to tap into popular concepts of history and Hungarianness, rather than scholarly narratives. Through this approach, the sculptures—and the commemorative site they created in Freedom Square— condensed various events of Hungarian history into a unified space.

Layers of Memory

The evocation of the recent loss of territories through the commemoration of other events, such as Mohács or the execution of the Arad martyrs, was a standard feature of the remembrance of Trianon in the interwar period. The commemorative site in Freedom Square was an early expression of this idea. The square had already been a site of remembrance before 1920, and the monuments reinterpreted it by absorbing its old meanings, effectively colonizing the memory of 1848–1849.

The history of Freedom Square can be traced to the late eighteenth century, when a large military building known as the New Building (Neugebäude, Újépület) was constructed on a site then located on the outskirts of the town of Pest.[20] It consisted of four wings arranged around a large central area—the future urban square—with a smaller rectangular pavilion at each corner. Between 1793 and 1796, the building was used as a prison for French prisoners of war and later served as an army barracks and a military academy. After Hungary's defeat in the War of Independence of 1848–1849, prominent Hungarian freedom fighters were imprisoned here, and the revolutionary Prime Minister Lajos Batthyány (1807–1849) was executed by the wall of the New Building on 6 October 1849.

The New Building thus came to symbolize Habsburg oppression in the eyes of Hungarian nationalists, and its fate was sealed after the Austro-Hungarian Compromise of 1867. Plans to use the building for peaceful civic purposes were eventually overridden by calls for its demolition, which finally happened in 1897. The square designed in its place by the architect and city planner Antal Pálóczy (1849–1927) was pointedly named Szabadság tér: Freedom Square. By this time, Pest had been incorporated into Budapest, now a bustling metropolis, and Freedom Square was located in its very heart, close to the new Parliament building then under construction. The buildings surrounding the square housed important institutions underpinning Hungary's new status as quasi-independent nation state, such as the Stock Exchange (1897–1907) and the National Bank (1902–1905). The streets leading to the square were named after generals of the War of Independence.

The way the *Irredentist Sculpture Group* capitalized on the existing national symbolism of the square was not unique to this project; many monuments in interwar Central Europe, as well as elsewhere, were erected in such meaningful locations. One example is the Vítkov National Monument in Prague; built between 1928 and 1938 on the location of Jan Žižka's 1420 victory over Emperor Sigismund's forces, it commemorated the Czechoslovak legionnaires who had fought on the side of the Entente in the First World War. Presented as freedom fighters against Habsburg oppression, the legionnaires were fashioned as Žižka's heirs; an iconic location within the city received a new layer of meaning. Where Freedom Square differed, however, was that while in the case of Vítkov, the two meanings strengthened each other with no conflict within the overall message, in the Budapest example, the relationship between layers was more fraught. The aim was not just to exploit but also to obscure the old meanings—to efface them while still keeping them in plain sight. As I show later in this chapter, ultimately this strategy applied not only to Freedom Square but extended from the square to all of Budapest.

Freedom Square's original status as a site of remembrance arose from its direct relationship, as a physical space, to Batthyány and his fellow prisoners. For many decades, it had needed no purposely erected monument; indeed, the New Building itself could be demolished, and the square still remained a primary site for the remembrance of 1848–1849. At the same time, in the late 1890s, urban planners added a new interpretation, a layer of optimism, transforming the square into a site for immortalizing the fervent nation building of the post-Compromise years. Then, in 1920, tragedy settled over the site again. This not only created a new space for commemorating Trianon but also promoted the memory politics of the Horthy regime. Although fashioning itself as heir to the pre-1918 Hungarian Kingdom, the regime was uncomfortable with many elements of the legacy of both 1848–1849 and post-1867 Hungary—the plebeian Republicanism of the former and the classical liberalism of the latter.[21] The new monuments helped focus the meanings of Freedom Square in a way that suited the regime, transforming it from a commemorative space largely defined by its actual material connection to historical events—which made it especially suited to spontaneous acts of remembrance—into one built to promote the regime's interpretation of the past by immersing passersby in a particular understanding of historical space.

In 1926, a new monument erected in Freedom Square strengthened the conflation of the memories of 1848–1849 and Trianon. The so-called Batthyány Sanctuary Lamp is an ornamental lantern with an eternal flame standing on a stone pediment near the spot where the revolutionary prime minister had been executed in 1849. The Municipality of Budapest had decided to erect a memorial to Batthyány in 1905, and the architect Móric Pogány (1878–1942) had won the design competition, but the project was delayed by twenty years. Held on 6 October 1926, the anniversary of Batthyány's death, the inauguration ceremony was suffused with references to Trianon. According to Budapest Mayor Jenő Sipőcz (1878–1937), "Batthyány and the other martyrs were not dreaming about today's dismembered Hungary; they aimed for independence and freedom, but not as goals in themselves, but as means to make the nation great and glorious."[22] In a less explicit but all the more pointed reference, the writer Gyula Pekár (1866–1937) described the guns that killed Batthyány as "Czech weapons."[23] On the same day, right-wing university students held demonstrations and made speeches at each of the four irredentist statues.[24]

Hiding the remembrance of Trianon behind other commemorations was useful in a practical sense because it helped circumvent the ban on official campaigning against the peace treaties. It was, however, not just a handy ploy; it embodied a general feature of how societies remember. The way Trianon resonated in the remembrance of different historical events in interwar Hungary is a salient example of what Ann Rigney has called the convergence and coalescence of cultural memories. Analyzing the "scarcity" of memory, Rigney described how the "stories told about certain events also provide a cultural framework for remembering them, and just as actual locations serve to attract topographically unrelated memories, so too certain narratives provide a cultural framework for other stories. Later events are superimposed on earlier ones to form memorial layers as it were."[25] Narratives relating Hungarian history as a succession of tragic events had already been popular in the nineteenth century (the national *Anthem* written by Ferenc Kölcsey in 1836 being the seminal example), and even then, they had drawn on precedents: the so-called *jeremiads* lamenting the effects of the Ottoman wars in the sixteenth and seventeenth centuries. Trianon was easily incorporated into this tradition. Once that happened, it could serve as an all-illuminating lens, an interpretative framework for the understanding of previous tragedies. It did not have to be commemorated directly, because it was reflected in numerous other events in Hungarian history.

The interwar reinterpretation of the 1849 defeat as a prefiguration of Trianon allowed Freedom Square to seamlessly shift between commemorating the former and the latter. The metaphorical relationship between the two events was, however, not the only connection between them articulated in the square; there was also a metonymical one. On the day of Batthyány's death, the Arad martyrs had also been executed three hundred kilometers away. Their memory was closely intertwined with Batthyány's; the naming of three streets around Freedom Square after Arad martyrs (Károly Vécsey, Lajos Aulich, and Ernő Kiss) in 1908 is an example of their joint commemoration. In this way, Freedom Square encompassed a distant location, Arad, in its range of memories, and this gained crucial importance after 1920, when Arad became part of Romania. Before then, Freedom Square referenced Arad much like Trafalgar Square references Cape Trafalgar—as a historical moment detached from its spatial reality—but after Trianon, the reference inevitably evoked the locality itself. The symbolic importance of Arad in the national narrative of Hungarian history was used to bolster Hungarian territorial rights in the present. This coalescence of geographical space and historical time helped turn Freedom Square into a microcosm of Greater Hungary.

As already mentioned, Arad had had its own monument before state borders shifted.[26] Sculpted by Adolf Huszár (1842–1885) and György Zala (1858–1937) and erected in 1890, it consisted of a large pedestal with four seated allegorical figures and, in the middle, a higher pediment on which a statue of the victorious Hungaria—a female figure personifying Hungary—held up a laurel wreath in her right hand. The base was adorned with portraits of the martyred thirteen. As literature has pointed out, the monument was erected at a time when the official memory of 1848 shifted from commemorating the revolution as a fight for freedom toward emphasizing its national aspects—a shift that fit into the Hungarian government's increasingly assertive Magyarization policies in which nationalism and imperialism became one.[27] The Hungarian nationalist rhetoric that surrounded the unveiling of the statue was not designed to make the Romanian inhabitants of Arad feel included; in their eyes, the monument became a symbol of Magyarization. Romanian papers lamented how the monument erased the Romanian fight for freedom, which, in 1848, had meant supporting the Habsburgs against Hungarian nationalism. One article pointed out that the monument had been erected "in the center of a purely Romanian region loyal to the Monarchy."[28] To these commentators, the memorial colonized Romanian space both metaphorically—pushing out Romanian narratives from the public sphere—and physically. This sealed the monument's fate after 1918. In 1922, Romanian authorities surrounded it with a wall. Three years later, they took it down and transferred it to a storage space in Arad Fortress.

The Batthyány Sanctuary Lamp was, in a certain sense, a replacement for the Arad monument. In the framework of irredentist spacetime, it was able to preserve a spiritual connection that stretched across the border. As Pekár put it at the inauguration: "The Arad thirteen are looking at us today from the prison fortress of Arad and greet the fourteenth martyr of the Hungarian Calvary with a military salute. This Batthyány Sanctuary Lamp, piously lit here today by the municipality, burns on with another million flames in the heart of the nation, to nurture us with faith, to shine the light of hope in the Hungarian night."[29] If the Arad monument had originally carved out physical space to showcase the Hungarian narrative in a multiethnic locality, the new monument transformed this into a spiritual idea of national territory that could be metonymically transferred to a distant space in Budapest.

Trianon as a site of memory encompassed the memory of not only a 1920 treaty that reduced the size of Hungary but also of a series of other events interpreted as national tragedies. The monuments of Freedom Square led the way toward a reconceptualization of national identity in which these historical tragedies marked out the spatial expanse of the ideal homeland. The idea of national tragedy, of defeat, was hence central. In the irredentist sculptures, however, this was combined with an activist message that urged its public to break the cycle of defeat.

Sculpting Defeat

In the victimhood narrative of Hungarian history, consecutive national tragedies were conceptualized as blows of fate that were inevitable, like natural disasters. Yet, the whole point of irredentism was to take action, turn the tide, and regain the lost territories. As Urmánczy stated at the inauguration, the role of the sculptures in Freedom Square was to foment revenge. There was a tension within the ideology between passive victimhood and agency. The sculptors of the irredentist monuments expressed this tension in the manner of good professionals trained in the academic tradition—by drawing on artistic precedents and reshaping them in a way that merged old meanings with new ones.

The task the sculptors faced was complex. First, they had to represent geographical concepts in a recognizable visual form. Second, they had to create an imagery that conveyed a sense of defeat and loss but also a call to action. For the first, they could find ample precedent in the countless allegories depicting cities, countries, or continents in human—mostly female—form, produced through many centuries of Western art history. For the second, they could draw on more specific models from a country that had suffered similar territorial loss half a century before. It might seem surprising that the country in question was France, a member of the Entente to which irredentists assigned primary blame for Trianon. In 1871, due to its defeat in the Franco-Prussian War, France had lost Alsace-Lorraine. It had won it back after the First World War, due to the same treaties that had disadvantaged Hungary. Hence, paradoxically, the victory of the great adversary offered hope to Hungarian irredentists, as it exemplified the impermanence of borders drawn up in peace treaties.

The fact that the sculptures echoed French precedents was often brought up in the Hungarian press. The most important example was the statue of the city of Strasbourg erected on the Place de la Concorde in Paris in 1838, which gained additional significance as a memorial after 1871. As the *Pesti Hirlap* explained in 1929: "While Alsace belonged to the Germans, the statue of Strasbourg in the heart of Paris was covered with a veil of mourning. And in the hearts of all French people who passed by it in those decades, with their hats removed in tribute, it evoked one throbbing word: revanche!"[30] The French connection was clear early on; in December 1920, before the statues had even been unveiled, the periodical of the Pécs Socialist Party, the *Munkás* (*Worker*), mocked authorities for imitating France "in this respect too."[31]

These authors noticed a similarity in how the monuments created a space within the capital, in Freedom Square as in the Place de la Concorde, to mourn territories lost elsewhere. They did not remark on formal or iconographic parallels between the sculptures and French precedents. Nevertheless, these, too, are striking. In the 1880s, images of defeat proliferated in French public sculpture. Many works followed one basic format: they featured a strong, erect, armed figure supporting another figure who is inert, wounded, or dead.[32] Three of the four Hungarian sculptures followed the same scheme. In Pásztor's *East*, a mustached, stern ancient Hungarian warrior holds a nude young man who has collapsed in agony. In Sidló's *West*, another ancient warrior—one with a wide, muscular chest that does not conform to the classical idea of beauty and instead projects a stern heroism—towers over a dainty, wounded young man. In Kisfaludi Strobl's *North*, the dying figure is a woman: a personification of Hungary. She is taller than the man who supports her, but that man is a stocky, robust figure with a Hungarian mustache who props her up while grabbing his sword and throwing a fierce stare at anyone who might attempt to harm her.

Given that the *Irredentist Sculpture Group* had admittedly been inspired by the Place de la Concorde and that at least one of the sculptors had spent a longer time in Paris, it is safe to assume that the compositional similarity to French late nineteenth-century sculptures commemorating the war, such as Jean-Alexandre-Joseph Falguière's *Allegory of the Resistance* (1871), Marius-Jean-Antonin Mercié's *Gloria Victis* (1873), or Louis-Ernest Barrias's *Monument á La Defense de Paris* (1879–1881), is not a coincidence. There is, however, a fundamental difference between the Hungarian sculptures and their French precedents. As Michael Dorsch has argued, in France, the imagery of defeat featured strong female figures not afraid of weapons or combat.[33] The statue of Strasbourg that would be veiled after 1871—a work by James Pradier—was itself an example: it featured a robust woman calmly sitting on a cannon. In the post-1870 examples, it is the female figures who protect the wounded men. Mercié's and Barrias's works are important but far from unique examples.[34] According to Dorsch, the imagery expressed anxieties about the decline of French masculinity, already present earlier in the nineteenth century and strengthening after the defeat and the 1871 Commune.

In the Hungarian sculptures, by contrast, the strong characters are always men. This difference reflects the masculine character of the Horthy regime's official culture, in which women—whether real or depicted in artworks—could rarely take on leadership roles. If, in French art, the fear of "effeminacy" in defeat was expressed by representing strong militant women, in Hungary, it led to eschewing such figures altogether. Nevertheless, this difference in the social context only partly explains the difference in imagery. The messages conveyed by the French and the Hungarian sculptures were similar but not quite the same. While the French sculptures positioned the defeat as a thing of the past that needed to be mourned, the Hungarian sculptures focused more pointedly on "revanche."[35] However fierce the women looked in the French sculptures, by using female figures, the sculptors indicated that their compositions were allegories and not realistic representations of war. Although the Hungarian sculptures also were allegorical, they employed a different allegorical vocabulary. Through the well-known nine-teenth-century imagery of militant Hungarian masculinity, they presented militancy as the only source of hope in the dire present.

These images of masculinity drew on ancient Hungarian mythology (or, at least, on how nineteenth-century Romantic nationalism had reconstructed it) and on history. In *West*, sculpted by Sidló, the muscular figure protect-ing the young man who has collapsed over the Hungarian Holy Crown is the mythical war god Hadúr (lit. Warlord; a nineteenth-century invention). The group, which represents the most distant region conquered by ancient Magyars, is completed by a *turul*, the totemistic bird of Hungarian myth. In Kisfaludi Strobl's *North*, a *kuruc* warrior—an anti-Habsburg rebel of the sev-enteenth and early eighteenth centuries—supports the dying personification of Hungary, who has suffered mortal wounds, as she has been crucified. In the lower half of the composition, a child representing the Slovak popula-tion of former Northern Hungary huddles close to the woman. This detail alludes to the patronizing idea, often voiced by irredentists, that the Slovak minority belonged under the protection of the more developed Hungarian nation. In *East*, the work of Pásztor, the ancient Prince Csaba—mythical son of Attila, king of Huns—releases a figure personifying Transylvania from his chains. Although the myth of Hungarians being related to the Huns had been disproven by historians in the mid-nineteenth century, it lived—and still lives—on in the nationalist imagination. Finally, in Szentgyörgyi's *South*, a Hungarian man armed with a weapon and shield protects a woman who per-sonifies the German-speaking minority, while the sheaves of wheat before them symbolize the rich agriculture of the southern lands.[36]

The four sculptors employed the same visual sources that nineteenth-century artists had used to conjure up images of the past. They combined classical nudes with national imagery—helmets, mustaches, braided hair. With their headwear, facial hair, stern expressions, and stocky figures, the statues of Csaba and the kuruc warrior resemble the illustrations of the sev-enteenth-century series of prints *Mausoleum*, whose depictions of chieftains and kings had served as models for a host of paintings and sculptures in the nineteenth century. This imagery had also featured in the seven millennium monuments discussed earlier. Many of these represented figures of ancient warriors, often subsequently identified as Chieftain Árpád, the leader of the Conquest. Depicting similar characters in a similar visual idiom, the irre-dentist sculptures evoked the previous monuments and their message of hegemony. In late nineteenth-century Hungary, Árpád and his warriors were employed as symbols of the chauvinistic ethnic nationalism that increasingly challenged the multinational state envisioned by the liberal nationalists of the 1860s and 1870s.[37] Drawing on this imagery in 1920, the irredentist sculptures established continuity with the nationalist politics of the millennium.

The seven millennium monuments—as well as the better-known *Millennium Monument* in Heroes' Square, Budapest, which similarly featured ancient warriors—had not been intended as calls to action; rather, they glorified the existing status quo and warned against attempts to subvert it. In this, they resembled most monuments across the world, which either promote a similar message or mourn past losses and conflicts that are ready to become history. Exuding a sense of permanence is, after all, the central raison d'être of monuments. In this vein, the French sculptures of defeat had employed a formal language of closure, even though French society was far from seeing the issue as resolved. The sculptures of Freedom Square, by contrast, represented a status quo the Union of Defensive Leagues wanted to change. They would not be permanent; their success would in fact be marked by their eventual obsolescence. They were, by design, ephemeral, and in this respect, they ultimately had more in common with the delicate veil placed on the statue of Strasbourg than with the bronze and stone sculptures whose compositions they echoed. In Freedom Square, the monuments were seemingly made of stone—but this was, in fact, "artificial stone," a material usually used for tombstones. The impermanence of artificial stone and its inferiority to marble or bronze was evident to contemporaries. The organizers had probably opted for this material so that the monuments could be erected as swiftly as possible, but contemporaries endowed the gesture with symbolism.[38] A journalist writing for the *Pesti Hírlap* in 1929 explained that the inferior material had been chosen in the hope that the sculptures would not stand for long.[39]

While justifying the choice of material, the journalist nevertheless advocated for reerecting the sculptures in noble marble. He believed they had become so important as symbols of an unforgettable pain that they would remain relevant even after the (in his mind inevitable) return of the lost territories. The example highlights how central the idea of pain and suffering had become to Hungarian national identity. The irredentist sculptures articulated and promoted this model. At the same time, they helped frame Trianon as a military issue that could only be resolved by accepting future pain and suffering. This connotation became integral to Trianon as a site of memory. Despite subsequent interwar efforts toward a diplomatic resolution, the iconography of commemoration continued to strike the same notes, helping to radicalize Hungarian society.

Rites of Remembrance

Redemption through suffering is, of course, a Christian concept, and applied to Trianon, it fit well into the Horthy regime's instrumentalization of Christianity to further its political aims. As public life became suffused with Christian symbolism, irredentism was developing into a political religion. The imagery employed in Kisfaludi Strobl's *North*, the crucifixion of Hungary, was to become one of the most cited clichés of irredentism, in word and image alike. In 1928, the cover of a popular album titled *Justice for Hungary!* would be illustrated with the map of Greater Hungary nailed to the cross, creating the most influential visual articulation of the idea (fig. 2.3).[40]

But even before this happened, the idea of Hungary's sacrifice and—analogous to the New Testament story—inevitable resurrection was essential to irredentist thinking. Through rites performed in Freedom Square and its vicinity, irredentism gained a religious temporality; it grew into a larger framework encompassing not only political life but also the everyday. The rites were also cleansing rituals; they ceremoniously excluded everything and everyone who did not fit the framework. For the Horthy regime's political Christianity, a main enemy was Communism, and the copious religious imagery was to override all traces of the 1919 Soviet regime. Even more broadly, the ideology was also deeply antisemitic, and when it conceptualized Christianity as the core element of national identity, it made it clear whom it wanted to exclude.[41]

As Mabel Berezin has argued, urban rituals and their regular repetition helped Fascists reshape Italian identities by colonizing both the space and time where everyday life played out.[42] The rituals of Freedom Square, which inhabited the annual calendar through their connections to national and Christian holidays, functioned in a similar way. Their participants could experience a spiritual connection to the ideal Hungary envisioned by irredentists—ideal not just in its territorial extent but also in its societal "unity," its successful "marginalization of internal foes" such as Jews or Communists.[43]

On 16 January 1921, the inauguration ceremony of the irredentist sculptures included the consecration of the irredentist flag. This was a white silk flag embroidered with an image of the Virgin Mary in the center and the coats of arms of the sixty-three counties of historical Hungary along the edges. It bore an inscription referring to the traditional belief in Virgin Mary as the patron of Hungary ("Patrona Hungariae") and calling for her help. Blessed by all Christian churches, the flag was subsequently deposited in Saint Stephen's Cathedral, just two corners from Freedom Square.[44] There, it assumed a central position on one of the most significant Christian holidays.

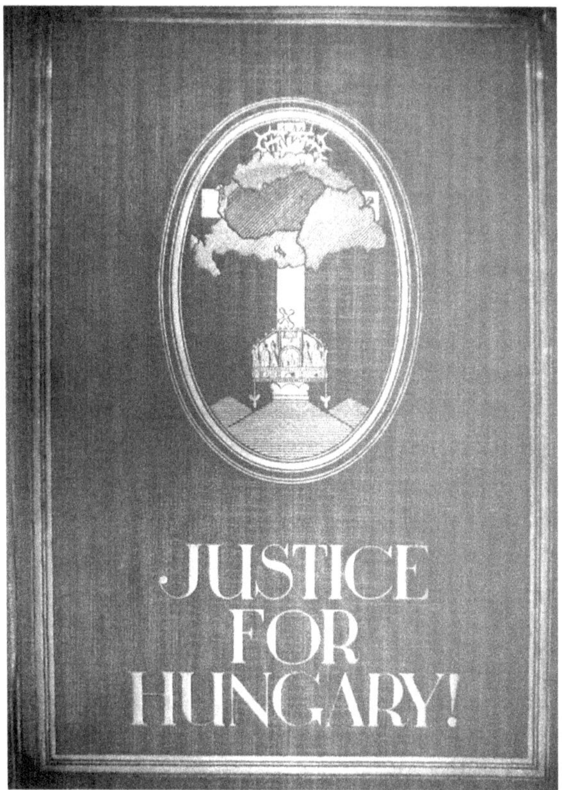

FIGURE 2.3.   Cover of Ottó Légrády, ed., *Justice for Hungary: The Cruel Errors of Trianon* (Budapest: Légrády Brothers, 1930).

Although not strictly mandated in liturgy, the "resurrection procession" held on Saturday or Sunday is a traditional part of Catholic Easter festivities in Hungary. In the interwar period, this religious ceremony morphed into a celebration of "Hungarian resurrection," during which the irredentist flag was carried along with the Eucharist to the irredentist sculptures, where a priest blessed the flag and the irredentist cause while an orchestra played the national anthem and the popular irredentist song "Hungarian Creed."[45] The procession would then ceremoniously return to the cathedral. Participants included members of the high clergy as well as prominent irredentist activists and representatives of the municipality.

Freedom Square had originally been designed to commemorate the 1848–1849 Revolution and War of Independence and celebrate the post-1867 semi-independent, liberal Hungarian state. The buildings that surrounded it and the names of the streets that ran into it all supported this concept. Although the overall message was one of secular liberalism and triumphant capitalism—our martyrs died so that today we can have our own Stock Exchange—nineteenth-century city planners provided the square with a hint of a religious aura by shaping it like a basilica. Exploiting this characteristic, each Easter, the quasi-religious rites of irredentism overwrote the secular meanings inscribed into this urban quarter in the dualist era. In this way, Freedom Square made room for the commemoration of Trianon both in geographical space by providing it with a designated location within the city and in the annual cycle of time. Each Easter was now a reminder that the Hungarian resurrection was still to happen. Furthermore, Easter was not the only holiday that took on irredentist undertones. The Day of Saint Stephen, 20 August, was suffused with similar meanings; to some commentators, it became the true irredentist holiday.[46] Trianon governed the commemoration of 1848–1849 in a similar way. Irredentist activists employed the memory of both 15 March (the start of the revolution) and 6 October (the execution of the Arad martyrs) to position themselves as twentieth-century successors of the revolutionaries. Freedom Square was a central venue on all these occasions.

One group that regularly exploited the memory of 1848–1849 was the Turul Association, an influential and notorious radical right-wing student organization.[47] Driven by vicious antisemitism, the Turulists sought to limit the number of Jewish students at universities to zero. They regularly raided universities and attacked students they perceived to be Jewish, with little resistance from the authorities. The *Irredentist Sculpture Group* was their favored venue for heated antisemitic speeches.[48] This was also bolstered by an iconographic connection: the Turul Association took its name from a mythical bird associated with ancient Hungarians, also depicted in Sidló's *West*. Although already mentioned in medieval chronicles, the turul became firmly embedded into Hungarian historical memory as the supposed totemistic bird of the ancient Magyars in the nineteenth century. Its depictions proliferated in that period, gradually taking on a military meaning. Sculptures of the turul appeared in important representative sites of state power, such as the Buda Royal Palace (sculpture by Gyula Donáth, 1905), but also in public artworks promoting the hegemony of ethnic Hungarians, such as the millennium monuments. *West* continued this iconography, associating the turul with another (supposed) figure from ancient Hungarian mythology—Hadúr—and with war.

At that point in time, it was still possible the turul would gradually fade away to become one of many commonplace national symbols. Instead, it became one of the most controversial, largely due to the activities of the Turul Association. In 1920, when Sidló sculpted his turul, it was one of several motifs in the composition. It was a symbol of Hungarian dominance, but no more so than

Hadúr or the crown. By August 1945, when the sculptures were removed by postwar authorities, it was perhaps the most inflammatory detail in the whole sculpture group—a motif that emblematically united right-wing extremism, militant irredentism, and the fanatical antisemitism that had, by then, culminated in the Hungarian Holocaust.

As a public monument, the *Irredentist Sculpture Group* consisted not only of the four sculptures but also of the space they marked out together. This was a physical space within Freedom Square, but it also offered a metaphorical space for a segment of public discourse, which it invited, encouraged, and nurtured. It is no exaggeration to compare this repositioning of central Budapest in cultural memory to a conquest. The monuments of Freedom Square could be seen as primary bases from where the capture of Budapest—the "sinful city" of the Soviet Republic—could victoriously unfold. In February 1921, soon after the inauguration of the monuments, the right-wing extremist paper *Gondolat* (*Thought*) asserted that "Hungarian irredentism must be promoted continuously and unceasingly in the capital of Hungary in such a way that it . . . inserts itself into the most mundane thoughts of passersby. . . . The irredentism of Freedom Square must be taken out into the streets . . . the names of detached Hungarian towns, counties, and notions related to them must be pinned to the corners of Budapest's busy roads and public squares on white signs visible from far away."[49] Boulevards and bridges—most of which bore the names of Habsburg family members—had to be renamed in this spirit: "Transylvania Boulevard, Sekler Boulevard, Upper Hungary Boulevard, Southern Region Boulevard, Carpathian Boulevard . . . Kolozsvár, Kassa, Temesvár, Arad, Pozsony Bridge. . . . You will see how this will change, as if by magic, the visage of Budapest; you will see how these street names will become eternal flames of Hungarian irredentism."[50]

In later years, especially after 1927, naming public spaces in Budapest after places in the lost territories gained great traction.[51] In some neighborhoods, these street names appeared in clusters. For instance, in a suburb named Szentimre, Transylvanian Hungarians who had resettled in Budapest after Trianon named the streets and squares after their old homeland, arranging their houses around a central square named after the Hargita (Harghita) Mountains.[52] This was, no doubt, a form of commemoration and a way to express personal and communal grief. Nevertheless, the projection of the lost territories onto Budapest was also an act of consecration, of cleansing. "Sin City" could hence be turned into a site of remembrance for all places lost, a monumental example of the transposition of "geographically unrelated memories which then become concentrated in that single place," as described by Rigney.[53]

Blood and Soil

The "reconquest" of Budapest was only the beginning. The irredentist sculptures had been erected to foment "hatred and revenge"; the end goal was to win back the lost lands. Throughout the interwar period, irredentism promoted the idea that Greater Hungary was an organic whole. At the same time, the irredentist sculptures represented the four detached regions separately and did not include the remaining area of Hungary at all. This valorization of the lost territories in comparison to those that remained was typical of irredentist thinking, especially in the 1920s. Yet, by the end of the decade, the ideology evolved to such an extent that the sculpture group had to be complemented with a new monument expressing the organic totality of Greater Hungary.

Initiated by the irredentist activist Urmánczy and designed by Lechner and the sculptor Richárd Füredi (1873–1947), the *Reliquary Country Flag* was erected with the support of the municipality and unveiled on 20 August 1928 (fig. 2.4). It stood facing the four sculptures, so that the five monuments created an imaginary circle, still leaving ample space for demonstrations. The base of the new monument consisted of a stone pulpit, accessible via the stairs surrounding it. At the back of the pulpit rose a second, taller pediment decorated with a row of plantlike ornaments inspired by Hungarian folk culture. On top of it, a bird of prey spread its wings; reminiscent of the eagle lecterns of medieval churches, it was a turul, guarding the flagpole on which the Hungarian flag flew at half-mast. The lower pediment was decorated with the coats of arms of Hungary as well as of the Houses of Árpád, Anjou, and Corvin, families whose scions had ruled the Kingdom of Hungary between the eleventh and the late fifteenth centuries.[54]

Although the monument still had to be erected by a grassroots organization rather than by the state, the fact that it was erected at all reflected the political shifts of the late 1920s and the new impetus they gave to revisionist activism. The friendship treaty signed with Italy in April 1927 seemed to finally improve Hungary's position in international diplomacy and hence its chances of achieving its revisionist goals.[55] In the summer of the same year, a new revisionist campaign was kick-started from Britain, in an article published in the *Daily Mail* by its owner, Harold Sidney Harmsworth, Lord Rothermere (1868–1940). In "Hungary's Place in the Sun," Rothermere argued against the perceived injustices of the Trianon Peace Treaty.[56] This, as well as his subsequent donations to revisionist campaigns, earned him a cultlike following among Hungarian nationalists. Enthused by the British lord's support and emboldened by the departure of the economic and

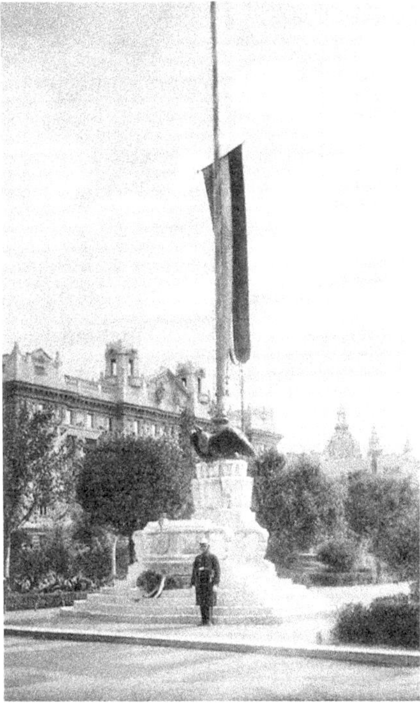

FIGURE 2.4.   Postcard depicting the *Reliquary Country Flag*, c. 1929.
Photo: Ády / kozterkep.hu

military control commissions of the League of Nations from Hungary in
1927, campaign groups supported by the government erected many Trianon
monuments across the country in the next years.[57] The *Reliquary Country Flag*
was the most prominent.

The inscriptions on the pediment reflected this historical moment. The
keystone of the reliquary bore the following sentence: "Be aware, oh human,
that you are standing here on the soil of Greater Hungary, consecrated with
blood, tears and sweat." The front of the pediment proclaimed: "Our country is the country of the Carpathians, Greater Hungary. It was founded in 896
by Prince Árpád and will endure until the end of times." On its back were the
words: "The foundations for our future greatness were laid by the greats of
our past." Underneath this inscription, the Hungarian Creed could be read.
Finally, two marble plaques just below the flagpole showed quotations from
two influential foreign supporters of the irredentist cause. "Hungary's Place
in the Sun" referred to Rothermere, while "I Trattati di pace non sono eterni"
("Peace treaties are not eternal") was a statement made by Mussolini in the
Senate in Rome on 5 June 1928.[58] Together, these inscriptions encompassed

virtually the entire mythology of Hungarian irredentism—the centuries-long suffering of the nation, its historical right to the territory, the importance of historical continuity, Rothermere's intervention, and the hopes pinned to Fascist Italy.

Reinterpreting the symbolic space defined by the irredentist sculptures, the *Reliquary Country Flag* helped connect the four disparate regions represented by the latter by providing a spiritual focus. While the sculptures reflected a picture of the country as fragmented, the country flag evoked it as a conceptual, if not legal, whole. It did so through the "relics" that it held—samples of soil collected from each of the former kingdom's counties, buried under the flag. Importantly, the reliquary did not distinguish between the counties of Dismembered Hungary and those of the lost territories; as part of the "country of the Carpathians," they all held the same spiritual importance. In this respect, the monument can be seen to reflect the revisionist politics of the Bethlen government, which emphasized the importance of the remaining territories and their economic and cultural prosperity. In this model, the central territory was not a black hole but a magnet whose allure could hopefully win back the lost lands. There was no need to draw up maps to refer to geographical realities like north, east, west, and south, because the emphasis was on completeness. The soil incorporated into the monument stood in for land and for territory. Visitors to the monument were, as its inscription proclaimed, standing on the soil of "Greater Hungary," which is the "country of the Carpathians"—of mountains that no longer legally belonged to Hungary but were still spiritually present. The emphasis on soil and the ground also recalled the idea of a tomb, while the flagpole reaching toward the sky, its flag to be raised to full mast upon the restoration of Greater Hungary, evoked the hope of future resurrection.[59]

The *Reliquary Country Flag* was not the only monument incorporating soil from other locations as relics; this had been done long before in Central Europe. More than a hundred years before, the people of Kraków volunteered to build a mound to commemorate the Polish national leader Tadeusz Kościuszko. Completed in 1823, the Kościuszko Mound contained samples of soil from battlefields in Poland and America where Kościuszko had fought. The idea behind such monuments was that the soil in these places had been consecrated by the blood of these heroes—just as the inscription of the country flag claimed. A more recent example—one that Hungarian irredentists were definitely aware of—was the commemoration of the Battle of Zborov in Czechoslovakia. On 2 July 1917, near the village of Zborov, Czechoslovak legions that had joined the Russian side successfully defeated the Habsburg army. In the postwar memory politics of the Czechoslovak state, the battle featured as a great milestone in the fight for independence, comparable to the 1620 Battle of the White Mountain. Zborov monuments were erected across the country, but the most important memorial, the one at the battlefield, was located outside the country's borders, as Zborov now formed part of Poland. On the tenth anniversary in 1927, many Czechs paid pilgrimage to the site, and the exchange of soil played an important part in the commemorations.[60] One Czechoslovak Parliament member brought soil from the White Mountain and added it to the memorial; others brought samples from their own localities and exchanged it for samples from Zborov, which they added to their Zborov memorials at home. Soil from other important First World War battlefields was also often added to the base of Zborov monuments.

The way samples of soil created a spiritual connection between places otherwise separated by distance or national borders is very similar to the concept of a spiritual Greater Hungary united by the deeds of heroic Hungarians of the past. Irredentism was a powerful ideology because, besides promoting specific geopolitical aims, it also mobilized deeper patterns of thinking. As the example of the monument in Zborov shows, spiritual connection through blood and soil did not necessarily come with territorial demands; Czechoslovakia had no intention to incorporate Zborov. Yet, as Nancy Wingfield has demonstrated, Zborov commemorations had a strong ethnic nationalist edge; they excluded the non-Slavic minorities of Czechoslovakia and even pushed Slovaks into the background, focusing mainly on the heroism of Czechs.[61] In combining ideas of place, history, blood, struggle, and nation, monuments with soil provided ethnonationalist concepts of the ideal nation with a tangible materiality and vehement emotional power. In 1934, a Nazi organization redesigned a memorial temple to Frederick Barbarossa, originally built between 1892 and 1896 on Mount Kyffhäuser, to instead memorialize war dead by incorporating urns with soil from Germany's lost territories and installing busts of Bismarck, Hitler, and others.[62] Six years had passed since the *Reliquary Country Flag* had been set up in Budapest. The devastating power of these embodied ideas was beginning to show.

Monuments into Icons

In Freedom Square, the *Irredentist Sculpture Group* and, later, the *Reliquary Country Flag* created a space designated for the commemoration of Trianon. Commemorations were not meant to be restricted to this space; instead, the location was intended to provide a focal point for a network. In 1928, the Freedom Square country flag gave rise to the Country Flag Movement, and a hundred similar monuments were erected across the country. Its inau-

FIGURE 2.5.   Lajos Márton, series of irredentist stamps, c. 1928, National Széchényi Library, Budapest, Map, Poster, and Small Print Collection.
Photo: National Széchényi Library

guration also prompted the Union of Defensive Leagues to issue a series of "letter-sealing commemorative stamps" (i.e., unofficial stamps with no monetary value) depicting the monuments of Freedom Square (fig. 2.5). Four of these showed the *Irredentist Sculpture Group*, while others depicted the country flag and other irredentist symbols. Designed by Lajos Márton (1891–1953), the images showed the sculptures as if they had come to life in front of backgrounds evoking the respective territories: mountains for north, a Transylvanian Sekler gate for east, fields of crops for south, and the ruined castle of Dévény/Devín for west. The sculptures were to inhabit public life far and wide, through as many channels as possible. In fact, the union waived all copyrights early on to aid the dissemination of the sculptures in the form of postcards and photographs.[63]

Three-dimensional reproductions were also created. In 1929, the *Gyógyszerészi Hetilap* (*Pharmacists' Weekly*) reported on the Annual Assembly of the Union of Pharmacists, which took place in the great hall of the Academy of Music. In the lobby, the "Pro Hungaria" Women's World Association of the Hungarian National Association exhibited miniature versions of the irredentist sculptures, while, in the same space, "interested colleagues could also examine the 'Capsulator' powder capsule maker."[64] Thanks to the activities

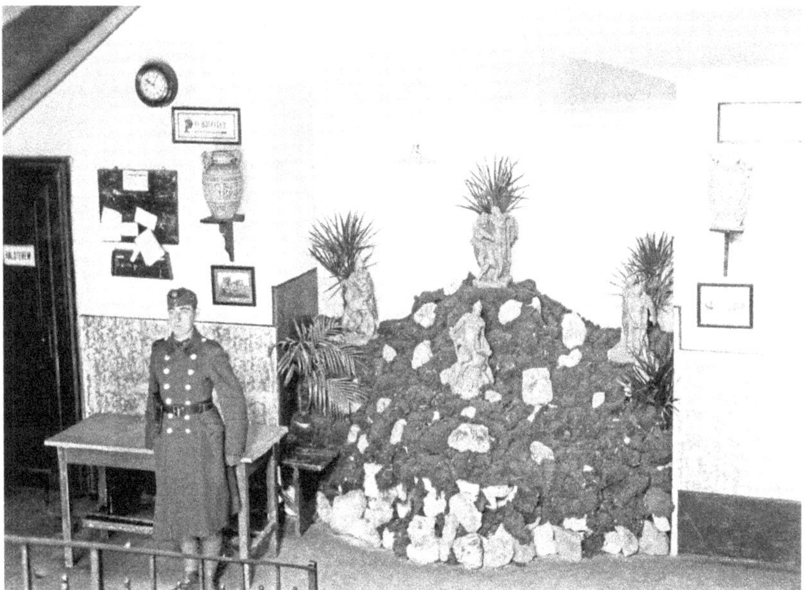

FIGURE 2.6.   Irredentist memorial in the Maria Theresa barracks, Budapest, 1927.
Photo: Tamás Konok Sr. / fortepan.hu

of a civil association, the sculptures materialized in an ostensibly apolitical professional space. Like the "powder capsule maker," they inhabited a world where supposed public interest intertwined inseparably with business venture: the Women's World Association did not disseminate the miniatures for free. Nevertheless, it also relied heavily on state patronage for its income. In 1931, the Social Democrat *Népszava* (*People's Voice*) reported that the Municipality of Budapest had confidentially instructed all its institutions to buy the miniatures for nine hundred pengős. The instruction came at a time of professed austerity in the wake of the Great Depression, and, the *Népszava* commented wryly, it was indeed a money-saving measure; had there been no austerity, the municipality would have made its institutions buy life-size versions of the sculptures.[65]

The story is a perfect encapsulation of the interwar Hungarian public sphere, where state ideology was disseminated by civil organizations and suffused all areas of life, sometimes in the most banal form. Embodying everyday irredentism, miniatures of the Freedom Square sculptures appeared in many places, in various installations. It is perhaps less surprising to find them in a military context, such as in the military barracks on Üllői Road, where a Calvary mound was built from soil and patches of grass with small versions of the sculptures on top (fig. 2.6).[66]

However, they were also present in places such as the Kiosk restaurant in Sashalom, near Budapest, where the owner, Lászlóné Göttler, had installed a Revisionist Room with miniatures of the four sculptures, the *Reliquary Country Flag*, and portraits of leaders of the revisionist movement.[67]

In these installations, the sculptures assumed a new spatiality that removed them from the material space of Freedom Square. At the barracks, they stood on top of a mound built from soil and pieces of rock. The installation evoked the idea of the Hungarian Calvary, an association strengthened by the palm leaves—symbols of redemption—placed behind each of the four sculptures. At the same time, the mound was a reminder of another important irredentist trope; the fact that Hungary had become a relatively flat country after losing the mountain ranges of Slovakia and Transylvania was incessantly bemoaned by activists. In Freedom Square, the four sculptures had created an imaginary space by projecting the four directions of the compass onto a semicircle. In the barracks, they were laid out to form a rhomboid shape but again did not correspond to the compass: north, positioned at the top, was faced by west, while south was located to the right and east to the left. They formed an imaginary space on top of a lost, sacred mound. The niche in which they stood was flanked by signs on the wall indicating the location of Kassa/Košice and Pozsony/Bratislava, opposite each other.

Memorials before the late twentieth century, especially urban figural sculptures such as those in Freedom Square, are often treated in later scholarly commentary as externalizations of memory that "do our memory-work for us," hence helping society to forget and absolve itself of responsibility.[68] In an influential essay, Young contrasted such monuments of national self-aggrandization with the "counter-monuments" installed in Germany from the 1980s onward, which handed the responsibility for commemorating the Holocaust back to society by involving members of the community in the memorialization process and reducing, or sometimes completely effacing, their own material and visual presence.[69] Politically, these monuments were diametrically opposed to the Freedom Square monuments and their encouragement of antisemitic discourse. Yet, unsettlingly, the Freedom Square monuments, too, transcend the limitations of "traditional" public monuments. This suggests that "participation" in memorialization is not necessarily a feature restricted to post-1945 democratic societies nor to the skeptical critique of monumental concepts of the nation. The monuments of Freedom Square expressed grandiose national martyrdom, but individual engagement with them in private and semiprivate spaces was part of how they functioned. They could be rearranged, like in the installation at the barracks, the designers of which self-evidently visualized irredentist spacetime

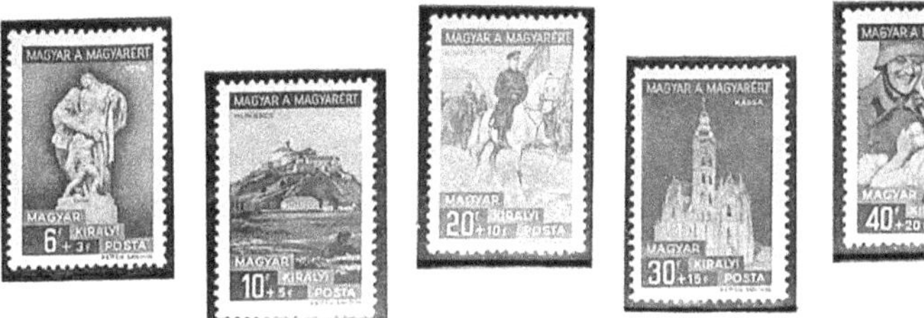

FIGURE 2.7.   Sándor Petten, *Hungarian for Hungarian*, series of stamps, 1939, private collection. Photo by author

while creating a new arrangement that did not need to mirror the one at Freedom Square. Handing memory back to society (after molding it into specific shapes) was precisely how the monuments helped mobilization for the irredentist cause.

The sculptures became icons in irredentist culture. Often removed from their original context, they signified allegiance to the cause in their mere form, without necessarily revealing their iconographic complexity. Given their ubiquity and frequent appearance in contexts not primarily related to irredentist activism, they aimed to assume the position of fundamental national symbols such as flags. Coming close to banality, they constructed irredentism as an inherent part of national identity. Yet, to use Michael Billig's term, the irredentist sculptures never became inconspicuous "unwaved flags"; however much they became part of the furniture in interwar Hungary, they were always activist symbols.[70] As images advocating territorial conflict, with their masculinity and wartime symbolism, they possessed a militant quality that only became more pronounced as the Hungarian political sphere radicalized.

In 1938, parts of Slovakia were reallocated to Hungary in the First Vienna Award orchestrated by Nazi Germany.[71] The next year, the Hungarian Royal Mail issued a series of stamps titled *Hungarian for Hungarian*, commemorating the occasion (fig. 2.7).[72] The stamps featured images of the castle in Munkács/Mukachevo, Horthy on a white horse riding into Komárom/Komarno, and Kassa/Košice Cathedral. The highest-value stamp showed a local Hungarian girl greeting a grinning Hungarian soldier and was inscribed with the year 1938. The lowest-price stamp showed an image from 1920: the sculpture of *North*. Its depiction of the dying Hungary was now the past; resurrection had begun. Yet, separated from its context in Freedom Square and depicted in front of a blank background, the sculpture was now an icon that lived on to depict Hungarian suffering as a general idea, one that served as a rallying cry for radicalization. The vision of the journalist who wished to preserve the monuments for the future was realized in this proliferating imagery, which could now resurface in homes, photographs, and stamp catalogues, even after the artificial stone sculptures were long gone.

Afterlives

Not all inhabitants of interwar Hungary were irredentists or revisionists. Liberal newspapers published articles promoting the acceptance of the new situation, and many left-wingers considered revisionism purely a device of government propaganda.[73] Nevertheless, when investigating the reception of Freedom Square's irredentist monuments in the interwar period, the researcher of newspaper archives is confronted by a curiously monolithic picture. The sole subversive act I have been able trace through these sources was reported in periodicals of émigré Hungarian Communists: the Vienna-based *Proletár* and the US-based *Előre (Forward)*.[74] According to these reports, the night after the unveiling of the irredentist sculptures in 1921, a group of left-wing workers hung inscriptions on them mocking Horthy and warning of the return of the proletarian dictatorship. The fact that this was only reported abroad was, of course, due to censorship in Hungary, and it is likely that this was not the only such episode. Nevertheless, the main impression one gets through the contemporary press is that there was widespread acceptance, not of the entirety of revisionist/irredentist ideology nor of its individual goals, which were debated even among revisionists and certainly by opponents of the right-wing regime, but of the general symbolism of irredentist spacetime. Papers reported on irredentist Easter and anti-Trianon 6 October as standard events of the year, without questioning the logic behind them. Ideology is pervasive if it goes beyond specific political goals, and monuments, built into the urban fabric and made to speak through ceremonies and rituals, are especially potent vessels for this.

The sculptures of Freedom Square were of course not solely responsible for the success of irredentism. Interwar Hungarian culture was saturated with revisionist and irredentist references in text and image, in every imaginable medium, especially after 1927. The monuments were, however, iconic and influential. By reframing the memory of 1848–1849 as part of the Trianon mythology, by defining irredentism as essentially militant, and by providing a focus for quasi-religious rites, they articulated some of the most fundamental tenets of the movement. By making irredentist spacetime tangible and helping it materialize in the urban space, they afforded these tenets with an immersive quality that was hard to escape. Through processions and street names, through new Easter and 6 October rites, irredentist spacetime enveloped not only the square but the city and the country.

The subsequent history of the square is a miniature reflection of Hungary's subsequent history.[75] The proliferation of irredentism in the 1930s saw the installation of further statues, such as the *Statue of Hungarian Pain*, a female nude by the French sculptor Émile Guilleaume (1932), and the *Hungarian Resurrection*, a muscular male counterpart by András Dózsa-Farkas (1935). The former statue was so generic that when the Communist authorities removed it in 1948, they transferred it to Margaret Island and reerected it in front of the Palatinus Baths with the title *Sunbathing Woman*.[76] The *Irredentist Sculpture Group* and the *Reliquary Country Flag* had already been destroyed in August 1945.

Today, Freedom Square exhibits a curious medley of memories. A monument to the liberating Soviet army, erected in 1948 in the center of the circle once circumscribed by the four sculptures and the *Reliquary Country Flag*, still stands. New sculptures set up after the fall of Communism include a memorial to the Swedish diplomat Carl Lutz, who saved Jews in the Holocaust (2006), statues of Ronald Reagan (2011) and George Bush (2020), and the *Monument of the German Occupation* (2014), heavily contested because of its whitewashing of Hungary's role in the Holocaust. It has engendered counter rituals, with demonstrators organizing discussions and leaving objects of Holocaust remembrance around the memorial, amounting to a permanent counter monument.[77] On the side of the square, a Calvinist church located in a modernist apartment block houses a bust of Horthy. Originally consecrated on 15 October 1940, to coincide with Horthy's victorious entrance into the "redeemed" part of Transylvania, the Church of Return had been built for Trianon refugees from the detached regions and has been decorated with many other symbols of Greater Hungarian history since the 1990s.

Outside the church, however, Freedom Square has ceased to be a commemorative site for Trianon. Under Communism, Trianon was largely a taboo subject.[78] Although concerns for Hungarian minorities could cautiously be voiced from the 1970s, this did not extend to wholly renouncing the treaty nor to prewar irredentist imagery.[79] Any direct commemorations of Trianon could only happen underground, in private spaces, if at all. In keeping memory alive, images and miniature versions of the irredentist sculptures—which still appear in the antiques trade in Hungary—must have played an important role. After 1989, the imagery resurfaced in public, and the various reproductions of Freedom Square's monuments were vastly more prominent than the square itself. Miniatures in museums serve as educational tools for schoolchildren.[80] The Trianon Museum, opened in 2003 in Várpalota, not only holds miniature versions but has also commissioned life-size reconstructions of the sculptures. One of its exhibitions tells the story of the Country Flag Movement.[81]

The imagery of interwar irredentism is back in Hungarian public life. It is, however, notable that when Viktor Orbán's government decided to erect a new, central Trianon memorial in Budapest, this was nothing like the Freedom Square sculptures. Unveiled in 2020, on the centenary of the treaty, and located in a street leading to the Parliament building, the memorial consists of a sanctuary with an eternal flame and a pathway, lowered into the ground, to the sanctuary. The walls flanking this path bear the names of places in present and former Hungary. Instead of the elaborate iconography of irredentism, the designers opted for abstract forms.[82] The approach is more reminiscent of Maya Lin's *Vietnam Veterans Memorial* in Washington DC than of interwar Freedom Square.[83]

Why this restraint? The 2020 memorial is conceptualized as the *Memorial Site of Belonging Together*, which—according to official explanations—would build a spiritual connection between Hungarians within and outside the borders; however, it also had a surprising message. It was conceived as part of a broader venture on the part of the Orbán government to establish an East Central European bloc within the European Union and take on a leadership role in this group. For a brief moment, the government attempted to use the memory of Trianon to build these connections, reframing it as a shared Central European catastrophe that destabilized and colonized the region.[84] The conventional imagery of Trianon was not suitable for this purpose because of its belligerency. The imagery of pain and suffering had been inextricably connected to a militant message, aimed at neighboring countries, early on; the *Irredentist Sculpture Group* had played a central role in this. This language had to be toned down if the goal was to strengthen cooperation. The Orbán government is otherwise known for its predilection for demodernizing the cityscape and rebuilding prewar scenery, but in this case, nonetheless, an abstract, postmodern formal language came in handy.

Still, by providing a "spiritual" model of Greater Hungary, the memorial reaches back to the devices of irredentist spacetime.[85] As Szabolcs László has observed, monuments such as Lin's in Washington or Michael Arad's 9/11 memorial in New York—which seem to have served as models in a formal sense—bear the names of dead people, in order to help society mourn and heal, while the 2020 Trianon monument lists the names of places. Its "focus is not on the human dimension of a truly difficult historical event, but on past territorial greatness and its loss," and hence not on the idea of healing but on "equating neighboring countries with ideas of death and destruction."[86]

Though the size of the lettering varies according to the size of localities, there is no other distinction; place names from present Hungary are interspersed with those from neighboring countries in a random order. All names are in Hungarian, even those of localities never inhabited by Hungarian speakers.[87] Yet again, the monument commemorates Trianon by obscuring the original geography and ethnic makeup of Greater Hungary and collapsing it all into a small, spiritualized space within central Budapest. Furthermore, that space was previously often used by antigovernment demonstrators to hold speeches and process toward the Parliament building. The Trianon memorial obstructs the path. As in the 1920s, the memory of Trianon reshapes the meanings and uses of public space in Budapest. Promoted as an overarching mindset—whether through abstract shapes or exalted images of suffering—irredentist spacetime can radically transform how people conceptualize the (national) space around them.

CHAPTER 3

History into Landscape

The dark silhouettes of warriors on horseback zigzag across a fragmented landscape, passing mighty castles and fortresses. The buildings are all individualized and identifiable. Their names are inscribed next to them, and so is the name of the river Danube (Duna), which flows across the image horizontally, cutting it in half. The dates next to the fortresses, all from the late sixteenth century, indicate that this is a picture of the Fifteen Years War fought by Hungarians against the invading Ottoman Turks from 1591 to 1606. It is an image of history that assembles details depicted from different viewpoints and at different scale, recalling avant-garde practices of image making.

The Turkish Wars is a sheet from the woodcut series *Hungarian Past* by Nándor Lajos Varga (1895–1978) (fig. 3.1). Raised in Transylvania, in the town of Sepsiszentgyörgy / Sfântu Gheorghe, Varga studied at the College of Fine Arts in Budapest in the 1920s and went on to become its professor of printmaking. He completed *Hungarian Past* in the mid-1930s, and the prints were first published in 1941.[1] As the brief introduction by Gyula Rajk (1893–1975)[2] explained, the aim was to evoke certain episodes from the "beautiful and painful" Hungarian past, which was "a mission, a vocation, and a faith. The closer it is to us, the more we feel its strength, its responsibility, and its promise, and the more we believe in Hungarian resurrection."[3] Hungarian history, as presented in the prints, largely aligned with the official narrative.

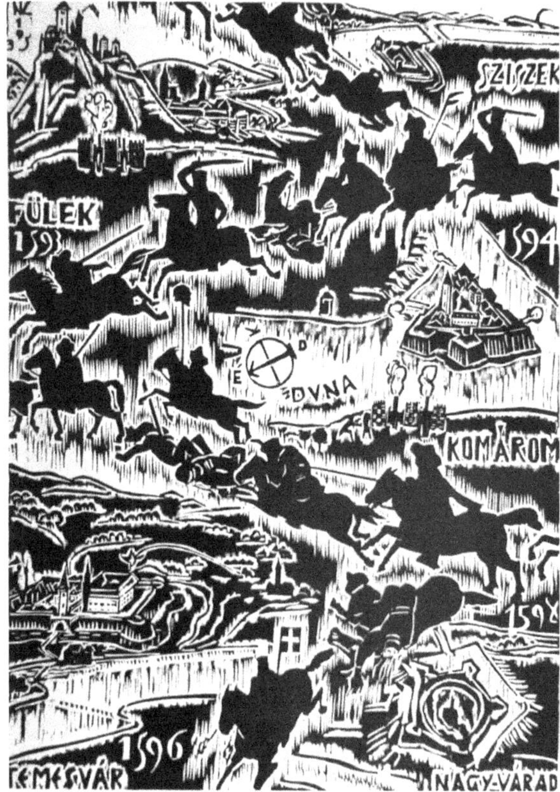

Figure 3.1.   Nándor Lajos Varga, *Turkish Wars (Hungarian Past XXII)*, early 1930s/1940, private collection.
Photo by author. Nándor Lajos Varga © OOA-S 2024

In the last sheets, the Soviet Republic appeared as the epitome of destruction and Horthy's ride into Budapest as a victorious moment (fig. 3.2). Trianon was, of course, the ultimate catastrophe. The preceding centuries were depicted as times of heroic struggles and national tragedies prefiguring the events of the early twentieth century.

By combining the imagery of history and landscape, Varga's *Turkish Wars* brought together two pillars of interwar nationalist and irredentist definitions of the nation's territory. The first of these, discussed in chapter 2, was "historical irredentism," which justified territorial claims by pointing to historical—often ancient and sometimes mythical—events that proved the nation had long possessed the regions in question. The second pillar, by contrast, invoked the timeless features of nature. From the nineteenth century, nationalist activism endowed elements of nature with symbolism.

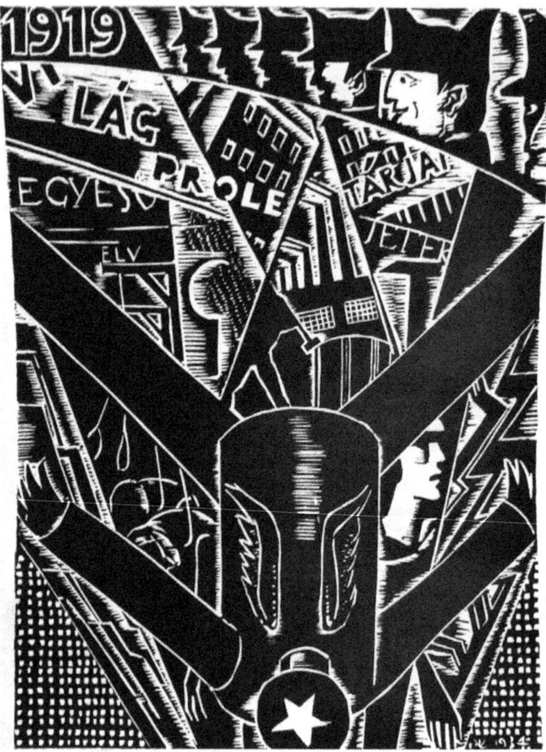

FIGURE 3.2.   Nándor Lajos Varga, *1919 (Hungarian Past XXXVIII)*, early 1930s/1940, private collection.
Photo by author. Nándor Lajos Varga © OOA-S 2024

For Slovaks, the Tatra mountains emerged as emblems of national identity marking the eternal homeland of a people without a state.[4] For Poles, one specific section of the Tatras gained increasing importance: nationalists—mainly from Warsaw—celebrated Zakopane and its surroundings as the region that had preserved true Polish identity and could rebirth the partitioned nation.[5] Throughout Central Europe and beyond, images and verbal descriptions of places and their histories—often produced in the context of the emerging tourism industry—helped disseminate nationalist ideas about people and place.[6] Stanislav Holubec has described, for instance, how the national "ownership" of the Giant Mountains, a site of Czech-German ethnic conflict, was contested in the literature and practices of tourism.[7] These ideas and debates continued in the interwar period, when new identities had to be forged and territories contested.[8] In Germany, descriptions of the post-Versailles country in scholarship and travel literature were crucial to creating new concepts of national space, within and outside the borders.[9] In Austria, the image of the Alps was employed to promote the country abroad and to build a postimperial Austrian national identity at home.[10] In Czechoslovakia, the Říp Mountain in central Bohemia, where, according to legend, the Czechs had first settled, was often represented as a site of national myth.[11] In interwar Hungary, the "detached" territories were commemorated not only by monuments but also at tourist sites such as the Palota Hotel at Lillafüred, built between 1925 and 1929 to replace the mountain resorts of Slovakia and hence symbolically "relocate" the High Tatras to Hungary.[12] The naturalization of national territory—or nationalization of the natural environment—was part and parcel with modern nationalism, which posited an unbreakable link between culture and place.[13]

In nineteenth-century Hungarian culture, the Great Plain took on the role of quintessential Hungarian landscape that had preserved the supposedly down-to-earth and straightforward yet passionate Hungarian national character.[14] One aspect that made the plains suitable for the role was that they were—rightly or wrongly—perceived as less ethnically mixed than the mountainous borderlands. In the interwar period, the image of the plains as a purely Hungarian region was still exploited in the tourism industry as well as in inland propaganda.[15] Located in "Dismembered" Hungary, it nevertheless had no function in irredentist activism. There, the emphasis was on the mountains located in the contested regions, the ethnically diverse former borderlands; it became imperative to prove that they, too, were inherently Hungarian. In *The Turkish Wars*, Varga laid out castles, rivers, and mountains—all from the lost territories—in a fictitious map where history and landscape became one.

This chapter explores how artists combined the imagery of nature and geography with that of history to visualize territorial claims and the ethnic identity of regions.[16] In doing so, they often drew on a nineteenth-century genre: the "historical landscape." Historical landscapes contrasted the eternal cycles of nature with the linear history of human civilizations by depicting human-built structures in ruin, surrounded and often overgrown by the lush vegetation of a picturesque, or sometimes threateningly sublime, landscape.[17] The various transformations of the genre discussed in this chapter highlight how different concepts of cultural heritage and tradition informed visions of national territory. In the previous chapter, the monuments of Freedom Square exemplified how public art visualized broader constructs of (national) space after the rupture of 1918. To be truly powerful, however, these abstract mental frameworks needed flesh and blood; they needed to be filled with representations of actual places replete with historical symbolism. By connecting landscape with history and anchoring both to a specific place, historical landscapes reflected and shaped how the inhabitants of interwar Central Europe filled their conceptual representations of the geographical space around them with meanings and values. The "mental maps" created this way were diverse and subjective, embodying the multiplicity of perspectives present in the fragmented space of the former Kingdom of Hungary.[18] Focusing on Slovakia as a contested territory, this chapter contrasts Hungarian irredentist imagery with a series of prints promoting Slovak nationalism as well as with a series depicting the complex social structure of Czechoslovak Bratislava. How these images represented the relationship between nature and culture, giving primacy to one or the other, reflected how the politics they promoted justified the nation's ownership of the land.

As historical landscapes united the timeless features of nature with the human-driven achievements of the nation, a group of people could serve as a bridge between the two. The idea that the peasantry preserved the true character of the nation, untainted by modern civilization, had already been influential in the nineteenth century. Peasants were one with the nation's land—combined with territorial claims, by the interwar period this notion was increasingly central to nationalist and radical right-wing thinking. This resulted in depictions of peasants that drew on older artistic traditions but transformed them to express new ideologies. In this chapter, I compare Ferdiš Duša's images of the Slovak landscape to images of the Hungarian countryside and its people created by the artist György Buday in the context of a movement aiming to regenerate the Hungarian nation from the "spirit and blood of the purely Hungarian peasantry."[19] The notion of regeneration runs through these images of the landscape and connects the works discussed here to European currents of (right-wing) modernism. At the same time, as the example of Buday's circle shows, the agency of the peasantry could be understood in different ways, some of which disrupted the fabric of overarching ideologies.

This chapter presents a multiplicity of perspectives, but this approach is certainly at odds with interwar nationalism, which proclaimed its vision of history and space as the only correct one. It is all the more striking, then, that Varga's *Hungarian Past* employed the avant-garde visual language of the montage, drawing attention to how its narrative was constructed from real and imagined historical sources. This is yet another artwork that problematizes oppositions between historical imagery and modernism and between modernity and conservative politics. Rather than being surprised at the modernity of irredentist art, asking why modernist visual devices seemed useful is more fruitful. The nineteenth-century imagery of the landscape helped naturalize irredentist claims, while its radical modernist transformations adapted it to the ideological context of the twentieth century.

Heritage and Landscape

The *Irredentist Sculpture Group* was an influential representation of the irredentist idea, but it was not the only prototype of commemoration produced in the immediate aftermath of Trianon. Edited by the brilliant poet and novelist Dezső Kosztolányi (1885–1936), better known as a leading contributor to the liberal modernist literary periodical *Nyugat* (*West*), the literary anthology *Bleeding Hungary* (Vérző Magyarország) was published in the same year.[20] The volume contained texts by several luminaries of early twentieth-century literature as well as by politicians and other public figures. The introduction was written by Horthy himself. Created by Ernő Jeges (1898–1956), the book's illustrations depicted locations outside the Trianon borders.

Jeges was born in 1898 in Torontálvásárhely/Debeljača.[21] In 1917, he moved to Budapest to study printmaking at the School of Applied Art. In 1918, he created one of the most influential anti-Trianon images in a poster commissioned by the National Propaganda Committee of the Károlyi government. It was probably this image of Greater Hungary cut up into pieces, accompanied by the forceful slogan "Nem! Nem! Soha!" ("No! No! Never!"), that drew the attention of the publishers of *Bleeding Hungary*.[22] In copper etching, the artist found the perfect technique to support the overall message of the volume. Made up of tiny fine lines, the images looked old-fashioned compared to the wood- and linocuts favored by the avant-garde (fig. 3.3). This effect, enhanced by the archaized lettering used for place names, articulated the idea that Hungary's claim to the depicted locations was rooted deep in history.

Many of Jeges's images depicted locations related to historical events and personalities. Their ensemble emphasized how Hungarian history had unfolded in the territory of Greater Hungary—a unified whole. Like the arrangement of the irredentist sculptures, the order of the illustrations and texts in *Bleeding Hungary* eschewed the realities of geographical space. Sometimes, consecutive images depicted locations in geographical proximity to each other, but at other times, they transported the reader from the North to Romania, then back, and then down to the Balkans. Sometimes, they matched the texts alongside which they appeared, sometimes not. Some were landscapes, while many depicted buildings—historical monuments that attested to the prominence of Hungarian culture in these lands.

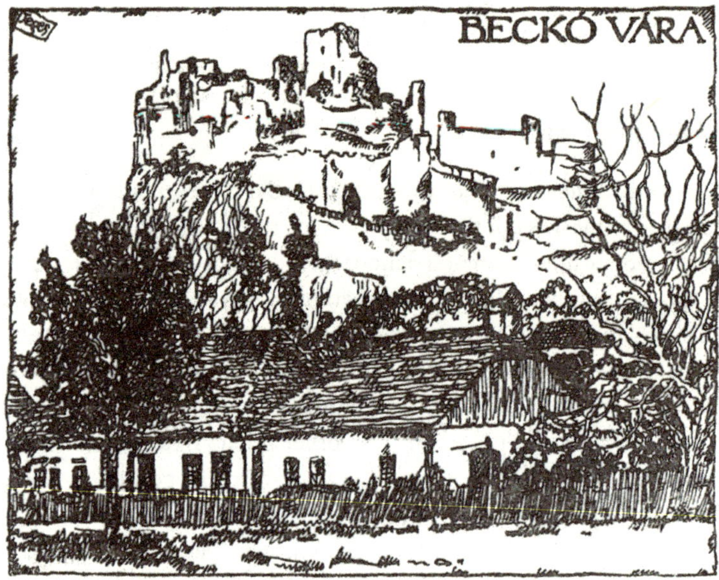

FIGURE 3.3. Ernő Jeges, *The Castle of Beckó/Beckov*, illustration from the volume *Vérző Magyarország: Magyar írók Magyarország területéért* [Bleeding Hungary: Hungarian authors for the territory of Hungary], ed. Dezső Kosztolányi (Budapest: Pallas Nyomda, 1921), 81, private collection.
Photo by author. Ernő Jeges © OOA-S 2024

In 1921, the idea of national cultural heritage was relatively new. Its roots reached back to the romantic nationalism of the early nineteenth century, which sought the traces of ancient history and myth in real and purported fragments of the past, be they ruined buildings, archaeological finds, manuscripts, or folk songs. National and regional museums founded across the Habsburg Empire channeled this enthusiasm into scholarship. By the second half of the century, institutions such as the Central Commission for the Research and Preservation of Artistic and Historical Monuments in Austria and the National Commission for Monuments in Hungary helped solidify the idea that remains of the past deserved to be protected for their historical value, articulating an enduring concept of cultural heritage. While stressing impartial, scholarly methods as opposed to romantic nationalism, their activities nevertheless implied that possessing these traces of the past was crucial to the existence of a nation and preserving them proved its sense of culture. In the past, the castles, churches, books, weapons, paintings, goblets, carpets, and hosts of other objects protected by the commissions had belonged to families, individuals, or religious communities. The idea that, regardless of these legal ties, the artifacts in question could also be spiritually owned by the nation was a new and revolutionary one and underpins how we conceptualize cultural heritage today.

Irredentists used the concept of cultural heritage to argue for the territorial integrity of Greater Hungary. If built heritage was Hungarian, then so was the land on which it stood. By merging castles and landscapes into dainty, archaizing images, Jeges's illustrations expressed this idea. They revived the genre of the historical landscape, which combined human-made remains of the past with the eternal features of nature, contrasting the transience of the former with the endurance of the latter. In the hands of irredentists, this imagery evoked not only the ancientness of the nation but also the inseparability of history, culture, and landscape and of nation and territory. Like most irredentist arguments, this line of thinking had to gloss over the multiethnicity of contested lands. Many towns in former northern Hungary had been founded by Saxons and thrived from the late Middle Ages thanks to their industrial and trading activities; nevertheless, in *Bleeding Hungary*, their picturesque townscapes supported Hungarian irredentism. The volume avoided uncomfortable questions simply by invoking the idea of Hungarian cultural hegemony and superiority, ever-present in irredentism. The view of Lőcse/Levoča/Leutschau, a town known for exquisite examples of Gothic architecture and art, was followed by an essay by the art historian Károly Lyka (1869–1965) arguing that the old territory of Greater Hungary was the natural space for Hungarian artistic production.[23] Despite Hungary's multiethnicity, claimed Lyka, many of the greatest artists had been Magyar-born, and those who were not had assimilated to Hungarian culture and absorbed its unique features.

These arguments lived on in irredentist activism in the next two decades, giving birth to one of the most elaborate attempts to promote the cause internationally. Produced by the Budapest publishing house Légrády Brothers, the revisionist album *Justice for Hungary!* was printed between 1928 and 1930 in five different language editions, to be distributed to institutions abroad (fig. 2.3).[24] Aiming to persuade readers of the "cruel errors of Trianon," the book's essays highlighted the injustices suffered by the Hungarian nation. The most spectacular feature, however, was the rich selection of images that provided an overview of Hungarian history and cultural heritage within and outside the new borders. The image section was introduced by a short text, "The Thousand Years' Struggles of the Hungarian Nation," followed by a selection of pictures from the nation's history; then, a piece titled "The Hungarian Genius" was illustrated by images of Hungarians' greatest cultural achievements.[25] The section, as a whole, could be characterized as a visual essay. It began with photos of the millennium monuments, destroyed, as the book put it, by the "fury," "spite," and "hatred" of the Czechs, Romanians, and Yugoslavs.[26] Subsequent images presented historical figures and events, such as King Stephen I, King Matthias Corvinus, or the battles against the Turks, in chronological order. In a manner familiar from *Bleeding Hungary*, the pictures showed places, buildings, and images associated with these personalities or events; some were contemporary photographs, and others reproduced nineteenth-century depictions. Instead of only focusing on the "lost" territories like *Bleeding Hungary*, the book emphasized connections between elements of heritage and historical memories throughout Greater Hungary.

In *Justice for Hungary!*, heritage served as a thread to hold together Greater Hungary across all historical periods. The castle of Trencsén/Trenčín/ Trentschin, which had also featured in *Bleeding Hungary*, was represented by a nineteenth-century English lithograph. Its significance was explained with a caption stating that it had been the center of a burgravate established by Stephen I.[27] Hence, it stood for the distant Hungarian past—the time when the kingdom was first established. However, it also evoked the nineteenth century, when the picturesque ruin was first appreciated as heritage. In this way, the album connected the period when the castle was built, the more recent past, when it was preserved, and the present, when Hungary claimed it as a rightful possession, into one continuous narrative. To build such narratives, however, irredentist publications had to leave certain parts of cultural memory by the wayside.

The ruined castle of Trenčín stands on a hill in western Slovakia, by the river Váh/Vág/Waag. Its picturesque environs had captivated travellers long before irredentist times. In 1818, the Austrian artist Joseph Fischer (1769– 1822) published a series of prints depicting sights along the river, then in Northern Hungary. The images did not garner much attention at first. Then, in 1826, the German-speaking Hungarian writer Baron Alajos Mednyánszky (1784–1844) republished them accompanied by a travelogue that he—a native of the Waag region—had compiled from his previous historical essays about the ruined castles by the river.[28] Some castles had featured in the grand events of history, but most had not, and Mednyánszky's essays combined historical facts and ethnographic observations with legends from local lore to engage his readers. Together, the images and the stories gained great popularity, providing writers and artists with inspiration throughout the century. They imprinted a unique image of the region into the historical imagination.

Mednyánszky was fascinated by the history and folklore of the region, but he also had an agenda. He belonged to a circle of authors—historians, writers, poets—associated with the historian Joseph Hormayr (1882–1848), who aimed to promote the integrity of the Austrian Empire under the banner of "imperial patriotism."[29] In this vein, Mednyánszky emphasized the multiethnicity of the region and focused on historical events in which the nations of the empire had cooperated or fought against a common enemy (the Turks) while downplaying the significance of rebellions against the Habsburgs. In this quest, the castle was a useful narrative device. According to Mikhail Bakhtin, who discussed it as one of the most evocative *chronotopes* (literary motifs that connect space and time), the castle "is saturated through and through with a time that is historical in the narrow sense of the word . . . the traces of centuries and generations are arranged in it in visible form. . . . And finally, legends and traditions animate every corner of the castle and its environs through their constant reminders of past events."[30] Aiming to show that the nations of the Habsburg Empire belonged together, inextricably connected by a shared history and intertwined traditions, Mednyánszky interspersed historical knowledge about the one-time owners of the castles—mostly Hungarian-, Polish-, or German-speaking aristocrats—with legends told and retold by the Slovak population of nearby villages. The chronotope of the castle helped him to present history as a multilayered entity spread out in space rather than as a chronological, continuous national narrative of the kind favored later in the nineteenth century. In this way, he provided an evocative account of how the histories of nations and ethnic groups overlapped in this multinational region. Their shared memories were inextricably intertwined, and in Mednyánszky's essays, the castles were like large, intricate knots that demonstrated their inseparability.

In representing ruined castles near the Vág, *Bleeding Hungary* drew on the tradition established by Fischer and Mednyánszky, as did *Justice for Hungary!* when it recycled a nineteenth-century print of Trencsén. Radically reinterpreting this piece of artistic and literary heritage, both publications used it to argue for the Hungarianness of the region rather than its multiculturality. They were not the first to do so; Mednyánszky's project had been coming apart at the seams right from the start. In the nineteenth century, when national narratives were being constructed and solidified, Mednyánszky's essays had been popular, but not quite in the way their author had intended. Instead of promoting togetherness, they served as a resource from which authors of all nationalist persuasions could cherry-pick elements that fit their national stories.[31] The editors of *Bleeding Hungary* and *Justice for Hungary!* followed this path. To them, the castles by the Vág mattered as examples of Hungarian built heritage and reminders of history, not as sites of—mostly Slovak—legends. Irredentist publications made no mention of the mysterious tales recorded by Mednyánszky, even though these were still in circulation.[32] Their visual imagery provided a sober and factual record of heritage and avoided the terrifying cliffs and stormy skies that Fischer—and nineteenth-century artists after him—had emphasized. For Hungarian irredentists, it was history, not nature or myth, that best bolstered the argument.

Jeges's sober images focused on the built environment, on towns, castles, and churches, and when hilltops and rivers were depicted, they were shown as benign, inhabited, and navigable. The editors of *Justice for Hungary!* focused on history, too. When they included a picture of a geographical feature, it was of the great Lake Balaton in remaining Hungary. The people of the nineteenth century had regarded storms on the Balaton with fear and awe, but to the Légrádys, it was the friendly "Hungarian sea," a beloved holiday destination that provided consolation for being "deprived of our real sea-board."[33] Nature was not a force to contend with in these irredentist publications.

A Montage of Sorts

By focusing on built heritage, irredentist publications showed Hungarian culture as reining in, and hence reigning over, the wild landscapes and multiethnic populations of Slovakia. This mirrored the argument, often made in irredentist literature, that the Hungarian nation was destined for hegemony in the region due to its cultural superiority. In *Hungarian Past*, Varga continued along the same lines; he depicted Hungarian history as a narrative constructed from primary sources, assembling the landscapes where history had taken place from cultural artifacts that supported Hungarian primacy.

Varga had embarked on his career under the tutelage of Viktor Olgyay (1870–1929), an influential teacher of printmaking at the Budapest College of Fine Art. Focusing mainly on etching, Olgyay recommended the study of Rembrandt to his pupils. Varga perfected this technique. Becoming a teacher himself, he wrote textbooks on printmaking. Around 1930, he began experimenting with a new technique, the woodcut, and *Hungarian Past* was his first large project, created on his own initiative.[34] The technique came with a new form of expression, and Varga abandoned his refined Rembrandtesque manner for forceful, expressive lines and agitated compositions. In this he was not alone; in the preceding decades, expressionism had made the woodcut widely popular with artists in Central Europe and developed a corresponding modern formal idiom. At the same time, woodcuts also evoked the past. The "primitivism" of medieval and early modern printmaking was embraced not only by expressionists but also by more conservative artists looking for traditional sources to renew the art of their time.[35] For a series depicting the (Hungarian) past, this was obviously a fitting formal language. Varga, how-

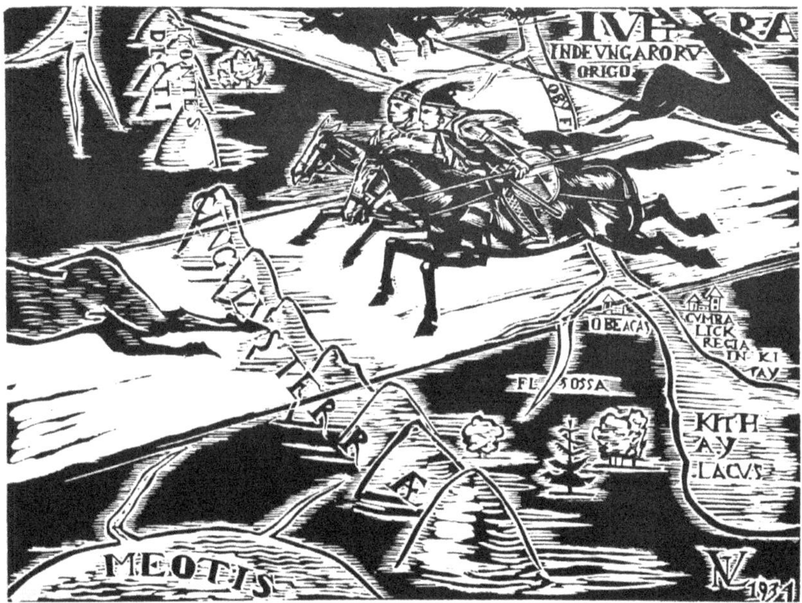

FIGURE 3.4. Nándor Lajos Varga, *The Miracle Stag (Hungarian Past I)*, early 1930s/1940, private collection.
Photo by author. Nándor Lajos Varga © OOA-S 2024

ever, went further. In addition to employing the general stylistic archaisms of expressionist woodcuts, he evoked the past in a number of ways, ultimately creating a work that can be read as a meditation on representing history from the perspective of the present.

This is immediately visible in the first print, *Miracle Stag*, which depicts a Hungarian origin myth (fig. 3.4). On an archaic-looking map drawn up in a few simple lines, a row of conical forms cuts vertically across the picture. Their inscription reads: "Montes dicti Cingulus Terræ" ("The mountains called the Girdle of the Earth"), a medieval name for the Urals. In the lower left-hand corner, a curvilinear shape denotes "Meotis," the ancient Greek name of the Sea of Azov. The river to the right of the mountains is the Ob, which emerges from a lake marked as "Kithay Lacus." In the top right-hand corner, "IVHRA INDE UNGARORUM ORIGO" marks the location of the ancient Hungarian homeland. The inscription is partly obscured by a dark stag dashing past, to disappear outside the picture frame. It is followed by two riders just visible at the top of the image. In the middle of the picture, two larger riders, stern and resolute warriors, race across the map in the opposite direction from the stag. On their giant horses, they traverse the river and the mountains with ease, spurred on by the promise of a yet-unknown future.

They are Hunor and Magor, legendary ancestors of the Huns and Hungarians. Encountering a wondrous stag on a hunt, the two brothers and their companions chased the animal until they reached a fertile land in the Maeotian Swamps, where they decided to settle. This was, according to myth, how Hungarians had left their original homeland, the first stage in a long journey that eventually led to the future Kingdom of Hungary.

A variety of visual devices employed in *Miracle Stag* recur throughout the series—setting the scene in a map, using the imagery of swift movement to animate it, integrating primary sources into the composition. In *The Miracle Stag*, Varga used a 1549 map from *Rerum Moscoviticarum Commentarii* by Sigismund von Herberstein, Maximilian II's ambassador to Russia.[36] This source was often quoted in Hungarian historical and geographical literature, as it provided rare information about northwest Siberian Finno-Ugric ethnic groups related to the Hungarians.[37] When "quoting" visual material such as Herberstein's map and assembling images without creating a unified pictorial space, Varga drew on the avant-garde practice of the montage. The frequent employment of lettering in his compositions originated from the same roots. Although these inscriptions mostly denote the names of places and people and hence seem integral to the old maps and prints Varga reproduced, their profusion and prominence within the compositions would not be possible without the experience of constructivist or cubist image making. Indeed, when the sheets were first displayed in 1941, this aspect was disparaged as not sufficiently "artistic" by the right-wing extremist—and aesthetically traditionalist—newspaper *Új Magyarság*.[38] While propagating one specific, highly politicized interpretation of history, the prints presented historical narrative as a construct—a patchwork sewn together from available sources, illuminated in different ways from different perspectives.

Herberstein's map is just one of many historical sources quoted in the prints. Sheet VIII, *Crusade of King Andrew II* (1177–1235, r. 1205–1235), features an image of the ruler on the throne taken from his seal preserved in the Hungarian National Archives. The depiction of King Ladislas IV in Sheet X is based on his image in the *Illuminated Chronicle*, a richly illustrated fourteenth-century manuscript containing Márk Kálti's *Chronicle of the Deeds of the Hungarians* (c. 1358–1373). Sheet XV, depicting King Matthias Corvinus, shows his portrait according to a relief in Wrocław Cathedral. The medallion is set against a backdrop assembled from the views of Buda Castle and Vienna in Hartmann Schedel's 1483 *Nuremberg Chronicle*—a reference to Matthias's successful 1485 siege of Vienna. These sources—most of them often reproduced and hence recognizable to many Hungarians—provided the prints in which they appeared with an air of historical accuracy that could be projected onto the rest of the images in the series. Many of Varga's compositions featured maps, most of which were the artist's own creations imitating historical maps such as Herberstein's. This artistic gesture positioned the narrative and message of the prints as historical truth while also showcasing the breadth of Hungarian heritage in a manner familiar from *Justice for Hungary!*. At the same time, it revealed to careful observers that, ultimately, the history told in the series was constructed by the artist.

There was another aspect that supported this suggestion. As one perceptive critic noted, Varga's pictures "speak in the illustrative style of their own time [i.e., the time depicted]," even though "they always evoke an artist with a culture and heart of today in their subjectivity."[39] In recreating the visual languages of the past, the images make a claim for historical authenticity but also highlight how historical facts are mediated through the mode of representation chosen by the artist. The most spectacular example is the print showing the Soviet Republic (fig. 3.2). The accompanying text describes this as a thoroughly negative and destructive event and—with rather thinly veiled antisemitism—its leaders as "elements foreign to our race."[40] Yet, while the image depicts destruction and chaos, it is also constructivist, in the manner of the avant-garde artists associated with the Soviet Republic. Its inclusion of the Communist slogan "VILÁG PROLETÁRJAI EGYESÜLJETEK" ("Proletarians of the world unite!") seems unironic at first, but a closer look reveals the gallows and nooses and the bodies of those executed by hanging, hidden among the shard-like, geometrical forms. Hence, the image makes the art of the Soviet Republic complicit in its violence, but by resurrecting that art, it nevertheless presents it as a valid idiom for expressing the turbulence of revolution and radical change.

The obviously constructed nature of the image *Turkish Wars—Sheet 22* in Varga's series—confounded the directions of cartographical space and merged them with historical time, creating a unified encapsulation of Hungary and its past in a manner reminiscent of the irredentist sculptures. The print indicates the locations of the most important sieges of the Fifteen Years War in a relief map, with their names and the dates of the battles next to the castles. Between them, black silhouettes of Turkish and Hungarian riders dash across the map. At first sight, their trajectories seem to indicate the chronological sequence of events. They are, however, not all riding in the same direction; they face each other on the left-hand side in the middle and split into two groups at the bottom right-hand side. The dates do not spell out a chronological sequence, either; from top to bottom, 1593 is followed by 1594 and 1598, but then by 1596. This leaves us with geographical space as the only system of orientation—but Varga's print does not provide a cartographically accurate depiction of space. In a gesture that seemingly serves as guidance, Varga included a compass in the middle of his composition. An illusory clue, this compass does not, however, serve as the ultimate key to the image. First, it is positioned differently from the usual convention, with north pointing to the left and slightly downward rather than toward the top of the sheet. Second, it does not accurately define spatial relations even within this modified framework. It is correct in indicating that Fülek/Fil'akovo, a castle in present Slovakia, is to the north of Sziszek/Sisak, now in Croatia. It is even right in suggesting that Komárom/Komarno is to the southwest of Fülek. But Temesvár/Timişoara is definitely not located in the north at the same latitude as Fülek and is also not to its west; Nagyvárad/Orodea is most certainly to the north of Temesvár, not to its south. The geography in the image is largely fictional.

Like other visualizations of irredentist spacetime, *Turkish Wars* associates places with historical events—important battles that had taken place there, whether won or lost. All castles in the image stood in the lost territories; Varga did not depict Győr or Eger, castles in remaining Hungary, despite their loss to the Ottomans in 1594 and 1596. The landscape is dissected by the rivers Danube and Temes/Timiş and, more violently, by the riders. This recalls irredentist images of the "dismembering" of Hungary, reminding viewers of the oft-cited parallel between the sixteenth-century tripartition-ing of Hungary into Ottoman, Habsburg, and Transylvanian territories and the Treaty of Trianon.[41] In the middle section of the image, Varga repre-sented Komárom/Komarno. The fortress fits well into the print's theme due to its successful defense against the Ottomans in 1594, but it is also a poignant symbol of Trianon. Located on the two banks of the Danube, the town of Komárom/Komarno had been split into two by the treaty, which had drawn up a new border along the river.

Here, it is necessary to refer to an essential aspect of the nationalization of the landscape: the way geographical features could define or, conversely, be used to dispute national borders. While borders had always been deter-mined by wars and negotiations, the idea that mountains or rivers delineate the "natural" borders of a country looks back on a long history.[42] Exploring borders as sites of memory in the French context, Daniel Nordman traced two distinct concepts: "frontières," which were disputed and malleable, and "limites," which had been fixed by sacrosanct, mutual agreements or by nature.[43] This duality conveys the inherent split within the idea of the border in Hungarian irredentism. On the one hand, it "only takes a pencil stroke" to change borders.[44] On the other hand, the old borders of Greater Hungary were considered eternal and immutable. In this vein, irredentism essential-

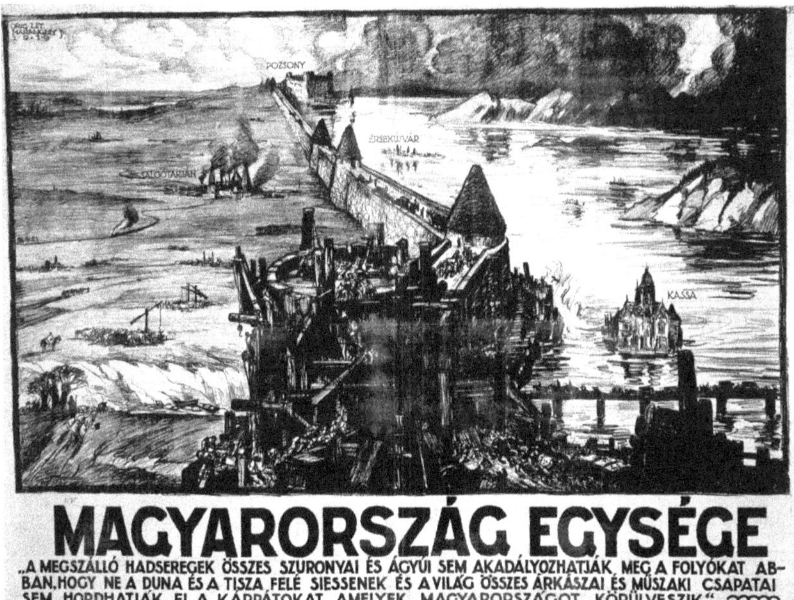

FIGURE 3.5.   Jenő Haranghy, *The Unity of Hungary*, poster, 1919, National Széchényi Library, Budapest, Map, Poster, and Small Print Collection.
Photo: National Széchényi Library

ized the territory of Greater Hungary as inseparable from the landscape. Elements of nature could be used to naturalize the old borders as well as to prove the arbitrariness of the new ones. The Danube, which featured prominently in Varga's *Turkish Wars*, marked the new border between Hungary and Czechoslovakia. Previously, the river had flowed through the kingdom, passing Hungarian lands on both sides. Irredentists often cited this fact as an example of how Trianon disrupted the natural order. Summing up this argument poignantly, a poster designed in 1919 by Jenő Haranghy (1894–1951) and published by the Hungarian Geographical Institute depicted Hungary's new northern border as a fortified stone wall (fig. 3.5).

On one side stretches new Hungary, with its plains and sweep-pole wells. On the other side, Pozsony / Bratislava, Érsekújvár / Nové Zámky, and Kassa / Košice are submerged in a flood. The text reads: "All the bayonets and cannons of the occupying armies cannot stop rivers from rushing toward the Danube and the Tisza, and all the world's sappers and technical teams cannot dismantle the Carpathians, which surround Hungary." The waters of the Danube and Tisza are destined to be Hungarian, while the true borders of the country are marked by the Carpathians. If Hungarian hegemony had pacified nature in Slovakia before Trianon, then the newly imposed borders had disrupted this peaceful order and caused the waters to rise.

In the naturalization of the borders of Greater Hungary, the most important reference point was the Carpathian Basin, the area enclosed by the Carpathian Mountains, the Alps, and the Dinarians, which irredentists conceptualized as a unified geographical space, as it largely corresponded with the territory of the former kingdom. Products of irredentist activism, from the poster described here to the inscription of the *Reliquary Country Flag*, designated the mountains as guardians of the nation's territory. Natural formations within these borders, such as the Hungarian section of the Danube, served as additional markers of nationality. Some of these had long functioned as national symbols, which proved their essential Hungarianness in irredentist eyes. One poster from 1920 protested that the negotiators of Versailles had "taken our rivers, taken our mountains" and lamented that the Hungarian coat of arms would have to be redesigned; according to tradition, the three mounds and four silver stripes symbolized three mountain ranges (the Tatras, the Mátra, and the Fatra) and four rivers (the Danube, the Tisza, the Drava, and the Sava) of the former kingdom, several of which were now lost.[45]

The assumption that certain geographical formations belonged to the nation by immutable natural law went hand in hand with the idea that only the nation had true, intimate knowledge of its land. One of the many myths circulating about the background of the Trianon Treaty in interwar Hungary was that borders had been determined in an illogical and unfair way because decision-makers lacked accurate information about the land and did not care enough to investigate; hence, tiny streams were identified as navigable by ship and consequently deemed suitable to serve as national borders.[46] These borders were seemingly adjusted to natural phenomena, but they were still artificial because they had been determined by ignorant foreigners and not by the nation to which the territory truly belonged.

In *Turkish Wars*, Varga drew on this imagery and its associated meanings. With its inscriptions and compass, the image imitates a map, but instead of providing a consistent aerial view, it incorporates small but detailed landscapes, evoking memory and emotion much in the manner of the posters discussed here. The viewpoint shifts throughout the image—some fortresses are seen from above, others from the front or at an angle. This, together with the warriors zigzagging across the image, creates a sense of fragmentation. Bringing together different spatial viewpoints in one image was an avant-garde device, one Varga borrowed from cubism and the technique of the montage. Here, however, it was not just an artistic idiom; it visualized a specific political message about the "dissection" of Hungary. The turbulences of history—personified by the warriors—had violently ruptured the landscape, and this state of rupture was best represented as a feature of modernity. As in the image of the Soviet Republic, the avant-garde appeared as something that disrupted the natural order. To deal with the disruptive forces of modernity, *Hungarian Past* called for regeneration.

Down the Slovak Váh

If culture ruled the landscape in the images of *Bleeding Hungary* what did these contested territories look like from an opposing viewpoint? Born in Frýdlant nad Ostravicí in Moravia but devoting a large part of his career to depicting Slovakia, the artist Duša (1888–1958) reimagined the tradition originating from Fischer and Mednyánszky from the perspective of Slovak nationalism. His series of prints *Down the Váh* was also an expression of regeneration; in his images, nature is unimpaired, majestic, thriving. Unlike the irredentist images discussed earlier, Duša's pictures emphasized the primacy and power of nature over history.

Duša's career was not exclusively dedicated to landscape; as a young artist, he was fascinated by industry in his home region.[47] In 1923, he created a series of prints featuring workers in mines, foundries, and factories. At the same time, however, Duša was interested in rural scenery and vernacular culture. Spending time in Slovakia around 1930, he created numerous woodcuts of landscapes. The most important ones were published together as *Down the Váh (Dolu Váhom)* in 1933 by the Bratislava-based publisher K. Jaroň, with an introduction by the Swiss writer William Ritter (1867–1955).[48] In 1934, Jaroň republished fifteen prints in a more representative album, accompanied not just by Ritter's text but also by descriptions of the individual locations.[49] This edition exists with two slightly different frontispieces. According to one, the purpose of the images was to decorate schools, offices, and homes, while the other stressed the use of the images in formal education: *Dolu Váhom* "originated from a love for Slovakia and Slovak schools," and its purpose was to provide the latter with an "artistic educational aid" in teaching the geography and history of the homeland.[50] In other words, the prints were intended as vehicles of promoting Slovak national identity, and as such, they—and the accompanying text—stereotypically characterized Slovakia as rural, romantic, and pure, stressing the close association between Slovak people and the lands they inhabited.

In the early nineteenth century, Mednyánszky's aim had been to demonstrate that the ethnically diverse Vág region belonged to the Habsburg Empire. Duša, by contrast, conceptualized the Váh as the Slovak river and avoided other ethnicities. This was explicit in the accompanying text by Ritter, which bore the title *Roman slovenskej rieky* (*Novel of a Slovak River*).[51] Ritter, a Slavophile who spent much time in Prague and Slovakia, believed that identity was a product of rootedness in a certain place.[52] His cultural conservatism made him oppose not only liberal internationalism but also the efforts of the Czechoslovak state to construct a Czechoslovak national identity built on ideas of modernity. In this, as well as in his devout Catholicism, his ideas corresponded with the increasingly radical Slovak nationalist movement.[53] He called the Váh the Slovak national river because it flowed exclusively through Slovak land and described it as "fidgety and swift then dreamy and calm . . . born in the most romantic place in the land, its extraordinary water reflects ruins along its banks and flows through the most beautiful region."[54]

Like so many examples of the "national landscape," the idea of the Váh as the quintessential Slovak river originated from the nineteenth century. Authors such as the Romantic poet Samo Chalupka (1812–1883) constructed an image of the landscape suffused with Slovak identity. In his poem "Sadness," Chalupka called the Tatras "mother" while lamenting that the Váh and Hron rivers were fed by Slovak tears and blood. Chalupka and other authors of the Slovak national movement often evoked Great Moravia and its powerful ninth-century ruler Svatopluk, inscribing bygone Slovak greatness into the land through landscape imagery.[55] Duša and Ritter continued this tradition, giving it modern visual form.

In line with the program outlined by Ritter, the human figures in Duša's prints are all Slovaks, identifiable by their traditional garments. They are peasants living a rural idyll while tending to their crops or animals. This exoticization of Slovakia as rustic and primitive, as opposed to industrialized Bohemia and Moravia, was part of the official ideology of the Czechoslovak state but—as exemplified by *Down the Váh*—also bolstered constructions of a separate Slovak national identity.[56] Slovakia, as depicted in these prints, could be characterized by three main elements: its dramatic yet fertile landscape; its ancientness, embodied by the ruined castles; and its people, whose lives, minds, and identities are inseparable from the land. In many prints, ruined castles appear in the background, while the Slovak peasants going about their day in the foreground receive more emphasis, as if to say that the past—the historical past when the region had belonged to Hungary and the castles to Hungarian aristocrats—has been overwritten by the blissful Slovak present. In one of the first prints, the towering figure of a Slovak shepherd sits on top of a hill surveilling the land that he now, apparently, possesses (fig. 3.6). In classical landscape painting, peasants had been tiny accessories

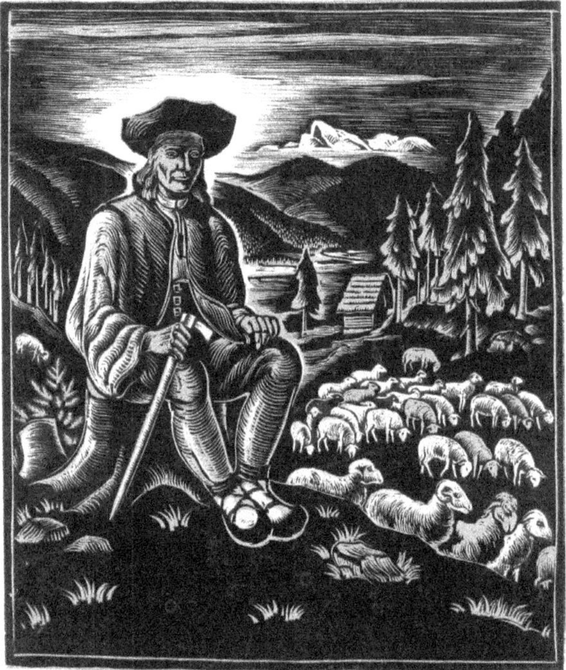

FIGURE 3.6.   Ferdiš Duša, *At the Black Váh* (from the series *Down the Váh*), 1930–1933, Slovenská národná galéria, Bratislava.
Photo: Slovenská národná galéria, Bratislava. Ferdiš Duša © OOA-S 2024

in picturesque views taken in by upper-class wanderers. Duša's print turned this artistic convention upside down.

Although the subject matter of *Down the Váh* differs from that of Duša's earlier work, the visual language—strong contrasts, hard lines—is similar. In *Strečno*, Duša depicted the stormy skies with crystalline straight lines, similar to how he represented the cavalcade of light and noise in foundries.[57] He often depicted old and modern in unity; in *Trenčín*, for instance, the ruined castle—made up of simplified, rectangular shapes, resembling a modernist building—stands above the town now populated by modern buildings and a factory chimney.[58] In other ways, however, *Down the Váh* recalls the suspenseful atmosphere of Mednyánszky's tales. In some images, past and present coexist as peacefully as in Fischer's pictures. In others, such as *Hričov*, the harmony is broken (fig. 3.7). Instead of allowing the eye to gradually take in the vista and its varied elements, this image demands attention for three prominent motifs—the tree, the castle, and the well—while obstructing the trajectory of our gaze with strong contours and pitch-black shapes.

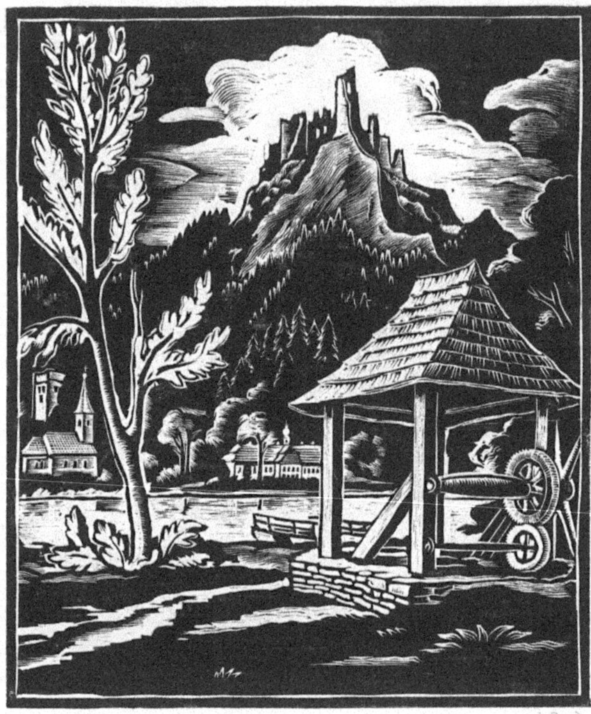

Figure 3.7. Ferdiš Duša, *Hričov* (from the series *Down the Váh*), 1930–1933, Slovenská národná galéria, Bratislava. Ferdiš Duša © OOA-S 2024

The tale of Hričov was one of the most chilling told by Mednyánszky. The young nobleman Ferenc Thurzó had taken advantage of a wealthy widow, marrying and then imprisoning her in her own castle. The desperate woman put a curse on the building. One day, a monk came to the castle to remind Thurzó of his sins. Standing in front of the castle, he gave a terrifying speech. Thurzó imprisoned the monk but continued to see the shape of the figure in one of the ominous cliffs visible from his window. His guilt drove him into madness. Taken over by ghosts that scared away all living beings, the castle finally burst into flames, never to be rebuilt.

Although Hričov had been owned by some prominent families, it never featured in the grand narrative of history. Nothing politically remarkable had happened there; the castle's main claim to fame was this gruesome tale. Castles such as Hričov symbolized the past as sublime and intriguing yet terrifying and not wholly knowable—a message at odds with the "rational" anti-Trianon arguments Hungarian irredentists aimed to make. Hence, the irredentist publications neglected Hričov. To Slovak nationalists, however, fragments of myth and elements of nature held greater significance than the remains of elite history. What is remarkable in Duša's series is how, while retracing and reimagining its nineteenth-century sources, it also faithfully preserved their atmosphere. The image of Hričov is disturbing because there is no balance between the foreground and the background, the past and the present. The tree and the well seem to be taking over, but the castle is too prominent, too threatening to let that happen. It is still haunted by ghosts. Published in the 1930s, the print could still make those familiar with the story of the stone monk shudder.

The two irredentist albums made the landscapes of the borderlands part of Hungarian history by emphasizing built heritage. Duša's prints, by contrast, dehistoricized the castles of the Váh by blending them into the landscape. Through this process, the landscape could appear as eternally, purely Slovak. The idea that the peasantry preserved "pure" national character because of how its life and culture was rooted in the nation's land was, however, not unique to Slovak nationalism.

The Heritage of the People

Contrasting "corrupt," "decadent," "alien" urban culture with the purity of the countryside was a recurring theme in early twentieth-century projects of national regeneration. In visual culture, it catalyzed diverse right-wing modernisms, such as the regionalist movements in Austria or traditionalism in Romania.[59] In Hungary, counterrevolutionary propaganda set up an opposition between sinful, Communist Budapest and the virtuous and loyal countryside, whose people had been immune to Communist agitation because it was at odds with true Hungarian spirit.[60] By the 1930s, several right-wing authors suggested that the renewal of Hungarian society must be rooted in peasant culture, producing a wealth of polemical literature often critical of official policies. The view of ideal Hungarian society promoted in such texts was often fundamentally racialized. The most influential author was Dezső Szabó (1879–1945), a fierce critic of Hungary's right-wing ruling class who blamed its failings on the supposed German origin of its prominent figures. At the same time, he also blamed economic and financial problems on supposed Jewish influence.

The so-called populist movement that grew out of these ideas was an increasingly important and complex phenomenon of interwar Hungarian culture.[61] Shaping into an ideology some populists described as "the third way," it incorporated elements from right and left, and, as its influence grew, it proceeded to change both. It was the populist movement that engendered the persistent opposition between "urban" and "popular" in Hungarian culture. The movement underwent decisive shifts and splits by the early 1940s, blurring simple dichotomies between right and left or modern and traditional. I return to this in chapter 5. For now, I want to introduce an artist who started his career in the center of the populist movement. His variations on the historical landscape amalgamated the depiction of "eternal" peasant culture and "elite" commentary on recent history.

The life of Buday (1907–1990) reflected the spatial ambiguity caused by shifting borders in interwar Central Europe.[62] Born in 1907 in Kolozsvár/Cluj in Transylvania, he moved to Szeged, in the southeast of post-Trianon Hungary, with his family in 1924. His father, Árpád Buday (1879–1937), was an archaeologist and head of the Collection of Antiquities at the Museum of Transylvania in Kolozsvár. In the wake of Trianon, the University of Kolozsvár relocated to Szeged, and the older Buday decided to follow his colleagues and friends. By then, the young György was respected as a burgeoning artist at the College of Nagyenyed/Aiud. Although his career subsequently unfolded in Szeged, he maintained close contacts with artists and writers in Transylvania and published several collections of his engravings in Cluj.

In 1928, a group of radical students formed a society called the Szeged Youth (Szegedi Fiatalok), and Buday became president. He studied law at the university at the time but had also developed an avid interest in printmaking. Influenced by authors such as Szabó, the Szeged Youth intended to carry out fieldwork among the peasants of the plains around Szeged. By bringing the culture of the city to the villages while studying peasant culture and drawing on it in their own work, they believed they could merge these two parts of society and rejuvenate the Hungarian nation. In 1931, they established the Art College of the Szeged Youth—not a formal teaching institution but an organizational framework for the cultural activities of the group.[63] Buday soon developed a fruitful collaboration with another key member, the ethnographer Gyula Ortutay (1910–1978). In the late 1920s and 1930s, Ortutay conducted extensive fieldwork collecting peasant lore. He compiled these into a series of beautifully crafted publications illustrated with Buday's wood engravings. The 1933 book of folk ballads and songs (*Mondotta Vince András béreslegény, Máté János gazdalegény* [*Said Farmhand András Vince, the Master's Son János Máté*]) was followed in 1935 by a book of peasant tales from the Nyír and Rétköz regions (*Nyíri és rétközi parasztmesék*) and one of Sekler folk ballads (*Székely népballadák*) and in 1937 by *Tales from Bátorliget* (*Bátorligeti mesék*).

In one image in *Tales from Bátorliget*, a figure stands in front of three hills, the middle of which has a cross on the top (fig. 3.8).[64] The triple mound with

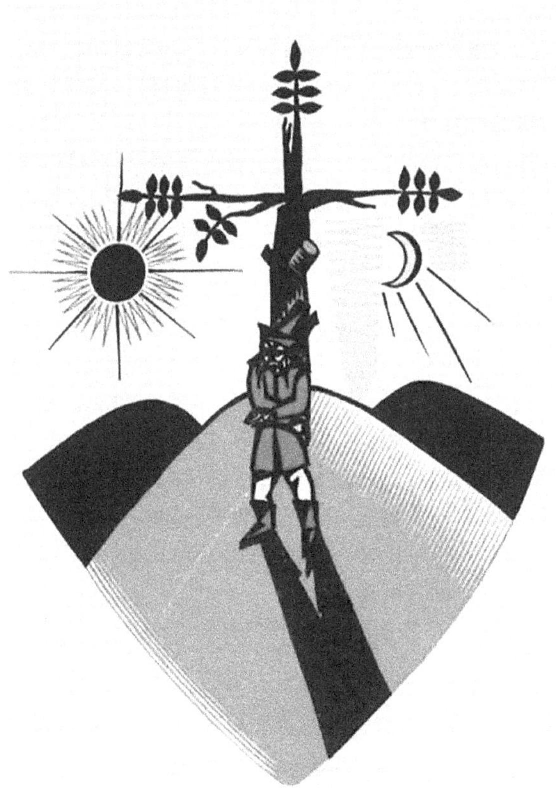

FIGURE 3.8. György (George) Buday, illustration from *Bátorligeti Mesék* (Tales from Bátorliget), 1937. Reproduced courtesy of the artist's estate.

a cross is a central motif in Hungarian heraldry and still features in Hungary's coat of arms. Although it probably originates in Christian symbolism—Mount Calvary—for centuries it had been interpreted as symbolizing three mountain ranges of historical Hungary: the Tatras, the Matras, and the Fatras. The significance to irredentists of losing two of them in 1920 was encapsulated by the poster *You Have Taken Our Rivers*. Buday's image naturalized the idea of the Hungarianness of these mountains in a similar way, this time by making them part of the "traditional" and "timeless" imagery of folktales.

Similar references to Trianon can be found in Buday's other work, too.[65] In *Sekler Folk Ballads* (1935), the first image, *Sekler Crucifixion*, depicts a Transylvanian Sekler man in traditional dress tied to a cross that leans precariously toward the beholder.[66] It rises monumentally above a vast landscape, with fertile agricultural lands in the foreground and mountains in the background. The Transylvanian landscape recurs in many images, even if not always as an explicit reference to Trianon. What is notable in Buday's pictures, when compared to others discussed in this chapter, is that he rarely represented built or material heritage. When buildings appeared, they were not specific. In works where the imagery evoked folk culture, Buday did not collect visual motifs from vernacular crafts and use them in his work, even when his friend Ortutay was collecting texts. Instead, he opted to create a fairy-tale atmosphere by inventing his own vernacular-surreal imagery.

Some of Buday's pictures made peasants and their culture part of the landscape; in images such as the one with the triple mound, it is the beholder, not the tiny peasants in the image, who can take in the view and hence its symbolism. The social activism of the Szeged Youth notwithstanding, this was essentially a scholarly rather than an activist depiction of the countryside and its people. It corresponded with Ortutay's ideas: to the ethnographer, peasants were "people of nature" who could not delight in the beauty of the landscape as external observers because they were one with nature and never outside it.[67] These observations recalled nineteenth-century ideas about the peasantry, conventional by the 1930s, that held that individualism had no place in rural societies.

Somewhat contradictorily, however, Ortutay's breakthrough as a scholar came when he developed a new approach, the "research of personalities," which stressed the agency of individual storytellers in the evolution of folktales.[68] *Tales from Bátorliget*, for instance, contained tales told by one immensely talented storyteller from a tiny village in northeastern Hungary: Mihály Fedics. Fedics's tales were unusual, often bizarre. They combined the well-known cast of kings, princesses, and clever peasant boys or girls with Christian imagery and playful humor, often bordering on the surreal. They mostly had some semblance of a happy ending, but sometimes they did not end at all, and they rarely had a moral. Instead of conjuring up a satisfying and ideologically useful image of a simple, pure, and fair village society, they were inherently weird, even unsettling. Buday's images expressed this by piecing together dainty fairy-tale-like motifs into surreal compositions, through strong contrasts of dark and light, or by juxtaposing giant figures with tiny ones. Sometimes, Buday constructed pictorial space so that it expressed his characters' emotions, taking a thoroughly modern approach and exploring the individual subjectivities of the supposed "people of nature."

The intangible heritage of the people of the countryside disrupted harmonious views of the landscape they were supposedly part of but could not see. Buday's artistic approach reflected the dissonance between the ideology of the Szeged Youth and the reality they encountered, which hindered simple conceptions of peasant identity and activism. As the group progressed with their fieldwork, they faced the grim realities of peasant life in the destitute homesteads of the Hungarian plains, and their views shifted considerably. Early iterations of their mission statements were conceived within an ethnonationalist framework. In 1929, Buday himself wrote: "Our race [fajtánk] can only conceivably gain a more prominent role in our homeland and become a self-sufficient nation state if today's intelligentsia regenerates from the spirit and blood of the purely Hungarian peasantry."[69] The original idea was to connect with the inhabitants of villages and homesteads by listening to their songs and stories and reciprocating with their own performances, such as poetry readings. Once there, however, the students realized that the people they wanted to draw into this high-minded cultural exchange lived in deep poverty, left behind by the elites of Horthy's Hungary. Consequently, many members of the Szeged Youth shifted toward class-conscious, left-wing movements and began to cooperate with Social Democratic and Communist groups in the city. Others underwent right-wing radicalization.

What happened next demonstrates the complexity of real and figurative landscapes and mental maps in a turbulent time. Shifting to the left himself, Ortutay came into contact with left-wing and anti-Fascist groups. In 1943, he joined the Independent Smallholders, Agrarian Workers, and Civic Party, and in 1944, he resigned as editor for literature at the state radio and joined the resistance. In 1945, he secretly joined the Hungarian Communist Party and facilitated its suppression of the Smallholders Party. From 1947 to 1950, through the Communist Turn, he was minister of culture and continued to hold various positions in culture and education in the next decades. He remained a notable scholar, but his legacy as a powerful actor in an oppressive system is controversial. In recent decades, his prewar hesitance between right and left has also been scrutinized more critically, complicating the simple picture of resistance hero.[70]

Buday left Hungary in 1936, when he received the Rome Scholarship awarded to artists by the government. The next year, another scholarship allowed him to travel to Britain where he—a long-standing Anglophile—had already spent time in 1928. Dismayed by Hungary's increasing political alignment with Nazi Germany, he settled in London. He did not know it at the time, but he was to remain in England his entire life. In 1940, he illustrated an edition of Shakespeare's *Timon of Athens*, and the next year, he produced a patriotic image of Britannia looking toward the continent for the *Times Literary Supplement*. After the war, he was appointed director of the Hungarian Cultural Institute in Britain but resigned in 1949, when Communist authorities began to prepare a show trial against him. Ironically, his application for British citizenship was rejected due to his suspected Communist sympathies.[71] All this took a toll on his mental health. Although he continued to work as an illustrator, he spent the last decades of his life in the hospital.

In 1943, Buday began producing a series of publications called *Little Books*, which he distributed among his friends, often recycling images from his Szeged Youth days. The second *Little Book* (1945), about "the man who fought for freedom," repurposed the illustrations of *Tales from Bátorliget*, accompanying them with an anti-Fascist parable about a man who stood up to the Nazis.[72] The first (1943) and fifth (1949) *Little Books* contained Hungarian ballads and folktales.[73] The fifth book reused Buday's old image of a Hungarian village church with an apple and rose on its typical baroque spire, but the inside page included a corresponding image of an English village with a stone church topped with holly (the *Little Books* were Christmas presents). Rather than being exclusive, the imagery of place became collectable, mobile, and transnational. Buday wrote about this eloquently in an autobiographical sketch: "Let me say that, by carefully, studiously drawing the landscapes by the river Tisza or the characteristic Szeged houses decorated with sunray motifs, I definitely felt that the peculiarities, landscapes and people of the second home, Szeged and the Plains, were now mine. . . . (Later I took possession in a similar way of Austria's beautiful landscapes, where I took many long walks, as well as of the towns, landscapes and people of Italy, and finally England.)"[74] If landscapes can be possessed, they are subjective, not national possessions. His historical experience, his own migration, made Buday reconsider the ideological constructs of his youth.

Imro/Imre Weiner-Kráľ and His Bratislava Series

In Hungarian irredentist publications, as well as in Duša's prints made from a Slovak standpoint, the nationalization of the landscape effaced the multiethnicity of contested regions. The conceptualization of the countryside as inherently more national than the city, which underlay Duša's and Buday's work, further bolstered exclusive definitions of national identity and territory. It is therefore useful to conclude this chapter with a work that synthesized history and landscape, urban and rural, nature and heritage in a way that evoked the spirit of the Fischer-Mednyánszky tradition.

Imro/Imre Weiner (1901–1978) was born in Vágbeszterce/Považská Bystrica/Waagbistritz, into a Jewish family.[75] From 1919 to 1922, he studied architecture and painting in Prague, first at the Czech Technical University, then at the School of Applied Arts. He subsequently trained at the art academies of Düsseldorf and Berlin and finally, in 1924, at the École des Beaux-Arts in Paris. He returned to Slovakia in 1924. From 1928 to 1932, he lived in Bratislava and then spent time in Berlin. In 1938, he emigrated to Paris, where he joined the resistance during the Second World War and earned the nickname Kráľ (king) for his bravery. He returned to Czechoslovakia in the 1950s. He was married to the photographer Irena Blühová / Irén Blüh (1904–1991), who studied at the Bauhaus. Weiner-Kráľ's art merged some of the avant-garde movements of his time but was most influenced by surrealism.

Today, Weiner-Kráľ has an important place in Slovak art history as a representative of Slovak surrealism, but he is also remembered as belonging to the Hungarian minority.[76] His life, as well as his art, reflects the diversity of interwar Slovakia and disrupts attempts at imposing exclusive ethnic designations.[77] He started his higher artistic training at the most heated moment of the border disputes, and he chose to go to Prague, rather than to Budapest, the destination of choice for many ethnic Hungarians from Slovakia. This decision does not necessarily mean Weiner-Kráľ did not identify with the Hungarian minority. As a Communist of Jewish descent, he must have seen Prague and its state-encouraged modernism as more hospitable than counterrevolutionary Hungary, with its violent antisemitism and relatively conservative art schools. Other biographical facts hint at Weiner-Kráľ's Hungarian identity. In 1935, he took part in the first annual art exhibition of the Czechoslovak Hungarian Association for Scholarship, Literature, and Art, and around the same time, he was part of an (unsuccessful) attempt to set up a Hungarian art school in Slovakia with artists such as Bertalan Pór (1880–1964), who had emigrated from Budapest to Slovakia due to his involvement in the Soviet Republic.[78] Additionally, Weiner-Kráľ's Jewish identity featured in his work depicting Slovakia's Orthodox Jewish communities.[79] Furthermore, as a Hungarian commentator in 1961 put it, he was also the "painter of the Slovak village" who drew on local folk culture in many of his pictures, developing his own brand of "village surrealism."[80]

Around 1937, Weiner-Kráľ briefly returned to Bratislava. It was at this time that he created a series of woodcuts representing aspects of the city, which he collected under the title *Bratislava*. The city had received this name less than twenty years earlier. Prior to 1919, its Slovak name had been Prešporok, while in Hungarian, it had been known as Pozsony, and in German, as Pressburg. It was a city of long-standing historical significance: before the Hungarian conquest in the ninth century, it had been an important center of Great Moravia; later on, during the Turkish Wars and the partition of the country, it had functioned as Hungary's capital. It hosted the Hungarian Diet until 1848, when the assembly was first held in Pest. Given its multiethnic population, Pozsony/Pressburg/Prešporok had been a prime target for the Hungarianizing efforts of the government in the late nineteenth century but nevertheless retained its diverse character.[81]

As part of Czechoslovakia, Bratislava had to be integrated into a new narrative of national identity as a site of both old and new. The ideology of the state revolved around modernity—starting a new chapter after a past hallmarked by Habsburg and Hungarian rule. The markers of Czechoslovak identity were social progress, cutting-edge industrial production, and modernist aesthetics. These characteristics were present in Bratislava's modern buildings, erected after 1918, and in its art school. The city was, however, also the center of Slovakia, whose image as rural and traditional diverged from this bigger picture. To counter Hungarian arguments, according to which Magyar tribes had conquered the region by virtue of their superior military skills, Slovaks emphasized the issue of primacy: they had been there first. Hence, the heritage of the Great Moravian Empire had to be brought to the fore. Bratislava held many such traces; the first stone castle on its hill had been built in the ninth century, in the time of Great Moravia, and the ruins of nearby Devín castle were similarly associated with the bygone empire. In guidebooks and other materials aimed at domestic and foreign audiences, this focus on ancientness had to be married with the celebration of progress.[82]

Weiner-Král''s prints expressed this subtlety through surrealist compositions and a mixture of gentle nostalgia and sharp satire. They combined the imagery of progress with that of traditionalism, the imagery of the present with that of the past. Many of the sheets had a layered structure; divided into horizontal sections, they superimposed motifs representing different aspects of the place. One example is *Devín*, which is also known as *The Past (Minulosť)* and as *Scene of Action (Dejisko)* (fig. 3.9).[83]

The last title is perhaps the most fitting. The image presents Bratislava and Devín as a stage where historical events had taken place throughout the centuries, witnessed by the two ancient castles. In the upper half of the composition, beneath Bratislava Castle, lie a medieval knight and lady. They represent the people of the past, who had once inhabited the region and shaped its history. Formerly flesh and blood, they are now reduced to faint silhouettes, like cut-out dolls. Devín is depicted in the bottom half of the image. To its right floats a steamship, drawn with a few simple lines. As in Mednyánszky's tales, the castle is a node that allows a simultaneous view of different historical times without building a broader, continuous narrative.

Located at the western edge of the nineteenth-century Kingdom of Hungary, on its border with Austria, the castle of Dévény/Devín/Theben fea-

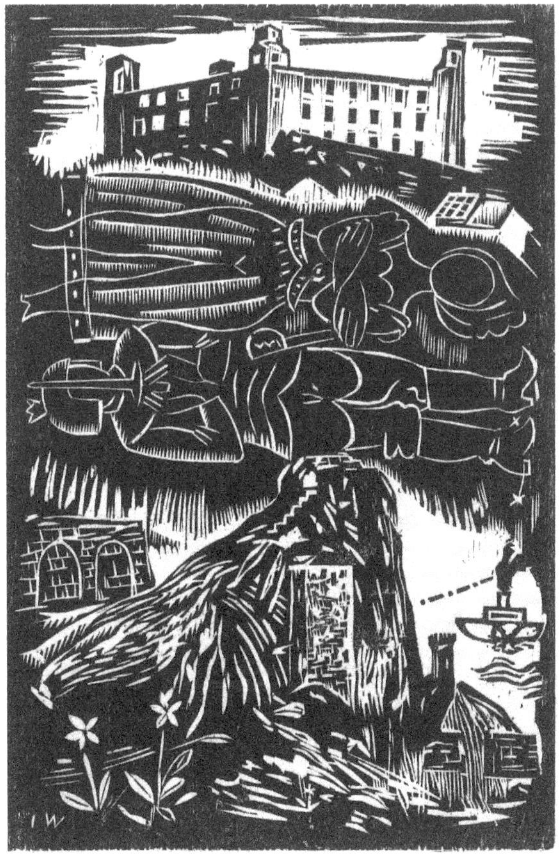

FIGURE 3.9. Imro Weiner-Král, *Devín* (from the series *Bratislava*), 1937, Slovenská národná galéria, Bratislava. Imro Weiner-Král © OOA-S 2024

tured in Slovak and Hungarian historical memory alike.[84] As a site of memory, Devín was, perhaps, of greatest importance to Slovaks, who remembered it as a fortress of Great Moravia. For Hungarians, then, Dévény was a place where Magyar tribes had defeated the Moravians.[85] It symbolized the westernmost point ancient Hungarians had reached—and hence their military strength—while also being the "Porta Hungarica" that greeted visitors arriving to Hungary from the west. Due to its historicity, its symbolic location on the border, and its arresting visual qualities, Dévény was favored by landscapists in the nineteenth century. Starting with a prototype painted by János (Johann) Hofbauer (1803–1839) in the early 1830s, these pictures frequently featured a steamship on the Danube, juxtaposing the ancientness of the castle with modern technological progress.[86] In 1896, one of the millennium monuments was erected on Devín Hill. Promptly removed by Czechs in 1918, the loss of the monument was oft lamented by interwar Hungarian nationalists.

No longer a symbol of cutting-edge modernity in 1937, the steamship nevertheless appeared in Weiner-Král's *Devín* as well. Overall, the print emphasized history and human civilization rather than nature. The knight and the lady are more prominent than any other element of the image. Yet, at the bottom in the foreground, two flowers grow, representing the present. The juxtaposition of the bygone past and vigorous present was a centuries-old feature of historical landscapes, but in this context, it had particular poignancy. For the liberal journalist Árpád Pásztor (1877–1940), reminiscing on the loss of the Devín column in 1932, it provided a way to transcend the militant rhetoric of irredentism: "The rock on which the Árpád monument once stood emerges from the water bare and solemn. Where once the bronze Turul [mythical Hungarian bird] had spread its wings, now a flagpole stands high, but on the grassy side of the castle hill a group of children are playing merrily in the spring sunshine—today's children, tomorrow's adults, who no longer ruminate on yesterday."[87]

This approach to the loss of heritage and landscape prioritized a peaceful future. Pásztor ultimately argued for the acceptance of Trianon borders and friendly cooperation with neighboring countries in an economic union. In the article, as well as in Weiner-Král's picture, the whimsical yet cheerful aspects of nature—grass, flowers, sunshine—are what represent the will to move on. As in nineteenth-century historical landscapes, nature, eternally renewed, thrives victoriously over fragments of human-made heritage. Pásztor was a Budapest-based journalist, but his background was similar to Weiner-Král's. He had been born into a Jewish family in Ungvár/Užhorod/Uzhhorod, in Subcarpathian Ruthenia, a former Hungarian region that now lay in Czechoslovakia. The thoughts he expressed would not have been alien to many minority Hungarians in Slovakia. As László Szarka has explained, the forceful irredentism of the Hungarian kin state found relatively little purchase among Hungarians outside the Trianon borders, who—even if dismayed by the new situation—acutely felt the need to adapt and go on with their lives.[88] In Slovakia, ideas of regionalism and "native inhabitant" organizing, which aimed to unite Hungarians, Slovaks, Ruthenians, and Germans in pursuit of regional autonomy within Czechoslovakia, had considerable popularity, even if their success was ultimately hindered by tensions between Slovak and Hungarian nationalists and by the wider political developments of the late 1930s. Slovak Hungarians developed a proud identity as the "westernmost," most progressive of Hungarians, ironically in line with the Czechoslovak state's self-representation.

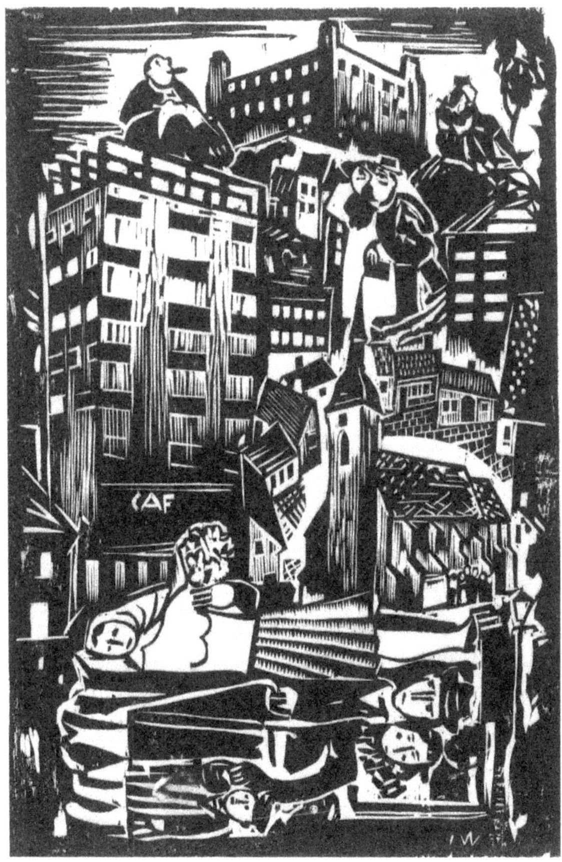

FIGURE 3.10. Imro Weiner-Král, *City and People* (from the series *Bratislava*), 1937, Slovenská národná galéria, Bratislava. Imro Weiner-Král © OOA-S 2024

Nature does not feature prominently in the *Bratislava* series, which focuses on life in the city. But nature in historical landscapes stands for the present, and in *Bratislava*, it is the present that lives on. The past, in the form of Bratislava Castle, is a constant but harmless presence. It appears in almost all images in the series, overlooking the city and its inhabitants. Like a pin poked into historical spacetime, it helps drill down into the past so that new and old, urban and rural, Slovak, Hungarian, and German can be viewed together at once. In *Mesto a ludia* (*City and People*), four horizontal figures in rural dress—a couple with a child and another woman holding a bouquet—lie in the bottom part of the image, much like the medieval figures in *Devín*; this time, it is they who represent the fundaments of present Bratislava and bear the weight of its modern prosperity (fig. 3.10).

In the layer above them stands Saint Martin's Cathedral, with its lone spire and gothic buttresses, juxtaposed with a tall modernist building. Completed in 1935, the Manderlák was the first modern high-rise apartment block in Bratislava. On the top sits a rich bourgeois smoking a cigar, perhaps a caricature of the owner, Rudolf Manderla. In the meandering alleyway that opens up between the sections of the image, a middle-class couple—a woman carrying an elegant clutch and a man in suit and hat—make their way downward, toward the church and the rural figures.

The castle appears in the background in the sheet titled *Port*, which depicts laborers unloading heavy sacks from the boats. It is there in *Funeral* and *Café Boon*, the latter depicting a popular café located on a boat on the river. In one print (*Pri Dunaji šaty perú* [*They Wash Clothes by the Danube*], the title of a folk song), an urban and a rural woman watch soldiers marching by, while in another (*Fajront* [*Work Is Over*]), a group of workers head home and the castle is encased by the smoke of factory chimneys.[89] Instead of separating the people of the city and the country, the prints highlight social tensions that cut across this constructed duality. The castle is certainly a marker of the city's identity, a symbol onto which all its diverse inhabitants can project their hopes and ideals. Nevertheless, as a vestige of the past, it does not determine modern life; it does not favor one Bratislava over the other. Grappling with the menaces of the present is the duty of those who live with them today.

A Multiplicity of Landscapes

The collapse of the Habsburg Empire, the formation of new nation states, the new borders drawn, and the resulting transformation of mental maps were all wide-reaching developments of modernity. Repurposing an old, nostalgic genre such as that of the historical landscape to express, lament, or try to intellectually resolve the ensuing tensions was a logical artistic approach. The genre allowed for a variety of transformations expressing a range of perspectives. Depending on the artists' politics, images could lay emphasis on either nature or history. Nevertheless, there were commonalities. Their diversity notwithstanding, the artworks examined in this chapter all aimed for regeneration. Relying on tradition, myth, politics, and, sometimes, scholarly research, they aspired to remedy a transformation of space and time that suffused all areas of culture in Central Europe.

The examples have all been prints on paper—series of woodcuts, book illustrations, and posters. Their imagery was produced for wider consumption. Rather than existing in isolation, they often supported each other; their powerful visualization of ideas would be picked up by subsequent artists, to be perpetuated into the future. Affinities such as these can be seen between the *You Have Taken Our Rivers* poster from 1920 and Buday's 1937 illustration. *Bleeding Hungary* and *Justice for Hungary!* employed archaizing images of castles to claim areas outside the new borders as inherently Hungarian. Varga assembled similar vignettes into artistically more complex and inventive compositions, making their historical allusions more concrete while taking a thoroughly modern approach to image making. Appearing in many forms, in different kinds of printed material, these images helped shift the meanings people associated with specific places, shaping a collective mental map that elevated the lost territories to a fundamental importance.

The imagery of the historical landscape contributed to the nationalization of landscapes in the nineteenth—and then again in the twentieth—century. In this chapter, Duša's *Down the Váh* exemplified how old imagery can gain a new meaning in a different political context. Yet, this series also reminds us of the overlaps between collective mental maps in multinational Central Europe and of how the same places can mean different things in different national narratives. In its versatility, the historical landscape also offered ways to express this multiplicity. In Weiner-Král's *Bratislava*, surrealist compositional devices helped evoke the multifaceted, multilayered nature of past and present through the imagery of ruined castles, hills, and rivers as well as that of the modern city.

In visualizing history and anchoring it into specific locations, artists drew on current knowledge about the past and its material heritage. Scholarly disciplines such as historiography, archaeology, and geography informed popular understandings of history, and hence its visual representations. Of the examples discussed in this chapter, Varga's *Hungarian Past* drew most obviously on academic research, but scholarship was never far removed from the politics of memory. The next chapter will take a closer look at the relationship between historical research, official expectations, and the visual arts.

CHAPTER 4

The Archive and the Ruin

The artworks and publications discussed in the previous chapter approached historical heritage in various ways. They made it a vehicle of nationalist agitation, subsumed it into its sublime natural surroundings, assembled its fragments into a montage, surrounded it with the vigorous life of a contemporary city. One thing none of them did was provide scholarly historical analysis. This was not their job; they were not scholarly publications. But is the gap between them and the latter as decisive as we might think at first sight? Scholarship does not exist in an isolated ivory tower; it is part of a broader cultural and political environment. Its institutions are formed by political will, and its practitioners are often involved in political developments. Art and scholarship are both inseparable from cultural politics, and interactions between the three are not exceptional but rather familiar aspects of our culture.

Interwar nationalisms across Europe drew profusely on historiography and archaeology, often in ways that haunt cultural memory to this day. Tracing the ancient roots of the nation supported territorial claims by proving primacy in the region. In Romania, the theory of Daco-Roman continuity, which posits that Romanians originated from the ancient Dacians who had absorbed Roman culture, was elaborated by distinguished archaeologists.[1] In Bulgaria, similar continuity was drawn up with the Thracians, an elusive ancient group of peoples.[2] Rather than focusing on the evolution and interaction of cultures, nationalist archaeology interprets the archaeological record as evidence of the history of specific modern peoples; early twentieth-century German archaeology, for instance, emphasized the lack of non-German groups in an area and highlighted this as a sign of the racial purity of German populations.[3] Mussolini supported grandiose archaeological projects in Italy and abroad to promote the ancient Roman Empire as a precedent of the Fascist state and its imperial ambitions.[4] In Rome itself, this amounted to a complete transformation of the cityscape, as nineteenth-century streets were demolished to create open spaces where ancient ruins could be revealed.[5] This was about not only imposing a specific interpretation of ancient history but also reframing the recent past—demolishing the traces of the prewar bourgeois liberal culture that Fascists had rebelled against. The ancient past was a crucial reference point, but the ambition to reconstruct historical narratives spanned the centuries that had since passed.

Similar developments can also be traced in Hungary. In this chapter, I look at two artistic projects as examples of the symbiosis between scholarship, politics, and art. Both involved reinterpreting elements of material heritage, and both were intended for a wider public, not just historians. The first example, the interior decoration of the National Archives of Hungary (1924–1929), not only visualized a historical narrative corresponding to the ideology of the early Horthy regime but also presented it as an objective truth supported by historical documents. Andor Dudits's murals brought this storyline to life using the venerable formal language of nineteenth-century art academies. In the second example, the Medieval Ruin Garden established in Székesfehérvár as part of the 1938 Saint Stephen jubilee, the conclusions of meticulous archaeological research were suffused by ideology. Artistic commissions that formed part of the project, such as Lili Sztehlo's stained glass window and Vilmos Aba-Novák's murals, started out with requirements of strict historical accuracy, but in the finished products, historical "truth" and state ideology became inseparable. Dudits endowed his images with the aura of pure art, far removed from the swamps of real life and politics. Aba-Novák, in turn, created a radical, dissonant, curiously modern formal language that transmitted the ideology at a gut level, overwhelming viewers with its monumentality. In both cases, art not only disseminated the desired message to a broader audience but packaged it in a way that made it seem self-evident.

Historiography and Politics

The central figure in the story I tell here is the minister of religion and education, Kuno Klebelsberg, and the beginnings reach back to the time before his ministership. On 16 February 1917, when he was a state secretary at the ministry, the Hungarian Historical Association elected Klebelsberg as its new president. He held a doctorate in law and had no scholarly publications in the field. To the numerous critics of the association's decision, this signaled the profession's "self-humiliation" before political power.[6] Nevertheless, Klebelsberg held the position until his death in 1932. From December 1921 to June 1922, he was also minister of interior affairs, following which he became minister of religion and education.[7] He served in this position for ten years and throughout this time showed unwavering commitment to historical research. He established research institutes at home and abroad, funded archival research, initiated publications, and instituted fellowships. Despite the successive radical political changes in the hundred years that followed, much of the infrastructure he created and the knowledge production he catalyzed remains fundamental to Hungarian historiography.

Klebelsberg was, however, a politician, and his support for research fit his ideological program. A close ally of Bethlen, he was instrumental in the "consolidation" of the Bethlen era. Cultural soft power was seen as essential to the prime minister's quest to peacefully revise Trianon, and Klebelsberg's pet project, the network of international Hungarian research institutes, fit into broader endeavors of cultural diplomacy.[8] The minister was a firm believer in Hungarian cultural superiority, but he saw it as an advantage that could be lost; hence, it was important to strengthen Hungary's cultural institutions at home, too, before neighboring countries could catch up. This would turn "Dismembered Hungary" into a cultural powerhouse whose territorial claims would be taken more seriously.

Through these projects, Klebelsberg ensured that the official politics of the state permeated scholarship in numerous, often seemingly innocuous ways. This had implications for art, too—first, because art history and archaeology often came under the umbrella of history and benefitted from this support, and second, because Klebelsberg was keen to use art to promote his model of Hungarian history and culture. The first project examined in this chapter demonstrates how this played out during Klebelsberg's ministership, while the second shows how the structures he built remained in place after his death, in a changing political environment. The decoration of the National Archives of Hungary was created when Klebelsberg was at the peak of his career. The murals were painted by one of his most favored artists, and the cycle included a full-length portrait of him wearing medieval armor. The Medieval Ruin Garden in Székesfehérvár opened in 1938, six years after Klebelsberg's death. By then, consolidation was over; the Hungarian government pursued more militant and radical policies of territorial expansion and antisemitism. The minister of religion and education, Bálint Hóman (1885–1951), was a historian, a scholar, and a promoter of openly racist policies. Yet, the artists who decorated the building had benefitted from a scholarship set up by Klebelsberg, and the entire project was shaped by the fusion between research and politics he had established.

Klebelsberg's dual tenure as president of the historical society and as minister was an important sign of the close relationship between professional history writing and the political sphere, but it was not the only one. Several of the most important ideological underpinnings of the Horthy regime were developed by historians. The first and most influential of these was Gyula Szekfű's polemic *Three Generations*, first published in 1920.[9] As highlighted in the introduction, Szekfű placed the blame for Trianon on the shoulders of the liberal political elite of pre-1918 Hungary, castigating them for their suppression of minorities and their liberal attitude to Jewish immigration. Rejecting the anti-Habsburg tendency of traditional Hungarian nationalism as well as Asian-oriented Turanism, Szekfű asserted that Hungary belonged to the "Christian-Germanic cultural community."[10] Within the imperial framework, non-Hungarian minorities had lived peacefully under a paternalistic Hungarian hegemony. In the nineteenth century, conservative reformers such as Count István Széchenyi had sought to modernize the feudal country while respecting these principles. The revolutionaries of 1848, followed by the nationalist elites of the dualist period, had destroyed these fundaments, setting the country on a course toward catastrophe. Of the *Three Generations*, symbolized by Széchenyi, the 1848 revolutionary Lajos Kossuth, and the turn-of-the-century politician and Prime Minister István Tisza, the latter two ultimately brought failure and decline.[11]

Three Generations received extensive critique from major figures, including the prominent older historian Henrik Marczali (1856–1940); the writer Zsigmond Móricz (1879–1942), known for his unidealized depictions of peasant life; and the left-wing sociologist Oszkár Jászi (1875–1957), a member of the revolutionary Károlyi government.[12] Nevertheless, the book was well received; it struck a chord with the elites of the Horthy regime as well as with the wider public. Its rejection of the revolutionary mindset, its positive evaluation of Habsburg rule, its staunch antiliberal stance, and its open antisemitism all matched the regime's political goals and provided them with an ideological grounding. Although more a political polemic than a piece of scholarship, it also signaled a shift in history writing. In the late nineteenth century, positivism had been hugely influential in Hungarian historiography, coupled with the *historicism* most famously represented by Leopold von Ranke (1795–1886), which focused on the evolution of states as the most important subject of historical inquiry. In the 1920s, however, a new trend became prevalent that sought to trace a driving force, a "spirit"—often the national spirit—in history and culture.[13] Initially, this meant the adoption of the German methodology known as Geistesgeschichte, which broadened the scope of inquiry from the history of politics and political elites toward that of ideas, society, and cultural production. In post-Trianon Hungary—as in post-Versailles Germany—the shift from the state toward culture had political implications. As the historian Elemér Mályusz (1898–1989) put it in 1931:

> The blows that hit the states that had lost the war proved that, first, the state has no primacy over other forms of organic unity and, second, that the latter also had their own individual lives, previously ignored by our historiography. . . . It became evident that land, population and culture had lived closely intertwined lives beneath the enormous vaulted construct of the state; that is, that people were not just citizens, but prior to that also members of religious, cultural, racial and national communities; their material lives may have been dependent on the land, but they also raised the area they inhabited to a level corresponding to their intellectual culture.[14]

A focus on culture and, increasingly, on ethnicity allowed Hungarian historians to envision a continuous narrative even when the borders of the Hungarian state had radically changed.[15]

Although categorized as Geistesgeschichte in the volume on new directions in Hungarian history writing in which it first appeared, Mályusz's essay heralded a further split within historiography. In Germany, the new "völkisch" trend that focused on "the people" rather than the elites was already well defined, but in Hungary in 1931, it was still hidden under the general umbrella of Geistesgeschichte. In the next years, the contrast became clearer as Szekfű—the most emblematic Hungarian representative of Geistesgeschichte who nevertheless still examined the state and its elites—and Mályusz found themselves on opposing sides in historiographical debates. The nationalist implications of the "völkisch" approach in Germany were clear to Mályusz. However, he advocated a Hungarian version of the methodology as a means to counter German expansionism.[16]

Klebelsberg's policies were inseparable from these intellectual developments. In 1928, he published several articles on "neonationalism" explaining that, with the dethroning of the Habsburgs and Trianon, Hungarian nationalism had lost the two main aims that had driven it previously: the struggle against Austrian centralization and Germanization and the goal of Hungarianizing the country's non-Hungarian populations.[17] Like Szekfű, he characterized both aims as fruitless. The "neonationalism" he advocated would be suited to Hungary's new situation. The goal was to become wealthier and more cultured than surrounding nations, to build a prosperous Hungary, where higher education levels would drive productivity, an independent mindset, and the solidification of a self-confident Hungarian identity.

The funding Klebelsberg provided for historiography was a pillar of his project. Besides providing support for the infrastructure of research, this funding went toward publications, ranging from broader surveys informed by Geistesgeschichte to positivistic collections of primary sources and other handbooks. He had already laid out his program in his opening speech at the 1920 general assembly of the historical society, at a time when the postwar state's budget was still lamentably scarce. Specifically mentioning the National Archives, he highlighted the untenable situation in which the new building was occupied by unrelated governmental offices.[18] Speaking with his chair-of-the-historical-society hat on, he demanded that these be moved elsewhere, so the archive could fulfill its intended role. For this to happen, it had to be placed under the authority of the Ministry of Education. With his member-of-the-government hat on, Klebelsberg accepted this suggestion and made sure it was implemented. In his speech, he stated that one of the causes of the political disorder of the last years was the decline in the public's historical knowledge. Those who had a strong concept of legal continuity and the moral and practical relevance of political tradition did not fall into the trap of dangerous, subversive ideas. Society needed to support history writing for the sake of its own survival.

One of those who benefitted from ministerial support was Szekfű, who contributed to several large projects in the 1920s. His recurring collaborator was the future minister, Hóman, then a talented medievalist and, from 1923, director of the Hungarian National Museum. From 1928, they published an eight-volume coauthored *Hungarian History*, with Hóman writing the chapters up to the fifteenth century and Szekfű the rest, providing an encompassing view of politics and culture.[19] In 1931, Hóman edited *New Directions in Hungarian History Writing*, in which a range of authors explained recent methodological shifts, mostly related to Geistesgeschichte, from the viewpoints of different subdisciplines, with Szekfű authoring the chapter titled "Political History Writing."[20] By the mid-1930s, however, Szekfű had grown critical of the Horthy regime. In his contribution to *Hungarian History*, he had described the eighteenth century as Hungary's golden age, with the baroque landlord—the ideal Hungarian character in Szekfű's eyes—presiding over a patriarchal, rural idyll where ethnic minorities lived in peace and the Hungarian nobility negotiated a mutually beneficial arrangement with the Habsburgs.[21] In his 1934 supplementary chapter to a new edition of *Three Generations*, he contrasted his own age with this idyllic picture, describing the former as a "Neobaroque society" that only imitated the eighteenth-century ideal in superficial details but not in its essence.[22] By the forties, despite his own antisemitism, Szekfű was horrified by the institutionalized racism of the state; he rejected Nazism and went into hiding during the German occupation and the terror of the Arrow Cross. Hóman, by contrast, grew more and more radical in his right-wing views. As a minister, he took part in preparing the anti-Jewish laws of 1938, 1939, and 1941.

Despite these contrasts, the 1920s and the 1930s, Klebelsberg's and Hóman's ministerships, belonged in a continuity. Klebelsberg himself had designated Hóman as his eventual successor.[23] The two projects examined in the rest of this chapter reveal the deeper connections underlying the apparent differences—a shared program of bolstering the illusions of ideology through the venerable aura of historical facts.

The Decoration of the National Archives of Hungary

During Klebelsberg's ministerial tenure, the building of the National Archives was what has been described as an "inhabited ruin."[24] Designed and partly built before 1918 but only finished and taken into possession by the Archives in the 1920s, the building was reinterpreted to suit the new circumstances. Hence, it expressed how the new political and intellectual elite perceived Hungarian history and within it its own role.

The story of the modern National Archives of Hungary began in 1756 with the establishment of the Archivum Regni, which was to preserve documents deposited by aristocratic families and state institutions.[25] In 1875, the Hungarian government decided to modernize and reorganize the Archives as part of its state-building administrative reforms. By this time, the role of the Archives was not only to document and uphold legal continuities but also to aid historical research by making available a wealth of primary sources. Given the strong focus on the development of the state in late nineteenth-century history writing, the relationship between the two was intimate. Through the documents accessible in the Archives, historians could describe the continuity and extent of the Hungarian state, a subject with obvious political implications.

An institution with such symbolic and practical importance needed a suitable and representative home. Construction of a new building in the Buda Castle area finally began in 1913 according to designs by Samu Pecz (1854–1922).[26] Pecz was a historicist architect who designed a range of public buildings, including churches, government offices, and market halls, in a characteristic, modernized medieval style, often employing colorful tiles from the Zsolnay factory on the roofs. The National Archives building followed this model. An imposing, robust structure, its facades are livened up by Romanesque arched windows, trefoil arches supported by dainty columns, carved rosettes, and bright yellow, green, red, and white patterns on the roof. While choosing a historicist formal idiom, Pecz aimed for cutting-edge modernity in functionality. Drawing on examples he had observed on a study trip across Western Europe, he provided the Hungarian archives with ample and eminently suitable space for storing, restoring, studying, and displaying historical documents.

When construction began in 1913, authorities had only approved the plans for the building, leaving the furnishings and interior decoration for later. By the time these were on the agenda again, a new protagonist had appeared on the scene and taken the matter into his own hands. Klebelsberg complemented the narrow budget of the archive with generous funding in order to turn the building into a "Hungarian Pantheon."[27] Advised by officers from the Archive and occasional juries, he took on a central role in determining the decorative program and selecting the artists. Among them were the sculptors Zsigmond Kisfaludi Stróbl, István Szentgyörgyi, and Ferenc Sidló, whom we encountered in chapter 2 as sculptors of the irredentist monuments and who had since become favorites for official commissions. The stained glass windows were the work of an older artist, Miksa Róth (1865–1944), whose colorful compositions had long been the jewels of historicist and art nouveau buildings across the country. Finally, Klebelsberg commissioned murals narrating Hungarian history to run along the walls of the building on several floors, in the hallways and in all representative rooms. The artist he commissioned was Dudits, who, in 1923, had just completed his monumental *Oath in the Vérmező* discussed in chapter 1.

Although Dudits drew attention with the *Oath in the Vérmező*, he had by then completed a number of other commissions for public buildings, most of them murals with historical subject matter. The *Oath*, a realistic group portrait, was exceptional in his oeuvre; he was more comfortable with painting dainty historical scenes imbued with a late nineteenth-century aestheticism that gave them a fairy-tale-like quality. He continued along these lines in his murals in the Archive. At first sight, therefore, the decoration of the Archive followed the late historicist artistic framework determined by Pecz's building. Within these conservative forms, however, the decoration embodied the new aims of a twentieth-century regime.

In 1928, Dezső Csánki (1857–1933), director of the Archives, guided a journalist around the building.[28] He described it as the Hungarian Pantheon, an idea he claimed he had pitched to Klebelsberg. Unlike its French counterpart, the Hungarian Pantheon would not house the mortal remains of great historical figures. Instead, it would collect documents, paintings, and works of artistic industry to preserve the memory of the Hungarian past. Some of Dudits's paintings were already finished, and the enthused journalist wrote that they conjured up, in a gripping yet classical manner, the most glorious times of Hungarian cultural history. The idea of such a collection functioning as a national pantheon originated from the nineteenth century. At several points in its early history, the Hungarian National Museum (founded in 1808) had been conceptualized as a national pantheon.[29] In 1875, Károly Lotz (1833–1904) and Mór Than (1828–1899) had decorated the main stairwell with a fresco cycle depicting the evolution of Hungarian culture over the course of history—a program similar to that of Dudits's murals. Csánki and Klebelsberg wanted to turn the Archives into a new pantheon—essentially a national museum fit for a new era.

To achieve this, the Archives had to represent the totality of Hungarian history, both in time and space. Dudits's frescoes visualized a narrative from the foundation of the state to recent times, but this was only one strand of the encompassing program.[30] Some of the decoration reached back to preceding times: a sculptural group by Sidló depicted ancient Magyar warriors in a battle. The building's Romanesque style had been determined before the First World War, but it fit postwar ideology, as it recalled the time of Stephen I, central to the Horthy regime's memory politics. In the interior, Róth—who described Klebelsberg's close oversight of the project in his memoirs—decorated the wall spaces between the historical scenes with medievalesque ornament, recalling nineteenth-century neo-medieval projects such as the interiors of the nearby Church of the Assumption (Matthias Church) or the neo-Gothic Parliament building.[31] Hence, the decoration stayed true to the spirit of the structure and connected the Archive to the nineteenth century, which had birthed similar national institutions. Totality was also present thematically. Dudits's frescoes focused on the evolution of culture in Hungary but were complemented by bronze sculptures depicting Hungarian military prowess, including, besides Sidló's ancient Magyars, early modern Hungarians fighting the Turks in Kisfaludi Strobl's composition.

In addition to representing totality in time, the Archives were conceived as a microcosm of historical Hungary in a spatial sense. In the arches of the windows in the stairwells, Róth represented the coats of arms of Hungarian cities. Csánki had conceived of this idea in 1915, before Trianon, but by the time Róth received the commission in the 1920s, the meaning of the imagery had changed. Many of the cities evoked in the windows no longer belonged to Hungary, and the building brought them together in one commemorative space much in the vein of the irredentist monuments discussed earlier in this book.[32] Indeed, Csánki had stressed this aspect in a memorandum about the windows addressed to Klebelsberg in 1928. According to a detailed plan submitted by Csánki in November 1928, the individual coats of arms were arranged so that from any point on the stairs, symbols of cities from both the lost and the remaining territories would be in view, creating a sense of unity.[33]

This amalgamation of historical time and geography is yet another manifestation of irredentist spacetime, but in this case, it shows how this mental framework, so widespread in public life, extended to—and was underpinned by—scholarship. Csánki had specialized in historical geography long before Trianon: the first installment of his multivolume project, *The Historical Geography of Hungary in the Age of the Hunyadis*, had come out in 1890. He was less active as a scholar following his appointment as director of the Archives in 1912, but his field gained new relevance in the next decade. The reason was summed up by Mályusz in his aforementioned essay, "The History of Ethnicity." Holding up German examples for emulation, Mályusz claimed that the cultural history of a nation could be best examined through monographs of individual localities, "as it is through such microscopic study that the most specific, typical characteristics of the lives of groups within the people can be revealed, which are usually obscured in studies of the totality, the entire people."[34] Revealing such characteristics was important because it would bolster revisionist arguments about the diversity, and yet organic unity, of historical Hungary. The documents in the Archives would aid such research, an aim expressed by the emphasis on places in the decorative program.

The importance of place in history is a theme evoked in Dudits's murals as well, which depicted significant moments in the history of Hungarian culture, education, and scholarship, often clearly showing where the events had taken place. They also included two landscapes showing medieval castles: the castle of Vajdahunyad/Hunedoara, the birthplace of King Matthias, now in Romania, and the castle of Diósgyőr, near the city of Miskolc, in post-Trianon Hungary. The inclusion of castles connects Dudits's frescoes to another nineteenth-century precedent: the Hungarian Academy of Sciences, whose great hall Than had decorated with scenes representing different eras of Hungarian culture, while its lecture hall held landscapes with castles by Antal Ligeti (1823–1890). Yet again, the program situated the Archives alongside the esteemed national institutions of the nineteenth century. These similarities make the differences even more revealing; they demonstrate where the Horthy regime broke with interpretations of history promoted in the previous era.

The cycles of murals at the academy and in the corridors of the Archives both began with medieval kings: Stephen I and some of his successors. They placed particular emphasis on Louis I and Matthias, the latter honored in several pictures in the Archive's Chivalry Room. Like Than's cycle at the academy, Dudits's murals represented baroque culture through Péter Pázmány (1570–1637), cardinal, writer, and intellectual leader of the Hungarian counterreformation; Miklós Zrínyi (1620–1664), seventeenth-century poet and military leader; and Francis II Rákóczi. The latter's exile in Tekirdağ, where he wrote his memoirs, was the subject of a large composition. Dudits's narrative diverged from the nineteenth-century precedent by placing greater emphasis on the eighteenth century, Szekfű's favorite age. Separate pictures celebrated Ferenc Nádasdy (1708–1783) and András Hadik (1710–1790), two Hungarian noblemen who had served as valiant leaders in Maria Theresa's army; Maria Theresa and her Ratio Educationis, a 1777 law that expanded primary education in Hungary; and Antal Grassalkovich (1694–1771), a wealthy aristocrat who had commissioned an exquisite baroque mansion in Gödöllő (fig. 4.1).

Staying true to this pro-Habsburg narrative, the next pictures downplayed the revolutionary aspects of the nineteenth century. The frescoes at the Academy of Sciences had included revolutionary figures such as Kossuth, Lajos Batthyány, and the poet Sándor Petőfi (1823–1848). By contrast, the Archives represented the nineteenth century through three images, celebrating, respectively: Palatine Joseph Habsburg (1776–1847), important early patron of the Hungarian National Museum; Széchenyi, originator of the Chain Bridge connecting Pest and Buda; and the Opera House—the only national institution in nineteenth-century Hungary built through imperial patronage.

The revolutionaries were not completely absent from the murals. They had appeared in the Research Room, the first space decorated by Dudits in 1925, before he received a commission encompassing the entire building. Here, one of two larger compositions—destroyed in the Second World War—was titled *The Eras of Hungarian History*. The image evoked an uncomfortable tension between Habsburg patronage and Hungarian rebellion, showing the severed heads of three dissident Hungarians at the feet of Emperor Leopold I, with Rákóczi turning his back on the scene and Kossuth solemnly looking on.[35] This was, however, a small and isolated reference. The narrative as a whole was driven by Szekfű's model rather than the equally influential narrative that told Hungarian history as a history of struggle for freedom.

The individual images reflected Klebelsberg's preferences in even more specific ways. The picture of Maria Theresa's Ratio Educationis was dedicated not to her but to József Ürményi (1741–1825), the Hungarian nobleman

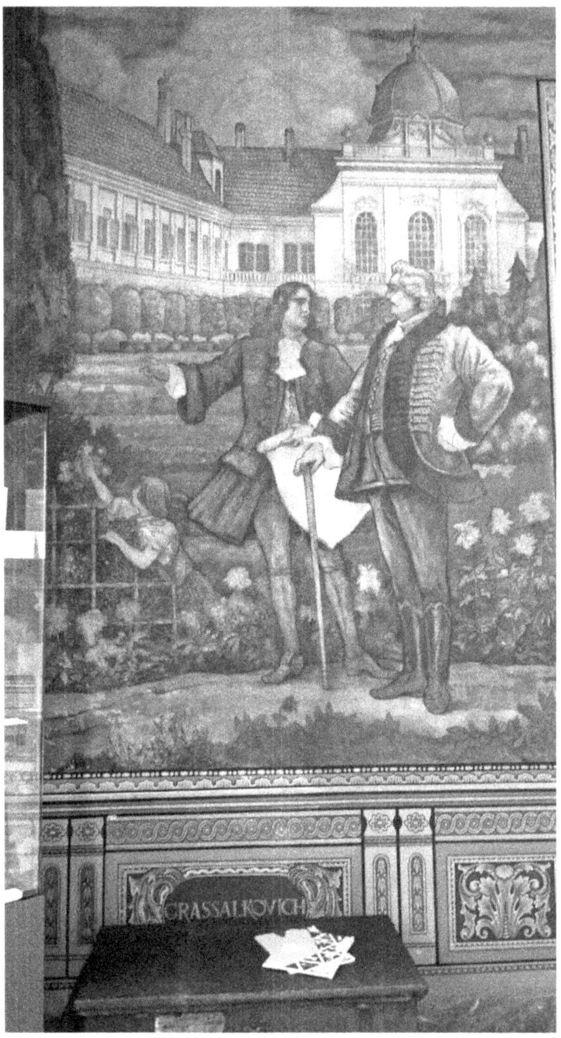

FIGURE 4.1.   Andor Dudits, *Antal Grassalkovich with András Mayerhoffer*, mural in the National Archives of Hungary, Budapest, 1927–1928.
Photo by author

who had drafted the legislation. In his programmatic speeches, Klebelsberg often referred to Maria Theresa's time as the golden age of Hungarian culture, specifically highlighting Ürményi, whom he considered his like-minded predecessor.[36] One of Klebelsberg's main achievements was his expansion of primary and secondary education, which was also celebrated in the murals; one of the last images (destroyed in 1950 and only known from sketches) showed peasant children on their way to school.[37] The motif of children with

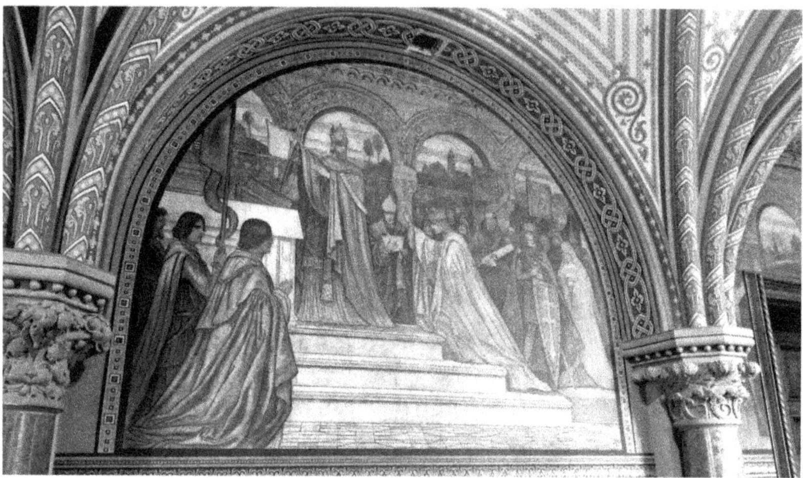

FIGURE 4.2.   Andor Dudits, *The Golden Bull*, mural in the National Archives of Hungary, Budapest, 1925–1926.
Photo by author

books connected this picture to the one of the Ratio Educationis, glorifying the twentieth-century minister through the historical precedent.

The fact that the murals reflect an interpretation of history favored by the government that commissioned them is not surprising. What makes them interesting is how they propped up this interpretation. In most images, a sheet of paper appears, representing a historical document that played a key role in the featured event. The first scene shows Stephen I founding the Benedictine Monastery of Pannonhalma, whose original founding document is still preserved. Another shows Béla III in 1181 ordering all official business in the court to be put into writing, hence establishing official literacy. Yet another picture shows King Andrew II issuing the Golden Bull of 1222, a fundamental law that limited the king's powers and established constitutional rights for the nobility (fig. 4.2). An example of Hungarian constitutionality enthusiastically cited by nationalist activists in the nineteenth century, the Golden Bull was a seminal milestone in any standard narrative of Hungarian history. Here, however, its importance lay in the fact that it was an example of history hinging on the written word. No copies of the original 1222 Bull survived, but the 1351 reissue belonged among the Archive's most cherished treasures.[38]

In centering documents that marked milestones in the legal and institutional history of Hungary, the murals recalled two aspects of nineteenth-century history writing: its positivism and its focus on the state. The pictures, and the documents they featured, represented the continuous constitutional existence of Hungary. This was an important point of reference in the irredentist memory politics of the Horthy regime, but it had been equally important in the late nineteenth century, when post-Compromise Hungary asserted itself as a legal entity whose unity overrode the requests of minority groups for autonomy. In this respect, what the murals expressed was not radically new. Nevertheless, some of the details, as well as the artist's overall approach, subtly shifted the picture.

In each of the scenes mentioned so far, a document featured prominently. Other scenes were not centered on one specific document, but the recurring motif of the sheet of paper was still present, holding the cycle together. Another recurring motif was a profusely decorated treasure chest—a metaphor of the Archive itself.[39] In one picture, King Louis I receives the relics of Saint Paul Eremite, brought to him in a chest-like reliquary from Venice after he defeated the city state in 1381. This image also features a document—the Turin Peace Treaty—presented to Louis by the delegation. The inclusion of the relics and the document in the same work and the imagery of the chest-reliquary suggest that historical documents are relics too. Hence, the Archive itself takes on a quasi-sacral role, less in line with nineteenth-century positivism than with the Horthy regime's instrumentalization of Christianity and sacralization of its own politics. Some important actors of that politics appeared in the pictures in person. In a lunette depicting Prince of Transylvania Gábor Bethlen (1613–1629), a late descendant of his family, Prime Minister István Bethlen stood next to the prince's desk. Klebelsberg himself was part of a group of kings and leaders from Hungarian history represented on the wall of the Reading Room. In the wider context of the murals, these contemporary figures became part of a storyline evidenced, and at the same time sacralized, by primary sources—instruments of scholarly research but also mystical relics of a venerable past.

Perhaps the most appealing of Dudits's pictures is the one depicting Grassalkovich with the architect András Mayerhoffer (1690–1771) in front of the Gödöllő mansion (fig. 4.1). Recalling the baroque and rococo of the eighteenth century, the murals lightened up both in color and composition on the second floor as they reached this point in the chronological narrative.[40] Grassalkovich and Mayerhoffer stand in the garden before a row of luscious roses that brighten up the composition with the emerald-green grass and the blue sky. To the left, under a yew tree, a peasant girl kneels in the grass and reaches up to pick a rose. It is as if Szekfű's paternalistic baroque idyll had materialized in a corridor of the neo-Romanesque building. The flowers, the bright colors, and the lovely girl reflect Dudits's vision of beauty, a pronounced expression of a certain kind of daintiness that permeates the whole cycle. This quest for aesthetic harmony constituted another aspect that turned the murals into a vessel of twentieth-century politics while seemingly serving to distance the artworks from anything political.

Those Who Don't Do Politics

Dudits had gained favor with authorities during the Horthy regime by completing one of the first large-scale political commissions. Yet—at least based on his public comments—he saw himself as an artist far removed from the political sphere. When he was interviewed in 1921 while working on the *Oath*, the article was titled "Those Who Don't Do Politics."[41] Almost a decade later, Dudits became embroiled in a political controversy sparked by the concluding scene of his cycle in the Archives. As a defense, he insisted on the apolitical purity of his art.

Painted on the vaulted ceiling in the staircase, this last scene was supposed to represent "the events that followed the collapse"—that is, the end of the First World War and with it of historical Hungary. Destroyed in the Second World War, the composition is today only known from descriptions.[42] According to the daily *Magyarország*, the painting

> symbolises the revolutionary times and provides an allegory of Trianon. . . . The bottom part depicts the collapse; to the right stand the participants of the Károlyi revolution with the flag of the National Council. Count Mihály Károlyi and János Hock are signing the agreement with Béla Kun. To the left, on a platform, under the five-pointed star, the bloodthirsty beasts of the Soviet regime are preparing for murder. (Among them the figures of Lenin and Bukharin appear.) Above, there is a symbolic group: the grieving mother—Hungary—as she holds her four children—the lost territories of the country—close to her heart. Next to her dogs are brawling—it is the Little Entente urging the Great Entente to break them [the group representing Hungary] up. At the very top, angels bring the Hungarian coat of arms, protecting it with flaming swords.[43]

The problem with the complex and dramatic scene was that it was completely fictitious. Contrary to official narratives conflating liberal revolutionaries with Communists, Károlyi and János Hock (1859–1936; president of the National Council when Károlyi was prime minister) had never signed anything with the Bolshevik leader Kun. The accord that created the Soviet Republic was signed by leaders of the Social Democratic and Communist parties (the latter included Kun).[44] Pointing this out, the *Pesti Napló* (*Pest Journal*) called it "historical mystification perfect in form and content—on view in the foremost workshop of Hungarian historical scholarship."[45] Like the scenes from the more distant past, this section of the murals was supposed to be based on a document; in this case, however, the document did not exist. Vince Nagy (1886–1965), once minister of interior affairs in the Károlyi government, promptly initiated a lawsuit for libel.[46]

On his part, Dudits distanced himself from the whole affair:

> I have no opinion on this court case. As an artist, I stand far removed from political affairs. Free artistic expression has nothing to do with politics, and if I did paint historical scenes, I could only interpret these allegorically. . . . There are no portraits there at all. . . . I have never seen them [Hock, Károlyi, Kun] in my life. Which makes the proposition that I painted their portraits impossible. . . . I did not paint a portrait, but an allegorical fresco. I wanted to depict the collapse, so I needed figures. These figures do not stand for living figures; next to them there are angels with flaming swords bringing the Hungarian coat of arms. I did not want any reality here, because it would have been impossible to unite reality with angels and the expression of hope.[47]

Dudits admitted that one of the figures was indeed wearing priest's garb but denied that this figure could be identified with Hock, an ordained Catholic priest. He concluded by calling the court case "interesting," as the figures bore no inscriptions and could not be identified.

As the ceiling fresco no longer exists, it is impossible to judge whether Dudits's defense was honest. This is, however, less important than the central premise of his statement. The idea that "free artistic expression has nothing to do with politics" recurred in Dudits's interviews again and again, as he aimed to describe himself as an original genius. In 1925, he rejected the label of conservative, arguing, "In art, speculation has little significance; only an original nervous system can create outstanding works. It is futile to try to be a conservative when one's whole personality is the exact opposite."[48] In 1931, the right-wing *Magyarság* claimed that Dudits's art "exists in a higher sphere and is not built on the realities of earthly life." It noted that in his "decorative murals," Dudits "composed majestic accompanying music to the highest ideals of faith and homeland. . . . In this ideal world there is no trace of the grating, random incidents of raw reality. Here, every line and color are united by a higher harmony."[49]

When accused of "doing politics," Dudits found refuge in the romantic myth of art as a sphere elevated above reality. By the early twentieth century, this myth had become widely accepted; it had turned into a cliché. This is precisely why it served so well as a refuge: it was dominant in popular culture across political fault lines. Reporting on the controversy surrounding Dudits's picture of the "Collapse," the Social Democratic daily *Népszava* disapproved of the political message but still declared that although the murals lacked truth, this did not mean that they lacked art.[50] At the same time, as the earlier excerpt from the *Magyarság* shows, the cliché of art as a separate sphere could easily serve to naturalize *political* conceptions of nation or history. Dudits was an artist, and artists do not paint politics; they only paint the "highest ideals of faith and homeland." That how they paint them happens to coincide with official interpretations of faith and homeland can surely only mean that these interpretations represent a higher truth.

In the decoration of the National Archives, politics, scholarship, and art cooperated in presenting a version of history as uncontested truth. Seals, coats of arms, and documents all highlighted that it was based on fact. An aestheticized style of painting suffused with beauty and grace positioned it above politics. Prime Minister Bethlen aimed for consolidation, which meant leaving room for a wider (although not unlimited) range of views. Klebelsberg's policies, too, focused on building up Hungarian culture in a broader sense. Yet, the plan also meant positioning this broader but still conservative and antiliberal culture as the default, as apolitical and self-evident, while construing everything that questioned it as vulgar politics. In this way, the frescoes of the Archive depoliticized politics through scholarship and aesthetics. This was not identical to what Walter Benjamin described as the "aestheticization of politics"; the National Archives, after all, did not incite ritualized mass events, and neither did it promote war.[51] Nevertheless, the approach it exemplified laid the groundwork for more militant entanglements of art, politics, and history.

The Rebirth of History Painting

Although Klebelsberg showered Dudits with commissions, he was acutely aware that the new official art, and within it history painting, could not be sustained solely by aging artists of the old guard. In 1929, he founded the Rome scholarships, a scheme that allowed young artists to spend a year at the Hungarian Academy in Rome studying old and new art in Italy, so they could develop the skills necessary for fulfilling state and church commissions. The intellectual architect of the scheme was the art historian Tibor Gerevich. Gerevich was primarily a scholar of medieval Italian and Hungarian art, but he had strong views on contemporary art as well. Interviewed in

1920 on the way forward for the art world after Trianon, he expressed a view that chimed with other regenerative ideas across Europe: the "inglorious" disruptive period of impressionism and the avant-garde would have to be followed by an era of quiet, monumental, new classicism.[52] From 1924 to 1930, Gerevich was director of the Hungarian Historical Institute in Rome, and from 1932 curator of its expanded successor, the Hungarian Academy in Rome. It was in these roles that he directed the Rome scholarship program for artists.

In an article published in 1932, Gerevich laid out the principles behind what would come to be known as the "School of Rome."[53] He presented the art shaped by the program as an antithesis of old academic painters, trained mostly in Munich, who "related to the Venetians, the Carraccis and Cortona through Makart and Piloty."[54] The new art of the School of Rome would be a public art that expressed the spirit of its own age. Nevertheless, much like Dudits, Gerevich denied that this art had anything to do with politics. "In an aesthetic sense," he wrote, "there is no right-wing or left-wing art, there is only good and bad art, past and future."[55] He rejected the claim advanced by proponents of the "decrepit" Munich style that only the latter style could produce truly Hungarian patriotic art.

He refrained from naming them, but when Gerevich talked about living representatives of the "decrepit" Munich style, Dudits was undoubtedly one of the prominent artists he had in mind. Although supported by the same Klebelsberg who patronized Dudits, Gerevich's project catalyzed a more modern, in some ways radical style. Klebelsberg himself was old-fashioned in his tastes, a fact his critics gladly pointed out.[56] The work produced by Rome fellows was often more modern than what he would have personally liked, but he was not one to censor art simply based on style and did not let his personal preferences get in the way. The conservative modern art born from the scholarship would go on to form the visual backdrop to the radical right-wing shift in Hungarian politics in the 1930s, contradicting, yet again, the received wisdom that modern art went hand in hand with progressive politics.[57] The Székesfehérvár Ruin Garden and its mausoleum decorated by Aba-Novák and Sztehlo is a case in point.

Having belonged to the first cohort of the Rome scholarship, Aba-Novák went on to develop a new style for monumental painting that shocked even some of those who shared the ideology behind the commissions. In 1933, Aba-Novák painted murals in the church in Jászszentandrás, a village in northeastern Hungary. With its frontal, wide-eyed figures and linear compositions, the cycle drew heavily on early Christian and Byzantine art. The representation of the Last Judgment was especially evocative and disturbing.

A local Franciscan named Father Odilo agitated particularly fiercely against the frescoes.[58] He decried all figures, including those of Christ and the saints, as distorted and lacking true religious feeling. Worried that this might imperil the frescoes, local notary Tibor Futó asked the art historian János Jajczay (1892–1976), a supporter of the School of Rome, for a counter opinion. Jajczay was—according to the notary—"delighted to hear" that locals had fainted upon seeing the frescoes; this meant that they had a profound effect.[59] This was the goal—to revive the power such images had once had on medieval crowds by targeting emotions and instincts rather than the intellect.

Aba-Novák's approach was controversial: Gerevich himself was wary of it, so much so that the painter kept his designs for Jászszentandrás hidden from him until the scandal was already brewing.[60] Nevertheless—as Gerevich no doubt realized—it was here that the new official art could break most decisively with the old. Dudits's frescoes sought harmony and beauty while employing historical sources to intellectually convince viewers of their truthfulness. Aba-Novák's paintings, by contrast, dealt in shock and dissonance, persuading their beholder by overwhelming them with their monumentality. It is not too far-fetched to relate this to the changing political context; just as Dudits gave way to Aba-Novák as a favored artist for public commissions, Bethlen and Klebelsberg's consolidatory politics was replaced by the more confrontative, radical right-wing politics of the prime ministers succeeding him.

In 1932, Bethlen's government was swept away by the repercussions of the global financial crisis. Klebelsberg died of a sudden illness a few months later. The new prime minister, Gyula Gömbös (1932–1936), not only built alliances with Fascist Italy and Nazi Germany—the Italian orientation of Hungarian foreign policy had already been established under Bethlen—but openly embraced their ideology and cult of leadership. It was in this milieu, in 1936, that Aba-Novák painted the murals of the Gate of Heroes in Szeged, a spectacular vestige of the Horthy cult I discuss in the next chapter. In 1938, then, the artist received a key commission as part of the Saint Stephen jubilee, one that would bring together art, scholarship, and politics in a way fit for the late 1930s.

Excavations in Székesfehérvár

Located sixty-five kilometers to the west of Budapest, the city of Székesfehérvár has a long history. Founded in 972 by the father of the future Saint Stephen, Prince Géza, near the site of the Roman town of Gorsium, it was Stephen's favored city; after becoming king, he expanded its fortress, built a royal cathedral, and established a provostry. Székesfehérvár became a key ecclesiastical and political center. Up until the Ottoman Turkish occupation in the sixteenth century, Hungary's kings and queens were crowned here and usually buried in the cathedral, and feudal parliaments also took place in the city. Székesfehérvár continued to play an important role in the Ottoman Empire but went into decline by the time of its recapture. Old buildings, including the cathedral, were damaged in the sieges and finally torn down to make way for a new baroque city. The political center of the kingdom was now elsewhere, in Pozsony (today's Bratislava) and later in Pest. The medieval castle and cathedral were completely gone. With the rise of interest in the national past in the early nineteenth century, excavations began at the site. In 1848, this led to the discovery of the grave of King Béla III (c. 1148–1196) and his wife, Agnes of Antioch (1153–1184), the only royal tomb that had survived intact.

In the years leading up to the 1938 jubilee, the National Commission for Monuments launched a new round of excavations. Soon, however, archaeologists realized it was unlikely they would make new discoveries matching the nineteenth-century finds in significance.[61] To mark the jubilee, something spectacular was needed, but authentic remains were too scarce to allow even a partial reconstruction of the medieval building. The president of the commission, who was no other than Gerevich, strongly opposed built reconstructions if they were not based on solid facts. Hence, a decision was made to create a ruin garden that would be "more scholarly than ideological" and contain "technical, architectural surveys and imaginary reconstructions [in pictures] illuminating Saint Stephen's Basilica."[62] Nevertheless, the "ideological" element was not to be downplayed. The plan was for the garden to include a mausoleum, which would house a sarcophagus discovered in 1814 and later identified as Saint Stephen's, while bones found during the excavations would be interred in a crypt in front of the mausoleum.

In the interwar period, Hungarian archaeologists achieved many lasting results by conducting extensive excavations and adopting up-to-date international methodologies. Like elsewhere, the field was suffused with the nationalist ambitions of the time. Research on early medieval times focused on finding and describing the characteristic culture of Magyar tribes.[63] Gerevich himself was somewhat cautious in this regard, as he opposed the Turanism that sought the origins of ancient Hungarians in Central Asia and interpreted a diverse range of imagery as proof of this thesis.[64] Nevertheless, he was clear and unapologetic about the political significance of archaeology. His consistent emphasis on the Italian sources of Hungarian Romanesque art had obvious geopolitical implications at a time when Fascist Italy was Hungary's main ally as well as a potential counterbalance to German influence.[65]

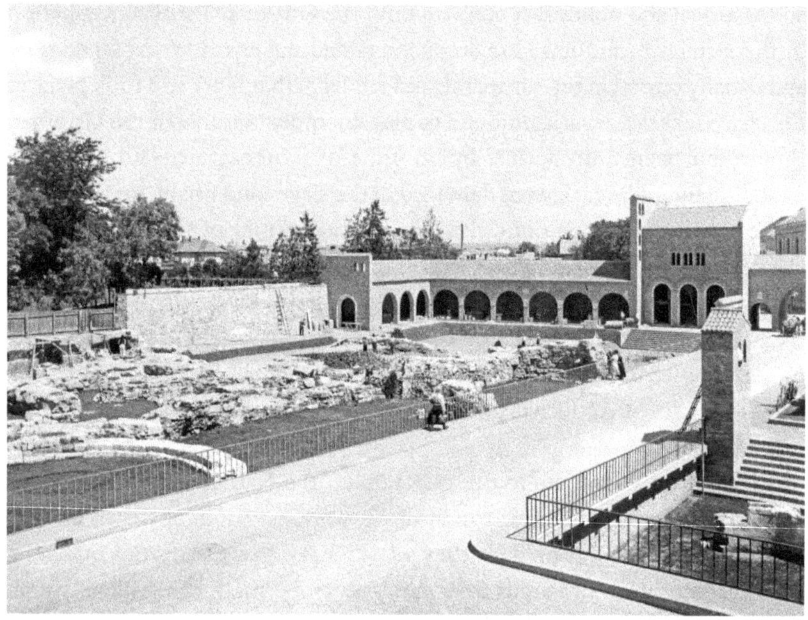

FIGURE 4.3.   The Székesfehérvár Medieval Ruin Garden in 1938 with Saint Stephen's Mausoleum in the background.
Photo: Tibor Somlai / Fortepan

Gerevich praised Mussolini as the "greatest innovator" of the time, who had "transformed the appearance of modern Rome within a few years by resurrecting the ancient."[66] By following the lead of this great figure, "whom we Hungarians always think of with a special fondness," Hungarians could not only invigorate tourism but prove the value of their culture to the world.[67] Unearthing the remains of medieval royal centers such as Székesfehérvár and comparing them to other finds from Greater Hungary offered the hope of reconstructing a unified Magyar culture that could prove—as Gerevich put it—the "supremacy" of Hungarian culture in the region.[68]

Designed by Géza Lux (1910–1945), Saint Stephen's Mausoleum comprised a taller building flanked on both sides by arched colonnades stretching along one side of the Ruin Garden (fig. 4.3).[69] The whole structure drew on Italian Romanesque architecture, especially from Lombardy and Ravenna, which was in line with how Gerevich and other scholars described the eleventh-century architecture of Saint Stephen's cathedral.[70] Analyzing finds from Székesfehérvár and other sites that they dated to the eleventh century, Gerevich and his student, Dezső Dercsényi (1910–1987), argued that these had been produced by itinerant stonemasons from Italy and local Hungarian artisans drawing inspiration from each other. The carvings followed models from Lombardy, Ravenna, and Dalmatia but also incorporated motifs from ancient Magyar culture, creating a special Hungarian Romanesque taste.[71] Dercsényi praised Lux for exhibiting the same independence when employing Italian forms in his modern building without becoming an imitator.[72] Although this comment referred to the influence of medieval Italy, Lux's building was Italian in another sense, too. Merging admiration for old and new Italy in a way that was, by then, usual in Hungarian culture, Lux's building exhibited a stern simplicity that also recalled the Italian rationalist architecture of the 1930s and hence the culture of Fascism.[73]

The details continued the idea of Italian models combined with Hungarian imagery. Sculptural decorations by Lux and the sculptor Walter Madarassy (1909–1994) employed motifs that were part of Christian iconography but also appeared on objects associated with ancient Hungarians, such as birds and stags. In reliefs by Lux, stags—totemistic animals of ancient Hungarians—drink water from a fountain beneath a cross, symbolizing how pagan Magyars converted to Christianity as Saint Stephen led them to the true source of faith.[74] Inside the mausoleum, Aba-Novák painted murals in his now-signature early Christian-modernist style. The large stained glass window in the center of the main wall, facing the entrance, was the work of Sztehlo (1897–1959). An inventive and prolific stained glass artist, Sztehlo had spent two years in Rome with her husband, the architect Bertalan Árkay, who had received the Rome Scholarship. Throughout the 1930s, she was often involved in group projects of the School of Rome.

Aba-Novák executed one of his murals, *The History of the Holy Right Hand*, for the 1938 jubilee (fig. 4.4). The other large composition, *The Mystery of the Holy Crown*, was only unveiled in 1940, alongside further scenes from the life of Saint Stephen decorating smaller spaces on the eastern and western walls of the mausoleum (fig. 4.5).[75]

The Holy Right Hand was a relic of Saint Stephen. Supposedly found naturally mummified when the king's tomb was opened for his canonization as a saint in 1083, the right hand was, in 1938, kept in the Saint Sigismundus chapel in Buda Castle. It provided occasion for one of the most propagandistic parts of the jubilee as it was festively transported across the country, a trip that eventually extended to the parts of Slovakia reannexed to Hungary in late 1938. In Aba-Novák's mural, the relic was symbolized by Stephen's monumental living right hand, represented on the lower right-hand side together with his left hand holding the orb, in a mandorla-shaped frame. The crowded

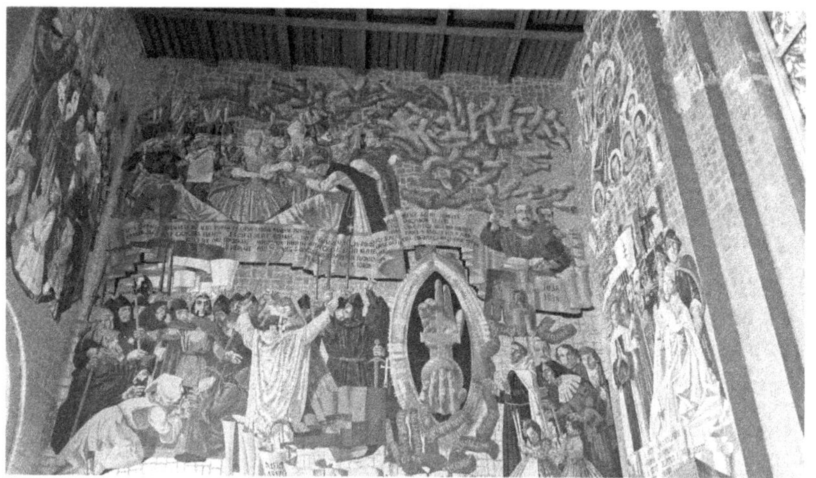

FIGURE 4.4.   Vilmos Aba-Novák, *The History of the Holy Right Hand*, 1938, reconstruction early 1990s, Székesfehérvár Ruin Garden.
Photo by author

scene to the left depicted the discovery of the relic under King Ladislas I, while the one in the top half showed Empress Maria Theresa institutionalizing the Cult of the Right Hand.

The political significance of the crown was similarly poignant. In 1000, Stephen decided to have himself crowned a Christian king, and the pope sent him a crown for the occasion. In feudal law, it was the crown, rather than the monarch, that represented the state and held the power to which Hungarian noblemen were subordinate. This idea—the "doctrine of the Holy Crown"—gained additional significance after Trianon, when the territories of Greater Hungary were referred to as the lands of the Holy Crown, thereby providing an additional argument for their organic—and divine—unity. In his mural, Aba-Novák represented the crown hovering in the center, flanked by two enormous raised swords and surrounded by personalities from Hungary's past and present (fig. 4.6). Unlike in the other mural, where the figures were composed into scenes, here they stood in rigidly arranged groups, all facing the viewer with a stern, penetrating gaze.

Before the jubilee, the minister of religion and education had announced a competition for paintings representing King Stephen. Selected entries would be exhibited at the National Museum in May 1938, and two of them—the best painting and the best study for a mural—would receive a prize.[76] The prize for best mural went to Aba-Novák, who had submitted his designs for the Székesfehérvár commission. As in many of Hóman's commissions during the jubilee, artists entering the competition were expected to draw on

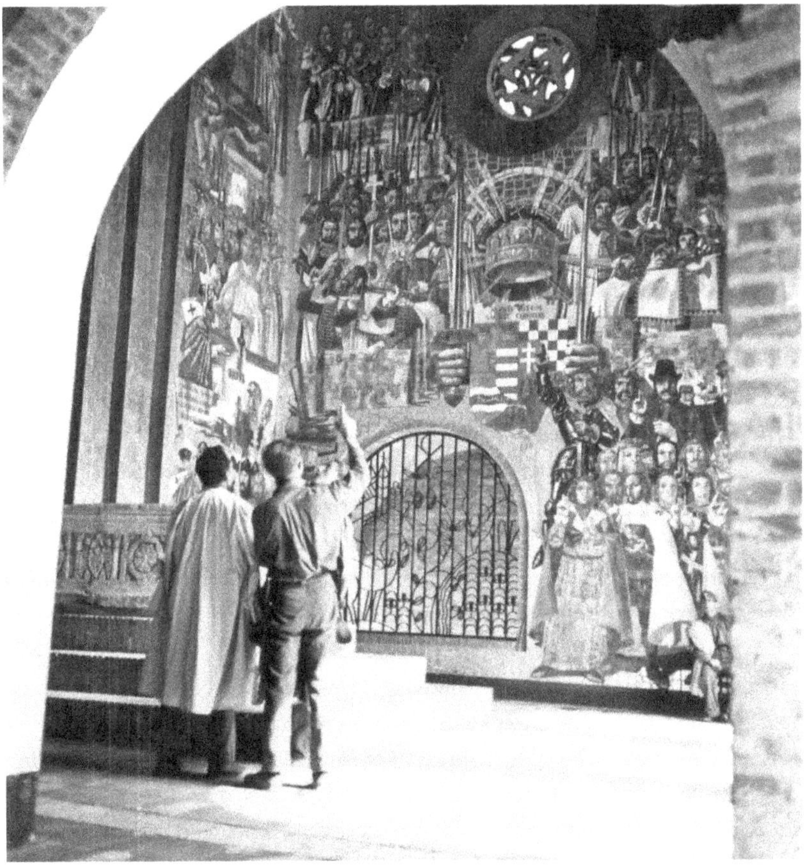

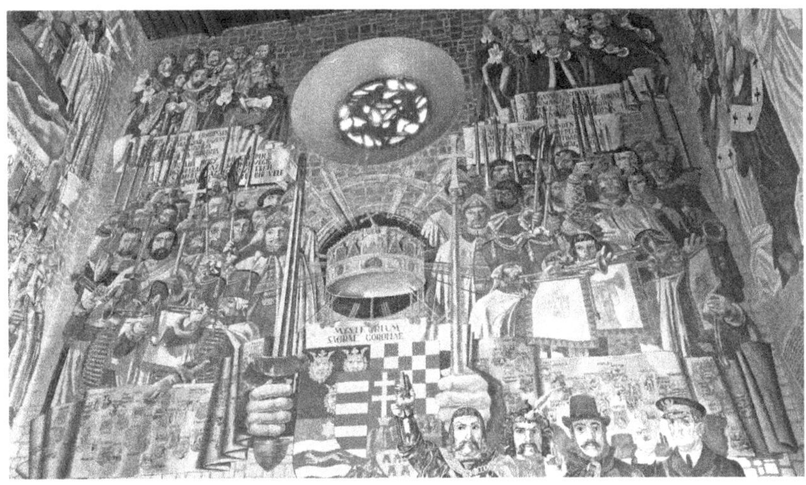

Figure 4.5.   The interior of Saint Stephen's Mausoleum, c. 1940, with Vilmos Aba-Novák's mural of *The Mystery of the Holy Crown*.
Photo: Dezső Dercsényi, *A székesfehérvári királyi bazilika* [The Royal Basilica of Székesfehérvár] (Budapest, 1943), 69

Figure 4.6.   Vilmos Aba-Novák, *The Mystery of the Holy Crown*, detail.
Photo by author

the latest results of historical research rather than the traditional and often fanciful interpretations depicted in nineteenth-century art and still cherished in cultural memory. Entries had to respect "historical, iconographical and archaeological findings of scholarly research (for instance that Saint Stephen was christened at three years of age, etc.)."[77] The requirement was, however, not absolute, as demonstrated by Aba-Novák's victory. The Hungarian Royal Crown known today—and since early modern times—is not the crown Pope Sylvester had sent to Stephen, but an object constructed one or two centuries later. This was well known to scholars in 1938; Gerevich argued that the upper part of the existing crown had originated from the pope, while the lower part had been attached later.[78] In the design competition for jubilee stamps (discussed in chap. 1), the ministry had specified that Stephen could not be depicted wearing the preserved crown and required artists to produce tentative reconstructions of his early eleventh-century crown.[79] Aba-Novák's Székesfehérvár murals eschewed this element of accuracy. In *The Mystery of the Holy Crown*, the known crown glows in the center of the composition— acceptable, as this is an allegorical image. However, Aba-Novák also depicted this crown in the scene showing Stephen's coronation. The same is true of Sztehlo's window, where the central, large standing figure of Saint Stephen wears the known Holy Crown, and the same object also features in the scene showing the pope sending the crown to Hungary. The need to represent the continuity of the doctrine of the Holy Crown overrode the requirement of historical accuracy.

In another sense, the murals adhered to "historical truth" as constructed in 1938; like the building itself, they drew on models from Italy. Dercsényi praised Aba-Novák profusely for his preference for Italy—not contemporary Italian art so much as older models, including early Christian mosaics.[80] Still, as he did with Lux, Dercsényi commended Aba-Novák for remaining original: "He developed his individual style, his extraordinary skill in characteristic representation of human figures, on his own, and it is incomparable to any foreign or Hungarian models. He lacks the phony pathos and romanticism of the Millennium. He formed his figures himself out of flesh and blood, and they differ fundamentally from the saints of the seventeenth and eighteenth centuries, which had been so distant from the Hungarian vernacular type."[81]

As the rejection of the seventeenth and eighteenth centuries suggests, the Székesfehérvár murals offer a different narrative of Hungarian history than that seen in the National Archives. In the lower right-hand corner of *The Mystery of the Holy Crown*, a group of monarchs and leaders congregate. The last figure in the top row is Horthy, and to his right stand three historical personalities represented as his predecessors (fig. 4.6). János Hunyadi, Francis II Rákóczi, and Kossuth had all been uncrowned leaders of Hungary like Horthy, with the first and the last holding the title of regent, and Rákóczi appointed as *dux* and *princeps* by the rebellious Parliament of 1705. A notable difference from the National Archives is the prominent position of Kossuth, the rebel. This narrative hearkened back to the anti-Habsburg narratives of the nineteenth century, rehabilitating Kossuth but positioning him as one who fought for the integrity of the nation rather than as a liberal reformer.

Dercsényi's claim that Aba-Novák's figures were closer to the "Hungarian vernacular type" than seventeenth- and eighteenth-century saints is notable for another reason, too; it is an example of the obsessive search for "Hungarianness" or "Hungarian spirit" in art, pervasive in interwar art history and criticism. Gerevich was one of the most high-profile art historians putting forward such arguments. His description of the fifteenth-century panel paintings he attributed to Tamás of Kolozsvár as expressing "the balanced nature, brave vitality, yet soberness of the Hungarian soul" was a prime example.[82]

In the late thirties, the "Hungarian spirit" became a cliché in art criticism. However vague, it produced a certain stylistic trend noticeable in the art of the time. As Julianna P. Szűcs has shown, critics celebrated a certain "hard Hungarianness" manifested in traits also present in Aba-Novák's work: rigid frontality and symmetry, hard contours, strong contrasts in color, crowded compositions.[83] These characteristics were regarded as similar to vernacular art, which was, in turn, seen as the vessel of true national spirit. Another visible consequence that also showed the increasing racialization of the idea of Hungarianness was the prominence of stereotypically Asian facial types. Anthropologists in interwar Hungary were keen to provide a scientific definition of the "Hungarian race," but the well-known intermingling of several ethnic groups in the historical kingdom over the centuries complicated these aims. Nevertheless, by the late 1930s, the so-called Mongoloid-Caucasian type, whose Hungarian version was referred to as the Alföld (Plains) type, emerged as the fundamental Hungarian type in racial anthropology.[84] Even if this phenotype was not commonly observed in twentieth-century Hungary, depictions of ancient Hungarians provided an opportunity to assert its existence. In the 1938 jubilee, it surfaced repeatedly, and we saw in chapter 1 how Sidló's statue of King Stephen was praised for this racialized Hungarianness. Sztehlo represented similar figures in her window; their almond-shaped eyes, prominent cheekbones, and thin mustaches all conformed to Asian stereotypes (fig. 4.7).

Sztehlo was a versatile artist who experimented with various modes of expression throughout her career. In the early thirties, she employed the geometric forms of cubism, veering toward abstraction in her compositions.

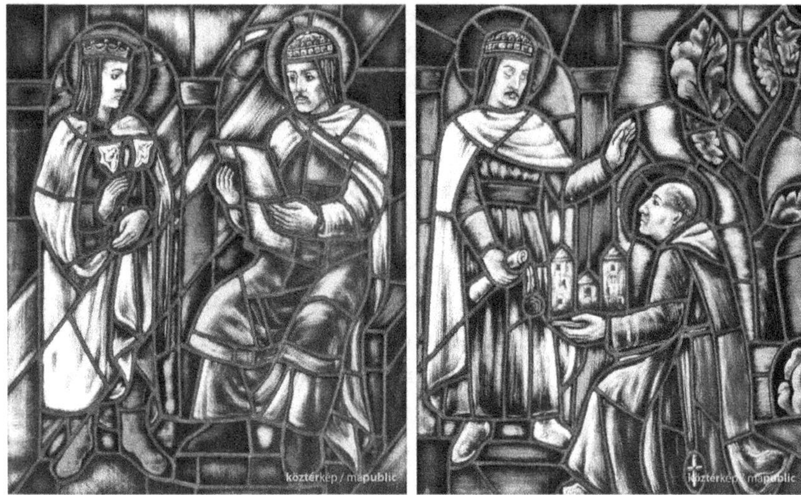

FIGURE 4.7.   Lili Sztehlo, two panels from the Saint Stephen window, 1938, reconstructed by Gábor Gonzales and Judit Fűri, 1997, Medieval Ruin Garden, Székesfehérvár.
Photo: Rolf Singer /kozterkep.hu CC BY-SA 4.0

By 1938, however, she returned to more detailed representations with more plasticity. In the Székesfehérvár window, this was necessary in order to make the ancient Hungarian faces recognizable. What remained of her earlier avant-garde experiments were the diagonal rays of light—represented with glass of a lighter color—that dissected the scenes and joined them into an encompassing abstract system. This feature of the windows may be connected to French Orphism, an avant-garde trend that emerged out of cubism but prioritized light and color and was linked to spiritualism (fig. 4.8).[85]

Sztehlo tamed her avant-garde tendencies to make her figures more realistic. Aba-Novák employed his signature unsettling style that was thought to recall the vernacular. Both were designed to be immediately legible and enthralling to the public of the Medieval Ruin Garden. A big difference between Dudits's frescoes in the Archives and Aba-Novák's in the Ruin Garden lies precisely here. The National Archives may have been intended as a pantheon, but in practice, they were visible to a select few: those who worked there, scholars who came to conduct research, and those who deliberately sought it out as a site to visit—people with a more than cursory interest in history and art. The Ruin Garden, by contrast, was inaugurated as part of a grandiose series of celebrations. It was an open space with a semi-open building—a site of pilgrimage. Aba-Novák's murals, as typical of his style, aimed to elicit awe, not intellectual pondering. In their formal language as

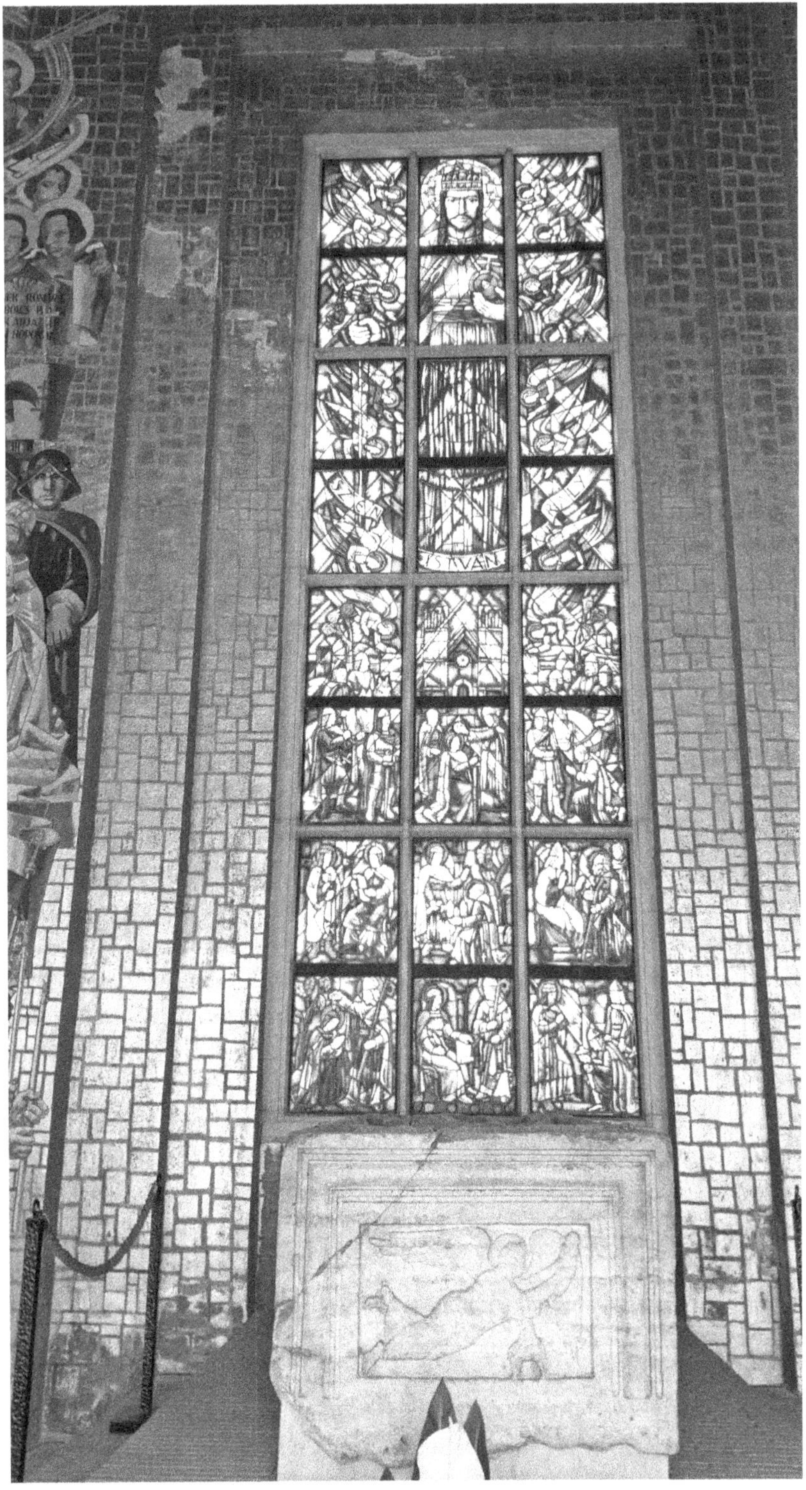

FIGURE 4.8. Lili Sztehlo's stained glass window with the Saint Stephen sarcophagus, Medieval Ruin Garden, Székesfehérvár, 2022.
Photo by author

well as the historical narrative they promoted, they lacked the lofty aristocratic refinement typical of Klebelsberg's commissions.

The differences point to a broader contrast between the two ministers of culture. His efforts to expand lower education notwithstanding, Klebelsberg was essentially an elitist whose main concern was to support excellence in higher education and improve access to universities for the middle class. Hóman, by contrast, initiated programs to guide children of the peasantry into higher education.[86] This apparently socially progressive stance was, however, tainted by the fact that it derived from an ethnicist mindset that sought to promote the Hungarian "race" in its supposed struggle against domination by other races in the country. The decidedly unrefined, rustic character of the frescoes of the Ruin Garden was one visual manifestation of this now official brand of populist nationalism.

The Illusions of Archaeology

The hypothetical Italian contacts of Hungarian art in Saint Stephen's time may have been convenient politically, but they were the fruit of serious research. Gerevich and Dercsényi supported their argument with meticulous comparisons between fragments; they used up-to-date scholarly methodologies. In 1943, Dercsényi employed such comparisons to describe an organized royal workshop consisting of Italian and Hungarian stonemasons who had supposedly worked on all the important construction projects in Saint Stephen's time.[87] Yet, the conclusions did not stand the test of time, as their fundaments were mistaken. Many carvings once believed to have been made in the early 1000s are today thought to have been produced later, which refutes the idea of sustained Italian contacts under Stephen. As one scholar wrote in 1994: "In 1943 Dezső Dercsényi constructed an eleventh century royal workshop out of stones that quietly slipped, twenty or thirty years later, into the following century."[88]

According to the principles of the National Commission for Monuments, the displays at the Ruin Garden had to be based on the results of archaeological research. At the same time, the project was part of the Saint Stephen jubilee and claimed a significance in public life that stretched beyond academia. Scholars searched for remains from Stephen's time and drew up connections that later proved to have been too convenient to be true. The murals presented a historical narrative spanning from medieval to current times and placed living personalities, most importantly Horthy, next to canonical heroes of the past. As in the National Archives, the presence of scholarship served to position the imagery of the murals not as politics but as well-established, uncontestable truth. Once viewpoints shifted, however, so did the truths.

Driven by the expectations of the jubilee year, excavations at Székesfehérvár focused heavily on the king's person and possible traces of his presence. After archaeologists discovered the fundaments of a Romanesque apse on the site, this came to be referred to as the Crypt of Saint Stephen without solid proof. Although the committee renounced fanciful reconstructions, it also planned a Romanesque rebuilding of this apse in the early stages of the project, even though, for lack of substantial original fragments, this would have been based on nothing more than general knowledge of the international Romanesque style.[89]

Although the legend of Saint Stephen compiled before his 1083 canonization described his 1038 burial in the basilica in detail, tracing the location centuries later was extremely difficult. It was only between 1970 and 1971 that the archaeologist Alán Kralovánszky (1929–1993) convincingly pinpointed where the crypt may have been, but the layout and decoration are still unknown.[90] In 1938, the newly built mausoleum was to serve as a substitute, a place to pay respect to Hungary's first king. It was to house the most significant material object contemporary scholars could connect to the king's burial: the so-called Saint Stephen sarcophagus (fig. 4.8).

The Saint Stephen sarcophagus is a marble sarcophagus probably originating from Roman times. Its decoration includes Christian motifs such as cherubs and an angel flying to heaven with a human soul depicted in the form of a baby. This imagery is the result of medieval recarving, as the old sarcophagus was recycled to be used in a new, obviously high-status burial. Found in Székesfehérvár in 1814, the sarcophagus was taken to the National Museum in Pest. When the art historian Imre Henszlmann (1813–1888) first described the sarcophagus, he was mistaken about its provenance and thought it to be Roman. Decades later, József Hampel (1849–1913) dated the object, on stylistic grounds, to the tenth or eleventh century. None of these nineteenth-century publications claimed that the sarcophagus had been King Stephen's. This conclusion was only drawn in 1930 by Elemér Varjú (1873–1945) based on the eleventh-century dating of the object, the Saint Stephen legend's description of a white sarcophagus used in the king's burial, and the assumption—suggested by nineteenth-century primary sources—that it had been unearthed from an intact layer in the Székesfehérvár basilica.[91]

The recent identification of King Stephen's sarcophagus obviously came in very handy in 1938, when scholars and authorities alike wished to celebrate a jubilee in Székesfehérvár based on solid historical facts despite few such facts having been established. This was a substantial, even spectacular, object, especially in comparison to the mostly smaller fragments that had been unearthed. The mausoleum was designed to contain the sarcophagus and highlight its importance. Unsurprisingly, Gerevich and Dercsényi sought to connect it to Italy and traced Venetian stylistic influences, as Stephen's successor, Peter I, had come from Venice.[92]

Scholars may have been politically motivated to accept the sarcophagus as Saint Stephen's, but this does not mean the claim was baseless. Varjú had employed primary sources and stylistic analysis on par with art historical methodologies of the time. His identification of the sarcophagus continued to be accepted after the demise of the Horthy regime, even though many of its premises came to be questioned over the decades. In the subsequent historiography of the sarcophagus, scholarly curiosity that never ceased to probe old claims constantly clashed with the enduring ability of such claims to linger, especially if their significance extended beyond the confines of academia.

In the 1970s, when Kralovánszky finally excavated King Stephen's crypt, it became apparent that the space he found could not have held a large stone sarcophagus, which meant that the king's original sarcophagus had to have been removed before the canonization and the construction of the new crypt.[93] In the next decades, Sándor Tóth argued on stylistic grounds that the carvings originated from the later eleventh century, not from Saint Stephen's time. He tentatively connected the recarving of the sarcophagus to the 1083 canonization rather than to the original burial of the king but implicitly questioned the identification itself by calling the object the "Székesfehérvár sarcophagus," not the sarcophagus of Saint Stephen.[94] By this time, Gerevich and Dercsényi's idea of Venetian connections had been disproven, as scholars emphasized Byzantine influences instead, which severed the connection to Stephen's successor, Peter.[95] Another blow to Varjú's hypothesis came in 2007, when Orsolya Bubryák scrutinized all available documentation on the discovery of the sarcophagus.[96] The meticulous reconstruction of the object's trajectory indicated that it had not been found within the site of the basilica. The misattribution arose because the sarcophagus was conflated with another object, a Roman tombstone that had once lain among the fundaments of the church. In the nineteenth century, this stone had been misidentified as the lid of the sarcophagus. Even though this claim had been refuted by the early twentieth century, the tombstone's original location was still projected onto the sarcophagus. All that can definitely be said about the latter is that it came into the museum from the garden of the bishop's palace, but how it had ended up there and where it had originated from are unknown. It once must have contained the body of someone of high status, and that someone may have been King Stephen, but given that the object no longer had a known connection to the basilica, there was nothing to conclusively prove this identification.

The sarcophagus now stands in the Székesfehérvár mausoleum, surrounded by Aba-Novák's murals and Sztehlo's window, just like in 1938. The murals, which had already started to decay in the 1940s, and the window had been covered up and destroyed in the 1950s, but they were restored after 1990.[97] This was when the sarcophagus, exhibited in the National Museum for decades, also returned to the site as Saint Stephen's sarcophagus. The role of the mausoleum is to shape the cultural memory of the nation, and this leaves little room for nuance. How can the complexities and uncertainties of scholarly research be made visible at sites of national memory? Inherited from the late 1930s as a time capsule containing that era's politicization of scholarship, the Székesfehérvár Medieval Ruin Garden is a perfect focus for pondering this question.

Scholarship in Changing Times

After 1945, the politicized conceptual frameworks and racialized assumptions of interwar Hungarian art history writing came under scrutiny. In 1951, when the philosopher and art historian Lajos Fülep, newly appointed as university professor and member of the Hungarian Academy of Sciences, defined new, sober tasks for Hungarian art historiography, he started out from a scathing critique of Gerevich and his peers.[98] Following Fülep's guidance, Hungarian art historians have been wary of attempts to construct narratives of "Hungarian" art before 1800 and instead mostly prefer the term *art in Hungary*. Having consistently distanced himself from official culture in the interwar period, Fülep possessed the moral authority to set out such a program, and, not being a Communist, he did so without forcing a new ideology onto his subject. More broadly, of course, historical scholarship was under severe ideological pressure after 1948. *Geistesgeschichte* became a dirty word, and its practitioners were hounded out of institutions. The connections between politics, official ideology, scholarship, and its institutional as well as conceptual frameworks became extremely fraught yet again.

Like the ocean in a drop of water, the general problems of examining culture and scholarship produced under repressive regimes are revealed in the examples of the National Archives and the Székesfehérvár Medieval Ruin Garden. It is tempting to try to separate useful institutions and good research from bad politics and controversial art or even to distinguish between worthy and disreputable features within the same project. It might feel inevitable when official ideologies produce mistaken research, as in the case of Gerevich and Dercsényi's theory of Italian contacts. Yet, it is important to keep in mind that this is not necessarily the case. Interconnected in many ways, all aspects of the official cultural establishment, whether "good" or "bad," formed part of the same greater whole. Confronting this historical experience might help with navigating the moral conundrums of the present.

CHAPTER 5

Heroes and Rebels

In 1929, the artist Gyula Derkovits (1894–1934) completed one of his most iconic works. The series of woodcuts, *1514*, narrated the peasant uprising led by Sekler nobleman György Dózsa (1470–1514) in the eponymous year (fig. 5.1).[1] The expressive, concise compositions did not shy away from depicting the desperation of the peasants nor the horrors of the retaliations that followed their defeat by the Hungarian nobility. A sympathizer of the Hungarian Communist Party (HCP), Derkovits chose not only a subject that resonated with left-wing radicals but also an art form—the narrative series of prints—often employed to express left-wing ideas in early twentieth-century Europe. Käthe Kollwitz's (1867–1945) series depicting the 1524–1525 German Peasants' War (1902–1908) and Frans Masereel's (1889–1972) "picture novels" about life in a capitalist society were direct precedents Derkovits drew on.

Hence, Derkovits affiliated himself with left-wing artistic tradition. At the same time, his work was not separate from other strands of contemporary Hungarian visual culture. Although produced in the context of the illegal Communist movement, *1514* became widely known outside of this circle when displayed at Derkovits's posthumous retrospective at the Ernst Museum in 1934. The quality of the series was recognized by many who did not share the artist's politics. The liberal *Pesti Napló* praised them as "mag-

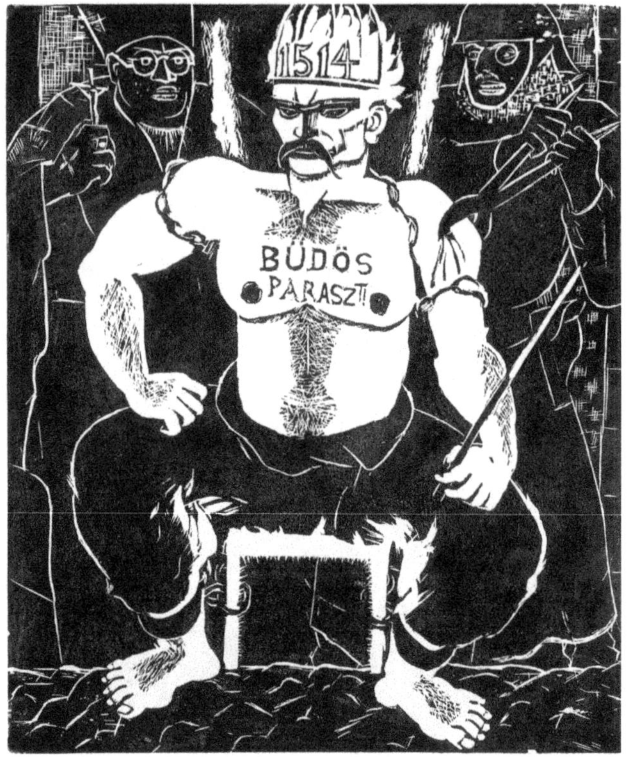

FIGURE 5.1.   Gyula Derkovits, *Dózsa on the Throne of Fire (1514 IX)*, 1928–1929, Budapest History Museum—Museum Kiscelli, Municipal Gallery, Budapest.

nificent woodcuts bursting with a robust, almost raw force."[2] More surprisingly, the extreme right-wing *Nemzeti Újság* also admired how the series represented misery "through the dreadfulness of brutal power."[3] Hungarian art history writing has often discussed left-wing art as if it had existed in its own microcosm—a historiographical perspective constructed in the years of state Socialism but not without its parallels outside the former Eastern Bloc. More recently, art historians have complicated this picture, calling attention to the complex institutional networks spanning the art world. Artists of different political persuasions exhibited together and even collaborated; the work they produced existed in a shared environment.[4] Politically antagonistic works were not necessarily different visually, and their imagery transcended political fault lines.

Dózsa was certainly no favorite of the official politics of the Horthy regime. Therefore, by centering him as a hero, *1514* questioned the official pantheon. But how stable was that official pantheon really? Certainly, the Horthy regime was keen to celebrate historical personalities, as exemplified by the Saint Emeric and Saint Stephen jubilees, by historical tableaux such as Aba-Novák's Székesfehérvár mural, or by Horthy's leadership cult, which encompassed the veneration of historical personalities presented as his prefigurations. Yet, as seen in the previous chapter, the position of many figures in the pantheon was far from secure. Different perspectives, such as pro-Habsburg versus pro-independence or Protestant versus Catholic, cohabited uneasily in official culture. The official backdrop to alternatives like *1514* was not really solid—it was a more fluid environment. Consequently, alternative ideas were not always perfectly distinct; they related to different aspects of official culture in more complex ways. This chapter examines these interactions by analyzing representations of historical personalities from the late 1920s to the early 1940s amid increasing political radicalization. Highlighting how styles and themes resonated across the artistic and political spectrum, it explores the universal appeal of the figure of the hero and how it could be used to promote different, and sometimes rebellious, interpretations of the present and past.

Heroes for All Times

Long-standing narratives that appear to be rooted in collective memory are in fact often perpetuated by institutions.[5] A striking example is the series of twenty "demonstrative images" first published by the Ministry of Religion and Education between 1913 and 1915 to aid the teaching of history in state schools. Some of the pictures were based on well-known nineteenth-century history paintings; others were new compositions. Together, they spelled out a canon of the most important events of Hungarian history, as befitted the memory politics of the late dualist state. The narrative began with the election of Árpád as leader and ended with the coronation of Emperor Franz Joseph. In between, it included scenes of Hungarian heroism (the self-sacrifice of Miklós Zrínyi fighting the Turks), strength (Matthias Corvinus capturing Vienna), and rebellion (Rákóczi elected as prince) and emphasized the indispensability of Hungarians to the Habsburgs (Rudolf Habsburg and the Hungarian King Ladislas IV triumphing in the Battle of Marchfeld, published under the title *The Hungarians Laying the Foundations of the Great Power of the Habsburgs*).[6]

A few years later, the empire fell, the great power of the Habsburgs dissolved, and Hungary was a much smaller country led by a regent. The educational images nevertheless remained available to schools, providing a mundane yet influential example of continuity between the memory politics of the dualist period and the Horthy regime.[7] The narrative drawn up by the

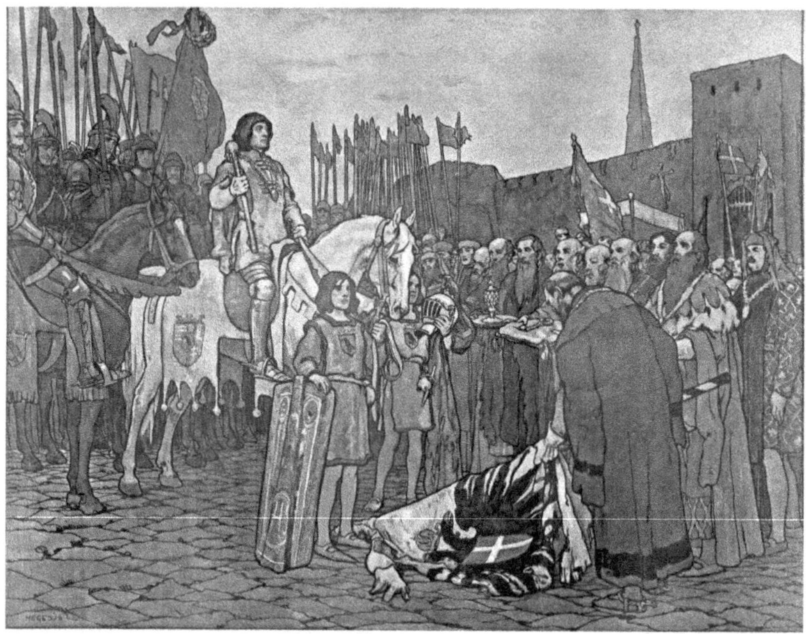

FIGURE 5.2.   Unknown lithographer after László Hegedűs, *Matthias at the Gates of Vienna*, teaching aid, 1913, Hungarian National Museum Historical Picture Gallery, inv. no. 59.1041.

images—one that accepted Habsburg rule but stressed Hungarian agency—was still valid. Moreover, the images presented not only a preferred storyline for the narration of Hungarian history but also models for how history should be visualized. The way they centered great personalities and their heroism, as well as their emphasis on great victories and defeats, helped prop up some of the more specific elements of interwar memory politics.

One of the images from 1913 seems especially ominous in the light of subsequent events. *Matthias Corvinus at the Gates of Vienna* was lithographed after a composition by László Hegedűs (1870–1911), a successful academic history painter (fig. 5.2). It showed Matthias on horseback, accepting the surrender of the burghers of Vienna. After 1919, the meanings of this image changed; the Renaissance king's white horse inevitably conjured up the image of Admiral Horthy victoriously entering Budapest. Indeed, similar representations of Matthias were integral to Horthy's self-representation. As part of the refurbishment of the Buda Royal Palace in the early 1900s, the veteran history painter Gyula Benczúr (1844–1920) had been commissioned to create two paintings depicting Matthias, *Matthias's Triumphal Procession into Buda* and *Matthias Welcoming a Delegation from the Pope*, for the Hunyadi Room of the palace, planned since 1904. By the time Benczúr completed the paintings in 1920, the context had changed. That year, the palace became Horthy's residence, and the Hunyadi Room came to visualize his identification with the Hunyadi family. The regime's highest award, the so-called Corvin Chain, was festively presented in this room.[8] In this context, the procession of the triumphant fifteenth-century king riding a white horse, painted by Benczúr in luscious colors and with neobaroque pomp, now served to recall Horthy's entrance into Budapest.[9] In chapter 1, I emphasized the relative lack of historicist spectacle in Horthy's procession. Nevertheless, the core symbol—the hero on horseback—was staged according to an existing iconographic tradition in Hungarian representative history painting. Viewers could imagine the pomp, and hence the scene's momentous significance, by drawing on their memories from school.

Such historical parallels were abundant in Horthy's leadership cult. Matthias and his father, János Hunyadi, a previous regent of Hungary, were two of his multiple prefigurations. Another was, of course, Árpád, whose election also featured in the series of teaching aids. The image of Árpád held up on a shield by his electors, the leaders of the seven Hungarian tribes, had been created by Mihály Kovács (1819–1892) in 1854 and oft reproduced in the following decades. Horthy was keen to identify with Árpád, the strong leader elected by representatives of the nation according to the ancient constitution. The frameworks for his cult were in place well before 1919, constructed by decades of official memory politics and ready to use.

While the twenty-piece series of teaching aids remained the same throughout our period, these were not the only historical images available in schools. A new addition discussed in chapter 1 was Andor Dudits's *Oath in the Vérmező* (fig. 1.3). The Ministry of Religion and Education ordered schools to acquire this image by raising funds for the Archduke Joseph Sanatorium Association. Depicting a heroic figure who stands out from the crowd and conceptualizing its subject as a key event in Hungarian history, the picture shared many characteristics with the canonical series. The crowd of flags on the left-hand side is similar to Hegedűs's *Matthias Corvinus*, and the basic composition of one man facing a crowd characterizes several of the demonstrative images. This is not to say that Dudits deliberately based his painting on this series of teaching aids; rather, it highlights a trend of representing authority—and deference to it—in Hungarian history painting that lived on in the self-representation of the Horthy regime, its organic revival assured by the fact that it was already well disseminated in society.

In addition to seeing the teaching aids, which would probably have been displayed on classroom walls, schoolchildren could also encounter images of history in their textbooks. Pál Madai's *History of Hungary*, one of the most widely used books, illustrated many events with reproductions of nineteenth-century history paintings.[10] This changed in the sections about the nineteenth century, which were mostly illustrated with portraits of the great men of the time, from István Széchenyi and the revolutionaries of 1848 to Ferenc Deák, architect of the Compromise. From the late nineteenth century to the present time, the book did not contain any illustrations, except for one on the penultimate page: a photograph of Horthy in his decorated uniform, looking sternly at the schoolchild about to close the book. The illustrative material reflects that interpretations of national history produced in the nineteenth century were still crucial in the interwar period. It also shows that mainstream historical narratives promoted a history of great personalities—of venerable heroes. Finally, it demonstrates that this view of history was part and parcel with Horthy's leadership cult.

The narration of history through great personalities was, of course, not unique to Hungary. Horthy's leadership cult, too, was one of many similar cults in Europe. With the widening of political participation, the emergence of mass politics, and the decline of monarchies, political leaders appealed to the broader electorate through a new form of representation.[11] In Poland, Józef Piłsudski (1867–1935) was celebrated as a great military commander and savior of the nation much like Horthy.[12] In Austria, the Austro-Fascist dictator Engelbert Dollfuß (1892–1934) was venerated after his assassination as a saintly figure, which included his identification with Saint Engelbert (1185/1186–1227), medieval bishop of Cologne.[13] Even in Czechoslovakia, Tomáš Garrigue Masaryk (1850–1937) was likened to historical figures such as the fifteenth-century religious reformer Jan Hus in the cult that developed around him despite the fact that he was a democratic rather than authoritarian leader.[14] It was not unique to the Horthy regime to create a pantheon of historical figures who served as models and predecessors. Something that was notable, however, was the almost unsurmountable rift within the regime's memory politics, which made the pantheon surprisingly mutable.

The Problem with Revolutions

The Habsburg past was remembered in the interwar period in two antagonistic ways, both of which influenced official memory politics but were still impossible to reconcile. Promoted by Kuno Klebelsberg, Gyula Szekfű's pro-Habsburg narrative of Hungarian history had been influential in official representation from the regime's early days. At the same time, the pro-independence narrative of the late nineteenth century, which Szekfű had originally rebelled against, lived on. Szekfű had rejected the legacy of 1848ers such as

Lajos Kossuth, but the regime's memory politics had to encompass their veneration so as not to alienate large sections of society. The Horthy cult incorporated Kossuth by turning him into one of Horthy's prefigurations, but his status in the pantheon was not rock solid. In chapter 4, two representative cycles of murals exemplified two different approaches to his memory.

These two strands of remembrance strongly correlated with religion: the pro-independence narrative was seen as Protestant, while the one more accommodating to the (Catholic) Habsburgs was associated with Catholics. This split was well observable in school textbooks. Calvinist educational institutions favored Madai's *History of Hungary* for its uncompromising anti-Habsburg stance and emphasis on the persecution of Protestants under imperial rule. The Calvinist Universal Convention commissioned a group of Calvinist historians to evaluate the suitability of different textbooks for their schools, and some of the other books did not meet these standards. For instance, the series written by the outstanding cultural historian Sándor Domanovszky (1877–1955), recommended by Klebelsberg's ministry, was rejected because of its reconciliatory tone in discussing conflicts between Hungary and the imperial government.[15]

The legacy of 1848 was problematic for a further reason, too. In a regime that self-defined as counterrevolutionary, describing any revolution in positive terms threatened to open the floodgates toward a more positive evaluation of 1918–1919. Children, especially, had to be protected from such ideas, which is why the history textbooks of the era rarely used the word *revolution* to describe 1848. Instead, they emphasized events that symbolized Hungarian constitutionality, such as the April Laws of 1848, and devoted minimal space to what happened in the streets of Budapest.[16] If 1848 threatened to raise the specter of 1919, then the revolutionary past of "sinful" Budapest was the most sensitive issue of all. Its reminders had to be appropriated carefully, as in Freedom Square, where the memory of 1848 was subsumed into the commemoration of Trianon.

It was in this ideological context that the government erected a new memorial to Kossuth in Budapest. The idea had been around since 1894, the year of Kossuth's death, when fundraising for the project began. János Horvay (1873–1944) won the design competition in 1906 and set to work in 1911. The war interrupted the plans, and it was only in 1927 that the monument was finally unveiled next to the Parliament building. In 1898, when the building was under construction, the square it stood on had been christened Parliament Square. This was renamed Lajos Kossuth Square when the monument was unveiled.

Horvay's sculptural group depicted Kossuth with other members of the revolutionary government (fig. 5.3). Lacking compositional focus, it was

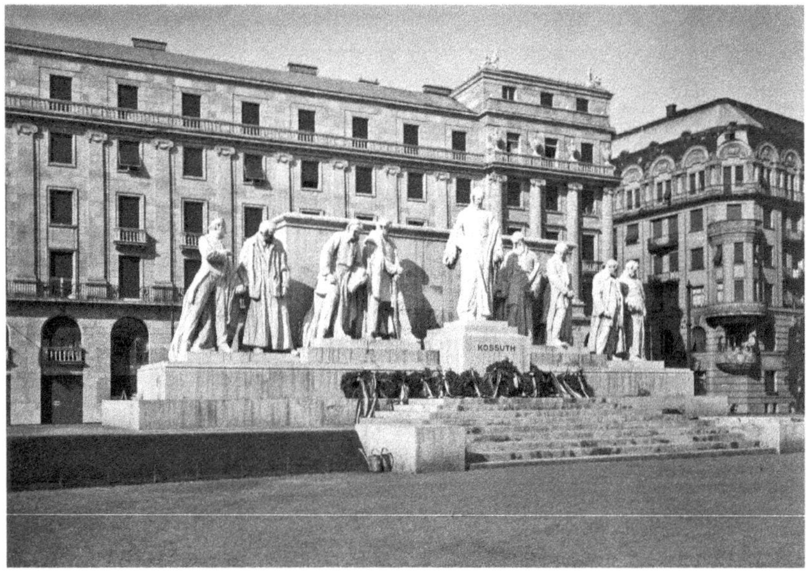

FIGURE 5.3.   János Horvay, Lajos Kossuth monument, 1911–1927, Budapest, Kossuth Square.
Photo from 1937, Új Nemzedék daily / Fortepan

criticized as clumsy from the start. In its awkwardness, however, it was a perfect encapsulation of the regime's conflicted relationship to 1848, even though Horvay had designed it long before the regime's inception. By then, Horvay was a true specialist in Kossuth statues, having created around twenty likenesses of the revolutionary leader between 1902 and 1908. Some of these depicted Kossuth giving a rousing speech, but the version designed for Parliament Square lacked such revolutionary fervor. It represented Kossuth as a brooding intellectual, with a cape thrown over his Hungarian dress for a more classical impression. The monument showed him as minister of finance—his first role in the revolutionary government, before he became regent and hence primary leader during the War of Independence. Nevertheless, he stood in the center, with other members of the government lined up on both his sides. This created an iconographical absurdity, as the prime minister, Lajos Batthyány, appeared in a subordinate position to him. All figures seemed melancholy, hanging their heads and turning inward instead of interacting with each other or facing the viewer.

As one of the few regents of Hungary, Kossuth could easily be fashioned as a prefiguration of Horthy. One of the representative rooms in the Parliament building was redecorated in 1929 for Horthy's ten-year anniversary with scenes showing Hungary's regents: Hunyadi defeating the Turks at Belgrade, Kossuth giving a speech to the 1848 Parliament, and Horthy opening the Parliament of 1920.[17] In Kossuth Square, however, this allusion was missing. Instead of presenting Kossuth as an inspiring leader, Horvay showed him as a tragic hero. In 1923, he explained that in the postwar years, his main artistic concern was to represent the passing of time, loss, and death. "The Kossuth statue is, in effect, a statue of the great graveyard we call Hungary; it was so close to my heart because it allowed me to express the suffering and great sorrow of the Hungarian."[18] Reiterating the tragic narrative of Hungarian history, Horvay did not have to explicitly mention Trianon; it was implicit in his assertion that the "sorrow of the Hungarian" was ongoing.

Like a curious time capsule, Horvay's design for the Kossuth statue arrived in Horthy's Hungary from prewar times and assumed new meanings fit for the regime's memory politics. The tragic Kossuth, rather than Kossuth the revolutionary, was suited to how the regime aimed to reshape the memory of 1848. The reshaping was not universally influential, however. Horvay's approach was widely critiqued, and not just by the regime's detractors. Responding to those who wished to see the orator Kossuth, the sculptor resorted to citing technical concerns: marble "does not permit great gestures," making it impossible for him to carve a raised arm or extended foot.[19]

The original design competition had located the sculptural group in the middle of the square, in front of the Parliament building. On the advice of a committee led by State Secretary K. Róbert Kertész, it was ultimately moved to the side of the square. Instead of the Parliament building, a nineteenth-century apartment block now served as its backdrop. Horvay was, as contemporary reports attest, rather dismayed, but the demotion of the statue happened anyway.[20] The reasons are not quite clear. According to these reports, some thought the sculpture would ruin the view of the Parliament. The flaws of the composition may also have been the reason, judging from the fact that one of the plans for modification, supported by Kertész, recommended splitting up the sculptural group and placing the figures on opposite sides of the building. Despite all the ado, the monument was finally unveiled festively, demonstrating that the Horthy regime still honored Kossuth. Nevertheless, the history of the sculpture, from the very fact that it was a commitment inherited from prewar times to its controversial iconography and the indecisiveness over its final location, reflects the hesitation around the memory of 1848 and its central hero.

The Horthy regime's ambivalence about the revolutionary heritage of the nineteenth century was characteristic but not unique. In Italy, the memory of Giuseppe Garibaldi (1807–1882) and his movement presented similar difficulties. Claudio Fogu has described how the cult of Garibaldi and the Risorgimento had been completely subsumed into Fascist self-representation, which held up Garibaldi's Redshirts as precedents to the Blackshirts, with Mussolini himself keeping the 1932 Garibaldi anniversary under tight control so that the memory of the nineteenth-century hero could never overshadow the celebration of the Fascist present.[21] Given that both regimes defined themselves in opposition to nineteenth-century liberalism, handling the latter's legacy in memory politics was crucial. As a totalitarian leader, however, Mussolini held stronger control over the public sphere than Horthy and the Hungarian political elite did. In Hungary, the regime had to allow for different interpretations to hold together the coalition of social groups its power depended on. This made it impossible to shape the past into a monolith. There was not just one pantheon, but several, and they largely contained the same historical figures but still interpreted or ranked them in different ways. If opponents of the regime wished to disrupt strategies of memorialization, it was precisely these rifts that they needed to target.

The 1514 Uprising and Its Remembrance

The 1514 uprising was a seminal event in the history of Hungarian feudalism.[22] It all began with a call to a crusade that gathered peasants in the field of Rákos, in present Budapest. Kept on meager supplies, the crowd soon turned against the nobles on whose land they toiled and who now failed to supply the army with provisions. The Transylvanian nobleman Dózsa—who had been appointed leader of the crusaders—took the helm of the peasant insurgency. Following a series of successful sieges and battles, the rebels were finally defeated at Temesvár (now Timișoara, Romania). Dózsa suffered a horrible punishment: he was burned alive on a throne set aflame, and his flesh was fed to his soldiers. A collection of new laws, the so-called *Tripartitum* compiled by István Werbőczy (1458–1541), radically curtailed the rights of peasants and solidified the rigid institution of serfdom until the nineteenth century.

The memory of the 1514 uprising constituted one of many rifts in Hungarian history writing, memory politics, and popular understanding. Madai's textbook described the uprising as righteous, given the exploitation of peasants by the nobility. It emphasized the cruelty of the retaliations as well as the unjust, oppressive measures codified in Werbőczy's *Tripartitum*.[23] Domanovszky, author of the textbook rejected by Calvinist schools for its Habsburg-friendly stance, promoted a different view. In *The Cultural History of Hungary*, which he edited in the 1930s, the relevant essay (written by Domanovszky's son, György Domanovszky [1909–1983]) argued that the *Tripartitum* was not a product of revenge but of long-term historical developments and that the Hungarian nobility did not universally mistreat peasants.[24]

The Dózsa uprising had always formed a controversial chapter in Hungarian history. In the early nineteenth century, historians described it as a violent rebellion against the natural order. In 1847, the writer and liberal politician József Eötvös (1813–1871) published a novel, *Hungary in 1514*, that presented a more nuanced picture and described the desperate situation of serfs while not condoning the violence of the uprising. This improved the image of the event, but Dózsa largely remained a negative character in nineteenth-century cultural memory. The exceptions were maverick eternal 1848ers and left-wing sympathizers like the artist Viktor Madarász (1830–1917), who painted several pictures of the uprising and its leader that would never be exhibited in his lifetime. The official view was summed up by Madarász's daughter, Adeline (1871–1962), who recalled that her teachers had called Dózsa's army a raggle-taggle assembly of crooks and robbers.[25] By the interwar period, alternative viewpoints emerged in education, as demonstrated by Madai's textbook. Nevertheless, comprehensive surveys of Hungarian history still treated the uprising as a small episode rather than as a cornerstone. To left-wingers such as the sociologist Róbert Braun, its significance was downplayed.[26]

Because it was little discussed in official narratives, the Dózsa uprising lent itself as an anchor point for left-wing counternarratives of history. From the late nineteenth century, Hungarian Social Democrats and Communists had included it in publications promoting their concepts of the historical past.[27] Dózsa was part of the left-wing pantheon of historical heroes—his bust had appeared in the 1 May decorations of the Hungarian Soviet Republic—even though that pantheon was largely an internationalist one. Unlike many other Hungarian national heroes, Dózsa had not been previously used as a symbol by other political actors. As a rebel and hero, he offered a point of identification for those who sought to subvert the system. The real ingenuity of the choice, however, lay in the fact that it was not completely alien to official narratives; rather, it filled a gap and made a forceful claim where those narratives tended to be ambivalent. It offered a clear alternative for people disillusioned with the state's trepidation over heroes of independence and rebellion.

Derkovits's *1514* was a series of woodcuts created on a commission from the illegal HCP, but the specific circumstances are unclear. The only known account by a contemporary witness can be found in the memoirs of Derkovits's wife, Viktória Derkovits, published in 1955.[28] A recent monograph questioned the truthfulness of this account, suggesting that Viktória made up a story about the couple's involvement in the Communist movement in order to construct a narrative fit for the 1950s.[29] Subsequent research, however, unearthed sources that supported Viktória's claims.[30] I have explained elsewhere why I believe Viktória's account can overall be trusted, despite the undoubtedly complicated time of its publication.[31] What she revealed about *1514* fits perfectly with other contemporaneous events in the illegal party. In the following, I analyze how *1514* encapsulated debates about the party's strategy and visualized these through the lens of memory politics.

Derkovits was born in the Western Hungarian town of Szombathely on 13 April 1894.[32] His father was a cabinetmaker, and in 1910, the young Gyula started training as his apprentice. In 1914, he was drafted and sent to war. Following a serious injury, he was declared unfit for military service in 1915. Living with his brother Jenő in Budapest, he worked as a cabinetmaker and studied drawing at an independent art school. Derkovits sympathized with the Communist movement and the Soviet Republic, but his involvement did not go further, and he did not face any repercussions after the counterrevolution. His brother, who had been more active politically, emigrated to Vienna with many of his comrades.

On 18 April 1920, Derkovits married Viktória. He exhibited his pictures regularly and gained paid commissions as an artist. Nevertheless, the couple struggled financially, and in May 1923, they were evicted from their Budapest flat. They subsequently spent three years with Jenő in Vienna, and Derkovits became familiar with the Austrian art world. After returning to Budapest in January 1926, Derkovits continued to show his works at various venues. Having built connections with the illegal HCP (Kommunisták Magyarországi Pártja, KMP—literally Party of Communists in Hungary) in Vienna, the couple moved into a flat paid for by the party, which used it for secret meetings. This arrangement, however, did not last long, and in August 1931, they were evicted again due to rent arrears. Their living situation became increasingly precarious. Derkovits's already fragile health deteriorated rapidly. He died of heart failure on 18 June 1934, at the age of forty.

Although Derkovits struggled to make a living from his art, this was at least partly due to his uncompromising personality. Many contemporaries regarded him highly as an artist. Several retrospective exhibitions were held in his memory in the 1930s, and the critical reception of his art was very positive. Although this chapter focuses on his woodcuts, Derkovits was primarily a painter. Sometimes satirical, sometimes tragic, his pictures critiqued bourgeois society and highlighted the misery of the urban proletariat. A modernist through and through, Derkovits treated the pictorial plane as a flat surface and the composition as a construction of the artistic intellect. Scholarship has described some of his paintings as montage-like "picture-essays" because they bring together a variety of reality-inspired yet symbolic motifs that make up the political-social-artistic message of the composition.[33]

Writing about *1514* in 1955, Derkovits's widow stated that the idea originated from the "Vienna comrades"—that is, the Vienna-based group of Hungarian Communist émigrés with whom the Derkovitses had come into contact through the artist's brother.[34] Known as the "Landler faction" after its central figure, Jenő Landler (1875–1928), this group included the philosopher György (Georg) Lukács (1885–1971) and József Révai (1898–1959), who was to become the much-feared minister of culture in the Stalinist early 1950s.[35] It is accepted as a fact that the subject matter of *1514* was suggested to Derkovits by someone from this circle, but the identity of that person is debated.[36] Nevertheless, although Viktória did not connect the original inspiration to a specific person, she related how a number of comrades, among them Révai, perused the finished prints with satisfaction at Christmas 1929.[37] According to Viktória, in January 1930, Lukács informed them that the party would soon pay for the first portfolio of the series.[38] In a much later interview, she also identified Lukács as the person who had first communicated the party commission to Derkovits.[39]

The original purpose of the prints is obscure. According to Viktória, the commission concerned postcard-sized sheets, which would have been cheaper and easier to distribute. This suggests the woodcuts were intended as agitative material. However, Derkovits then came across eleven large pearwood panels in a shop and decided to use them instead.[40] The sheets became larger and more expensive, but this does not seem to have been a problem for the party.

Viktória claimed that the woodcuts were first distributed in Vienna.[41] According to a contemporary newspaper, they were sold in the Ottó Bookshop in Bratislava, Czechoslovakia (formerly Pozsony, Hungary), in 1930.[42] In 1934, they were displayed at the memorial exhibition organized at the Ernst Museum in Budapest—a venue not associated with the Communist Party. Finally, in 1936, the prints were published in a smaller format as an album by the periodical *Gondolat* (*Thought*), a legal publication of the illegal Communist Party. The publication was initiated and overseen by Viktória, and the images were accompanied by forewords by the left-wing art critics György Bálint (1906–1943) and Ernő Kállai.[43] They described Derkovits as a painter of the poor and downtrodden who had intended the prints for "the people." Deriving the subject matter of the series from Derkovits's personal credo, rather than from the agitative activities of the party and a clear Communist conviction, softened the political message. This did not necessarily mean, however, that the prints no longer had an agitative purpose. Indeed, in the same year and a year later, the woodcuts were sold with great success at the June outdoor fêtes organized for workers by the Social

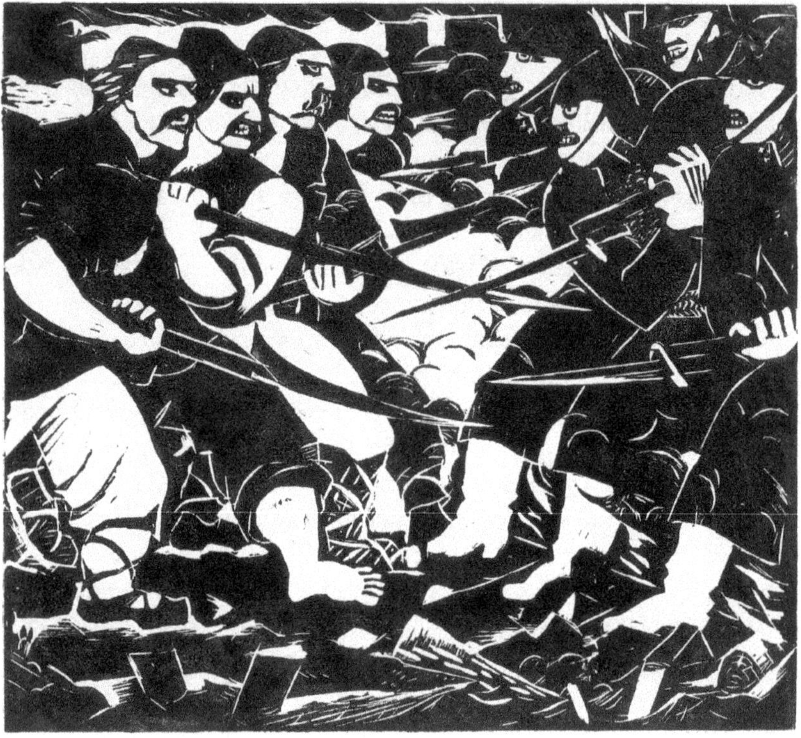

FIGURE 5.4.   Gyula Derkovits, *Clash (1514 VI)*, 1928–1929, Budapest History Museum—Museum Kiscelli, Municipal Gallery, Budapest.

Democratic Party, where the original printing plates to *1514* were eventually confiscated by the police.[44]

Derkovits's series consists of eleven prints narrating the story from the assembly at Rákos to Dózsa's death and the ensuing oppression symbolized by Werbőczy. The woodcuts present the sixteenth-century peasant revolt as analogous to the situation of the twentieth-century proletariat, conveying this message through anachronisms: in Sheet VI, *Clash*, the peasants face twentieth-century gendarmes (fig. 5.4), and in Sheet IX, *Dózsa on the Throne of Fire*, a bishop wearing modern spectacles oversees the peasant leader's torture (fig. 5.1).

The Marxist view of history as a continuous class struggle is reflected here. Friedrich Engels had similarly compared the 1524–1525 German Peasants' War to the revolutions of his own time: "Three centuries have passed and many a thing has changed; still the Peasant War is not so impossibly far removed from our present struggle, and the opponents who have to be fought are essentially the same. We shall see the classes and fractions of classes which everywhere betrayed 1848 and 1849 in the role of traitors, though on a lower level of development, already in 1525."[45]

In visual culture, the most emblematic depiction of the German Peasants' War as a prefiguration of modern struggles had been created between 1902 and 1908 by Kollwitz in her series of etchings *Peasant War*. Like many other artists in Central Europe, Derkovits was a great admirer of Kollwitz's art.[46] This is obvious in *1514*, too, down to the specific choice of some of the scenes (e.g., *Sharpening the Scythe*). At the same time, Derkovits opted for the technique of the woodcut instead of the etching. He employed a formal language of strong, simple black lines, more reminiscent of the expressionist woodcuts of the Belgian Masereel, also hugely influential in European interwar printmaking.[47] In these respects, Derkovits connected to international models; in other ways, however, his work was tightly rooted in a very specific Hungarian context.

The Hungarian Communist Party, Trianon, and Derkovits's *1514*

The year Derkovits completed *1514* was a momentous one in the history of the HCP. Tensions bubbling under the surface for years came to a head with decisive consequences. If the woodcuts were produced in this environment, they also reflect the issues and conflicts driving the events.

The HCP was founded on 24 November 1918. In March 1919, it merged with the Hungarian Social Democratic Party, and on 21 March, it declared the Hungarian Soviet Republic. After the latter's collapse, most of the party's prominent personalities left the country. Some, like the leader of the Soviet Republic, Béla Kun, went to the Soviet Union; others settled elsewhere in Europe. Personal rivalries and disagreements over strategy led to bitter infighting between different factions. The most important division lay between Kun's Moscow group and the Vienna group headed by Landler. While Landler focused on slowly developing a strong, victorious Communist movement in Hungary, Kun sought to rapidly enforce decisions made in Moscow, regardless of the effect on the actual Hungarian situation.[48]

In the late 1920s, the party started planning a congress, and in September 1928, Lukács was tasked with drafting a strategic document as part of the preparations. The resulting text, known as the *Blum Theses* (*Blum* was Lukács's conspiratorial pseudonym), summed up the antidogmatic realpolitik of the Landler faction by providing a detailed account of the Hungarian political situation and proposing strategies for navigating it.[49] The essay stirred up controversy within the party, sparking a series of events leading to Lukács's eventual withdrawal from political action. Instead of an immediate "proletarian dictatorship," the *Theses* argued for an intermediate "democratic dictatorship" better suited to the Hungarian circumstances. To Lukács, retaining democratic principles such as free speech or the freedom of assembly were crucial in opposing the Bethlen government. Moreover, to counter the government's irredentist agitation, Lukács proposed that the party take an antirevisionist stance by employing the slogans "Down with territorial integrity! Down with the revisionist swindle!"[50] The Communist International (Comintern) rejected the *Blum Theses* as opportunism and instructed the HCP to practice self-criticism. The congress had to be delayed several times, and when it finally happened in 1930, members of the Vienna faction, who had formed the Committee of Foreign Affairs of the HCP, faced severe ostracization and had to publicly denounce their previous views.[51] The clear winner was Kun, who presided victoriously over the congress, having decisively humiliated his rivals.

The interwar HCP operated underground, employing extensive conspiratorial safety measures. Due to this, as well as potential manipulation of the archives in the next decades, it is impossible to build up a complete picture of their activities from surviving primary sources. Nevertheless, with this in mind and despite a degree of uncertainty, the 1930 congress can be reconstructed relatively well from a large cache of drafts, minutes, and other documents held at the Institute of Political History in Budapest.[52] My examination of this material did not reveal any references to Derkovits or *1514*. In the following, I argue that the prints were produced in close connection to what was happening within the party, but I cannot support this claim with explicit direct primary sources. Nevertheless, I believe that the correspondences are too uncanny to be accidental. The lack of evidence can plausibly result from the inconvenient nature of the events evoked by the prints—events not of 1514, but of 1929.

The first clue leading me toward this interpretation was Sheet V, *Dózsa on the Bastion*, which exhibits a surprising resemblance to irredentist imagery (fig. 5.5). The woodcut shows Dózsa victoriously holding up a flag with the names of ten localities where the peasants had triumphed in battle. Of the ten places, only two still lay in Hungary in Derkovits's time. The rest had been awarded to neighboring countries: Csanád (Cenadu Vechi), Arad (Arad), Zádorlak (Zădăreni), Világos (Șiria), Solymos (Șoimoș), and Lippa (Lipova) to Romania; Csála (Чалма / Čalma) and Becse (Бечеј / Bečej) to the Kingdom of Serbs, Croats, and Slovenes. Treating place names as icons of anti-Trianon sentiment was a usual device in irredentism; an example was the practice of naming streets after locations outside the new borders (see

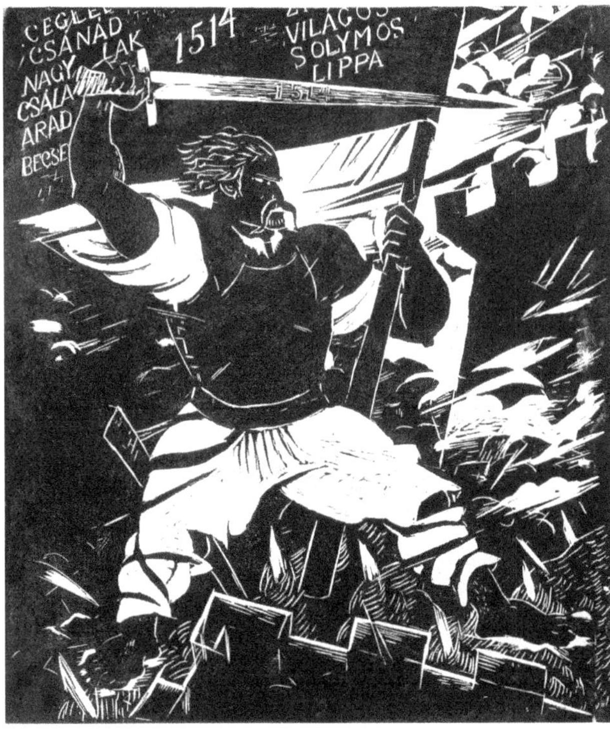

FIGURE 5.5.   Gyula Derkovits, *Dózsa on the Bastion (1514 V)*, 1928–1929, Budapest History Museum—Museum Kiscelli, Municipal Gallery, Budapest.

chap. 2). Moreover, Derkovits's emphasis on *where* the events of the uprising had taken place, on the spatiality of a historical narrative meandering across the former territory of Hungary, is a notable manifestation of irredentist spacetime. In 1929–1930, when irredentist activism was reaching new heights, it was impossible for a Hungarian viewer to see this image and not think of Trianon.

As mentioned earlier, Trianon was one of the contentious issues that led the Comintern to denounce Lukács's *Blum Theses*. The official view of the Comintern, formulated at its Second World Congress in 1920, was that the Versailles peace treaties were the products of imperialist violence and needed to be shattered.[53] To members of the practically minded Landler faction, however, this meant that the HCP would have to agree with official irredentist rhetoric and support one of the government's most dangerous tools in moving Hungarian society to the right. Hence, in July 1927, an editorial in *Új Március (New March)*, the HCP's periodical, proclaimed that the revision of Trianon and the reestablishment of Hungary's "thousand-year-old" borders were imperialist slogans employed with the purpose of inciting a war against the Soviet Union.[54] To counter it, Hungary's revolutionary workers had to connect the goal of defending the Soviet Union with anti-Trianon aims. Lukács completed the *Blum Theses* in January 1929. By spring, Révai went even further, arguing that, in the current political and social situation, the revision of Trianon served the interests of the ruling classes and consequently had to be dropped by Communists as a political aim.[55] In May 1929, the party distributed pamphlets with the slogan "Down with revisionism!," probably on Révai's initiative.[56]

Upon the Comintern's denunciation of the *Blum Theses* and Révai's editorial, Révai did a U-turn and in autumn 1929 published a new article on revisionism.[57] Refuting his own previous arguments, he now held that the party should explain to workers that it was possible to fight jointly against imperialism and Trianon. There was a difference between the imperialist revisionism of the ruling classes and the justified demands of the working class, because the latter stemmed from their opposition to international imperialism. Reading between the lines, we can see Révai's real reasoning: he assumed that the working class was overwhelmingly against Trianon, and consequently believed that dismissing these views would be politically disadvantageous.

On Christmas 1929, a few months after the publication of Révai's self-critical article, he and other comrades were approvingly scrutinizing the finished woodcuts in Derkovits's home. By then, the U-turn was complete. Did the allusions to revisionism in the images serve as visual proof that the problematic slogan "Down with revisionism!" had now been abandoned? We have no way of knowing for certain. It is, however, striking how the series encapsulated the Comintern's official view that the tension created by the peace treaties should be resolved by achieving national self-determination within a Central European federation, brought about by the triumph of fraternal Communist movements cooperating internationally. The Dózsa uprising was a pertinent symbol; the majority of Dózsa's rebels had been non-Hungarian speakers. The events of 1514 provided a model for a workers' revolution stretching across borders. Derkovits's images acknowledged the grief Hungarian workers felt over Trianon but identified the ruling classes as the real enemy and proposed solidarity as a way out of their dire situation.

Interpreted in this way, the series reconciles the Landler faction's focus on the specific Hungarian situation with the Comintern's doctrines. There was, however, another aspect of the prints that broached a sensitive subject. Earlier, I wrote that *1514* was a model for a workers' revolution—but the story it told was not one of workers, but of peasants. The relationship between those two groups was a constant headache for the international Communist movement.

Workers and Peasants

Marxism, and hence the politics of early twentieth-century Communism, focused on workers—the proletariat. The Industrial Revolution and capitalism had produced the conditions Marx described, which would ignite a revolution in which workers would seize the means of production and help society proceed toward Communism. Nevertheless, the Soviet Union, the first country that elevated Communism to state ideology, was far from the most industrially advanced in Europe. A large part of the population lived off agriculture and resisted rigid policies of collectivization and the requisitioning of grain according to targets set in Moscow. This ignited "the Great Soviet Peasant War," a struggle between peasants across the Soviet Union and state leadership that lasted until the mid-thirties and claimed millions of lives.[58] In 1928, around the time Derkovits began working on *1514*, Stalin launched a new, more violent round of forced collectivization and purges that resulted in famines in Ukraine and elsewhere and eventually broke all opposition. Around 1930, the situation of peasants was not an easy subject.

Peasants—or "agricultural workers," as Communists preferred to call them—posed a challenge for the Communist movement in Hungary, too. Agriculture formed a very significant part of the Hungarian economy that involved more than half of the population. Some owned enough land to make a living; others found it harder to scrape by. Two-thirds of the peasantry lived in poverty. Those who owned no farmland and lived off day labor were the most destitute. Their situation could well be described as more desperate than that of urban industrial workers, and not only because their wages were considerably lower. By the 1920s, 90 percent of industrial workers benefitted from compulsory health insurance and other forms of welfare. In the countryside, none of these were available.[59]

Given the large numbers of people working in agriculture, the HCP had a strong interest in recruiting them to the movement. However, due to their social stratification and diverse employment conditions, it was harder to categorize them as one group than industrial workers. Agitation among peasants was thus highly important but could also easily become ideologically suspect. Besides the issue of Trianon, it was due to this question that the "Vienna comrades" found themselves in hot water before the 1930 congress. As a draft resolution prepared at the congress put it, Lukács's theses had shifted toward suggesting a "bourgeois-democratic revolution, a democratic dictatorship of workers and peasants."[60] This was anathema: the revolution had to be a proletarian revolution and the dictatorship a dictatorship of the proletariat. Kun's opening remarks at the congress described previous mistakes in more detail. "The leader of the village caucus" (referred to by the alias *Simonyi,* which belonged to Imre Nagy [1896–1956], future prime minister and emblematic figure of the 1956 revolution) had acted too independently in certain issues, arguing for agricultural reform when the party fought for the distribution of land and claiming that the peasantry formed a class of its own, when in fact the party only represented landless, poor peasants and classed wealthy peasants with the bourgeoisie.[61] The revolution would necessarily destroy feudal structures in agriculture and distribute land among councils of landless peasants, said the draft resolution; there was no need to identify them as a class for that to happen. Instead of highlighting their specific issues, the party was to include them by using the slogan "Workers' and Peasants' Government."

As mentioned earlier, Derkovits employed anachronistic imagery to signal that the sixteenth-century peasants' uprising was to be interpreted as a prefiguration of the workers' movement of his time. In modern left-wing rhetoric, peasants often stood in for revolutionaries from other social classes, as evidenced by Engels's comparison between the German Peasants' War and the 1848 revolutions. The dissemination of *1514* at Social Democratic workers' fêtes shows that this kind of appropriation was easily performed in this case, too. In 1930, Derkovits himself assembled the woodcuts into a placard for a workers' demonstration, inscribing, in the center: "1514 / 193" (fig. 5.6). In this new artwork, he replaced the eleventh image, which showed Brother Lőrinc (a Franciscan friar and Dózsa's ally) and his men, with an alternative image showing one anonymous figure—dressed more like a worker than a peasant—breaking through prison rails.[62]

This conflation notwithstanding, the fact that Derkovits was commissioned to depict peasants, rather than workers, had deeper significance in the Hungarian context. The "Vienna comrades" had already commissioned a similar artwork at least once: in 1923, Béla Uitz (1887–1972) had produced *General Ludd,* a series of etchings about the Luddites, for the party.[63] Uitz's series depicted a movement of factory workers, rather than peasants; furthermore, the subject was taken from Britain, not Hungary, fitting into the internationalist pantheon that characterized the party's memory politics in its early years. With *1514,* something shifted. The choice of subject matter may have been related to the HCP's attempt to bring the peasantry into stronger focus in its activism. Moreover, it signaled the intention to find heroes in *national* history that Hungarian peasants and workers could iden-

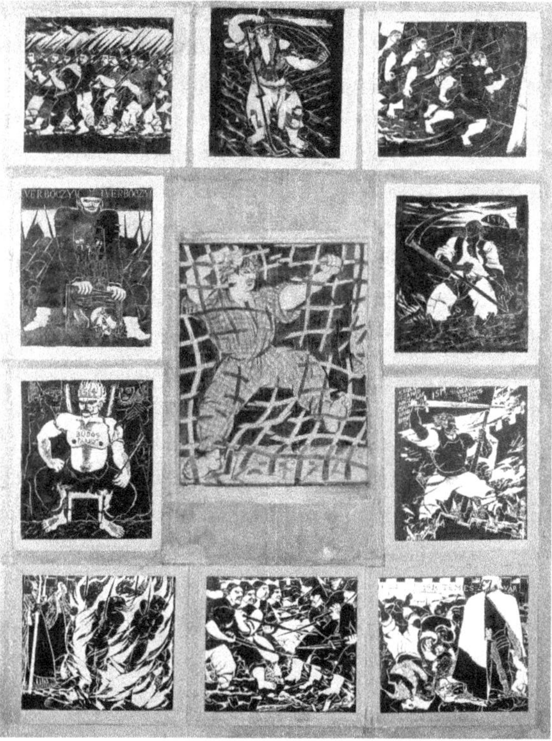

FIGURE 5.6. Gyula Derkovits, placard for workers' demonstration, 1930, Hungarian National Gallery, Budapest.
Photo: Szépművészeti Múzeum / Museum of Fine Arts, Budapest, 2025

tify with. This was a logical decision in the Hungarian circumstances, but it also fit into international developments.

It may seem surprising that the Moscow-based Comintern supported nationalist ideas of revisionism over Lukács's internationalist approach to Trianon, but nationalism was not completely absent from European left-wing thought and activism.[64] The Comintern had no qualms about instrumentalizing nationalism, or even xenophobia and antisemitism, to further its aims outside the Soviet Union. In Germany, for instance, it had ordered that the Communist Party of Germany use such slogans to win over right-wing voters several times in the 1920s and 1930s.[65] The late 1920s brought a shift in attitude toward nationalist propaganda within the Soviet Union, too; 1927 was the year of the War Scare, when the Soviet leadership panicked over a supposedly imminent attack by Western powers. They came to realize that, when it came to mass mobilization, socialist slogans of class struggle were not enough. Instead, as Stalin himself soon declared, flesh-and-blood heroes, preferably from national (that is, Russian) history, were needed to fire up the imagination. By the mid-1930s, this new approach developed into "national Bolshevism"—a Russocentric repackaging of the Marxist-Leninist worldview.[66] Derkovits's Dózsa series preceded the full unfolding of national Bolshevism by a few years, but it signaled a similar shift within the memory politics of the Hungarian Communist movement. This time, the goal was not just to provide a historical example of class struggle but also to reach out to Hungarian workers by appealing to their national sentiments.

The aim of addressing the Hungarian political environment specifically can explain why Derkovits's *1514* stands relatively alone in the Central European context. Narrative series of prints were popular with left-wing artists in the interwar period, but they mainly depicted internationalist and contemporary themes. An example is the Austrian Otto Rudolf Schatz (1900–1961), a Social Democrat who created many wood engravings showing the struggles of workers, but in general terms rather than in a historical perspective.[67] In a broader sense, however, *1514* fits into the search for historical models and concepts of national identity that permeated post-1918 Central European culture. A peasant hero whose interwar symbolism is somewhat comparable was Juraj Jánošík (1688–1713), a legendary bandit shaped into a national hero by the Slovak national movement. In new Czechoslovakia, he offered a counterpoint to previous Austro-Hungarian rule, an example of a hero of the lower classes, as well as a point of identification for Slovaks within the multinational but Czech-dominated state. Jánošík was depicted in paintings and prints by a range of Slovak artists, most of whom treated the theme as an opportunity to employ an imagery inspired by vernacular culture and the atmosphere of folktales. In 1923, Ľudovít Fulla (1902–1980) told Jánošík's story in a series of colored linocuts.[68] Softly delineated and composed with a balladistic taciturnity, these images have little in common with Derkovits's expressive and openly agitative compositions.

The problem of addressing questions of national identity may have been a general one for the international Communist movement, but visual artists reacted to it in different ways, as prompted by their specific situations. In Czechoslovakia, the central elements of the official image of the state were modernity and progress, and references to history were secondary, while in Hungary, official propaganda prioritized the idea of "historical Hungary" and hence a wide range of historical imagery to further the revisionist cause. The series *1514* exemplifies how the Communist movement adapted to this situation by appropriating some of the rhetoric while offering an alternative narrative of history.

A Wider Perspective

The way Derkovits's *1514* visualized a distinct Communist memory politics while engaging with issues debated at the time suggests that the project was closely linked to party strategy. Nevertheless, by the mid-thirties, the series also made a broader impression in the art world. In 1934, it garnered attention from the press when shown at Derkovits's memorial exhibition, and in 1936, it was published in accessible album form. Moreover, it appeared at group exhibitions, where it was surrounded by works by artists of various political persuasions. In 1935, for instance, it was on view at the exhibition of the Association of Hungarian Copper Etchers at the National Salon (Nemzeti Szalon). Other artists present included Pál Molnár-C. (1894–1981), a member of the School of Rome often involved in official and ecclesiastical commissions, György Buday, the Szeged artist exploring the life of "the people" discussed in chapter 3, and Nándor Lajos Varga, whose irredentist *Hungarian Past* I explored in the same chapter.[69]

Being present together at a group exhibition means that two artists inhabit, in some way, a shared section of the art world, but it does not necessarily point to deeper connections. In showing how Derkovits's work resonated on the right side of the political spectrum, exhibition reviews are more revealing. The Dózsa series—and the 1934 retrospective as a whole—received very favorable reviews in the right-wing press. Even the reviewer writing for the Catholic *Magyar Kultúra* (*Hungarian Culture*), a magazine edited by the Jesuit Béla Bangha (1880–1940), an arch-ideologue of the counterrevolution, celebrated Derkovits's work.[70] Instead of being viewed with suspicion as a sign of Communist sympathies, the artist's preoccupation with the poor was presented as a virtue both here and in the hard-right *Magyarság*.[71] The similarly inclined *Nemzeti Újság* also praised Derkovits as a painter of misery and hence "the truest and greatest Hungarian natural talent."[72]

By the mid-1930s, the political landscape was changing. The "populist" (*népi*) movement, discussed in chapter 3, had always nurtured visions of racial purity, but some of its adherents, disillusioned with the German orientation of Hungarian official politics, began shifting toward the left, shedding at least some of their antisemitic views. At the same time, their ideas of racial purity found in the countryside were becoming absorbed into mainstream right-wing politics. When the *Nemzeti Ujság* called Derkovits a "Hungarian natural talent" and praised *1514* for its raw energy, it evoked racialized notions of a pure national culture, untainted by sinful (Jewish) city life. This was not the kind of praise, nor the ideological context, that Derkovits had ever sought. Nevertheless, the art he created to express his left-wing ideals struck a chord with those who wished for a new kind of modern art capable of expressing right-wing visions of Christian Hungary. The critic of *Magyar Kultúra* who waxed lyrical about Derkovits was the same János Jajczay who had championed Aba-Novák's ecclesiastical work (see chap. 4).

If *1514* was conceived the late 1920s as an effective intervention in current Hungarian political culture, then by the mid-thirties, its choice of subject matter fit even more seamlessly into wider developments. The appeal of Derkovits's formal language, too, stretched past the Communist movement. The rawness highlighted by the *Nemzeti Ujság* was also praised by others; the liberal critic Artúr Elek (1876–1944), for instance, called *1514* "rudimentary" and "imperfect" in its technique but "greatly powerful in form and gripping in expression."[73] With their simple forms and hard lines, the images recalled sixteenth-century broadsheets. As mentioned in chapter 3, archaization was often employed in expressionist woodcuts, but Derkovits's emphasis on angular forms, sharp weapons, and straight lines cutting through the composition distinguish *1514* from more lyrical examples, such as Ferdiš Duša's *Down the Váh*. In Hungarian graphic arts, the work that perhaps most shared its focus on tight composition and geometry was a polar political opposite: Varga's *Hungarian Past*. Varga, a professor of printmaking and author of books on the history and practice of this art form, was well aware of Derkovits's series and mentioned it in his survey of Hungarian wood engraving.[74]

Some official narratives of Hungarian history neglected the Dózsa uprising, but *Hungarian Past* was not one of them. Sheet 16 of Varga's series bears the title *Dózsa* (fig. 5.7). A nude male figure in shackles lies in the right-hand foreground, threatened from above by figures with spears. A group of others are torturously pushing a large stone slab inscribed "Verbőczi Tripartitum" up a hill. The hill is, in fact, a volcano, from which—as the accompanying text explains—the dissatisfaction of peasants had erupted like flaming hot lava. The *Tripartitum* sealed this valve, robbing peasants of their last resort: the right of free movement. The image does not visually cite Derkovits's *1514*, but both works depict the *Tripartitum* as a crucial turning point. The Dózsa uprising was an episode from history where the memory politics of radical left- and right-wing movements could intersect. The meaning of the episode was, of course, different: in *Hungarian Past*, it was yet another incarnation of the recurring Hungarian tragedy, while in *1514*, it critiqued the social conditions of the present. The two were not necessarily antagonistic, however. Both works visualized ideas existing in the same political culture. The movements they represented did not simply battle over the interpretation of the same sites of memory; they exploited each other's interpretations to gain broader appeal.

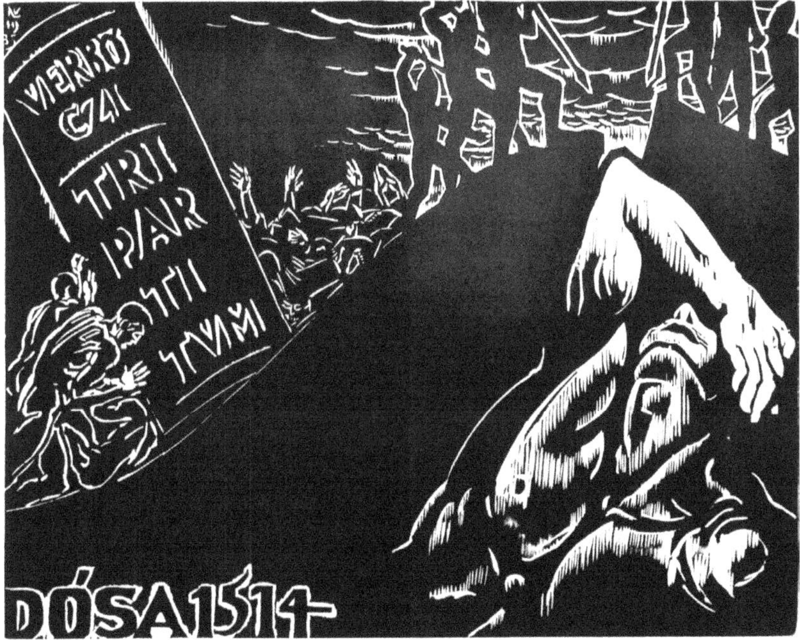

FIGURE 5.7.   Nándor Lajos Varga, *Dózsa (Hungarian Past XVI)*, early 1930s/1940, private collection.
Photo by author. Nándor Lajos Varga © OOA-S 2024

The Cult of the Hero

Derkovits's *1514* presented a hero who had a natural place in a left-wing pantheon but could also appeal to the right—a hero who had valiantly fought against injustice, be it the injustice of class oppression or of the recurring tragedies afflicting the Hungarian nation. The imagery of heroism was central to the series: six of the eleven sheets depicted one large figure towering over its surroundings, sending a message of strength. Four of these were positive heroes of the uprising, while two represented the oppressors. As iconic images, they were central to the message—so much so that when Derkovits arranged the sheets into a placard, he placed these into the center, pairing them to spell out a new message of oppression followed by defiant rebellion. The appeal of this kind of imagery stretched across political divides. Official culture was wary of its connotations of rebellion—resulting in brooding, melancholy depictions of Kossuth—but gladly placed depictions of heroism into the service of the regent's self-representation. The tone of this official imagery of heroism shifted, however, as the political environment radicalized.

In interwar Europe, the word *heroes* often referred to the fallen of the First World War. In Romania, for instance, the memorial day of the war was called Heroes' Day, and the society responsible for preserving the memory of the dead was called the Heroes' Cult.[75] Similar phrasing was used in Hungary, where a new central war memorial, the Memorial Stone of Heroes, was installed in front of the Millennium Monument in Budapest in 1929. Conceived by the ever-present Kertész, the project was another instance of appropriating a commemorative space designed in the dualist era.[76] A large, flat, tomblike structure, the stone bore two inscriptions: "1914–1918" and "For the Thousand-Year-Old Borders" ("*Az ezeréves határokért*"). A site that commemorated the 896 Conquest now also commemorated Trianon. In 1932, the square was renamed Heroes' Square, a name it still bears today.

The way the war monument was used as an opportunity to create another Trianon monument reflects the ubiquity of revisionism in Hungarian public life, but it is also a manifestation of a broader, international phenomenon in war commemoration. Across Central and Eastern Europe, in states asserting themselves within expanded borders or lamenting territorial loss, the remembrance of the First World War was an occasion for defining the nation in a territorial, political, and cultural sense. Indeed, the Heroes' Memorial Stone may be seen as a response to the Bucharest Tomb of the Unknown Soldier, erected in 1923, which featured a shield with the symbols of all territories Romania had acquired in 1918 and an inscription stating that the Unknown Soldier "sleeps happily," having given his life for the unity of the Romanian people.[77] Commemorations on Heroes' Day were often conceived in a way that prioritized the Romanian ethnicity and Orthodox religion, marginalizing other ethnic and religious groups.[78] In Czechoslovakia, commemorations associated with the Czechoslovak Legion often had similar exclusionary connotations.[79] In Hungary, the most spectacular war monument of the 1930s would leave behind the minimalism of the Heroes' Memorial Stone to promote a more forceful and militant image of the hero, using an expressive, "raw" formal language that could satisfy the requirement of energetic "Hungarianness" increasingly voiced by right-wing critics.

As the center of counterrevolutionary activity during the Soviet Republic, the city of Szeged featured prominently in the memory politics of the Horthy regime. It had given a new home to the University of Kolozsvár (Cluj), which had relocated from Romania. To provide a counterpoint to "sinful" Budapest, the government aimed to build up Szeged as a major cultural hub. The new university buildings occasioned major construction works, which included a cathedral (designed in the prewar years), a representative square around the cathedral with colonnades and a historical pantheon, and a road leading out-

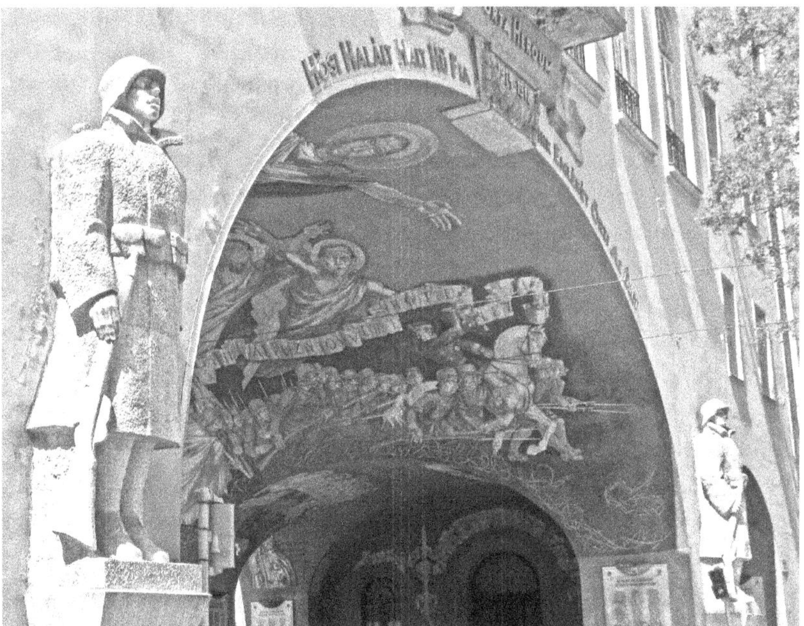

FIGURE 5.8.   The Gate of Heroes with Éva Lőte's statues and Vilmos Aba-Novák's *Christ* and *Allegory of Action*, 1936.
Photo: Batomi / Wikimedia Commons CC BY-SA 3.0

ward from the square. A monumental gate was to provide a festive entrance to the square while also serving as a bridge across the road, connecting two buildings. Designed by Móric Pogány, it was completed in 1936 (fig. 5.8).

Around the same time, the municipality of Szeged was planning a First World War monument elsewhere in the city center and ran a competition for the sculptures.[80] The winner was the sculptor and applied artist Éva Lőte (1906–1966). The two projects were subsequently merged; the gate became a war monument, and its decoration was devised with the commemorative function in mind. Two statues from Lőte's design were to be placed on its facade, while Vilmos Aba-Novák was commissioned to paint its frescoes. The monument was to be named the Gate of Heroes. Work was finished in October 1936.

Pogány's building is austere and geometrical, resembling contemporary Italian rationalism. Lőte's statues on the facade facing Cathedral Square are similarly reserved; upright figures flanking the gate, they represent the *Dead* and the *Living Soldier*. Aba-Novák's frescoes, by contrast, exhibit the same propensity for shock and horror as the frescoes of the Jászszentandrás church. The murals combined religious imagery with gruesome depictions of the devastation of war, enclosing it all in an irredentist framework. In the middle of the ceiling of the central arch, a frontal, Byzantine representation of Christ in Judgment confronts those who pass through (fig. 5.8) The group of figures to Christ's right represent *Piety and Hope*: priests and monks consoling women and children mourning their loved ones.[81] Beneath them, soldiers' graves appear, with an empty helmet and in it a red exclamation mark—the missing face of the Unknown Soldier. The allegory to the left of Christ is that of *Action*. Living soldiers are encouraged by angels and led into battle by Horthy, who looks back at them while charging ahead on a white horse. The side arches contain religious motifs and inscriptions referring to the future heroism of Hungarians. The text above Saint George slaying the dragon reads: "This is how the horse-riding people will subjugate their enemies." The one accompanying the figure of Saint Stephen declares the reason behind the impending military conflict: "Let the realm of Saint Stephen be, again, how it once was." The grisliest composition shows a choir of angels and the bleeding hands of Christ above a group of ghosts—dead soldiers, some in gas masks, hovering over their graves (fig. 5.9).

The sculptor of the gate, Lőte, was the daughter of a professor of medicine who had relocated to Szeged from Kolozsvár / Cluj with the university.[82] Having studied at the School of Applied Art, she gained public commissions such as altarpieces, tomb sculptures, and World War monuments. Her statues, the *Dead* and the *Living Soldier*, had been designed for the originally planned monument but form an essential conceptual entry point to the iconographic program of the Gate of Heroes (fig. 5.8). This suggests that the unrealized monument may have been the originator of the gate's basic theme: the juxtaposition of death and new life. Within the context of irredentism, this evoked the idea of Hungarian resurrection. With his bulging dead eyes and ghostly face, Lőte's dead soldier matched Aba-Novák's more spectacular ghost soldiers hovering under the arch. Her living soldier, then, introduced the corresponding scene on the right side: Horthy leading his army. Given the location in Szeged, the primary interpretation of this scene is that it represents Horthy at the helm of the National Army in 1919, taking on the Soviet Republic. Paired with the idea of Hungarian resurrection, however, it also referred to a future war, one that would help "the realm of Saint Stephen be, again, how it once was."

Like other First World War monuments across Europe, the Gate of Heroes aimed to provide the local community with a location to mourn their dead while also placing those individual deaths into a broader narrative.[83] However, unlike many other monuments, it eschewed the serene formal language of cemeteries for agitated depictions of the horror and devastation of war.

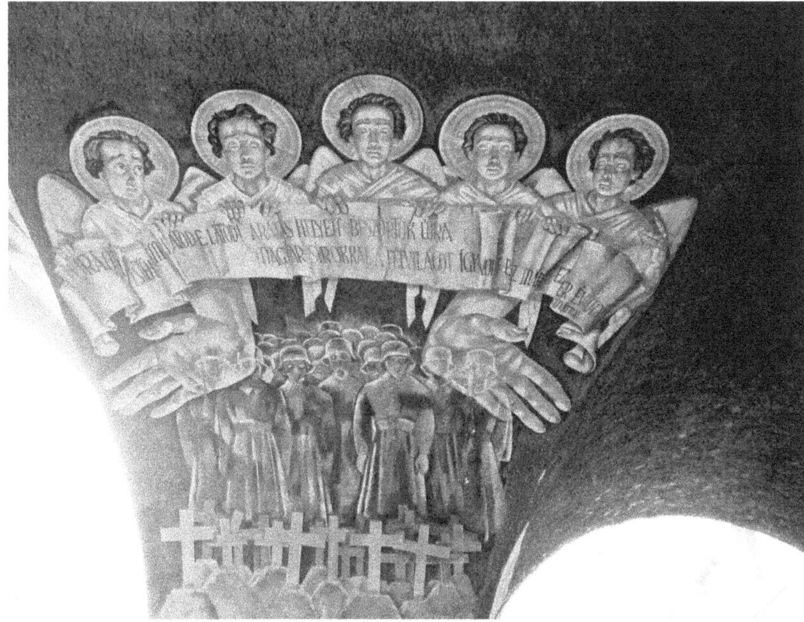

FIGURE 5.9.   Vilmos Aba-Novák, *Soldiers with Their Graves*, detail from the Gate of Heroes, 1936. Photo: Wikimedia Commons, public domain

This imagery could easily have found a place in antiwar activism, but, placed into the interpretative framework of death and resurrection borrowed from Christianity, it took on the opposite meaning. The sacrifice of the soldiers was the same as that of Christ, and it had to be followed by resurrection brought about by a new group of soldiers. They would be led by the heroic leader of the country, Horthy himself, the only one able to bring redemption.

In the early 1920s, as Horthy solidified his power, his image had shifted from that of powerful military leader to constitutional monarch. Dudits's *Oath in the Vérmező* (chap. 1) had visualized this new image. By the mid-1930s, the image of the warlord returned, and the Gate of Heroes was the prime example. At the same time, the leadership cult gained increasingly irrational, quasi-religious elements.[84] This intensified after 1938, the First Vienna Award, but the Gate of Heroes foreshadowed the shift. Horthy was usually compared to historical figures such as Árpád, Hunyadi, or Matthias Corvinus, but in the gate, this historical framework was replaced by a purely religious one. Horthy emerged as a singular hero worthy of literal worship. The sacral aura around Horthy in the late thirties was not dissimilar to the veneration of the assassinated Austro-Fascist Chancellor Dollfuß in contemporary Austria.[85]

This was official memory politics in the late 1930s. On the one hand, historical parallels and allusions were prominently visible in the grandiose spectacle of the Saint Stephen jubilee and commissions such as Aba-Novák's Székesfehérvár murals. On the other hand, they were eschewed in projects such as the Gate of Heroes, where the only past that mattered was the recent past and the only personality worth celebrating was the regent himself. In this framework, the cult and imagery of great historical personalities only seemed to underscore the regime's politics. To seek alternatives, its opponents turned to narratives of rebellion.

Memory and Resistance

In 1938, the HCP again commissioned a series of prints about history. Károly László Háy (1907–1961), a founding member of the Group of Socialist Artists, met Révai in Prague, where the Communist activist explained that it was time for the party to employ historical analogies from the "centuries-long anti-German tradition of independence in Hungarian culture."[86] Inspired by this idea, Háy planned a series of linocuts depicting the struggles of Hungarians against the Ottomans and Habsburgs in the seventeenth and eighteenth centuries. In 1942, he pitched the series, which he had titled *Between Two Pagans for One Homeland*, to the leadership of the HCP. The party urgently relieved him from other duties and tasked him with completing the series, which they intended to publish legally under the auspices of the Hungarian Historical Memorial Committee.

The committee had been founded in 1942 by a coalition of intellectuals, from Communists to populists, opposed to the German orientation of Hungarian politics. A year before, immediately after the German attack on the Soviet Union, the Comintern had instructed all Communist parties to desist from pursuing Socialist revolution and instead aim to build a national front of resistance in each country to support the patriotic war fought by the Soviet Union.[87] In the process, they were to employ national rhetoric and imagery. The committee was part of the HCP's efforts to do so.[88] In their first proclamation, published on 1 March in the Social Democratic daily *Népszava*, they encouraged the public to submit mementoes of the 1848 revolutions in preparation for its anniversary on 15 March.[89] Calling for national unity, the proclamation contained both the stated aim of the committee (to nurture the memory of 1848) and its covert one (to foster national resistance against Nazism through historical precedents). The committee president was the populist writer Imre Kovács (1913–1980).

Just as in the case of Viktória Derkovits's reminiscences, Háy's account of the origin of his series of prints is hence corroborated by the political context. The title and subject matter reveal, yet again, the Communist Party's strategy to embed its memory politics into a broader political context in order to disseminate its message widely. "Between two pagans for one homeland" ("*Két pogány közt egy hazáért*") was a phrase originating from *Te vagy a legény, Tyukodi pajtás*, a song from the seventeenth-century anti-Habsburg kuruc uprisings. In the 1930s, it was often employed by opponents of German-friendly governmental politics as a reference to Hungary's position between Nazi Germany and the Soviet Union. Kovács himself had published his thoughts under this title in 1938.[90] This shows that the Communist Party was ready to tactically employ this rhetoric, seemingly even at the expense of the Soviet Union, in order to build a coalition of resistance. In 1942, this was in line with the new strategy of the Comintern. According to the artist, however, Révai had already recommended this subject matter to him in 1938, which suggests a more direct link to the party's previous employment of national themes in its activism.

Háy never completed the series, but a few of the images have survived. One of these is a curious composition. It shows Miklós Zrínyi (1620–1664), a powerful Hungarian-Croatian military leader who was killed by a wild boar on a hunt but whose death was often blamed on the Habsburgs in cultural memory (fig. 5.10). Háy depicted this ambivalence: in his image, Zrínyi is attacked by a boar but also shot at with a rifle. The artist claimed that Communist activist Zoltán Schönherz (1905–1942) had advised him that the "the centuries-old image of Zrínyi's demise in the consciousness of the people was now itself a historical truth; furthermore, it was a historical necessity for the Germans to get rid of Zrínyi sooner or later, and it was just a random occurrence that they were preceded by the boar."[91] The rifle strengthened the anti-German message of the image, made explicit in the inscription. Háy's composition has been described as clumsy, not without reason.[92] Nevertheless, it was a more explicit statement than any other on the power of art to evoke, visualize, and transmit cultural memory, to give it form and meaning. All the images examined in this book had similar aims, even if they went about them in different ways and in the service of different agendas. They all exemplify the constant and continuous work that constructs sites of memory—"the consciousness of the people."

The early 1940s saw an eruption of historical imagery in Hungarian visual culture and public life. History was undoubtedly a battleground. That the most important legal organization of broad resistance was the Historical

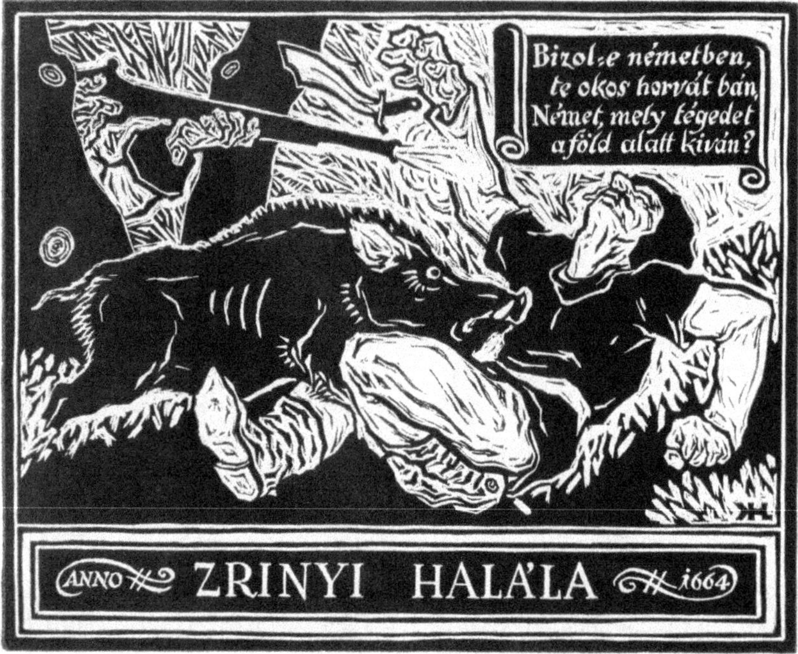

FIGURE 5.10.   Károly László Háy, *The Death of Zrínyi (Between Two Pagans for One Homeland)*, 1941, Hungarian National Gallery, Budapest.
Photo: Szépművészeti Múzeum / Museum of Fine Arts, Budapest, 2025. Károly László Háy © OOA-S 2024

Memorial Committee is itself obvious proof. The committee and its supporters organized rallies related to the anniversaries of 1848, commemorating its individual heroes. These continued along the path set by Schönherz with similar protests in 1941. The memory of 1848 was now central to Communist activism. However, as Háy's series demonstrates, the opposition's pantheon also included other heroes: Zrínyi, Rákóczi, the kuruc rebels. Some of these overlapped with official memory politics; we have seen how Kossuth sometimes functioned as a prefiguration of Horthy, and Rákóczi, too, was cited as a parallel.[93] Given the regime's ambivalence about some of these figures, wrestling them away from officialdom was a logical goal for the opposition.

The art of dissent was not separate from official art but provocatively evoked it. In 1942, the Group of Socialist Artists organized the exhibition *For the Freedom of Art*. Closed down by authorities after three days, the show aimed to counter official propaganda and included a section called *Freedom and the People*, dedicated to sketches for frescoes. Háy displayed a sketch with the motto "History" (fig. 5.11).

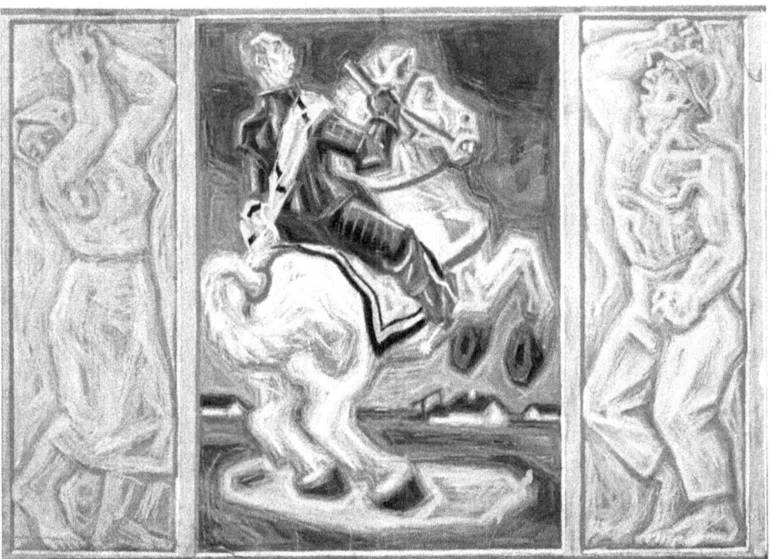

FIGURE 5.11.   Károly László Háy, *History*, sketch for a fresco, 1941, Hungarian National Gallery, Budapest.
Photo: Szépművészeti Múzeum / Museum of Fine Arts, Budapest, 2025. Károly László Háy © OOA-S 2024

The composition consists of three panels. In the center, a figure in military uniform sits on a prancing white horse, his caricaturistic face resembling that of his steed. The two side panels depict two figures in grisaille, a peasant woman and a male worker, twisting their bodies in anguish. The message is clear: wars bring glory to the powerful but misery to the lower classes. As Sára Bárdi has shown, the figure in the center echoes Horthy's iconography, recognizable even though there is no portrait-like resemblance.[94] A stamp published in 1940 for Horthy's anniversary, designed by Ferenc Márton, the ill-tempered painter of the allegorical *Oath in the Vérmező*, depicted the regent on the back of a prancing horse, and so did a 1941 ceiling fresco, by Molnár-C., commemorating the "return" of Upper Hungary in the Dob Street Post Office. A historical precedent, according to Bárdi, was Francis II Rákóczi, whose statue—on a prancing horse—had been erected next to the Parliament building in 1937.

By 1942, Hungary was at war. In 1941, it had joined the German invasion of Yugoslavia and had subsequently attacked the Soviet Union. The stakes in political activism, and hence in activist art, were very high. Several of the artists participating in *For the Freedom of Art* were jailed, and many of those mentioned in the previous section of this chapter did not live to see the end of the war. Schönherz was arrested in July 1942 and executed in October. In this situation, the organizers of the exhibition reached back to older utopias; when encouraging artists to design frescoes, they optimistically envisioned a future where left-wing artists could carry out large-scale commissions as for 1 May 1919. Most of the submissions recalled the images of a bright Socialist future that had then decorated Budapest.[95] Háy's design was, however, a reminder that to construct a new future, it was also necessary to rebuild the past.

Pantheons in Conflict

This chapter starts with the "consolidated" 1920s and ends with the Second World War. Throughout the period, the representation of history functioned as a medium through which different political actors aimed to influence society. When Derkovits created *1514*, the way the work forcefully claimed an episode from national history for the left-wing cause was relatively new. By 1938, as Háy's conversation with Révai shows, national history had emerged as a crucial weapon of resistance.

In the culture that surrounded left-wing activists, history had been an essential element right from the start. Horthy's power and cult were propped up by historical precedents, and irredentism drew on concepts of the past through its influential construct of irredentist spacetime. When those opposed to the regime held up their alternative heroes, they did not do so in a self-imposed vacuum. Derkovits's Dózsa or Háy's Zrínyi were not just symbols created to promote general Communist or anti-Fascist values but carefully thought-out interventions in a specific place and time, a specific political context. They engaged with issues and adopted imagery from a wider sphere than just their own.

The appeal of the hero is universal. Heroes are indispensable reference points in any narrative, shaped by any political perspective. Instead of regarding the pantheons of different movements as solid and distinct from each other, this chapter argues for a more fluid view. Derkovits's *1514* shows how history can be employed in activism to intervene in official discourses, exploit their vulnerabilities, and reach out to audiences across the political spectrum. The series of prints did so by focusing on a heroic figure that held a precarious position in official memory culture but appealed to emerging populist and radical right-wing movements. Derkovits's powerful "raw" depiction of desperate peasants was a rallying cry to Communists, but it resonated with right-wing populism and with those who sought a similarly raw, nationalist modernism in the late 1930s. The prints spoke to the specific situation within the Communist Party, to specific debates happening at the time, but they could also break out of their narrow context to become canonical artworks in any narrative of Hungarian art history.

In interwar Europe, heroes could mean many things—the fallen of the Great War, venerable personalities from the historical past, new leaders around whom cults had emerged. In Mussolini's Italy, the greatest hero was the Duce, so much so that he had to overshadow the revolutionary hero Garibaldi even in Garibaldi's memorial year. In Hungary, a similar cult developed around Horthy, taking a quasi-religious and at the same time militant form by the late 1930s. For left-wing activists such as Háy, the imagery of Horthy as hero offered opportunities for critical perspectives and satire precisely because it was so ubiquitous, so flexible. It could be employed to aggrandize its subject but also to expose the imagery of official memory politics as banal and clichéd. The imagery of heroism—valiant fighters, outstanding leaders, great men on horseback—was not new in the interwar period; its roots reached back to nineteenth-century nation building and even further back into centuries of art history. Nevertheless, the artists discussed in this chapter used it to navigate and influence a modern public sphere heavy with the problems of the early twentieth century, repurposing the imagery in ways that would prove resilient. At a time when catastrophic violence was about to erupt, these struggles over memory soon paled in significance. In the many decades that followed, however, the mutable yet persistent nature of historical pantheons continued to shape narratives of the past.

Epilogue

The ending of one the most important and beloved works of postwar Hungarian literature evokes the 1926 Mohács anniversary. *School at the Frontier*, a coming-of-age novel by Géza Ottlik (1912–1990), follows the trials and tribulations of a group of boys attending a military academy in the 1920s. First published in 1959, under Communism, but set during a previous period of authoritarianism, the book achieved cult status, as it came to be seen as an allegory of survival under oppressive regimes, even though—or perhaps because—it sharply focuses on the microworld of the school and rarely dwells on wider social issues. At the end of the book, however, the historical background comes into slightly stronger focus, signaling that the boys have reached the cusp of adulthood. Having graduated middle school in 1926, the three friends travel down the Danube with the rest of their class toward Mohács. Ottlik does not explain it further, but readers of this book will know that the characters joined thousands of pilgrims floating down the river to attend the anniversary celebrations. The boys do not discuss this on the ship. They have more important things to talk about: friendship, personal freedom, belonging. Looking back, the novel's main narrator, Bébé, is nevertheless prompted to muse on history:

> The four hundredth anniversary of the Battle of Mohács was coming
> up at the time. It might seem like a strange thing, to celebrate a defeat,

but the one who could have celebrated a victory, the great Ottoman Empire, was no more. The Tartars had also disappeared, and so had, in the meanwhile, almost in front of our eyes, the resilient Habsburg Empire. Hence, we had become used to such solitary celebrations of our great lost battles, the ones we had survived. Perhaps we had also become used to regarding defeat as something more exciting, more important, than victory; something made of a more dense material; or, at least, as more truly ours.[1]

To Bébé, the "celebration" of the Mohács anniversary revealed a deeper characteristic of Hungarian cultural memory. The excerpt reiterates the tragic narrative of Hungarian history—a narrative evoked many times in the previous chapters of this book. Admittedly, Ottlik strikes a different tone; instead of national death and resurrection, he talks about survival, and instead of grandiose pathos, he employs a gentle irony. Yet, the passage shows how the narrative itself endured, continuing to serve as an explanatory framework. According to the novel's fiction, Bébé put his thoughts and memories to paper in 1957, a year after the defeated Revolution of 1956. The revolution itself was taboo; had the book mentioned it, it would not have been published in 1959. In the next decades, however, many of *School at the Frontier*'s readers viewed it as a commentary on the 1950s and a beacon of comfort under a new authoritarianism. Through the oppressive microworld of the military school, Ottlik's novel explored the possibilities of preserving an inner freedom when choices are severely limited. It allowed readers to draw parallels between the Horthy regime and Communism and think of survival strategies as a constant feature of Hungarian history, as if living with defeat and enduring oppression had become part of the Hungarian national character.

Such statements about how a nation's history shaped its character are ubiquitous, from major literary works such as Ottlik's novel to tourist guides and recipe blogs. This book has taken a different approach. It discussed some enduring tropes of Hungarian culture, placing them into their historical context, but has also shown how they were formed and perpetuated by political will rather than by innate streams of cultural memory, some sort of national subconscious. The images and objects I have examined not only reflected how certain events or people were remembered at the time but also shaped their remembrance in the next decades. To what extent they were able to do so depended on their visibility, accessibility, and relationship with broader cultural narratives. A brief look at the afterlives of some of these objects will highlight how their loss—or, by contrast, continued existence—contributed to general shifts in social remembrance.

Whether or not artworks exist in their objecthood inevitably shapes how they, and the events they commemorate, live on in cultural memory. Mihály Bíró's *Horthy* series was strictly banned in interwar Hungary, and copies found in the country were condemned to destruction. To this day, few copies are accessible to researchers. The National Széchényi Library holds a full series of the original lithographs, safely preserved in the Collection of Posters and Pamphlets but rarely on view.[2] According to the department's librarian, Anita Szarka, the prints survived because their one-time custodians, librarians of the early 1920s, had hidden them from the prying eyes of authorities—probably led not as much by left-wing convictions as by their professional ethos.[3] After 1945, further institutions acquired copies of *Horthy*, but the prints are rarely reproduced. This might be due to their exceptionally naturalistic depiction of highly gruesome scenes, but since 1989, it has been nevertheless inseparable from a general tendency to forget about, gloss over, or minimize the events of the White Terror.[4] How much more clearly would these events live on in cultural memory if Bíró's prints had been more visible and available in larger numbers? We can only speculate on the degree, but it is not far-fetched to claim that the interwar ban still contributes to the low visibility of the prints and their subject in the 2000s.

The visibility of many works discussed in this book shifted several times in the past hundred years—so much so that assessing their one-time significance requires the reconstruction of a fundamentally different cultural context, one in which objects little known today were influential icons. In chapter 2, I analyzed the monuments of Freedom Square in such a way, exploring how they not only expressed but also promoted the widespread mindset of irredentist spacetime. In August 1945, the monuments were removed from the square and destroyed. Their influence dissipated and only lived on in their miniature reproductions, limited to homes and hidden even there. After the Communist turn of 1948, the new regime consciously obliterated the remains of old memory politics and replaced them with its own commemorative signs. Vilmos Aba-Novák's murals on the Szeged Gate of Heroes and in the Székesfehérvár Saint Stephen Mausoleum were covered up with lime. The building of the National Archives was heavily damaged in the Second World War. The controversial fresco *The Collapse* was irretrievably lost.[5] When reconstruction work began in the late 1940s, the original plan was to paint over all the pictures, which were deemed artistically worthless, creating blank spaces on the walls instead. Additional expert opinions, however, persuaded decision-makers to keep most of the pictures and only repaint the details that directly recalled the Horthy regime.[6] István Bethlen's portrait was replaced by a generic face in the mural showing Gábor Bethlen, and the image celebrating Klebelsberg's school reforms was never restored. The armor-clad portrait of Klebelsberg was, however, allowed to remain by the building's entrance.

Besides these radical changes, there were also continuities between the memory politics of the interwar period and the postwar Communist regime. The heroes of 1848, for instance, remained important political symbols. An interesting example that embodies both continuity and rupture is the fate of János Horvay's Kossuth monument in Kossuth Square. The postwar government retained the name Kossuth Square and continued the veneration of the revolutionary prime minister next to the Parliament building but decided to change the tone. In 1951, authorities removed Horvay's monument, which was seen as too pessimistic due to its melancholy mood, and replaced it with a more upbeat representation of Kossuth the orator by Zsigmond Kisfaludi Strobl. The Communist regime promoted an optimistic view of history rather than one made up of tragedies, and Horvay's memorial, which—in the sculptor's words—represented "the suffering and great sorrow of the Hungarian," was not suited to this message.[7] Nevertheless, it was not destroyed; instead, after standing for a few years in a cemetery in Budapest, it was transferred to the town of Dombóvár and erected as a public monument.[8] As during the Horthy regime, the memory of 1848–1849 could not be rejected, but it could be manipulated by shifting emphases between its different elements and controlling their visibility. Horvay's sad Kossuth was thought to be inappropriate for a central national space of remembrance, but it could still serve a purpose as a focus of more limited local commemorations.

Kisfaludi Strobl, maker of one of the irredentist sculptures and favored artist of the Horthy regime, was obviously a great survivor; he continued to carry out public commissions, including statues of Stalin and Lenin, up until his death in 1975. Other artists discussed in this book remained less prominent. With many of their works destroyed, artists such as Andor Dudits or Aba-Novák fell largely into oblivion. In the case of the latter, research on the School of Rome in the 1980s gradually restored his renown, while the former has remained one of many late academic painters whose conservative art is rarely analyzed.[9] A discussion of the many shifts in cultural politics, art historical canons, and historiographical trends that have shaped the reception of artists since 1945 would far surpass the scope of this book. One artist worth mentioning, however, is Gyula Derkovits, whose reputation was closely linked with Communist memory politics. As a left-wing artist who had depicted the miseries of the proletariat, Derkovits, the historical figure, was always viewed favorably by Communist authorities. His art, however, raised problems in the Stalinist 1950s. At a time when Socialist Realism was held up as an artistic ideal, Derkovits's professed modernism counted as bourgeois formalism.[10] By the 1960s, the art policies of the state loosened, and the prewar modernism of left-wing artists emerged as a preferred artistic idiom. Seizing this opportunity, art historians researched and promoted the work of Derkovits, who emerged as the model Socialist artist. He lent his name to, among other things, a scholarship for young artists, a state-run commercial art gallery, and a housing estate in his birthplace, Szombathely. Like most Socialist icons, Derkovits lost some of his appeal after 1989 but nevertheless continues to be viewed as one of the most significant artists of the interwar period. The major retrospective exhibition organized in 2014 emphasized his principled, thoughtful modernism and the complexity and inventiveness of his "picture-essays" while also placing him more firmly into the context of interwar left-wing activism.[11]

The year 1989 brought a plethora of changes. The visible memoryscape of Hungary transformed yet again, as some of the previously obliterated images and artworks returned to the public eye. Aba-Novák's frescoes were restored both in Szeged and Székesfehérvár in the 1990s. At the time, the restoration of the murals garnered broad support across the political spectrum.[12] It was seen as the rightful salvaging of artistic heritage that had been obliterated for political reasons. But can public artworks that encapsulate not only a pointed political message but also a whole ideology ever become the subjects of pure aesthetic consumption? Certainly, perhaps, in times when the ideology no longer resonates. Until then, they embody the cultural environment in which militant irredentism thrived. In Székesfehérvár, for instance, they provide a political framing for archaeological research, even if the results of that research question some of the fundaments of the framing, as explained in chapter 4.

Not all artworks removed after 1945 have been restored, however. In the National Archives, restoring the lost or repainted parts is either impossible—for lack of photos of the originals—or deemed unnecessary. In other, more high-profile cases, the possibility of reconstruction sometimes emerges in public discourse. With the fall of Communism, it became possible to openly discuss the commemoration of Trianon and the Horthy regime. In the early 1990s, under the right-wing Hungarian Democratic Forum (Magyar Demokrata Fórum, MDF) government, many different projects emerged to rehabilitate the regime and its ideology, receiving varying degrees of governmental support. In August 1990, timed for the anniversary of the Second Vienna Award, a group named the Holy Crown Association created a foundation with the aim of restoring the irredentist monuments of Freedom Square.[13] Opponents of the project pointed out that the *Reliquary Country Flag* had been inscribed with a quotation from Mussolini. Faced with strong push-back, including from the minister of defense, the foundation disbanded.[14] By the next year, however, its chairman, the military historian Ernő Raffay, was state secretary at the Ministry of Defense and regarded the plan as unproblematic apart from the Mussolini reference.[15] In 1993, Horthy's remains were brought to Hungary from Portugal, where he had died, to be festively reburied in his family's plot in Kenderes. The event was initiated by a nongovernmental organization, the Association of Hungarian Sailors, but received tacit governmental support, with MDF politicians attending the ceremony and Prime Minister József Antall sending a wreath—a constellation remarkably similar to the cooperation between grassroots organizations and the state in interwar memory politics.[16]

Under Communism, the memory of Trianon was suppressed and rarely talked about; it only surfaced, from the 1970s onward, in cautious discussions about the rights of Hungarian minorities in neighboring countries.[17] This meant that the memory of Trianon shifted. As the rhetoric and imagery of irredentism disappeared from the public sphere, the remembrance of the territorial changes lost its militant edge and came to be embodied, instead, in the consumption and fostering of Hungarian minority culture "outside the borders." Irredentist spacetime no longer functioned as an encompassing interpretative framework. Today, as discussed at the end of chapter 2, the imagery of the irredentist memorials is often on public view, thanks to their miniature versions. Initiatives to reerect the monuments surface now and then; one researcher observed a temporary monument, erected to call for the restoration of the originals, in Freedom Square in 2008.[18] The restoration has not happened, but the imagery and ideas of irredentism are back in the political sphere and the everyday. As Margit Feischmidt has shown, Trianon in the twenty-first century works as a "national mythomoteur" that "speaks to current feelings of loss and disenfranchisement, offering symbolic compensation through the transference of historical glory" without necessarily reviving all the elements of interwar irredentism.[19]

Irredentism offered compensation for a sense of disenfranchisement in the interwar period, too. Still, at least according to my own perceptions, irredentist spacetime as a way of viewing the totality of Hungarian history has not returned, and many of its elements remain largely forgotten. This might not always remain so; as I noted in the relevant chapter, the latest central Trianon monument erected by the Fidesz government combines geometrical forms very dissimilar to the Freedom Square monuments with an evocation of Greater Hungary as a unified historical space that is much in their spirit. New school textbooks emphasize Hungarian victimhood in Trianon while also reviving interwar perspectives such as Turanism in the discussion of earlier historical periods.[20] However, the fact that the direction is not a given and depends on further political action proves how memory is the product of constant work.

According to Myra Waterbury, in post-1989 Hungarian mainstream politics, references to Trianon and the "lost" territories serve "the interests and perceptions of political elites, who desire access to three sets of resources represented by ethnic diasporas: the extraction of material resources for economic gain; the utilization of those abroad as a culturo-linguistic resource to be used in defining the boundaries of national identity; and as political resources to help create or maintain legitimacy and support for kin-state elites."[21] In other words, influencing the present inhabitants of former Hungarian regions is more important than the land itself as historical territory, which makes irredentist spacetime obsolete. Waterbury's book was published in 2010, and much has happened since then: Fidesz's hard-right shift; its granting of Hungarian citizenship to minority Hungarians despite the fact that—as a failed referendum in 2004 attested—this decision was not particularly popular with the Hungarian electorate; the Russian full-scale invasion of Ukraine, which seems to have removed the taboo from certain forms of irredentist speech and imagery.[22] Still, I believe the point about the lower salience of territory in today's kin-state nationalism still stands and explains the differences between the imagery and commemoration of Trianon then and today. The attempt to conceptualize the treaty as shared Central European trauma through the 2020 Trianon memorial is a case in point.

The Trianon memorial is an abstract postmodern one, but the memory politics of Viktor Orbán's government generally employs a different visual language, one resembling historicism but better described perhaps as selective reconstruction. In 2010, after Fidesz won the elections in a landslide, the new government instructed all public institutions to display a framed copy of the Declaration of National Cooperation, a text sanctioned by the Parliament on 14 June 2010. The declaration defined the 2010 elections as a revolution "in the voting booths" through which Hungary had finally regained its independence after losing it in 1944, with the German occupation. This model of history, which not only rehabilitated and asserted continuity with the Horthy regime but also assigned the blame for the Holocaust fully to Germany, drives the government's politics of memory in its most visible form.[23] A prominent project has been the reconstruction of Kossuth Square, which explicitly aimed to restore the pre-1944 state of this public space.[24] This meant reproducing and reerecting monuments to nineteenth-century Prime Minister Gyula Andrássy (1823–1890; equestrian statue originally erected in

1906 and removed in 1945) and Prime Minister (during the First World War) István Tisza (1861–1918; monument erected in 1934 and toppled in 1945). It also meant removing some more recent statues, such as those of Mihály Károlyi (erected in 1975) and Imre Nagy (erected in 1996). Even Kisfaludi Strobl's Kossuth monument had to go. Replaced by a newly made reproduction of Horvay's memorial, it was resurrected, in a scrambled and somewhat puzzling composition, near the recently founded National University of Public Service. Edit András has described the new appearance of Kossuth Square as "postsocialist nationalist sublime," which invoked historical time in a grandiose gesture of "time travel" in order to erase the Communist past.[25]

The removal of Horvay's statue in the 1950s had been motivated by specific ideological concerns, including the wish to promote an optimistic view of history. By contrast, its reinstatement in the 2010s was just one element in a broader project to visually reconstruct the public environment of a chosen time. A similar aim drives the rebuilding of the Buda Royal Palace and its surroundings. Heavily damaged in 1945, the palace had been reconstructed in the 1960s according to a reduced plan, with some of its more elaborate historicist parts lost and several surrounding structures never rebuilt. Today, these surrounding buildings are being reerected out of concrete, and the refurbishment of the palace according to its prewar state is ongoing. The centrality of such projects to the Orbán government's self-representation and the proliferation of figurative, stylistically conservative public sculptures like the controversial *Monument of the German Occupation* in Freedom Square (mentioned in chap. 2) easily prompt an identification of the government with antimodernism and historicism. This view is supported by the government's self-promotion as a defender of traditional values against new "Western" trends such as feminism, multiculturalism, gender studies, or LGBTQ activism and its revival of traditionalist movements such as Turanism in its education policies and external cultural diplomacy.[26]

This is, however, only part of the picture. The abstract Trianon monument is not a unique exception; it is one example of "up-to-date," "progressive" elements nestling within the government's institutionalized cultural frameworks. State-run Hungarian museums host exhibitions of renowned international contemporary artists from the "Western" art world; the buildings of the planned new museum quarter are constructed in contemporary styles, some designed by international architects. In reaching back to 1944 in its politics of memory, the Orbán government professes to reestablish a continuity with the Horthy regime. Like then, modernity and modernism have a place and function in a right-wing culture that defines itself as antiliberal. The past can help understand the present and the present the past; in both cases, strict dualities are insufficient to describe the politics of culture.

A simple model of a dual culture with two separate halves cannot account for a large section of the Horthy regime's cultural production, nor can it satisfyingly describe how the system and its ideology worked. Examples such as Noémi Ferenczy's Saint Stephen tapestry, a work produced for one of the regime's greatest celebrations of its ideology by a left-wing artist who usually worked in isolation, remain hard to understand in such a framework. After 1945, this tapestry unsurprisingly disappeared from public view. As part of the representative culture of the Horthy regime, it was removed from the Nyíregyháza town hall immediately after the war. Its whereabouts were unknown until 1966, when a curator at the town's András Jósa Museum decided to open a mysterious cylindrical container lying in storage, uncatalogued and unmarked.[27] The tapestry has since been on view at a 2000 exhibition of the tapestries commissioned for the Saint Stephen jubilee as well as at Ferenczy's retrospective in Szentendre in 2020.[28] The accompanying publications contextualized Ferenczy's work within the larger commission and the artist's oeuvre but did not address the underlying issues. How did Ferenczy, with her strongly held artistic and political convictions, get involved in official projects—not just the commission for the Saint Stephen jubilee but also the Hungarian pavilion for the 1937 Paris World's Fair? How did her modernism appeal so much to a regime supposedly engaging in neobaroque historical pretense?

Writing her introduction to Ferenczy's retrospective in 1956, the well-established Communist art historian and painter Anna Oelmacher (1908–1991) must have felt the cognitive dissonance. She stated that when the Gobelin artist received the commission, authorities performed a background check on her and disapprovingly noted her Communist contacts. This, together with the fact that the wanderers, representatives of "the people," had to be removed from the design, restored Ferenczy's oppositionary credentials in Oelmacher's eyes.[29] Nevertheless, even in this account, the authorities' reservations concerned Ferenczy's friend group and subject matter, not her artistic style. Indeed, Ferenczy's modernism seems to have raised more eyebrows under Communism than under the Horthy regime. As a long-time left-winger, the artist was nominally a celebrated artist after 1945; in 1948, she received a Kossuth Prize, the highest award for contributions to Hungarian culture. However, as internal documents from the Ministry of Culture show, she was increasingly under suspicion for her "formalism," and while she was appointed professor of Gobelins at the College of Applied Art in 1950, her tenure was marked by constant conflict until she retired in 1956.[30] Looking back from the 1950s, as Oelmacher did, it was tempting to try to fit all the small tensions, controversies, and shifts of the 1930s into a strictly dualist political framework, just as it is tempting to do today, looking back onto the 1950s, when Oelmacher thrived. Tempting; but it does not explain why, in the end, Ferenczy's Saint Stephen tapestry came into being regardless.

This book aims to provide a more nuanced framework for understanding these issues by examining different ways in which modernity, and sometimes modernism, could serve official purposes in interwar Hungary. I discuss Ferenczy's tapestry as an example of how, by the late 1930s, modernism and modernity had been subsumed into official representation, helping to promote Hungary as a highly civilized state that draws on its long history while remaining open to technological and cultural progress; a state worthy of achieving its revisionist goals. By involving modernist artists of different political persuasions, the state was able to draw a larger section of the cultural sphere under its influence without exerting totalitarian control. Analyzing these processes seems more fruitful to me than trying to investigate the perspectives of individual artists, whose personal reasons for being involved, their ambitions or existential needs, may never be fully known. My goal has been to sketch up some of the blurred areas, whether within politics or the art world, and to map some of the contact zones where official and subversive, conservative and progressive, touched each other in unexplored ways. In chapter 1, I trace how the modern metropolis became part of official representation. In chapter 2, I highlight how the memory politics of irredentism suffused the modern public sphere. In chapter 3, I examine the transformations of landscape imagery in modern art and how they visualized a diversity of perspectives on history. In chapter 4, I explore how the modern establishment of historical scholarship existed in symbiosis with the official politics of memory and analyze artworks born from this institutional cooperation. Finally, in chapter 5, I describe how the memory politics of opposition movements reacted to official memory politics by aiming to puncture its vulnerable points.

The visual art that grew out of this last aim did not stand in splendid isolation within a culture that shifted increasingly to the right but borrowed right-wing iconography (that of irredentism) and created a formal language that could elicit praise from political opponents. Derkovits's *1514* certainly remained on view after 1945; indeed, it became one of the most reproduced and best-known artworks of the interwar era, celebrated as a visual articulation of revolutionary Socialism. Nevertheless, the shades of meaning I discuss in this book—the work's connections with conflicts over strategy within the Communist movement, its evocation of the Communist instrumentalization of nationalism—fell into oblivion in the second half of the century. Under Communism, these were all uncomfortable memories.[31] Reconstructing them helps us see the culture of the period in its complexity.

Because it took peasants as its subject matter, *1514* evokes another broader cultural phenomenon that is extremely hard to fit into a dualist model of interwar culture and has therefore proved particularly hard to digest in Hungarian cultural memory: the populist movement. Thanks in part to populist writers, whose influence spread across the political spectrum, peasants gained increased salience in Hungarian politics in the 1930s, which undoubtedly contributed to the overall favorable reception of *1514* after Derkovits's 1934 memorial exhibition. Evaluating populism as a cultural phenomenon, especially in relation to left-wing culture, is not easy, however. As discussed in chapters 3 and 5, populism had a pronounced antisemitic element and fostered visions of racial and cultural purity. At the same time, many populists exhibited genuine concern for the poor, based on firsthand experience rather than propaganda, which related them to left-wing movements and put them at odds with governmental policies. To complicate things further, by the mid-thirties, populism was to some extent appropriated by official politics, while populists themselves shifted across the political spectrum. Some remained staunchly right-wing, others joined the anti-Fascist resistance or moved even further to the left. After 1945, many former populists ended up in governmental positions, and some remained there after 1948, as their party, the Independent Smallholders', Agrarian Workers', and Civic Party, merged into the Communist Party. The most prominent example was the ethnographer Gyula Ortutay, who held official positions from 1947 up until his death in 1978.

In this book, the artist most closely related to populism is György Buday. Due to the mutability of the populist movement and the broad spectrum of views held by its members, locating the activities of Buday and the Szeged Youth within the contemporary ideological context is a complicated task. Published in 1967, the most comprehensive monograph on the artistic endeavors of the Szeged Youth did not leave the racist and antisemitic roots of their outlook unmentioned; it discussed how some members went on to support German Nazism but ultimately emphasized the left-wing tendencies of the group.[32] It is true that, as quoted in chapter 3, even Buday himself had written passages echoing Dezső Szabó's racialized conception of Hungarian identity. It is also true that the ideas and activities of the group were varied and that it included several members of Jewish descent. To gain a deeper understanding of the movement, it is essential to transcend dualist models of Hungarian culture—even if, paradoxically, one of the original proponents of that model was Ferenc Erdei, a sociologist who had himself been a member of the Szeged Youth. In a book about visual culture, the central question is, however, how Buday's prints fit into this picture. What the images tell us is that the Szeged Youth certainly fostered a form of modernity. Instead of nostalgically dwelling on elements of peasant culture, as many of his contemporaries did, Buday rarely borrowed specific motifs from vernacular culture and composed his images in a veritably modern way. When the atmosphere of folktales was ominous, strange, scary, or stifling, Buday did not hesitate to express this. Populists set out to examine peasants as a separate class that would rebirth the Hungarian nation; even in the 1940s, in his dualist model of Hungarian culture, Erdei conceptualized the peasantry as a separate category isolated from the otherwise encompassing opposition of traditional and modern. Yet, in a sense, populists drew attention to peasants not as objects of nostalgia nor of snobbish social disdain but as members of contemporary Hungarian society and active individuals. Buday's images suggest that while they may have been left behind by modernization, they were not alien to modernity, and their creative sensibilities matched those of urban intellectuals. This also meant that peasants were participants—agents as well as victims—of history, and this was a message that, in the end, corresponded with Derkovits's Marxist portrayal of the subject.

Untangling these issues after observing the full extent of their entanglements is a formidable task for art history writing. In drawing attention to connections and blurred areas that cut across the model of two cultures, I am not suggesting that all actors and products of culture were equally part of the Horthy regime; on the contrary, the diversity of career strategies, the different forms that modernity could take, and the wide spectrum of institutions and organizations all suggest that there was a choice. In its restriction of parliamentarism and forceful dissemination of its ideology, the Horthy regime was certainly authoritarian, but it was not a totalitarian system. In cultural life, certain views deemed politically subversive were censored, but there was no centrally imposed doctrine of taste and style. It was not compulsory to contribute to state-sponsored projects or to propagate state ideology. Navigating the cultural landscape was, however, more complex than a simplified model would suggest, and the overlaps and surprising connections best reveal how ideology was transmitted through culture.

The heritage of the interwar period is a difficult one to deal with, and not just in Hungary. The First World War, the collapse of empires, and the competing irredentist claims of nations resulted in the proliferation of historical narratives that aimed to explain the recent past or justify territorial claims. Many of these live on, adapted to new political contexts and methods of dissemination.[33] The regime changes of 1989 saw the removal of Communist monuments across the former Eastern Bloc, but public spaces did not remain bare for long; new monuments were erected and sometimes old ones restored as different political movements struggled for control over the politics of memory and post-socialist governments aimed to use these public spaces for their own self-representation. In multiethnic regions, conflicts between different national narratives of history are often centered around monuments, which help clashes between Hungarian grievances over Trianon and Slovak or Romanian resentment over the preceding Hungarian domination play out in the public sphere, sometimes also occasioning acts of reconciliation.[34] Today's new nationalisms and illiberal governments draw on interwar precedents in their memory politics.[35] At the same time, contemporary artists across the region draw on the same imagery to creatively disrupt old narratives, critique their present incarnations, and offer more flexible, open, and interconnected models of national history and memory.[36]

In *School on the Frontier*, Ottlik chose a motto to encapsulate the dilemmas faced by the boys. "Non est volentis, neque currentis, sed miserentis Dei," a line from Saint Paul's *Letter to the Romans*, is inscribed on the façade of the famous Renaissance Sgraffito House in Kőszeg, where the novel's protagonists attended the military school.[37] "So, then it is not of him who wills, nor of him who runs, but of God who has mercy." The novel's exploration of the existence of free will in an oppressive environment is a historical lesson that has resonated with readers for seven decades. From their strict and unpredictable teachers, ruthless bullies, and submissive peers, Ottlik's characters learn that they live in a chaotic world that not only restricts their choices but also robs them of meaning. When rules are so numerous and invasive that it is impossible not to break them but transgressions are punished randomly and with no possibility of appeal, the choice between collaboration and resistance is no longer consequential. Yet, the book's central message is that the choice is still there; even if it is weightless, it embodies an inner freedom.

Does this provide an appropriate lens through which to view the cultural production of the Horthy regime? Dealing with different historical periods of oppression and forms of collaboration and resistance is so ingrained in Hungarian cultural memory that—as my reader may have noticed—I cannot extricate myself from its conceptual hold in this epilogue. It is, I suspect, a form of the tragic narrative of Hungarian history, mentioned so many times in the previous chapters. To look back into the mists of time from a different angle, let me finish with the Sgraffito House, a magnificent piece of built heritage that has survived hundreds of years to transport a biblical phrase, originally inscribed, no doubt, as an expression of religious piety, into the twentieth century.[38] There, its black-and-white yet cheerfully decorative facade became part of a much-loved novel, locating the plot in our mental maps by anchoring it in Kőszeg, a border town whose old military academy recalled the Habsburg past of 1920s Hungary. The biblical phrase morphed into a secular statement about individual freedom and—according to subsequent readings of the book—broader forms of social oppression. Works of visual art transport memory into the present, and in doing so, they not only reflect how the past was interpreted in their own time but also offer themselves up for reinterpretation today. Their historian must wade through memory layers, and these layers all shape their scholarly investigation. Their future lives, their new interpretations, depend on what we make of them in the present.

Notes

Introduction

1. Mabel Berezin, *Making the Fascist Self: The Political Culture of Interwar Italy* (Ithaca, NY: Cornell University Press, 1997), 141–195.

2. Sándor Kontha, ed., *Magyar művészet 1919–1945* [Hungarian art 1919–1945], vol. 1 (Budapest: Hungarian Academy of Sciences, 1985), 171–222.

3. For example, Julianna P. Szűcs, *A Római Iskola* [The School of Rome] (Budapest: Corvina, 1987); P. Szűcs, "A 'Modern' Official Art: The School of Rome," in *A Reader in East-Central-European Modernism 1918–1956*, ed. Beáta Hock, Klara Kemp-Welch, and Jonathan Owen (London: Courtauld Institute of Art, 2019), accessed 11 November 2024, https://courtauld.ac.uk/research/research-resources/publications/cour tauld-books-online/a-reader-in-east-central-european-modernism-1918–1956/20-a -modern-official-art-the-school-of-rome-julianna-p-szucs/; András Zwickl, ed., *In the Land of Arcadia: István Szőnyi and His Circle 1918–1928 / Árkádia tájain: Szőnyi István és köre 1918–1928* (Budapest: Hungarian National Gallery, 2001); Anna Kopócsy, "A jelen történelmi értelmezése fa- és linóleummetszet-sorozatokban a két világháború között" [The historical interpretation of the present in series of woodcuts and linocuts in the interwar period], in *A modern magyar fa- és linóleummetszés 1890–1950* [Modern Hungarian wood- and linocuts], ed. Enikő Róka (Miskolc: Miskolci Galéria, 2005), 137–157; Zwickl, "Between Conservatism and Modernism: Classicisms and Realisms of the 1920s in Central Europe," in *Local Strategies, International Ambitions: Modern Art and Central Europe 1918–1968*, ed. Vojtěch Lahoda (Prague: Artefactum, 2006), 77–83.

4. Róka has insightfully analyzed this in "Construction of Continuity: Nationalism and Art in Interwar Hungary," keynote lecture at "In the Shadow of the Habsburg Empire," ERC CRAACE research group, Moravian Gallery, Brno, 12–14 September 2014.

5. Roger Griffin, *Modernism and Fascism: The Sense of a Beginning under Mussolini and Hitler* (Houndmills, UK: Palgrave Macmillan, 2007).

6. Ruth Ben-Ghiat, *Fascist Modernities: Italy, 1922–1945* (Berkeley: University of California Press, 2001); Claudio Fogu, *The Historic Imaginary: Politics of History in Fascist Italy* (Toronto: University of Toronto Press, 2003).

7. Matthew Affron and Mark Antliff, eds., *Fascist Visions: Art and Ideology in France and Italy* (Princeton, NJ: Princeton University Press, 1997); Irena Kossowska, ed., *Reinterpreting the Past: Traditionalist Artistic Trends in Central and Eastern Europe of the 1920s and 1930s* (Warsaw: Institute of Art of the Polish Academy of Sciences, 2010); Julia Secklehner, "A New Austrian Regionalism: Alfons Walde and Austrian Identity in Painting after 1918," *Austrian History Yearbook* 52 (2021): 201–226; Christian Drobe, *Verdächtige Ambivalenz: Klassizismus in der Moderne 1920–1960* (Weimar: Arts and Sci-

ence Weimar, 2022); Małgorzata Sears, *The Warsaw Group Rytm (1922–1933) and Modernist Classicism* (Kraków: Universitas, 2022).

8. On the limits on parliamentarism and on political and public life, see Levente Püski, *A Horthy-korszak parlamentje* [The parliament of the Horthy era] (Budapest: Országház Könyvkiadó, 2021).

9. Róka, "Construction of Continuity."

10. Walter Benjamin, "The Storyteller," in *Illuminations*, trans. Harry Zohn (London: Fontana, 1992), 84.

11. Miklós Zeidler, *Ideas on Territorial Revision in Hungary: 1920–1945* (Boulder, CO: Social Science Monographs, 2007).

12. Marina Cattaruzza, Stefan Dyroff, and Dieter Langewiesche, eds., *Territorial Revisionism and the Allies of Germany in the Second World War: Goals, Expectations, Practices* (New York: Berghahn, 2012).

13. Wolfgang Kemp, *Wir haben ja alle Deutschland nicht gekannt: Das Deutschlandbild der Deutschen in der Zeit der Weimarer Republik* (Heidelberg: Heidelberg University Publishing, 2016).

14. Nancy Wingfield, *Flag Wars and Stone Saints: How the Bohemian Lands Became Czech* (Cambridge, MA: Harvard University Press, 2007).

15. Jade McGlynn, *Memory Makers: The Politics of the Past in Putin's Russia* (London: Bloomsbury Academic, 2023), 4.

16. Margit Feischmidt, "Memory-Politics and Neonationalism: Trianon as Mythomoteur," *Nationalities Papers* 48, no. 1 (2020): 130–143.

17. On the concept, see Pierre Nora, "Preface to English Language Edition: From *Lieux de memoire* to Realms of Memory," in *Realms of Memory: Rethinking the French Past*, ed. Nora, English edition ed. Lawrence D. Kritzman, trans. Arthur Goldhammer, vol. 1 (New York: Columbia University Press, 1996), xv–xxiv; Nora, "Between Memory and History: Les Lieux de Mémoire," *Representations* 26 (1989): 11–12; Pim den Boer, "Loci memoriae–Lieux de mémoire," in *A Companion to Cultural Memory Studies*, ed. Astrid Erll and Ansgar Nünning (Berlin: Walter DeGruyter, 2010), 19–26.

18. In Hungary, see, for example, Zeidler, *Ideas on Territorial Revision in Hungary*; Balázs Ablonczy, *Trianon-legendák* [Trianon legends] (Budapest: Jaffa Kiadó, 2015), and *Ismeretlen Trianon* [Unknown Trianon] (Budapest: Jaffa Kiadó, 2020).

19. Steven Seegel, *Map Men: Transnational Lives and Deaths of Geographers in the Making of East Central Europe* (Chicago: Chicago University Press, 2018); Larry Wolff, *Woodrow Wilson and the Reimagining of Eastern Europe* (Stanford, CA: Stanford University Press, 2020). For an analysis of Hungarian "national cartographies" in the present, see Máté Zombory, *Maps of Remembrance: Space, Belonging and Politics of Memory in Eastern Europe* (Budapest: L'Harmattan, 2012).

20. Frithjhof Benjamin Schenk, "Mental Maps: The Cognitive Mapping of the Continent as an Object of Research of European History," *European History Online* (EGO), 8 July 2013, http://www.ieg-ego.eu/schenkf-2013-en; Norbert Götz and Janne Holmén, "Introduction to the Theme Issue: Mental Maps: Geographical and Historical Perspectives," *Journal of Cultural Geography* 35, no. 2 (2018): 157–161.

21. Schenk, "Mental Maps," 2.

22. For a discussion of the Lillafüred Palota Hotel that explores similar issues, see Gergely Kunt, "Creating the New Hungarian Tatras: Symbolic Politics as a Means of

Repositioning Tourism in Northern Hungary During the Interwar Period," *Journal of Tourism History* 15, no. 1 (2023): 20–42.

23. James E. Young, "The Counter-Monument: Memory against Itself in Germany Today," *Critical Inquiry* 18, no. 2 (1992): 270, 273.

24. Ann Rigney, "Plenitude, Scarcity and the Circulation of Cultural Memory," *Journal of European Studies* 35, no. 1 (2005): 19.

25. Rigney, "Plenitude, Scarcity," 19.

26. Zombory, *Maps of Remembrance*.

27. Jessica Rapson and Lucy Bond, eds., *The Transcultural Turn: Interrogating Memory Between and Beyond Borders* (Berlin: De Gruyter, 2014); Chiara de Cesari and Rigney, eds., *Transnational Memory: Circulation, Articulation, Scales* (Berlin: De Gruyter, 2014).

28. Rogers Brubaker, "National Minorities, Nationalizing States, and External National Homelands in the New Europe," in *Nationalism Reframed: Nationhood and the National Question in the New Europe* (Cambridge, UK: Cambridge University Press, 1996), 55–76.

29. Jeffrey Olick, "From Collective Memory to the Sociology of Mnemonic Practices and Products," in *A Companion to Cultural Memory Studies*, ed. Erll and Nünning (Berlin: Walter de Gruyter, 2010), 159.

30. Rigney, "The Dynamics of Remembrance: Texts Between Monumentality and Morphing," in *A Companion to Cultural Memory Studies*, ed. Erll and Nünning, 345–346; Rigney, "Remembrance as Remaking: Memories of the Nation Revisited," *Nations and Nationalism* 24, no. 2 (2018): 240–257.

31. Peter J. Verovšek, "Collective Memory, Politics, and the Influence of the Past: The Politics of Memory as a Research Paradigm," *Politics, Groups, and Identities* 4, no. 3 (2016): 529–543.

32. Emily Hanscam and James Koranyi, "Digging Politics: The Ancient Past and Contested Present," in *Digging Politics: The Ancient Past and Contested Present in East-Central Europe*, ed. Koranyi and Hanscam (Berlin: Walter de Gruyter, 2023), 1–4.

33. See the essays in Koranyi and Hanscam, *Digging Politics*.

34. For a monograph that evocatively describes the chaotic nature of the Soviet Republic, see Pál Hatos, *Rosszfiúk világforradalma: Az 1919-es Magyarországi Tanácsköztársaság története* [A world revolution of bad boys: The history of the 1919 Hungarian Soviet Republic] (Budapest: Jaffa Kiadó, 2021). On the Red Terror, see 357–374.

35. On the Horthy regime's self-defining in opposition to the Soviet Republic, see Péter Csunderlik, *A "vörös farsangtól" a "vörös tatárjárásig": A Tanácsköztársaság a korai Horthy-korszak pamflet- és visszaemlékezés-irodalmában* [From "red Fasching" to the "invasion of the red Tartars": The Soviet Republic in pamphlets and memoirs of the early Horthy era] (Budapest: Napvilág Kiadó, 2019).

36. For a deconstruction of the myth of Jewish dominance in the Soviet Republic, see Hatos, *Rosszfiúk világforradalma*, 95–117.

37. Iván Zoltán Dénes, *A történelmi Magyarország eszménye: Szekfű Gyula a történetíró és ideológus* [The ideal of historical Hungary: Gyula Szekfű the historian and ideologue] (Bratislava: Kalligram, 2015); on the Rákóczi book and the ensuing scandal, see 61–179. See also Ignác Romsics, *Clio bűvöletében: Magyar történetírás a 19–20. században—nemzetközi kitekintéssel* [Under the spell of Clio: Hungarian historiog-

raphy in the 19th and 20th centuries—with an international overview] (Budapest: Osiris, 2011), 279–282.

38. Gyula Szekfű, *Három nemzedék: Egy hanyatló kor története* [Three generations: The history of a declining age] (Budapest: Élet, 1920).

39. Tara Zahra, "Against the World: The Collapse of Empire and the Deglobalization of Interwar Austria," *Austrian History Yearbook* 52 (2021): 1–10.

40. Fogu, *The Historic Imaginary*, 25.

41. Dávid Turbucz, *A Horthy-kultusz 1919–1944* [The Horthy cult] (Budapest: Research Centre for the Humanities, 2016), 99.

42. Béla Bodó, *The White Terror: Antisemitic and Political Violence in Hungary, 1919–1921* (London: Routledge, 2019).

43. On the ideology, see Paul Hanebrink, *In Defense of Christian Hungary: Religion, Nationalism and Antisemitism, 1890–1944* (Ithaca, NY: Cornell University Press, 2006). On the antisemitism of the Horthy regime, see Krisztián Ungváry, *A Horthy-rendszer és antiszemitizmusának mérlege: Diszkrimináció és társadalompolitika Magyarországon 1919–1944* [The Horthy regime and an assessment of its antisemitism: Discrimination and social policy in Hungary] (Budapest: Jelenkor, 2017).

44. Romsics, *Bethlen István: Politikai életrajz* [IB: Political biography] (Budapest: Helikon, 2019). A shorter English version: Romsics, *István Bethlen: A Great Conservative Statesman of Hungary, 1874–1946* (Boulder, CO: Social Science Monographs, 1995).

45. Jan Bröker, *"Horthy Is a Nobody": Trials of Lèse-Régent in Hungary 1920–1944* (master's diss., Central European University, Budapest, 2011), https://www.etd.ceu.edu/2011/broker_jan.pdf.

46. Hanebrink, *In Defense of Christian Hungary.*

47. Katalin Sinkó, "Árpád versus Saint István: Competing Heroes and Competing Interests in the Representation of Hungarian History," *Ethnologia Europeana* 19, no. 1 (1988): 67–84.

48. Klimó, Árpád von, *Nation, Konfession, Geschichte: Zur nationalen Geschichtskultur Ungarns im europäischen Kontext (1860–1948)* (Munich: Oldenbourg, 2003).

49. Romsics, *Clio bűvöletében*, 125–152.

50. Hanebrink, *In Defense of Christian Hungary*, 17–19.

51. Ablonczy, *Go East! A History of Hungarian Turanism* (Bloomington: Indiana University Press, 2022).

52. Ablonczy, *Go East!*

53. Seegel, *Map Men*, 50–51; Ablonczy, *Go East!*

54. Zeidler, *Ideas on Territorial Revision in Hungary.*

55. Turbucz, *A Horthy-kultusz*, 92.

56. Raymond Williams, "When Was Modernism," in *Art in Modern Culture*, ed. Francis Frascina and Jonathan Harris (London: Phaidon, 1992), 24.

57. For a summary of such definitions, see Griffin, *Modernism and Fascism*, 54–58.

58. Peter Childs, *Modernism* (London: Routledge, 2000), 17, quoted in Griffin, *Modernism and Fascism*, 55.

59. Griffin, *Modernism and Fascism.*

60. Emilio Gentile, "The Myth of National Regeneration in Italy: From Modernist Avant-Garde to Fascism," in *Fascist Visions*, ed. Affron and Antliff, 25–45.

61. P. Szűcs, *A Római Iskola*; P. Szűcs, "A 'Modern' Official Art."

62. Tibor Gerevich, "Római magyar művészek" [Hungarian artists in Rome], *Magyar Szemle* (1932): 235–240.

63. Ferenc Erdei, "A magyar társadalom a két háború között" [Hungarian society between the wars], I and II, *Valóság* 19, no. 4 and 5 (1976): 22–53, 36–58.

64. Márk Áron Éber, "Melyik kettő? Miért kettős? A magyar szociológia kettőstársadalom-elméleteinek hasznáról és káráról" [Which two? Why dual? On the uses and disadvantages of theories of dual society in Hungarian sociology], *Szociológiai Szemle* 21, no. 3 (2011): 4–22. On dualities in describing interwar Hungarian society in contemporary accounts and subsequent scholarship, see also Romsics, "Magyarország(ok) a két világháború között" [Hungary(s) between the two World Wars], in Romsics, *A Horthy-korszak* [The Horthy Era] (Budapest: Helikon, 2018).

65. Gábor Gyáni, "Érvek a kettős struktúra elmélete ellen" [Arguments against the dual structure theory], *Korall* 2, no. 3–4 (2001), 221–231, esp. 227–228.

66. For a summary, see Béla Tomka, "A Horthy-korszak társadalom- és gazdaságtörténetének kutatása: Újabb eredmények és viták" [The study of the social and economic history of the Horthy era: New results and debates], in *A Horthy-korszak vitatott kérdései* [Debated issues of the Horthy era] (Budapest: Kossuth Kiadó, 2020), 23–24.

67. Verovšek, "Collective Memory." On these channels in Hungary, see Ildikó Szabó, *Nemzet és szocializáció: A politika szerepe az identitások formálódásában Magyarországon, 1867–2006* [Nation and socialization: The role of politics in shaping identities in Hungary] (Budapest: L'Harmattan, 2009).

68. Berezin, *Making the Fascist Self.*

69. Zsolt Nagy, *Great Expectations and Interwar Realities: Hungarian Cultural Diplomacy 1918–1941* (Budapest: CEU Press, 2017).

70. Nagy, *Great Expectations and Interwar Realities.*

71. See, for example, Éva Forgács, *Hungarian Art: Confrontation and Revival in the Modern Movement* (Los Angeles: Doppelhouse, 2016); Ralf Burmeister et al., eds., *Magyar Modern: Hungarian Art in Berlin 1910–1933* (Berlin: Hirmer, 2022).

72. Kopócsy, *Új Nyolcak: Festőnők a modern művészet sodrában* [The new eight: Women painters in the current of modern art] (Budapest: Holnap, 2021); on Bartoniek and history, see 189–191.

1. Spectacles of Renewal

1. For a photo, see, for example, *Vasárnapi Ujság*, 30 November 1919, 358, accessed 2 July 2024, https://dka.oszk.hu/html/kepoldal/index.phtml?id=74487#.

2. Fogu, *The Historic Imaginary*, 9–10.

3. On Szekfű's concepts of baroque and neobaroque, see Péter Erdősi, "Barokk és neobarokk: Két fogalom kölcsönhatása Magyarországon" [Baroque and neobaroque: The interaction of two concepts in Hungary], *Korall* 23 (2006): 155–186.

4. Ben-Ghiat, *Fascist Modernities.*

5. Griffin, *Modernism and Fascism.*

6. Fogu, *The Historic Imaginary*; Simonetta Falasca-Zamponi, *Fascist Spectacle: The Aesthetics of Power in Mussolini's Italy* (Berkeley: University of California Press, 1997).

7. Griffin, *Modernism and Fascism*, 54–58.

8. Gentile, "The Myth of National Regeneration in Italy," 25–45.

9. On the legionary movement and modernism, see Roland Clark, *Holy Legionary Youth: Fascist Activism in Interwar Romania* (Ithaca, NY: Cornell University Press, 2015), 137–140.

10. Mark Antliff, "La Cité française: Georges Valois, Le Corbusier, and Fascist Theories of Urbanism," in *Fascist Visions*, ed. Affron and Antliff, 134–170.

11. Quoted in Falasca-Zamponi, *Fascist Spectacle*, 20.

12. Falasca-Zamponi, *Fascist Spectacle*, 21.

13. Benjamin, "The Work of Art in the Age of Mechanical Reproduction," in Benjamin, *Illuminations*, ed. Hannah Arendt, trans. Zohn (London: Jonathan Cape, 1970), 243.

14. Horthy accused the city of having "dressed in red rags" in his speech on Gellért Square on 16 November 1919. See e.g., "Bevonultak a nemzet katonái: Horthy és hadserege Budapesten" [The soldiers of the nation have made their entrance: Horthy and his army in Budapest], *Pesti Napló*, 18 November 1919, 3. Unless otherwise indicated, translations from Hungarian are my own.

15. Csunderlik, *A "vörös farsangtól" a "vörös tatárjárásig,"* 298–305.

16. For the most detailed reconstruction of the decorations, see Csilla Markója, "'Vörös posztó': Városinstalláció 1919. május 1-én a források tükrében" [Seeing Red: The urban installation on 1 May 1919 in the light of the sources], *Enigma* 94, no. 25 (2018): 147–215. See also Boldizsár Vörös, "Károlyi Mihály tér, Marx-szobrok, fehér ló: Budapest szimbolikus elfoglalásai 1918–1919-ben" [Mihály Károlyi Square, statues of Marx, white horse: Symbolic occupations of Budapest in 1918–1919], in Vörös, *Eszmék, eszközök, hatások: Tanulmányok a magyarországi propagandáról, 1914–1919* [Ideas, devices, influences: Studies on propaganda in Hungary] (Budapest: MTA Bölcsészettudományi Kutatóközpont, 2018), 139–161; Bob Dent, *Painting the Town Red: Politics and the Arts during the 1919 Hungarian Soviet Republic* (London: Pluto, 2018), 44–86.

17. Markója, "Vörös posztó," 152–153.

18. Many of the individual works are connected to specific artists in Markója, "Vörös posztó."

19. Markója, "Vörös posztó," 173–175.

20. On the tension, see Merse Pál Szeredi, "A 'Mácastílus irodalmi diktátora Lukács György sznob uszályában': Az Aktivisták a Tanácsköztársaságban" ["The literary dictator of Máca style in the snobbish entourage of György Lukács": The activists in the Soviet Republic], *Enigma* 94, no. 25 (2018): 128–146.

21. Vörös, "Történelmi hősök, új rendszerek: Emlékszobrok Szovjet-Oroszországban és a Magyarországi Tanácsköztársaságban 1917–1918" [Historical heroes, new regimes: Memorial statues in Soviet Russia and the Hungarian Soviet Republic], *Mozgó Világ* 24, no. 5 (1998): 85–105; Markója, "Vörös posztó," 173.

22. Markója, "Vörös posztó," 159.

23. [Untitled photo of Ferenciek tere in Budapest on 1 May 1919], 1919, donated by Frigyes Schoch, *Fortepan*, accessed 19 September 2024, https://fortepan.hu/hu/photos/?id=27908.

24. Vörös, "Térfoglalás Budapesten—térfoglalás a történelemben? A Nemzeti Hadsereg budapesti bevonulási ünnepsége 1919. november 16-án" [Occupying space in Budapest—occupying space in history? The celebrations of the Hungarian National Army's entrance into Budapest on 16 November 1919], in *Ünnep–hétköznap–*

emlékezet: Társadalom és kultúrtörténet határmesgyéjén, ed. Cecília Pásztor (Salgótarján: Nógrád County Archives, 2002), 180–190.

25. "Bevonultak a nemzet katonái…" 3.

26. Quoted in Turbucz, *A Horthy-kultusz*, 74.

27. Markója, "Vörös posztó," 184.

28. Markója, "Vörös posztó," 183.

29. Turbucz, *A Horthy-kultusz*, 144–148.

30. Turbucz, *A Horthy-kultusz*, 149.

31. Berezin, *Making the Fascist Self*, 73.

32. "Márton Ferenc—a képrombolásáról" [FM—on his destruction of his painting], *Nemzeti Ujság*, 29 September 1920, 5.

33. "Eskü a Vérmezőn képpályázat" [Oath in the Vérmező painting competition], *Budapesti Hírlap*, 1 August 1920, 4.

34. T. Csaba Reisz, "Eskü a Vérmezőn" [Oath in the Vérmező], *Magyar Nemzeti Levéltár*, 17 May 2013, accessed 4 December 2024, https://mnl.gov.hu/a_het_doku mentuma/esku_a_vermezon.html.

35. "Márton Ferenc—a képrombolásáról".

36. On the Hungarian Jacobins in Social Democratic activism, see Vörös, *"A múltat végképp eltörölni"? Történelmi személyiségek a magyarországi szociáldemokrata és kommunista propagandában 1890–1919* ["We'll change henceforth the old tradition"? Historical personalities in Hungarian Social Democratic and Communist propaganda] (Budapest: MTA History Research Institute, 2004), 52–54.

37. "Mi ünnepélyesen esküszünk . . ." [We solemnly swear . . .], *Pesti Napló*, 13 April 1920, 3.

38. Photo, *Vasárnapi Ujság*, 25 April 1920, 88; National Széchényi Library Digital Picture Archive, accessed 2 July 2024, https://dka.oszk.hu/094000/094066.

39. *Vasárnapi Ujság*, 25 April 1920, 89, accessed 19 September 2024, https://epa .oszk.hu/00000/00030/03435/pdf/VU_EPA00030_1920_08.pdf.

40. [Caption on front page], *Képes Krónika*, 20 April 1920, 411.

41. "Meghívó" [Invitation], *Világ*, 16 May 1920, 4. See T. Csaba Reisz, *Dudits Andor családja, élete és munkássága* [The family, life, and oeuvre of Andor Dudits], manuscript, 161. I am grateful to T. Csaba Reisz for giving me access to his discussion of *The Oath in the* Vérmező in his upcoming monograph on Dudits.

42. István Szirmay, "Ahol mindenki csak egy ujjal zongorázik" [Where everyone plays the piano with just one finger], *Ujság*, 18 September 1927, 36.

43. Lajos Kassák, "A budapesti második nemzetközi fényképkiállítás" [The second Budapest international photography exhibition], *Századunk* 2, no. 2 (1927): 526–528.

44. "Eskü a Vérmezőn képpályázat," 4.

45. Miklós Szabó, "Politikai évfordulók a Horthy-rendszerben" [Political anniversaries in the Horthy regime], *Világosság* 19, no. 8–9 (1978): 507–516; Turbucz, *A Horthy-kultusz*, 9–10, 99, 129.

46. "Eskü a Vérmezőn" [Oath in the Vérmező], *Pesti Napló*, 13 May 1923, 8.

47. Turbucz, *A Horthy-kultusz*, 93–94.

48. "Eskü a Vérmezőn," 8.

49. Reisz, *Dudits Andor családja, élete és munkássága*, 165–167.

50. *Páter Zadravecz titkos naplója* [Secret diary of Friar Zadravecz], ed. György Borsányi (Budapest: Kossuth, 1967), 245, quoted in György Szücs, "'Pictura irre-

denta': Egy Csók István-kép elemzése" [Unredeemed painting: Analysis of a paint-
ing by István Csók], in *A Magyar Nemzeti Galéria Évkönyve / Annales of the Hungarian
National Gallery 1997–2001*, eds. Erzsébet Király and Anna Jávor (Budapest: Hungarian
National Gallery, 2002), 304.

51. Reisz, *Dudits Andor családja, élete és munkássága*, 167–172.

52. Reisz, *Dudits Andor családja, élete és munkássága*, 170.

53. "Dudits Andor felajánlotta a kormányzónak a 'Vérmezei eskütétel' vázlatát"
[AD has offered a study of the Oath in the Vérmező to the Regent], *8 Órai Ujság*, 26
May 1923, 7.

54. Turbucz, *A Horthy-kultusz*, 129, 161. On trials of *lèse-régent*, see 184–189; Jan
Bröker, *"Horthy Is a Nobody": Trials of Lèse-Régent in Hungary 1920–1944* (master's diss.,
Central European University, Budapest, 2011), https://www.etd.ceu.edu/2011/bro
ker_jan.pdf.

55. "Zehn Jahre Horthy," *Der Abend*, 27 February 1930, 8.

56. On Bíró, see Éva Bajkay, *Bíró Mihály* (Budapest: Reflektor, 1986); Peter Noever,
ed., *Mihály Bíró: Pathos in Rot* (Vienna: MAK, 2010). On the Horthy series, see Michael
Diers, "Colorful Images of Horror: The Horthy Portfolio by Mihály Bíró," in *Mihály
Bíró*, ed. Noever, 31–47.

57. "Biró Mihály Horthy-albuma a biróság előtt" [MB's Horthy album in court],
Jövő, 25 November 1922, 4; "Több külföldi sajtótermék postai szállitási jogának
megvonása tárgyában" [On banning the postal distribution of some foreign printed
material], *Pénzügyi Közlöny*, 1 September 1924, 532.

58. Annette Lechner, *Die Wiener Verlagsbuchhandlung "Anzengruber-Verlag, Brüder
Suschitzky" (1901–1938) im Spiegel der Zeit* (master's diss., University of Vienna, 1994),
https://www.wienbibliothek.at/sites/default/files/files/buchforschung/lechner
-annette-anzengruberverlag.pdf.

59. "Biró Mihály rajzai" [Drawings by MB], *Előre*, 10 February 1921, 2.

60. Ernő Kállai, "Tendencművészet és fotográfia" [Tendentious art and photog-
raphy], *Korunk* 2, no. 11 (1927): 766–771.

61. Kállai, "Tendencművészet és fotográfia," 767.

62. Kállai, "Tendencművészet és fotográfia," 770.

63. *Hansard*, Commons Chambers, vol. 126, 2 March 1920, https://hansard.parlia
ment.uk/Commons/1920-03-02/debates/3b858272-559e-453f-ab49-7c905aec361c
/Hungary.

64. British Joint Labour Delegation to Hungary, *The White Terror in Hungary*
(London: Trade Union Congress and the Labour Party, 1920).

65. Diers, "Colorful Images of Horror," 31–43.

66. British Joint Labour Delegation to Hungary, *The White Terror in Hungary*;
Bodó, *The White Terror*, 229–235. Despite the fact that her story was widely disseminated internationally by left-wing opponents of the Horthy regime, the first
name of "Mrs. Hamburger" never appears in any documents. See Emily Gioielli,
"The Woman with No First Name," *fernetzt—Junges Forschungsnetzwerk Frauen—und
Geschlechtergeschichte*, accessed 19 September 2024, https://fernetzt.univie.ac.at/the
-woman-with-no-first-name/.

67. Kállai, "Tendencművészet és fotográfia," 769.

68. Kállai, "Tendencművészet és fotográfia," 769.

69. "Zehn Jahre Horthy," 8.

70. "A magyar kormány felhívta az osztrák kormány figyelmét a durva támadásokra" [The Hungarian government has made the Austrian government aware of the aggressive attacks], *Nemzeti Ujság*, 1 March 1930, 5.

71. "Die Hüter der (Horthy-)Sittlichkeit," *Der Abend*, 14 June 1930, 1; "Osztrák ítélet Horthy kormányzó megsértéséért" [Austrian verdict for offending Regent Horthy], *Friss Ujság*, 14 June 1930, 4.

72. János B. Szabó, ed., *Mohács* (Budapest: Osiris, 2006); Pál S. Varga, Orsolya Száraz, and Miklós Takács, eds., *A magyar emlékezethelyek kutatásának elméleti és módszertani alapjai* [Researching sites of memory in Hungary: Theory and methodology] (Debrecen: Debrecen University Press, 2013).

73. Paul Hanebrink, "Islam, Anti-Communism, and Christian Civilization: The Ottoman Menace in Interwar Hungary," *Austrian History Yearbook* 40 (2009): 114–124.

74. Miklós Zeidler, *Ideas on Territorial Revision in Hungary: 1920–1945* (Boulder, CO: Social Science Monographs, 2007), ix, 234.

75. "Mohács: Bemutató a Nemzeti Színházban" [Mohács: Premiere at the National Theater], *Szinházi Élet* 9, no. 5 (1922): 3.

76. "Mohács: Bemutató a Nemzeti Színházban," 3–6, accessed 2 July 2024, https://epa.oszk.hu/02300/02343/00393/pdf/EPA02343_szinhazi_elet_1922_05.pdf.

77. "II. Lajos: Szomory darabja a Magyar Színházban" [Louis II: Szomory's play at the Magyar Theater], *Szinházi Élet* 11, no. 6 (1922): 3–12, accessed 2 July 2024, https://epa.oszk.hu/02300/02343/00394/pdf/EPA02343_szinhazi_elet_1922_06.pdf.

78. "II. Lajos: Szomory darabja a Magyar Színházban," 9.

79. *Mohács és Pécs részletes útmutatója: a mohácsi kiállítás, ünnepségek, kongresszusok, pécsi dalosünnepségek részletes műsoraival* [A detailed guide to Mohács and Pécs with detailed programs of the Mohács exhibition, festivities, congresses, and Pécs song festivals] (Budapest: Magyarság, 1926), 6.

80. *Mohács és Pécs részletes útmutatója*, 3.

81. "Mohács," *Pesti Napló Képes Melléklete*, 28 August 1926, 36; *Pesti Napló Képes Melléklete*, 5 September 1926, 34–35.

82. "A mohácsi vész 400. évfordulójának ünnepe Mohácson" [Festivities on the 400th anniversary of the Mohács disaster in Mohács], *Magyar Híradó*, 132, August 1926, accessed 20 September 2024, https://filmhiradokonline.hu/watch.php?id=8531&fbclid=IwAR0AzBxq69BgFGg4BQQ8hVchtE_jVvkMu6nof392IIPZAduS8Adpqzygvw0.

83. Tamás Csáki, "Árkay Bertalan építészete 1925–1945" [The architectural work of BÁ], in *Árkay: Egy magyar építész- és művészdinasztia* [A Hungarian architects' and artists' dynasty], ed. Csáki (Budapest: Holnap, 2020), 192–194.

84. Zeidler, *Ideas on Territorial Revision in Hungary*, 92–93.

85. *A Szent Imre év főünnepségeinek, nemzetközi gyűléseinek, kongresszusainak, értekezleteinek, kiállitásainak részletes sorrendje Budapest, 1930 augusztus 16–23* [Detailed schedule of the main celebrations, international congresses, meetings, and exhibitions of the Saint Emeric Year] (Budapest: Pallas, 1930).

86. Ambrus Seidl, "Szent Imre kultusza a budapesti Szentimrevárosban" [The cult of Saint Emeric in Saint Emeric's Town, Budapest], in *Szent Imre 1000 éve: Tanulmányok Szent Imre tiszteletére születésének ezredik évfordulója alkalmából* [1,000 years of Saint Emeric: Essays in honor of Saint Emeric on the thousandth anniversary of his birth], ed. Terézia Kerny (Székesfehérvár: Székesfehérvár Diocesan Museum, 2007), 186–187. For a photograph of the church, see "Budai Ciszterci Gimnázium Épülete"

[Building of the Buda Cistercian Secondary School] Wikimedia Commons, accessed 2 July 2024, https://commons.wikimedia.org/wiki/File:Budai_Ciszterci_Szent_Imre _Gimn%C3%A1zium_%C3%A9p%C3%BClete.png.

87. Gyula Szekfű, *Három nemzedék és ami utána következik* [Three generations and what comes after] (Budapest: Egyetemi Nyomda, 1934).

88. On Isabella's donation, see *A Szent Imre év főünnepségeinek*, 8.

89. Tibor Gerevich, "Római magyar művészek" [Hungarian artists in Rome], *Magyar Szemle* (1932): 235–240.

90. P. Szűcs, "A 'Modern' Official Art."

91. István Bizzer, "A Szent Imre-kultusz és a modern magyar szakrális művészet 1930–1950 között" [The cult of Saint Emeric and modern Hungarian sacral art], in *Szent Imre 1000 éve*, 158–175.

92. Private collection; for a photo, see "Szent Imre királyfi, 1930" [Prince Saint Emeric], Kieselbach Gallery, accessed 2 July 2024, https://www.kieselbach.hu/alkotas /szent-imre-kiralyfi.

93. Gentile, "The Myth of National Regeneration in Italy," 34–35.

94. Clark, *Holy Legionary Youth*, quote from 65.

95. For the Romanian examples, see Clark, *Holy Legionary Youth*, 177–183.

96. Hanebrink, *In Defense of Christian Hungary*, 134. On the political symbolism of Saint Stephen, see Klimó, *Nation, Konfession*, 244–289.

97. *A Szent István Emlékév, kiadja a Szent István Emlékév Országos Bizottsága* [The Saint Stephen Jubilee Year] (Budapest: National Committee of the Saint Stephen Jubilee Year, 1940), 189–191.

98. *A Szent István Emlékév*, 23–24.

99. *A Szent István Emlékév*, 31–32. For more on the murals, see chapter 4.

100. Pauliina Raento and Stanley D. Brunn, "Picturing a Nation: Finland on Postage Stamps, 1917–2000," *National Identities* 10, no. 1 (2008): 49–75, 50.

101. Sheila A. Brennan, *Stamping American Memory: Collectors, Citizens, and the Post* (Ann Arbor: University of Michigan Press, 2018), 98.

102. Brennan, *Stamping American Memory*, 99–100.

103. *A Szent István Emlékév*, 40.

104. Quoted in the official publication of the jubilee, *A Szent István Emlékév*, 43–44. For the stamps, see Hamza Imre et al., *A magyar bélyegek monográfiája* [Monograph of Hungarian stamps], vol. IV (Budapest: Közlekedési Dokumentációs Vállalat, 1971), 463–467.

105. *A Szent István Emlékév*, 44.

106. Ernst Kállai, "Kunstgewerbe und Volkskunst in Székesfehérvár," *Pester Lloyd*, 29 November 1938, 3.

107. For a large selection of advertisements for various products, see Kerny and András Smohay, eds., *István a szent király* [Stephen, the holy king] (Székesfehérvár: Székesfehérvár Diocesan Museum, 2013), 400–418.

108. Michael Billig, *Banal Nationalism* (London: Sage, 1995).

109. Alexander Vari, "Re-territorializing the 'Guilty City': Nationalist and Right-Wing Attempts to Nationalize Budapest during the Interwar Period," *Journal of Contemporary History* 47, no. 4 (2012): 725–729.

110. "Megelevenedik a magyar mult . . ." [The Hungarian past is brought to life], *Pesti Hírlap*, 22 August 1928, 7.

111. "Fényes felvonulás" [A dazzling procession], *Budapesti Hírlap*, 19 August 1938, 4.

112. *A Szent István Emlékév*, before pp. 241 and 257.

113. Nagy, *Great Expectations and Interwar Realities*, 196–227.

114. Ilona P. Brestyánszky, *Kovács Margit* (Budapest: Képzőművészeti Alap and Corvina, 1977), 27, 207; Kata Rákos, "Művészet és technika a modern életben—Magyar bemutatkozás az 1937-es párizsi világkiállításon" [Art and technology in modern life—Hungarian participation at the 1937 Paris World's Fair], in *Opus Mixtum I*, ed. Miklós Székely (Budapest: CentrArt, 2012), 104–111.

115. Vari, "Re-territorializing the 'Guilty City,'" 731–732. On the Saint Stephen jubilee and tourism, see also Nagy, *Great Expectations*, 220–224. Due to the worldwide decline in tourism, the efforts in 1938 did not draw in the desired number of visitors.

116. István Zombori, ed., *Szent István emlékezete falikárpitokon 1938–2000* [The memory of Saint Stephen in tapestries] (Szeged: Móra Ferenc Museum, 2001).

117. Károly Tolnai [Charles de Tolnay], *Ferenczy Noémi* (Budapest: Bisztrai Farkas Ferenc, 1934). On the book, see Ferenc Gosztonyi, "'Cézanne után': Tolnai Károly 1934-es Ferenczy Noémi-monográfiájáról" [After Cézanne: On Károly Tolnai's 1934 Noémi Ferenczy monograph], *Enigma* 26, no. 100 (2019/2020): 112–124.

118. Rákos, "Művészet és technika a modern életben"; Judit Pálosi, "Szent István kárpitok," [Saint Stephen tapestries], in *Szent István emlékezete falikárpitokon*, 22–26; Emőke Bodonyi, *Teremtés: Ferenczy Noémi művészete / Creation: The Art of Noémi Ferenczy* (Szentendre: Ferenczy Museum Center, 2020), 72–73, 162–163.

119. "The Admonitions of King Stephen," in Gergely Bisztray, ed., *Thousand Years of Hungarian Thought*, special issue, *Hungarian Studies Review* 27, nos. 1–2 (2000): 32.

120. Sinkó, "Árpád versus Saint István," 67–84.

121. Quoted in Péter Németh, "Ferenczy Noémi gobelinje Nyíregyházán" [NF's Gobelin in Nyíregyháza], in *Szent István emlékezete falikárpitokon*, 31. On the celebrations, see 29–32.

122. For a history of the commission and Ferenczy's designs, see Pálosi, "Szent István kárpitok," 22–25.

123. See her letter to Tolnai quoted in Pálosi, "Szent István kárpitok," 24.

124. On the Italian model, see Ben-Ghiat, *Fascist Modernities*.

2. Irredentist Spacetime

1. "A négy szobor: Az irredenta emlékművek leleplezése" [The four sculptures: The unveiling of the irredentist monuments], *Pesti Hirlap*, 18 January 1921, 2. On the militant tone of the inauguration, see János Pótó, "A Neugebäude helyén: A Szabadság tér és emlékművei" [Replacing the Neugebäude: Freedom Square and its monuments], *Mozgó Világ* 46, no. 1 (2020): 27–28.

2. Zeidler, *Ideas on Territorial Revision in Hungary*.

3. On the difference between the two concepts, see Zeidler, *Ideas on Territorial Revision in Hungary*, 11–13.

4. Pierre Nora, "Between Memory and History: Les Lieux de Mémoire," *Representations* 26 (1989): 11–12.

5. Young, "The Counter-Monument," 273.

6. Holly Case, "Revisionism in Regional Perspective," in *Territorial Revisionism and the Allies of Germany in the Second World War*, ed. Cattaruzza, Dyroff, and Langewiesche, 72–91. See also the rest of the essays in the same volume.

7. Aristotle A. Kallis, "To Expand or Not to Expand? Territory, Generic Fascism and the Quest for an 'Ideal Fatherland,'" *Journal of Contemporary History* 38, no. 2 (2003): 237–260, esp. 245–252.

8. Endre Liber, *Budapest szobrai és emléktáblái* [Sculptures and plaques in Budapest], Budapesti Statisztikai Közlemények 69/1 (Budapest: Budapest Székesfőváros Statisztikai Hivatala, 1934), 312. On the sculptures, see Zeidler, *Ideas on Territorial Revision in Hungary*, 188–195; Juliet Kinchin, "'Caught in the Ferris-wheel of History': Trianon Memorials in Hungary," in *Heritage, Ideology and Identity in Central and Eastern Europe: Contested Pasts, Contested Presents*, ed. Matthew Rampley (Woodbridge: Boydell and Brewer, 2012), 21–40; Erik Thorstensen, "The Places of Memory in a Square of Monuments: Conceptions of Past, Freedom and History at Szabadság Tér," *AHEA* 5 (2012), http://ahea.net/e-journal/volume-5-2012; Pótó, "A Neugebäude helyén," 26–28.

9. Zeidler, *Ideas on Territorial Revision in Hungary*, 94–98, 191.

10. Markója, "'Vörös posztó,'" 172–173.

11. Billig, *Banal Nationalism*.

12. On the monuments and their political and social context, see Bálint Varga, *The Monumental Nation: Magyar Nationalism and Symbolic Politics in Fin-de-siècle Hungary* (New York: Berghahn, 2016).

13. "A láthatatlan emlékmű" [The invisible monument], *Pesti Hirlap*, 6 October 1937, 1.

14. "A láthatatlan emlékmű."

15. Kallis, "To Expand or not to Expand," 252–253.

16. On the links between the memory of Barbarossa and Germany's defeat in the First World War, see Stefan Goebel, "Re-membered and Re-mobilized: The 'Sleeping Dead' in Interwar Germany and Britain," *Journal of Contemporary History* 39, no. 4 (2004): 492–496.

17. Kallis, "To Expand or not to Expand," 244, 253, 256.

18. Borut Klabjan, "Erecting Fascism: Nation, Identity, and Space in Trieste in the First Half of the Twentieth Century," *Nationalities Papers* 46, no. 6 (2018): 958–975.

19. Kemp, *Wir haben ja alle Deutschland nicht gekannt*, 229. See Martin H. Geyer, "'Die Gleichzeitigkeit der Ungleichzeitigkeit': Zeitsemantik und die Suche nach Gegenwart in der Weimarer Republik," in *Ordnungen in der Krise: Zur politischen Kulturgeschichte Deutschlands. 1900–1933*, ed. Wolfgang Hardtwig (Munich: R. Oldenbourg, 2007), 182.

20. For a concise history of the square and its monuments, see Pótó, "A Neugebäude helyén," 25–45.

21. On the memory of 1848–1849 see Klimó, *Nation, Konfession*; see chapters 4 and 5.

22. "Október hatodikán kigyulladt a Batthyány-örökmécses" [The Batthyány Sanctuary Lamp was lit on 6 October], *Nemzeti Ujság*, 7 October 1926, 2.

23. "Október hatodikán kigyulladt a Batthyány-örökmécses," 2.

24. "Az egyetemek ifjúsága az irredenta-szobrok előtt és a Vigadóban ünnepelte október 6-át" [University youth celebrated 6 October in front of the irredentist statues and in the Vigadó], *Nemzeti Ujság*, 7 October 1926, 2.

25. Rigney, "Plenitude, Scarcity and the Circulation of Cultural Memory," 19.

26. Jenő Murádin, *Az aradi Szabadság-szobor* [The Statue of Liberty in Arad] (Cluj-Napoca: Glória Kiadó, 2003); Margit Feischmidt, "Die Verortung der Nation an den

Peripherien: Ungarische Nationaldenkmäler in multiethnischen Gebieten der Monarchie," in *Grenzen und Räume in Österreich-Ungarn 1867–1918*, ed. Wladimir Fischer et al. (Tübingen: A. Francke, 2010), 119–123; James Koranyi, "The Thirteen Martyrs of Arad: A Monumental Hungarian History," in *Sites of Imperial Memory: Commemorating Colonial Rule in the Nineteenth and Twentieth Centuries*, ed. Dominik Geppert and Frank Lorenz Müller (Manchester: Manchester University Press, 2015), 53–69.

27. Koranyi, "The Thirteen Martyrs of Arad," 54.

28. Margit Feischmidt, "Lehorgonyzott mítoszok. Kőbe vésett sztereotípiák? *A lokalizáció jelentősége az aradi vértanúk emlékműve és a millenniumi emlékoszlopok kapcsán*" [Anchored myths, stereotypes carved into stone? The significance of localization in the Arad Martyrs Memorial and the Millennium Monuments], in *Mindennapi előítéletek: Társadalmi távolságok és etnikai sztereotípiák* [Everyday prejudices: Social distances and ethnic stereotypes], ed. Boglárka Bakó et al. (Budapest: Balassi, 2006), 370–391, 379.

29. "Október hatodikán kigyulladt a Batthyány-örökmécses," 2.

30. Imre Farkas, "Irredenta-szobrok" [Irredentist sculptures], *Pesti Hirlap*, 20 August 1929, 7.

31. "Elmaradt az irredenta szobrok leleplezése" [The unveiling of the irredentist sculptures has been postponed], *Munkás*, 10 December 1920, 3.

32. Michael Dorsch, *French Sculpture Following the Franco-Prussian War, 1870–80: Realist Allegories and the Commemoration of Defeat* (Farnham, UK: Ashgate, 2010), 23–53.

33. Dorsch, *French Sculpture*, 23–53.

34. Dorsch, *French Sculpture*, 107–132.

35. According to Dorsch (*French Sculpture*, 2–3), the French public invested a faith in historical closure into public sculpture.

36. For the details, see Pótó, "A Neugebäude helyén," 27.

37. Sinkó, "Árpád versus Saint István," 67–84.

38. On the practical reasons behind the material, see Pótó, "A Neugebäude helyén," 27.

39. Farkas, "Irredenta-szobrok."

40. On the imagery, see Sinkó, "The Offended Hungária," in *War of Memories: A Guide to Hungarian Memory Politics*, ed. Dóra Hegyi, Zsuzsa László, and Zsóka Leposa (Budapest: tranzit.hu, 2015), 13–38.

41. Hanebrink, *In Defense of Christian Hungary.*

42. Berezin, *Making the Fascist Self*, 141–195.

43. According to Kallis, the Fascist ideal fatherland encompasses three separate elements: societal, territorial, and missionary. See Kallis, "To Expand or Not to Expand," 245.

44. "Leleplezték a megszállt területek szobrait" [The statues of the occupied territories have been unveiled], *Új Barázda*, 18 January 1921, 1–2.

45. See, for example, "A Szent István Bazilika feltámadási körmenete az Irredenta szobrokhoz" [The resurrection procession of Saint Stephen's Basilica to the irredentist sculptures], *Pesti Hirlap*, 1 April 1923, 8; "Fényes pompával hordozták körül Nagy-Magyarország irredenta lobogóját Feltámadás napján" [The irredentist flag of Greater Hungary was carried in the procession with great pomp on Resurrection Day], *Pesti Hirlap*, 17 April 1938, 15.

46. "Esti levél: Vegyes ünnep" [Evening letter: A mixed holiday], *Pesti Hirlap*, 19 August 1928, 4.

47. Róbert Kerepeszki, "Nationalist Masculinity and Right-Wing Radical Student Movements in Interwar Hungary: The Case of the Turul Association," *Hungarian Studies Review* 41, no. 1–2 (2014): 61–88.

48. See, for example, "A kormányzó, a kormány, a nemzetgyűlés, a hadsereg és az egész nemzet ünnepelte ma október 6. vértanúit" [The governor, the national assembly, the army, and the whole nation celebrated the martyrs of 6 October today], *Magyarság*, 7 October 1926, 5.

49. Zsoldosházi, "Irredenta utcaneveket!" [A request for irredentist street names], *Gondolat*, 26 February 1921, 14–15, quoted in Miklós Zeidler, *A revíziós gondolat* [The revisionist idea] (Budapest: Osiris, 2001), 169–170. See also Zeidler, *Ideas on Territorial Revision in Hungary*, 203–204.

50. Zsoldosházi, "Irredenta utcaneveket!", quoted in Zeidler, *A revíziós gondolat*, 169–170.

51. Zeidler, *Ideas on Territorial Revision in Hungary*, 202–206.

52. Balázs Ablonczy, "Menekülés" [Escape], in Ablonczy, *Ismeretlen Trianon: Az összeomlás és a békeszerződés történetei, 1918–1921* [Unknown Trianon: Stories of the collapse and the peace treaty] (Budapest: Jaffa Kiadó, 2020), 278.

53. Rigney, "Plenitude, Scarcity and the Circulation of Cultural Memory," 19.

54. For a description, see Liber, *Budapest szobrai és emléktáblái*, 344–345.

55. Zeidler, *Ideas on Territorial Revision in Hungary*, 92–93.

56. Lord Rothermere, "Hungary's Place in the Sun: Safety for Central Europe," *Daily Mail*, 21 June 1927.

57. Zeidler, *Ideas on Territorial Revision*, 191.

58. For the inscriptions see Liber, *Budapest szobrai és emléktáblái*, 344–345.

59. Thorstensen, "The Places of Memory in a Square of Monuments," 9.

60. Wingfield, "National Sacrifice and Regeneration: Commemorations of the Battle of Zborov in Multinational Czechoslovakia," in *Sacrifice and Rebirth: The Legacy of the Last Habsburg War*, ed. Mark Cornwall and John Paul Newman (New York: Berghahn, 2016), 141–142.

61. Wingfield, "National Sacrifice and Regeneration," 141–142.

62. Goebel, "Re-membered and Re-mobilized," 494–495.

63. "Az irredenta szobrok reprodukcióját szabaddá tették" [Reproduction rights for the irredentist sculptures have been waived], *Nemzeti Ujság*, 18 June 1921, 5.

64. "Közgyülés után" [After the assembly], *Gyógyszerészi Hetilap*, 23 June 1929, 139.

65. "Sajnos, muszáj takarékoskodni" [Alas, money is tight], *Népszava*, 17 October 1931, 8.

66. Known from [Untitled photo of an interior space at Maria Theresa barracks], Üllői Road, 1927, donated by Tamás Konok Sr., *Fortepan*, accessed 27 September 2024, https://fortepan.hu/hu/photos/?id=43613.

67. "Özv. Göttler Lászlóné Kioszk-vendéglője" [The Kiosk restaurant of the widowed Mrs. László Göttler], in *Magyar városok és vármegyék monográfiája* [Monograph of Hungarian cities and counties], vol. 24, *Rákospalota és Rákosvidék*, ed. Oszkár Zsemley (Budapest: Magyar Városok Monográfiája Kiadóhivatala, 1938), 371.

68. Quotation from Young, "The Counter-Monument," 273.

69. Young, "The Counter-Monument."

70. Billig, *Banal Nationalism*, 40.

71. On the consequences, see Leslie Waters, *Borders on the Move: Territorial Change and Ethnic Cleansing in the Hungarian-Slovak Borderlands, 1938–1948* (Rochester, NY: University of Rochester Press, 2020).

72. Imre Hamza et al., *A magyar bélyegek monográfiája* [Monograph of Hungarian stamps], vol. IV (Budapest: Közlekedési Dokumentációs Vállalat, 1971), 480–481.

73. For a liberal view, see, for example, Árpád Pásztor, "A cseh Dunán" [On the Czech Danube], *Pesti Napló*, 3 June 1932, 4. For left-wing perspectives, see chapter 5 in this book.

74. George Mesenaki, "A megtréfált szobrok" [Sculptures pranked], *Előre*, 6 March 1921, 6.

75. Thorstensen, "The Places of Memory in a Square of Monuments"; Pótó, "A Neugebäude helyén," 25–45.

76. Zsóka Leposa, "The Statue of Hungarian Pain," in *War of Memories*, 63–75.

77. Ilona Fekete, "Unburied Bodies: Hungarian National Identity 1989–2020," *Australian Journal of Politics and History* 66, no. 3 (2020): 422–425; Edit András, *Határsértő képzelet: Kortárs művészet és kritikai elmélet Európa keleti felén* [Imaginary transgression: Contemporary art and critical theories in the eastern part of Europe] (Budapest: Humanities Research Centre Institute of Art History, 2023), 158–159.

78. Zsuzsa L. Nagy, "Trianon a magyar társadalom tudatában" [Trianon in the consciousness of Hungarian society], in *Trianon*, ed. Miklós Zeidler (Budapest: Osiris, 2008), 843–845.

79. On 1970s–1980s discourse on minorities, see Myra A. Waterbury, *Between State and Nation: Diaspora Politics and Kin-State Nationalism in Hungary* (New York: Palgrave Macmillan, 2010), 42–49.

80. László Kostyál, "Trianon szobor-emlékezete" [Statue memory of Trianon], Göcsej Museum, Zalaegerszeg, accessed 29 November 2024, https://web.archive .org/web/20240715081057/https://gocsejimuzeum.hu/muzeum-iskola-szertar /trianon-szobor-emlekezete.

81. See the website of the museum: "Feltámadnak a budapesti irredenta szobrok" [The Budapest irredentist sculptures are resurrected], Trianon múzeum, accessed 29 November 2024, https://www.trianonmuzeum.hu/index.php?page=post&id=64; "Kincsek a raktárból 22: Irredenta szoborcsoport—Észak" [Treasures from storage 22: Irredentist Sculpture Group: North], Trianon múzeum, accessed 29 November 2024, https://www.trianonmuzeum.hu/index.php?page=post&id=441; "Az országzászló mozgalom története" [The history of the country flag movement], Trianon múzeum, accessed 29 November 2024, https://www.trianonmuzeum.hu/index .php?page=post&id=194.

82. On the imagery of the memorial, see Fekete, "Unburied Bodies, 425–430.

83. For a comparison between the two monuments see András, *Határsértő képzelet*, 162–165.

84. Gábor Egry, "The Greatest Catastrophe of (Post-)colonial Central Europe? The 100th Years Anniversary of Trianon and Official Politics of Memory in Hungary," *Rocznik Instytutu Europy Środkowo-Wschodniej / Yearbook of the Institute of East-Central Europe* 18, no. 2 (2020): 123–142.

85. According to Edit András, the memorial "projects an imaginary map of Greater Hungary into the fantasies of visitors"; see *Határsértő képzelet*, 165–166.

86. Szabolcs László, "Memory Politics in an Illiberal Regime: Hungary's New Trianon Memorial," *ASEEES Blog*, accessed 4 December 2024, http://www.web19b.aseees.pitt.edu/news-events/aseees-blog-feed/memory-politics-illiberal-regime%C2%A0hungary%E2%80%99s-new-trianon-memorial.

87. László Szarka, "Soknyelvű ország—egynyelvű álom és emlék(mű)," *Új Szó Online*, 30 May 2020, https://ujszo.com/panorama/soknyelvu-orszag-egynyelvu-alom-es-emlekmu.

3. History into Landscape

1. Nándor Lajos Varga and Gyula Rajk, *Magyar múlt*, Varga Nándor Lajos 40 fametszete Rajk Gyula szövegével [Hungarian past, 40 woodcuts by Nándor Lajos Varga, with text by Gyula Rajk] (Budapest: Globus, 1941).

2. As an example of the complicated relationships shaped by the turbulent twentieth century in Hungary, the author Rajk is probably identifiable with the then-director of Globus Press, brother of prominent right-wing extremist Endre Rajk, who was a member of the Arrow Cross government in 1944 and 1945, and of illegal Communist László Rajk, victim of a famous Stalinist show trial in 1949.

3. Varga and Rajk, *Magyar múlt*.

4. István Kollai, "Mátyás király és a szlovákok: Az emlékezet transznacionalizálódásának aktorai Szlovákiában" [King Matthias and the Slovaks: Actors of the transnationalization of memory in Slovakia], *Regio* 25, no. 4 (2017): 142–143.

5. Patrice M. Dabrowski, *The Carpathians: Discovering the Highlands of Poland and Ukraine* (Ithaca, NY: Cornell University Press, 2021), 11–62.

6. Pieter Judson, "Marking National Space on the Habsburg Austrian Borderlands, 1880–1918," in *Shatterzone of Empires: Coexistence and Violence in the German, Habsburg, Russian, and Ottoman Borderlands*, ed. Omer Bartov and Eric D. Weitz (Bloomington: Indiana University Press, 2013), 122–235.

7. Stanislav Holubec, "Between the Czech Krkonoše and the German Riesengebirge: Nationalism and Tourism in the Giant Mountains, 1880s–1930s," *Nationalities Papers* 52, no. 2 (2024): 337–359.

8. See, for example, Judson, "Reisebeschreibungen in der 'Südmark' und die Idee der deutschen Diaspora nach 1918," in *Zwischen Exotik und Vertrautem: Zum Tourismus in der Habsburgermonarchie und ihren Nachfolgestaaten*, ed. Peter Stachel and Martina Thomsen (Bielefeld: transcript Verlag, 2014), 59–76; Holubec, "Between the Czech Krkonoše and the German Riesengebirge."

9. Kemp, *Wir haben ja alle Deutschland nicht gekannt*, 103–271.

10. Christian Rapp, "Schnelle Neue Alpen. Schnappschüsse der Moderne aus Österreichs Bergen," in *Kampf um die Stadt: Politik, Kunst und Alltag um 1930*, ed. Wolfgang Kos (Vienna: Czernin, 2010), 122–130.

11. Kaliopi Chamonikola, Markéta Zácková, and Terezie Petisková, "New Content, New Images," in *Budování státu: Reprezentace Československa v umění, architektuře a designu*, ed. Milena Bartlová and Jindřich Vybíral (Prague: UMPRUM, 2015), 10.

12. Kunt, "Creating the New Hungarian Tatras," 20–42.

13. Zombory, *Maps of Remembrance*, 11–50.

14. Erzsébet Király, Enikő Róka, and Nóra Veszprémi, eds., *XIX: Nemzet és művészet—Kép és önkép* [XIX: Nation and art—image and self-image] (Budapest: Hungarian National Gallery, 2010), 332–349.

15. Nagy, *Great Expectations and Interwar Realities*, 196–220.

16. The chapter is partly based on my article "Whose Landscape Is It? Remapping Memory and History in Interwar Central Europe," *Austrian History Yearbook* 52 (2021): 227–252.

17. On historical landscapes in nineteenth-century Hungary, see Júlia Szabó, *A mitikus és a történeti táj* [The mythical and historical landscape] (Budapest: Balassi, 2000).

18. On the concept of mental maps as employed here, see Schenk, "Mental Maps."

19. György Buday, *Ifjúságunk népnevelési feladatai és az alföldi rádióleadó* [The tasks of our youth in community education and the radio channel in the plains] (Szeged: Bethlen Gábor Kör, 1929), 12.

20. Dezső Kosztolányi, ed., *Vérző Magyarország: Magyar írók Magyarország területéért* [Bleeding Hungary: Hungarian authors for the territory of Hungary] (Budapest: Pallas, 1921). Contributors included other writers from the circle of *Nyugat* (Árpád Tóth, Aladár Schöpflin, Frigyes Karinthy, Mihály Babits) as well as prominent conservative authors, such as Ferenc Herczeg (subsequently a leading figure of the revisionist movement), and some on the more extreme right, like Cécile Tormay and József Erdélyi. For a detailed examination of the book and its ideology, see András Lengyel, "A 'Vérző Magyarország': Kosztolányi Dezső irredenta antológiájáról" [Bleeding Hungary: On the irredentist anthology edited by Dezső Kosztolányi], *Literatura 33*, no. 4 (2007): 399–424. On Kosztolányi and revisionism, see also Mihály Szegedy-Maszák, "Vérző Magyarország," *Kalligram* 19, no. 4 (2010): 83–96. On the second edition (Kosztolányi, ed., *Vérző Magyarország: Magyar írók Magyarország területéért* [Budapest: Bethlen Gábor Kör, 1928]), see Tamás Bíró-Balogh, "A Vérző Magyarország második kiadása: Kosztolányi 'jelentősen átdolgozott' irredenta antológiája" [The second edition of Bleeding Hungary: Kosztolányi's "significantly revised" irredentist anthology], *Kalligram* 18, no. 11 (2009): 65–70.

21. Emőke Bodonyi, *Jeges* (Szentendre: Pest Megyei Múzeumok Igazgatósága, 2008).

22. The illustrations of *Bleeding Hungary* and hence the circumstances of the commission are not discussed in studies of the artist's work.

23. Károly Lyka, "Magyar művészet—magyar határok" [Hungarian art—Hungarian borders], in *Vérző Magyarország*, ed. Kosztolányi (1921), 87–92.

24. This book refers to the English version: Ottó Légrády, ed., *Justice for Hungary: The Cruel Errors of Trianon* (Budapest: Légrády, 1930). The volume was also published in Hungarian, German, French, and Italian.

25. "The Thousand Years' Struggles of the Hungarian Nation" and "The Hungarian Genius: What It Has Achieved During Ten Centuries of History," in *Justice for Hungary!*, ed. Légrády, 41–108, 109–164.

26. Légrády, ed., *Justice for Hungary!*, 45. For more on the monuments, see chapter 2.

27. Légrády, ed., *Justice for Hungary!*, 50.

28. Aloys Freyherr von Mednyánsky, *Malerische Reise auf dem Waagflusse in Ungern* (Pest: Hartleben, 1826). The tales were also retold in Mednyánszky's subsequent pub-

lication: *Erzählungen, Sagen und Legenden aus Ungarns Vorzeit* (Pest: Hartleben, 1829), as well as in its later editions. On Fischer, Mednyánszky, and the influence of the images, see Nóra Veszprémi, *Fölfújt pipere és költői mámor: Romantika és művészeti közízlés a reformkori Magyarországon* [Overblown makeup and poetic frenzy: Romanticism and popular taste in Hungary c. 1820–1850] (Budapest: L'Harmattan, 2015), 43–56.

29. On Mednyánszky's "imperial patriotism," see Edit Szentesi, "Birodalmi patriotizmus: Történelemszemlélet, történetírás, történeti publicisztika és történeti témák ábrázolása az Osztrák Császárságban 1828-ig [Imperial patriotism: History writing, historical journalism, and the visual representation of history in the Austrian Empire before 1828]," in *Történelem-kép: Szemelvények múlt és művészet kapcsolatából Magyarországon [History–image: Examples of the relationship between past and art in Hungary]*, ed. Árpád Mikó and Sinkó (Budapest: Hungarian National Gallery, 2000), 73–91.

30. Mikhail M. Bakhtin, "Forms of Time and of the Chronotope in the Novel: Notes toward a Historical Poetics" (1981), in Bakhtin, *The Dialogic Imagination: Four Essays*, ed. Michael Holquist, trans. Caryl Emerson and Michael Holquist (Austin: University of Texas Press, 1990), 245–246.

31. See Veszprémi, *Fölfújt pipere*, 37–77. For more detailed analysis of the two irredentist publications and their relationship to nineteenth-century representations of the Vág/Váh/Waag region, see also Veszprémi, "Whose Landscape Is It," on which this section of this chapter is partly based.

32. They appeared in travel guides published in Czechoslovakia; see, for example, Leopold Wolfgang Rochowanski, ed., *Columbus in der Slovakei* (Bratislava: Eos, 1936), 251–253.

33. Légrády, ed., *Justice for Hungary!*, 138.

34. Zoltán Nagy, "Varga Nándor Lajos," *Szépművészet* 2, no. 2 (1941) 91–92; Kopócsy, "A jelen történelmi értelmezése," 140–142.

35. On these meanings of wood engraving, see Katalin Bakos, "Fametszet és illusztráció: könyv, album, mappa, sorozat 1920–1940" [Wood engraving and illustration: Book, album, folder, series], in *A modern magyar fa- és linóleummetszés (1890–1950)* [Modern Hungarian wood and linoleum engraving], ed. Enikő Róka (Miskolc: Miskolci Galéria, 2005), 71–72.

36. On the map, see Denis Sinor, "Western Information on the Kitans and Some Related Questions," *Journal of the American Oriental Society* 115, no. 2 (1995): 264–265.

37. See, for example, Josef Pápay, "Im Lande der Nord-Ostjaken," *Abrégé du Bulletin de la Société Hongroise de Géographie*, supp. *Földrajzi Közlemények* 34 (1906): 4–5.

38. R. Sz. I., "Az erdélyi művészek kiállitása" [The exhibition of Transylvanian artists], *Uj Magyarság*, 27 February 1941, 6.

39. R., "Varga Nándor Lajos történelemkönyve fametszetekben" [NLV's history textbook in woodcuts], *Magyar Nemzet*, 5 June 1941, 7.

40. Varga and Rajk, *Magyar múlt*, XXXVIII.

41. On the imagery of the violently dissected map of Greater Hungary, see Sinkó, "The Offended Hungária," 13–38.

42. Bernard Guenée, "From Feudal Boundaries to Political Borders," and Daniel Nordman, "From the Boundaries of the State to National Borders," in *Rethinking France: Les Lieux de mémoire*, ed. Nora, vol. 1, *The State* (Chicago: University of Chicago Press, 2001), 81–103, 105–132.

43. Nordman, "From the Boundaries of the State to National Borders," 120–123.

44. "A láthatatlan emlékmű" [The invisible monument], *Pesti Hirlap*, 6 October 1937, 1. See chapter 2.

45. Designed by Lajos Tary, Hungarian National Museum, Poster Collection, inv. no 57.0044, accessed 3 July 2024, https://www.museummap.hu/record/-/record/dis play/manifestation/oai-aggregated-bib10629129/69b03df6-72c0-4e14-a182-be1af53 c2060/solr/0/24/0/2/score/DESC.

46. Balázs Ablonczy, "A hajózható patakok balladája" [Ballad of the navigable streams], in Ablonczy, *Trianon-legendák* [Trianon legends] (Budapest: Jaffa Kiadó, 2015), 91–106.

47. Karel Bogar, *Muž s beraní hlavou: Ferdiš Duša a Frýdlant nad Ostravicí* [Man with a ram's head: FD in Frýdlant nad Ostravicí] (Frýdlant nad Ostravicí: Montanex, 2008).

48. Ferdiš Duša, *Dolu Váhom* / Viliam Ritter, *Roman slovenskej rieky* [Down the Váh / Novel of a Slovak River] (Bratislava: K. Jaroň, 1933).

49. Duša, *Dolu Váhom* I. diel, introduction by Rudolf Kratochvíl (Bratislava: K. Jaroň, 1934).

50. Duša, *Dolu Váhom* I. diel.

51. Duša, *Dolu Váhom* / Ritter, *Roman slovenskej rieky*, 5–9.

52. On Ritter, see Philippe Kaenel, "William Ritter (1867–1955): Un critique cosmopolite, böcklinien et anti-hodlérien," *Schweizerische Zeitschrift für Geschichte* 48, no. 1 (1998): 73–98; Lenka Bydžovská, "'Heart in a Trance': William Ritter and Czech Modernism," *Centre Interdisciplinaire de Recherches Centre-Européennes*, accessed 1 December 2024, https://web.archive.org/web/20211008153727/http://www.circe .paris-sorbonne.fr/IMG/pdf/lenka_bydzovska_william_ritter_22_2_2011_fini.pdf; Marta Filipová, *Modernity, History and Politics in Czech Art* (New York: Routledge, 2019), 38, 76.

53. See Thomas Lorman, *The Making of the Slovak People's Party: Religion, Nationalism and the Culture War in Early 20th-Century Europe* (London: Bloomsbury Academic, 2019), 149–218.

54. Duša, *Dolu Váhom* / Ritter, *Roman slovenskej rieky*, 5.

55. See Samo Chalupka, "Smútok" (Sadness), *Magyarul Bábelben*, accessed 1 December 2024, https://www.magyarulbabelben.net/works/sk/Chalupka%2C_Samo-1812 /Sm%C3%BAtok/hu/55825-B%C3%A1nat, and *Bolo i bude* (Was and Will Be), https:// www.magyarulbabelben.net/works/sk/Chalupka%2C_Samo-1812/Bolo_i_bude /hu/55827-Volt_%C3%A9s_lesz; Kollai, "Mátyás király és a szlovákok," 142–143.

56. For examples, see Marta Filipová, "'Highly Civilized, yet Very Simple': Images of the Czechoslovak State and Nation at Interwar World's Fairs," *Nationalities Papers* 50, no. 1 (2022): 152–159.

57. *Strečno*, Slovak National Gallery, Bratislava, inv. no. G 1115, *Web Umenia*, accessed 1 December 2024, https://www.webumenia.sk/dielo/SVK:SNG.G_1115.

58. *Trenčín*, Slovak National Gallery, Bratislava, inv. no. G 1122, *Web Umenia*, accessed 1 December 2024, https://www.webumenia.sk/dielo/SVK:SNG.G_1122.

59. Secklehner, "A New Austrian Regionalism," 201–226; Clark, *Holy Legionary Youth*, 179–180.

60. Csunderlik, *A "vörös farsangtól" a "vörös tatárjárásig,"* 298–305.

61. For a succinct overview in English, see Hanebrink, *In Defense of Christian Hungary*, 124–126.

62. For a thorough assessment of Buday's interwar artistic output, see Róka, "A fametszet nagymesterei: Buday György, Gáborjáni Szabó Kálmán, Molnár-C. Pál"

[The great masters of the woodcut: György Buday, Kálmán Gáborjáni Szabó, Pál Molnár-C.], in *A modern magyar fa- és linóleummetszés 1890–1950* [The modern Hungarian wood- and linoleumcut], ed. Róka (Miskolc: Miskolc Gallery, 2005), 107–118. Parts of the section on Buday in this chapter are based on my previous essay, "Tales from Bátorliget," in *George Buday: Surreal Fairy Tales*, ed. Robert Waterhouse (Manchester: Baquis, 2022), 11–49.

63. Ferenc Csaplár, *A Szegedi Fiatalok Művészeti Kollégiuma* [The Art College of the Szeged Youth] (Budapest: Akadémiai Kiadó, 1967).

64. Gyula Ortutay and Buday, *Bátorligeti mesék*, Ortutay Gyula gyűjtése, Buday György rajzaival [Tales from Bátorliget, collected by GyO, illustrated by GyB] (Budapest: Hungária, 1937). See Veszprémi, "Tales from Bátorliget."

65. Róka, "A fametszet nagymesterei," 114.

66. *Székely népballadák* [Sekler folk ballads], collected by Ortutay, ill. Buday (Budapest: Egyetemi Nyomda, 1935).

67. Attila Paládi-Kovács, *Ortutay Gyula* (Budapest: Akadémiai Kiadó, 1991), 156.

68. Paládi-Kovács, *Ortutay Gyula*, 185–191.

69. Buday, *Ifjúságunk népnevelési feladatai*, 12.

70. János Pelle, "Ortutay Gyula, a helyezkedés nagymestere" [GyO, great master of jockeying for positions], *HVG online*, 17 June 2021, https://hvg.hu/velemeny/20100617_ortutay_naplo.

71. Waterhouse, ed., *Their Safe Haven: Hungarian Artists in Britain from the 1930s* (Manchester: Baquis, 2018), 193–211.

72. George Buday, *George Buday's New Little Book of Hungarian Folktales and Illustrations* (London: Westminster, 1945).

73. Buday, *George Buday's Little Book of Hungarian Folktales and Illustrations* (London: Favil, 1943); Buday, *George Buday's Fifth Little Book: Hungarian Folktales and Illustrations* (London: Westminster, 1949).

74. Buday, "Életemről, művészetemről" [On my life, on my art], in *Buday György fametszetei* [György Buday's wood engravings] (Budapest: Magyar Helikon, 1970), 20.

75. On Weiner-Kráľ, see Marian Váross, *Imro Weiner-Kráľ* (Bratislava: Slovak Fine Arts Fund, 1963); Dagmar Srnenská and Alma Münzová, *Imro Weiner-Kráľ* (Bratislava: Petrus, 2001).

76. Váross, *Imro Weiner-Kráľ*; Srnenská and Münzová, *Imro Weiner-Kráľ*; "Weiner (Král) Imre," *Szlovákiai Magyar Adatbank* (Slovak Hungarian Database), accessed 4 December 2024, https://adatbank.sk/lexikon/weiner-kral-imre/.

77. For a discussion of this problem, see Secklehner, "Artwork of the Month, December 2021: Židovská Street III (1935–36) by Imrich Weiner-Kráľ," *CRAACE blog*, accessed 1 December 2024, https://doi.org/10.17605/OSF.IO/KGAZH.

78. Kálmán Brogyányi, "A Csehszlovákiai Magyar Tudományos, Irodalmi és Művészeti Társaság művészeti osztályának kiállítása" [Exhibition of the art section of the Czechoslovak Hungarian Association for Scholarship, Literature, and Art], originally published in *Forum* 3, no. 5 (1935), republished in Lajos Turczel, "Szemelvények Brogyányi Kálmán műkritikai és művészettörténeti munkásságából" [Excerpts from KB's art criticism and art history writing], *Limes* 9, no. 4 (1996): 38–41; Edgár Balogh, "Valóság és kultúra a csehszlovákiai magyarság életében" [Reality and culture in the life of the Hungarian minority in Czechoslovakia], *Korunk* 10, no. 7–8 (1935): 514.

79. Secklehner, "Artwork of the Month, December 2021: Židovská Street III."

80. Imre Barsi, "Nyugtalan ifjúság tükre" [Mirror of restless youth], *A Hét*, 30 April 1961, 17. On village surrealism, see Secklehner, "Artwork of the Month."

81. Eleonóra Babejová, *Fin-de-siècle Pressburg: Conflict and Cultural Coexistence in Bratislava 1897–1914* (Boulder: East European Monographs and Columbia University Press, 2003).

82. See Jozef Tancer, "Die Geburt Bratislavas auf den Seiten der lokalen Stadtführer 1918–1945," in *Zwischen Exotik und Vertrautem: Zum Tourismus in der Habsburgermonarchie und ihren Nachfolgestaaten*, ed. Stachel and Thomsen (Bielefeld: transcript Verlag, 2014), 225–230.

83. Slovak National Gallery, Bratislava, inv. no. G 985 and G 3010; for *Scene of Action*, see Srnenská and Münzová, *Imro Weiner-Kráľ*, 30.

84. Gabriela Kiliánová, "Ein Grenzmythos: Die Burg Devín," in *Heroen, Mythen, Identitäten: Die Slowakei und Österreich im Vergleich*, ed. Hannes Stekl and Helena Mannová (Vienna: Facultas, 2003), 49–80; Kiliánová, *Identität und Gedächtnis in der Slowakei: Die Burg Devín als Erinnerungsort* (Frankfurt am Main: Peter Lang, 2011).

85. See Kiliánová, "Ein Grenzmythos"; Kiliánová, *Identität und Gedächtnis in der Slowakei*, 11–56. See also Varga, *The Monumental Nation*, 47–73. According to Kiliánová, the castle did not feature prominently in German historical memory; the local German population accepted the Hungarian narrative.

86. For more on images of Devín in the nineteenth century and interwar period, see Veszprémi, "Whose Landscape Is It?," 244–252.

87. Árpád Pásztor, "A cseh Dunán" [On the Czech Danube], *Pesti Napló*, 3 June 1932, 4.

88. László Szarka, "Hungarian National Minority Organizations and the Role of Elites between the Two World Wars: Addenda to the History of Minority Nationalism in Central and Eastern Europe," *Hungarian Historical Review* 2, no. 3 (2013): 431–441.

89. For images, see "Imrich Weiner-Kráľ," *Web Umenia*, accessed 1 December 2024, https://www.webumenia.sk/katalog?related_work=Bratislava&author=Weiner-Kr%C3%A1%C4%BE%2C%20Imrich.

4. The Archive and the Ruin

1. Alexander Rubel, "Dacian Blood: Autochthonous Discourse in Romania during the Interwar Period," in *Digging Politics*, ed. Koranyi and Hanscam, 257–286.

2. Florian-Jan Ostrowski, "Thracian Archaeology and National Identity in Communist Bulgaria: The Ideological Pattern of Museum Exhibitions," in *Digging Politics*, ed. Koranyi and Hanscam, 45–76.

3. Bruce G. Trigger, "Romanticism, Nationalism, and Archaeology," in *Nationalism, Politics, and the Practice of Archaeology*, ed. Philip L. Kohl and Clare Fawcett (Cambridge, UK: Cambridge University Press, 1995), 263–279.

4. Oliver Gilkes, "The Voyage of Aeneas: Myth, Archaeology and Identity in Interwar Albania," in *The Politics of Archaeology and Identity in a Global Context*, ed. Susan Kane (Boston: Archaeological Institute of America, 2003), 31–49.

5. Paul Baxa, *Roads and Ruins: The Symbolic Landscape of Fascist Rome* (Toronto: University of Toronto Press, 2010), esp. 54–75.

6. As formulated by the literary historian and journalist Zsigmond Kunfi (1879–1929), a Social Democrat who would soon be responsible for cultural policy in the

revolutionary governments; quoted in Gábor Ujváry, *"Egy európai formátumú állam-férfi": Klebelsberg Kuno (1875–1932)* ["A statesman of European stature"] (Budapest: Kronosz Kiadó and Magyar Történelmi Társulat, 2014), 46.

7. For a monographical study of Klebelsberg, see Ujváry, *"Egy európai formátumú államférfi."* This is a useful biography that nevertheless downplays the authoritarian and antisemitic elements of interwar Hungarian cultural politics. For more critical perspectives, see, for example, Ungváry, *A Horthy-rendszer és antiszemitizmusának mérlege*; the section "Nem a 'kard,' hanem a 'kultúra!' Oktatás és művelődés" [Not the "sword," but "culture!" Education and culture], in *A Horthy-korszak vitatott kérdései* [Debated issues of the Horthy era], conference proceedings (Budapest: Kossuth, 2020), 95–131.

8. Nagy, *Great Expectations and Interwar Realities*, 109–164.

9. Szekfű, *Három nemzedék*. The text more often referenced today is that of the 1934 expanded edition: *Három nemzedék és ami utána következik* [Three generations and what comes after] (Budapest: Egyetemi Nyomda, 1934).

10. Szekfű, *Három nemzedék* (1920), 4.

11. On *Three Generations*, see Dénes, *A történelmi Magyarország eszménye*, 217–263.

12. Dénes, *A történelmi Magyarország*, 233–261.

13. On this shift, see Gergely Romsics, *The Memory of the Habsburg Empire in German, Austrian, and Hungarian Right-wing Historiography and Political Thinking, 1918–1941* (Boulder, CO: East European Monographs, 2010), 7–81.

14. Elemér Mályusz, "A népiség története" [The history of ethnicity], in *A magyar történetírás új útjai* [New directions in Hungarian History Writing], ed. Bálint Hóman (Budapest: Magyar Szemle Társaság, 1932), 238.

15. On developments in German scholarship and the concepts of Volksboden and Kulturboden, see Kemp, *Wir haben ja alle Deutschland nicht gekannt*, 159–181.

16. Romsics, *The Memory of the Habsburg Empire*, 306–307. On Szekfű and Geistesgeschichte, see Romsics, *Clio bűvöletében*, 293–316.

17. The articles were also collected into a volume: Kuno Klebelsberg, *Neonacionalizmus* [Neonationalism] (Budapest: Athenaeum, 1928). See Ujváry, *Egy európai formátumú államférfi*, 160–171.

18. Klebelsberg, [Opening speech, 14 May 1920, General Assembly of the Hungarian Historical Society] in Klebelsberg, *Beszédei, cikkei és törvényjavaslatai 1916–1926* [Speeches, articles, and legislative proposals] (Budapest: Athenaeum, 1927), 20–39, esp. 36.

19. Hóman and Szekfű, *Magyar történet*, 8 vols. (Budapest: Egyetemi Nyomda, 1928–1934). Several subsequent editions followed.

20. Szekfű, "A politikai történetírás" [Political history writing], in *A magyar történetírás új útjai*, ed. Hóman (Budapest: Magyar Szemle Társaság, 1932), 397–344.

21. Szekfű, "A barokk műveltség" [Baroque culture], in Hóman and Szekfű, *Magyar történet*, vol. 6, *A tizennyolcadik század* [The eighteenth century] (Budapest: Egyetemi Nyomda, n.d. [1932]), 130–173, 470–474.

22. Szekfű, *Három nemzedék* (1934), 407–421. See Erdősi, "Barokk és neobarokk;" Dénes, *A történelmi Magyarország eszménye*, 335–337.

23. Ujváry, *Egy európai formátumú államférfi*, 135.

24. Dariusz Gafijczuk and Derek Sayer, eds., *The Inhabited Ruins of Central Europe: Re-imagining Space, History, and Memory* (London: Palgrave Macmillan, 2013).

25. For a new, comprehensive history of the Archive and its collections, see T. Csaba Reisz, ed., *A nemzet levéltára: Fejezetek az Országos Levéltár történetéből* [The archive of the nation: Chapters from the history of the National Archives] (Budapest: Hungarian National Archives, 2023). For a shorter overview, see Géza Érszegi, ed., *Archivum Regni Regnum Archivi: A Magyar Országos Levéltár palotája* [The palace of the Hungarian National Archives] (Budapest: Hungarian National Archives, 2005).

26. On the planning and construction process, see Iván Borsa, "Az Országos Levéltár épületei 1874–1974" [The buildings of the National Archives], *Levéltári Közlemények* 50, no. 1 (1979): 23–50.

27. Borsa, "Az Országos Levéltár épületei," 34–38; on the building as Pantheon, see up., "Okmányokban, művészi és iparművészi remekekben fogja megőrizni a nemzeti múlt emlékeit az Országos Levéltár magyar Pantheonja" [The Hungarian Pantheon of the National Archives will preserve memories of the national past in documents, artworks, and works of artistic industry], *8 Órai Ujság*, 12 May 1928, 4.

28. "Okmányokban, művészi és iparművészi remekekben fogja megőrizni," 4.

29. Sinkó, "A művészi siker anatómiája 1840–1900" [The anatomy of artistic success, 1840–1900], in *Aranyérmek, ezüstkoszorúk: Művészkultusz és műpártolás Magyarországon a 19. században* [Gold medals, silver wreaths: The cult of artists and the patronage of art in nineteenth-century Hungary], ed. Sinkó (Budapest: Hungarian National Gallery, 1995), 15–47; Veszprémi, "An Introspective Pantheon: The Picture Gallery of the Hungarian National Museum in the Nineteenth Century," *Journal of the History of Collections* 30, no. 3 (2018): 453–469.

30. For a discussion of the complete decorative program with ample photographic material, see Reisz, ed., *A nemzet levéltára*, 352–455.

31. Miksa Róth, *Egy üvegfestőművész emlékei* [Memories of a stained glass artist] (Budapest: Hungária, 1943), 73–75.

32. For images, see "Category: Interior of State Archives of Hungary (Bécsikapu branch)," *Wikimedia Commons*, accessed 2 December 2024, https://commons.wiki media.org/wiki/Category:Interior_of_State_Archives_of_Hungary_(B%C3% A9csikapu_branch).

33. Reisz, ed., *A nemzet levéltára*, 329–331.

34. Mályusz, "A népiség története," 250–251.

35. Reisz, ed., *A nemzet levéltára*, 400–402.

36. See, for example, his parliamentary speech justifying his own draft legislation on education, in Klebelsberg, *Beszédei*, 413–416.

37. Reisz, ed., *A nemzet levéltára*, 443–445.

38. Reisz, *A nemzet levéltára*, 424.

39. Érszegi, ed., *Archivum Regni Regnum Archivi*, 31.

40. As already observed by the art historian Ervin Ybl in 1930, see "Az Országos Levéltár freskói" [The frescoes of the National Archives], in *Az Országos Magyar Képzőművészeti Társulat Évkönyve az 1929. évre* (Budapest: OMKT, 1930), 86, 94, 97. See Reisz, ed., *A nemzet levéltára*, 428–429.

41. F. M., "Akik nem politizálnak. . . ." [Those who don't do politics], *Magyarország*, 20 November 1921, 6.

42. T. Csaba Reisz, "Trianon ismeretlen emléke az Országos Levéltár mennyezetén" [An unknown memorial to Trianon on the ceiling of the National Archives], *Magyar Nemzeti Levéltár*, June 4, 2019, accessed 4 December 2024, https://mnl

.gov.hu/mnl/ol/hirek/trianon_ismeretlen_emleke_az_orszagos_leveltar_menny
ezeten; Reisz, ed., *A nemzet levéltára*, 449–452.

43. *Magyarország*, 10 October 1929, quoted in Reisz, "Trianon ismeretlen emléke."

44. See Hatos, *Rosszfiúk világforradalma*, 67–69, 529, note 150.

45. "Az egyesség okmánya" [The document of accord], *Pesti Napló*, 10 October 1929, 10.

46. Reisz, "Trianon ismeretlen emléke."

47. K-f, "Károlyi Mihály, Hock János és Kun Béla—nem szerepelnek az Országos Levéltár freskóján" [MK, JH, and BK are not depicted in the fresco of the National Archives], *Az Est*, 12 October 1929, 5.

48. Endre Sós, "Dudits Andor tiltakozik az ellen, hogy megcsökönyösödött akadémikusnak tartsák" [AD protests against being regarded as a stuffy academician], *Esti Kurir*, 30 August 1925, 6.

49. P. Z., "Dudits Andor," *Magyarság*, supp. 2, 1 March 1931.

50. "Festessünk freskókat!" [Let's commission frescoes!], *Népszava*, 13 October 1929, 14.

51. Benjamin, "The Work of Art in the Age of Mechanical Reproduction," in Benjamin, *Illuminations*, ed. Arendt, trans. Zohn (London: Jonathan Cape, 1970), 243–244.

52. See Béla Zsolt Szakács, "Gerevich Tibor (1882–1954)," *Enigma* 13, no. 47 (2006): 179.

53. Tibor Gerevich, "Római magyar művészek" [Hungarian artists in Rome], *Magyar Szemle* (1932): 235–240. See P. Szűcs, *A Római Iskola*; P. Szűcs, "A 'Modern' Official Art."

54. Gerevich, "Római magyar művészek," 238.

55. Gerevich, "Római magyar művészek," 239.

56. See, for example, Zoltán Farkas, "Gróf Klebelsberg Kunó képzőművészeti politikája" [The fine art policies of Count Kuno Klebelsberg], *Nyugat* 26, no. 5 (1933): 321–324.

57. For an insightful analysis of the School of Rome's modernism, see P. Szűcs, "A 'Modern' Official Art."

58. Péter Molnos, *Aba-Novák* (Budapest: Kieselbach, 2006), 60–62.

59. See Futó's account in Molnos, *Aba-Novák*, 60–61.

60. P. Szűcs, *A Római Iskola*, 71.

61. Viola Pleskovics, "Építőkövek az államalapító korából—Az 1938-as jubileum székesfehérvári romkertje" [Building stones from the time of the founder of the state—The Székesfehérvár Ruin Garden of the 1938 jubilee], *Építészfórum*, 20 August 2021, accessed 4 December 2024, https://epiteszforum.hu/kovek-az-allamalapito -korabol--az-1938-as-jubileum-szekesfehervari-romkertje. See also Pleskovics, "Additions to the History of Hungarian Medieval Royal Centre Rehabilitations in the Interwar Period," *Acta Historiae Artium* 63 (2022): 333–338.

62. Quoted in Pleskovics, "Építőkövek az államalapító korából."

63. Melinda Harlov-Csortán, "Roman Heritage in Hungary: The Case of the Fertőrákos Mithraeum on the Iron Curtain," in Koranyi and Hanscam, eds., *Digging Politics*, 165.

64. Szakács, "Gerevich Tibor," 196–197.

65. Szakács, "Gerevich Tibor," 195.

66. Gerevich, "A legújabb magyarországi ásatások" [The newest Hungarian excavations], *Magyar Szemle* 23, no. 1–4 (1935): 69.

67. Gerevich, "A legújabb magyarországi ásatások," 69–70. For more on the influence of Mussolini and Italian approaches to heritage on Hungarian heritage protection in the interwar period, see Pleskovics, "Additions to the History of Hungarian Medieval Royal Centre Rehabilitations," 327–346.

68. Ella Megyery, "A kultuszminiszter római utja s a magyar-olasz kulturkapcsolatok: Beszélgetés Gerevich Tiborral az olaszországi magyar manifesztációkról" [The Roman trip of the minister of culture and Hungarian-Italian cultural relations: A conversation with TG about Hungarian manifestations in Italy], *Magyarság*, 27 February 1927, 5, quoted in Pleskovics, "Építőkövek az államalapító korából."

69. On the excavations and the building, see also Pál Lővei, "Székesfehérvár, Romkert—1936–1938" [Székesfehérvár, Ruin Garden], *Építés—Építészettudomány* 29, no. 3–4 (2001): 379–388; Petra Gärtner, "Az idézet bűvöletében" [Under the spell of quotation], in *Szent István király bazilikájának utóélete: A Középkori Romkert 1938-tól napjainkig* [The afterlife of King Saint Stephen's Basilica: The Medieval Ruin Garden from 1938 to the present day], ed. Gärtner (Székesfehérvár: Szent István Király Múzeum, 2016), 7–21.

70. On Lux's medieval sources in more detail, see Pleskovics, "Additions to the History of Hungarian Medieval Royal Centre Rehabilitations," 334–336.

71. Gerevich, *Magyarország románkori emlékei* [Hungary's Romanesque monuments] (Budapest: Műemlékek Országos Bizottsága, 1938), 13; Dezső Dercsényi, *A székesfehérvári királyi bazilika* [The Royal Basilica of Székesfehérvár], with an introduction by Gerevich (Budapest: Műemlékek Országos Bizottsága, 1943), 32–35.

72. Dercsényi, *A székesfehérvári királyi bazilika*, 67–68. See also Pleskovics, "Építőkövek az államalapító korából."

73. Viola Pleskovics argues that these contemporary echoes are less significant than the medieval inspirations; see Pleskovics, "Additions to the History of Hungarian Medieval Royal Centre Rehabilitations," 336.

74. Pleskovics, "Építőkövek az államalapító korából."

75. On the commission and the phases of the work, see Molnos, "Aba-Novák Vilmos falképtervei a székesfehérvári Szent István-mauzóleumhoz" [VAN's designs for the murals of Saint Stephen's Mausoleum], in *István a szent király*, ed. Kerny and Smohay, 221–230.

76. *A Szent István Emlékév*, kiadja a Szent István Emlékév Országos Bizottsága [The Saint Stephen Jubilee Year, Published by the National Committee of the Saint Stephen Jubilee Year] (Budapest: National Committee of the Saint Stephen Jubilee Year, 1940), 31–32.

77. *A Szent István Emlékév*, 31.

78. Gerevich, *Magyarország románkori emlékei*, 237.

79. *A Szent István Emlékév*, 40.

80. Dercsényi, *A székesfehérvári királyi bazilika*, 68.

81. Dercsényi, *A székesfehérvári királyi bazilika*, 68–69.

82. Gerevich, "Kolozsvári Tamás," *Az Országos Magyar Régészeti Társulat Évkönyve* 1 (1920–1922): 163.

83. P. Szűcs, *A Római Iskola*, 113. On the racialized requirement of Hungarianness in the late 1930s and the School of Rome's consequent stylistic shift, see also P. Szűcs, "A 'Modern' Official Art."

84. Marius Turda, "From Craniology to Serology: Racial Anthropology in Interwar Hungary and Romania," *Journal of the History of the Behavioral Sciences* 43, no. 4 (2007): 368.

85. Gärtner, "Az idézet bűvöletében," 13.

86. Ujváry, "Nem a kard, hanem a kultúra: A Horthy-korszak kulturális politikája," in *A Horthy-korszak vitatott kérdései*, 110.

87. Dercsényi, "XI. századi királyi kőfaragóműhely Budán" [An eleventh century royal stonemasons' workshop in Buda], *Budapest Régiségei* 13 (1943): 257–293.

88. Sándor Tóth, "A 11. századi magyarországi kőornamentika időrendjéhez" [On the chronology of eleventh-century stone ornament in Hungary], in *Pannonia Regia: Művészet a Dunántúlon 1000–1541* [Art in Western Hungary], ed. Mikó and Imre Takács (Budapest: Hungarian National Gallery, 1994), 54.

89. Pleskovics, "Építőkövek az államalapító korából."

90. Olivér Kovács and Gergely Buzás, "Szent István sírja" [The tomb of Saint Stephen], *Altum Castrum*, accessed 2 December 2024, https://archeologia.hu/szent-istvan-sirja.

91. Tóth, "A székesfehérvári szarkofág és köre" [The Székesfehérvár sarcophagus and its circle], in *Pannonia Regia*, 82; Kovács and Buzás, "Szent István sírja."

92. Tóth, "A székesfehérvári szarkofág és köre," 82.

93. Kovács and Buzás, "Szent István sírja."

94. Tóth, "A székesfehérvári szarkofág és köre," 82–86.

95. Tóth, "A székesfehérvári szarkofág és köre," 82–86.

96. Orsolya Bubryák, "'E meditullio basilicae erutum'? Megjegyzések a székesfehérvári Szent István szarkofág provenienciájához" ["Unearthed from the middle of the basilica?" Comments on the provenance of the Saint Stephen sarcophagus], *Ars Hungarica* 35, no. 1 (2007): 5–28.

97. On the afterlife of the murals and for reproductions of original designs, see Molnos, "Aba-Novák Vilmos falképtervei."

98. For an annotated English translation, see Lajos Fülep, "The Task of Hungarian Art History (1951)," *Journal of Art Historiography* 6, no. 11 (2014), accessed 2 December 2024, https://arthistoriography.wordpress.com/wp-content/uploads/2014/11/veszprc3a9mi-trans-fulep.pdf.

5. Heroes and Rebels

1. My discussion of Derkovits's *1514* in this chapter is partly based on my article "Sites of Memory and Forgetting: Gyula Derkovits's Woodcuts of the 1514 Peasant War," *Oxford Art Journal* 46, no. 3 (2023): 379–405.

2. K. A., "Derkovits Gyula emlékkiállítása az Ernst-Múzeumban" [GyD's commemorative exhibition at the Ernst Museum], *Pesti Napló*, 28 October 1934, 14.

3. K. M., "Derkovits Gyula gyűjteményes kiállítása az Ernst Muzeumban" [GyD's retrospective exhibition at the Ernst Museum], *Nemzeti Ujság*, 28 October 1934, 28.

4. See, for example, Kopócsy, "A jelen történelmi értelmezése, 137–157.

5. For a study of the channels through which ideas of the nation, among them ideas of national history, were disseminated in Hungarian society from 1867 to the present, see Szabó, *Nemzet és szocializáció.*

6. Urhegyi Alajos, "A népiskolai történelmi szemléltető faliképek" [The historical demonstrative wall pictures for public schools], *Magyar Tanítóképző* 30, no. 10 (1915): 356–360. See Katalin Lányi, ed., *Történelmi szemléltetőanyag az első világháború korából* [Historical demonstrative material from the time of the First World War] (Budapest: Fekete Sas and Magyar Pedagógiai Társaság, 2003); Szabó, *Nemzet és szocializáció*, 58–62.

7. "Falitáblák, szemléltetőképek" [Wall tableaux, demonstrative images], *Hivatalos Közlöny*, 1 May 1930, IV; "Történelmi szemléltetőképek," *Nemzetnevelés*, 17 August 1937, 259. For a wide range of examples of administrative and ideological continuities between the Habsburg Empire and the successor states at a local level, see the European Research Council–funded project NEPOSTRANS (Negotiating Post-Imperial Transitions), led by Gábor Egry at the Institute of Political History in Budapest: *NEPOSTRANS*, accessed 2 December 2024, https://1918local.eu/.

8. "A kormányzó ünnepi külsőségek közt adta át a kitüntetetteknek a Corvin-Rend jelvényeit" [The regent has awarded the insignia of the Corvin Order to the recipients at a formal ceremony], *Budapesti Hirlap*, 24 February 1931, 7.

9. Turbucz, *A Horthy-kultusz*, 238. The painting is now in the collection of the Hungarian National Gallery (inv. no. 59.151T); see "The Triumphant Matthias (Matthias's entry into Buda)," *MNG*, accessed 3 July 2024, https://en.mng.hu/artworks/52705/.

10. Pál Madai, *Magyarország történelme gimnáziumok, reálgimnáziumok és reáliskolák III. osztálya számára* [The history of Hungary for secondary schools, grade 3] (Budapest: Franklin, 1926).

11. For a comparison between Horthy's cult and other contemporary leadership cults, see Turbucz, *A Horthy-kultusz*, 33–52.

12. M. B. B. Biskupski, *Independence Day: Myth, Symbol, and the Creation of Modern Poland* (Oxford: Oxford University Press, 2021).

13. Lucile Dreidemy, "'Denn ein Engel kann nicht sterben': Engelbert Dollfus 1934–2012—eine Biographie des Posthumen" (PhD diss., University of Strasbourg and University of Vienna, 2012), https://theses.hal.science/tel-01249522/document, esp. 54–57.

14. Andrea Orzoff, "The Husbandman: Tomáš Masaryk's Leader Cult in Interwar Czechoslovakia," *Austrian History Yearbook* 39 (2008): 121–137.

15. B. Gábor Albert, "A református fiú-középiskolák történelemtankönyvhasználata 1926-tól az 1930-as évek közepéig" [The textbook usage of Calvinist boys' secondary schools from 1926 to the mid-1930s], *Magyar Pedagógia* 113, no. 2 (2013): 119–129.

16. Albert, *Súlypontok és hangsúlyeltolódások: Középiskolai történelem tankönyvek a Horthy-korszakban* [Focal points and shifts in emphasis: Secondary school history textbooks in the Horthy era] (Pápa: Pedagogy Research Centre of the Faculty of Humanities of Pannon University, 2006), 76–87.

17. Beáta Csákó and Dániel Samu Nagy, *Az Országház nevezetes termei* [Significant rooms of the Parliament] (Budapest: Országgyűlés Hivatala, 2019), 91–94.

18. János Horvay, "Önéletrajz" [JH: Autobiography], in *Az Est Hármaskönyve 1923* (Budapest: Az Est Lapkiadó Rt., 1923), 327–328.

19. Emil Kállai, "Két Kossuth-szobor: Beszélgetés Horvay Jánossal—'Nem lehetett őt itt szónoknak ábrázolnom'" [Two Kossuth statues: Conversation with JH—"I could not depict him as an orator here"], *Délmagyarország*, 12 January 1928, 4.

20. "'Kossuth Lajost nem illik sarokba állítani': Rákosi Jenő és Horvay János a Kossuth-szobor helye körül támadt vitáról" ["It is improper to put Lajos Kossuth in the corner": Jenő Rákosi and JH on the debate around the location of the Kossuth statue], *Pesti Napló*, 1 April 1926, 8; "Ma délben főpróbát tartottak a Horvay Kossuth-szobrának elhelyezéséről" [Today at noon a modelling of the location of Horvay's Kossuth statue took place], *Uj Nemzedék*, 4 July 1926, 2.

21. Fogu, *The Historic Imaginary*. See also Fogu, "Fascism and Historic Representation: The 1932 Garibaldian Celebrations," *Journal of Contemporary History* 31, no. 2 (1996): 317–345; Massimo Baioni, "Interpretations of Garibaldi in Fascist Culture: A Contested Legacy," *Modern Italy* 15, no. 4 (2010): 451–465.

22. The following three sections of this chapter are partly based on Veszprémi, "Sites of Memory and Forgetting."

23. Madai, *Magyarország történelme*, 118–119.

24. György Domanovszky, "A jobbágyság élete" [The life of serfs], in *Magyar művelődéstörténet* [Hungarian cultural history], vol. 2, ed. Sándor Domanovszky (Budapest: Magyar Történelmi Társulat, 1939).

25. See her letter quoted in Béla Bíró, "Levél Madarász Viktor képeiről; Kossuth Lajos levele Madarász Viktorhoz" [Letter about VM's paintings; letter from Lajos Kossuth to VM], *Szabad Művészet* 6, no. 2 (1952): 70.

26. Róbert Braun, "A Dózsa-féle parasztfölkelés a legújabb magyar történetírás tükrében" [The Dózsa peasants' uprising in the mirror of recent Hungarian history writing], *Századunk* 10, no. 4–5 (1935): 188–189.

27. Vörös, *"A múltat végképp eltörölni"? Történelmi személyiségek a magyarországi szociáldemokrata és kommunista propagandában 1890–1919* ["We'll change henceforth the old tradition"? Historical personalities in Hungarian Social Democratic and Communist propaganda] (Budapest: MTA History Research Institute, 2004), 29, 75–76.

28. Gyuláné Derkovits, *Mi ketten: Emlékezés Derkovits Gyulára* [Us two: Remembering Gy. D.] (Budapest: Képzőművészeti Alap, 1954), 89. The book bears the date 1954 but was published the following year.

29. Molnos, *Derkovits: Szemben a világgal* [Derkovits: Facing the world] (Budapest: Népszabadság and Kieselbach, 2008), 45–47.

30. Barbara Büki, "The Past Is Still Present: A Painter in the Public Arena," in *Derkovits: The Artist and His Times*, ed. Bakos and Zwickl (Budapest: Hungarian National Gallery, 2014), 136–149.

31. Veszprémi, "Sites of Memory and Forgetting."

32. The overview of the artist's biography is based on Bakos and Zwickl, eds., *Derkovits: The Artist and His Times*.

33. Bakos, "An Oeuvre with the Power to Engage," in *Derkovits: The Artist and His Times*, ed. Bakos and Zwickl, 26–47.

34. Derkovits, *Mi ketten*, 89.

35. For a list of names, see the signatories of the "Ultimatum to the Central Committee," dated 30 October 1921 and signed by Jenő Derkovits alongside other

members of the Landler faction. Archives of the Institute of Political History, Budapest; published on the website of the Lukács Archives, "Ultimátum a KB-hoz," *Lukács Archívum Nemzetközi Alapítvány*, accessed 2 December 2024, https://www.lana.info .hu/lukacs-gyorgy/lukacs-gyorgy-muvei/lukacs-gyorgy-publicisztikaja-1920-22 /ultimatum-a-kb-hoz/.

36. For a summary of the various possibilities proposed in previous literature, see Bakos, "The 'Grandchild of György Dózsa,'" 190.

37. Derkovits, *Mi ketten*, 91–93.

38. Derkovits, *Mi ketten*, 93.

39. Béla Hegyi, "A Vigilia beszélgetése Derkovits Gyulánéval—két emlékeztetővel" [The periodical Vigilia interviews Mrs. Gyula Derkovits—with two reminders], *Vigilia* 41, no. 1 (1976): 29.

40. Derkovits, *Mi ketten*, 89.

41. Pongrác Galsai, "'Nem a tárgyakban őrzöm . . .' Beszélgetés Derkovits Gyulánéval" ["I don't preserve it in objects" . . . Conversation with Mrs. Gyula Derkovits] (originally published in *Nők Lapja*, 17 November 1962, 6–7), *Enigma* 20, no. 74 (2013): 59.

42. Büki, "The Past Is Still Present," 137, 148, note 10.

43. György Bálint, "Derkovits Gyula," and Kállai, "A Dózsa-sorozat fametszetei" [The woodcuts of the Dózsa series], in Gyula Derkovits, *1514: 11 fametszet* (Budapest: Gondolat, 1936).

44. Büki, "The Past Is Still Present," 137–138.

45. Friedrich Engels, "The Peasant War in Germany," in *Collected Works*, vol. 10, Karl Marx and Engels (New York: International Publishers, 1978), 399.

46. On Derkovits and Kollwitz most recently, see Zwickl, "Gyula Derkovits and European Art," and Bajkay, "The Artist's Search for Identity in Vienna," in *Derkovits: The Artist and His Times*, ed. Bakos and Zwickl, 48–61, 62–75.

47. On the Dózsa series and Masereel, see Szabó, "Die Holzschnittfolge '1514' von Gyula Derkovits," *Acta Historiae Artium* 10, no. 1–2 (1964): 202–203.

48. On the factions, see Péter Sipos, *Legális és illegális munkásmozgalom (1919–1944)* [The legal and illegal workers' movement] (Budapest: Gondolat, 1988), 119–131. See also György Lukács, *Megélt gondolkodás: Életrajz magnószalagon* [Lived thought: A biography on tape] (Budapest: Magvető, 1989), 179–196.

49. Lukács, *Megélt gondolkodás*, 191. For the text, see Lukács, "Tézistervezet a magyar politikai és gazdasági helyzetről s a KMP feladatairól" [Draft theses on the Hungarian political and economic situation and the tasks of the Hungarian Communist Party], ed. Ágnes Szabó, *Párttörténeti Közlemények* 21, no. 4 (1975): 156–207. See also Miklós Lackó, "A Blum-tézisek" [The Blum Theses], *Történelmi Szemle* 17, no. 3 (1974): 360–371.

50. Lukács, "Tézistervezet," 206.

51. See the documents at the Archives of Political History and the Trade Unions, Budapest, fonds 878, series 1, files, 19, 21, 25, 27–29, 41.

52. Archives of Political History and the Trade Unions, Budapest, fonds 878, series 1.

53. László Kővágó, "A kommunista párt és Trianon" [The Communist Party and Trianon], *História* 3, no. 2 (1981): 7–9.

54. "Trianon revíziója: A Szovjetunió elleni háború jelszava" [The revision of Trianon: Slogan of the war against the Soviet Union], *Új Március*, July 1927, 326–330.

See Kővágó, "A magyar kommunista párt nemzetiségpolitikája a Tanácsköztársaság megdöntésétől a felszabadulásig" [Nationality politics of the Hungarian Communist Party from the fall of the council republic to liberation], *Párttörténeti Közlemények* 23, no. 2 (1977): 81.

55. [József Révai], "A magyar munkásosztály és a revízió" [The Hungarian working class and revision], *Új Március* (April/May/June 1929): 131–138.

56. See Kővágó, "A magyar kommunista párt nemzetiségpolitikája," 82–83.

57. Kővágó, "A magyar kommunista párt nemzetiségpolitikája," 83; Kemény [Révai], "Harcoljon-e a Kommunisták Magyarországi Pártja Trianon ellen?" [Should the Hungarian Communist Party fight against Trianon?], *Új Március* (August–November 1929): 315–324. Republished in Zeidler, ed., *Trianon* (Budapest: Osiris, 2008), 398–406.

58. Andrea Graziosi, *The Great Soviet Peasant War: Bolsheviks and Peasants, 1917–1933* (Cambridge, MA: Harvard University Press and Harvard University Ukrainian Research Institute, 1996). See also Nicolas Werth, "The Soviet State and Peasants," in *The Cambridge History of Communism*, vol. 1, ed. Silvio Pons and Stephen A. Smith (Cambridge, UK: Cambridge University Press, 2017), 399–423.

59. On the social stratification of the peasantry and their lack of welfare, see Romsics, *A Horthy-korszak*, 170–173, 389–390.

60. Archives of Political History and the Trade Unions, Budapest, fonds 878, series 1, file 21. See János Rainer M., "Nagy Imre szovjet emigrációban, 1930–1939" [IN in emigration in the Soviet Union], *Történelmi Szemle* 38, no. 3 (1995): 319–343.

61. Archives of Political History and the Trade Unions, Budapest, fonds 878, series 1, files 27, 169. See Rainer, "Nagy Imre szovjet emigrációban."

62. Hungarian National Gallery, inv. no. F 59.19.

63. Bajkay, *Uitz Béla* (Budapest: Képzőművészeti Kiadó, 1987), 58–59.

64. Ronald Grigor Suny, *The Revenge of the Past: Nationalism, Revolution, and the Collapse of the Soviet Union* (Stanford, CA: Stanford University Press, 1993), 84–90; Jeremy Smith, *The Bolsheviks and the National Question, 1917–23* (Houndmills, UK: Macmillan and St. Martin's, 1999), 15–22.

65. Martin Mevius, "Reappraising Communism and Nationalism," *Nationalities Papers* 37, no. 4 (2009): 383–384.

66. David Brandenberger, *National Bolshevism: Stalinist Mass Culture and the Formation of Modern Russian Identity, 1931–1956* (Cambridge, MA: Harvard University Press, 2002), 6.

67. Cornelia Cabuk, *Otto Rudolf Schatz: Monografie und Werkverzeichnis*, ed. Stella Rollig and Christian Huemer (Vienna: Belvedere, 2018), https://werkverzeichnisse.belvedere.at/groups/otto-rudolf-schatz/results.

68. For images, see "Jánosík," *Web Umenia*, accessed 2 December 2024, https://www.webumenia.sk/en/dielo/SVK:GPB.G_1034 .

69. András Péter, "Művészeti séták" [Walks through art], *Tükör* 3, no. 7 (1935): 64.

70. János Jajczay, "Képzőművészeti szemle" [A survey of fine arts], *Magyar Kultúra* 21, no. 22 (1934): 482–483.

71. F. Z., "Derkovits Gyula emlékkiállítása" [The memorial exhibition of GyD], *Magyarság*, 28 October 1934, 21.

72. K. M., "Derkovits Gyula gyűjteményes kiállítása az Ernst Muzeumban," 28.

73. Artúr Elek, "Az újabb magyar grafikai művészet" [Recent Hungarian graphic art], *Magyar Művészet* 13 (1937): 223.

74. Varga, *A fametszet* [The woodcut] (Budapest: pub. by author, 1940), 380–381. For a discussion of *Hungarian Past* in relation to *1514*, see Kopócsy, "A jelen történelmi értelmezése," 140–142.

75. Maria Bucur, *Heroes and Victims: Remembering War in Twentieth-Century Romania* (Bloomington: Indiana University Press, 2009), 100–109.

76. Melinda Harlov, "A budapesti Hősök terén található Hősök Emlékkövének történeti áttekintése és lehetséges értelmezései" [Historical overview and possible interpretations of the Memorial Stone of Heroes in Heroes' Square, Budapest], *A Nagy Háború* (blog), accessed 2 December 2024, https://m.blog.hu/na/nagyhaboru/image/workshop/emlekko/harlovmelinda_hosok_emlekkove.pdf; Vari, "Re-territorializing the 'Guilty City,'" 723–725.

77. Bucur, *Heroes and Victims*, 122.

78. Bucur, *Heroes and Victims*, 106–109.

79. Wingfield, "National Sacrifice and Regeneration," 129–150.

80. Attila Tóth, "'Egy új, tisztultabb élet felé': A Hősök kapuja építészeti és helytörténeti jelentősége" ["Toward a new, purer life": The significance of the Gate of Heroes in architectural and local history], *Szeged*, October 2000, 18.

81. See the artist's description of the frescoes, quoted in Tóth, "Mit rejt a vakolat? A Hősök kapuja freskóiról" [What is hidden under the lime? on the frescoes of the Gate of Heroes], *Szeged*, March 1993, 30–31.

82. Emil Szomory, "Egy fiatal szobrásznő, aki boldog és egy hajdani istállóban alkotja remekműveit" [A young woman sculptor who is happy and creates her masterpieces in a former stable], *Ujság*, 8 April 1928, 51.

83. Jay Winter, *Sites of Memory, Sites of Mourning: The Great War in European Cultural History* (Cambridge, UK: Cambridge University Press, 2014), 78–116; Stefan Goebel, "Cultural Memory and the Great War: Medievalism and Classicism in British and German War Memorials," in *Cultures of Commemoration: War Memorials, Ancient and Modern*, ed. Polly Low, Graham Oliver, and P. J. Rhodes (Oxford: Oxford University Press, 2012), 135–158.

84. Turbucz, *A Horthy-kultusz*, 219–120, 199–284.

85. Dreidemy, *"Denn ein Engel kann nicht sterben."*

86. Károly László Háy, "Egy félbemaradt metszetsorozatról" [On an unfinished series of prints] (originally published *Művelt Nép*, 17 April 1955), in *Szabadság és a Nép: A Szocialista Képzőművészek Csoportjának dokumentumai* [Freedom and the people: Documents from the Group of Socialist Artists], ed. Nóra Aradi (Budapest: Art History Research Group of the Hungarian Academy of Sciences, 1981), 303–305. See Kopócsy, "A jelen történelmi értelmezése," 145.

87. Mevius, *Agents of Moscow: The Hungarian Communist Party and the Origins of Socialist Patriotism 1941–1953* (Oxford: Oxford University Press, 2005), 26–42.

88. Mevius, *Agents of Moscow*, 43–44.

89. "A Magyar Történelmi Emlékbizottság felhívása" [A call of the Hungarian Historical Memorial Committee], *Népszava*, 1 March 1942, 7.

90. Imre Kovács, "Két pogány közt egy hazáért . . .," *Híd* (May 1938): 1. Another important example is Sándor Pethő, "Két pogány közt egy hazáért," *Magyarság*, 6 and 13 September 1936, 1–2, 1–2.

91. Háy, "Egy félbemaradt metszetsorozatról," 304.

92. Kopócsy, "A jelen történelmi értelmezése," 146.

93. Turbucz, *A Horthy-kultusz*, 65, 78, 92.

94. Sára Bárdi, "Politikai ikonográfia a két világháború közötti magyar képzőművészetben: Esettanulmány: Háy Károly László Történelem jeligéjű freskóterve (1942)" [Political iconography in interwar Hungarian art: Case study: KLH's fresco design submitted under the code-word *history*], in *Élő művek: Tanulmányok a Fiatal Művészettörténészek 7. Konferenciájának előadásaiból* [Living artworks: Papers from the 7th Conference of Young Art Historians], ed. Ilka Boér and Emese Pál (Budapest: Martin Opitz Kiadó, 2022), 185–203.

95. See, for example, "Szabadság és a Nép," figs. 123–130.

Epilogue

1. Géza Ottlik, *Iskola a határon* [School at the frontier] (Budapest: Magvető, [1999]), 422–423. Translation my own.

2. National Széchényi Library, Budapest, Collection of Posters and Pamphlets, inv. no. Alb.E 18.

3. Verbal communications of Anita Szarka (Budapest, 25 November, 2022), to whom I am grateful for sharing this information with me.

4. On the memory of the Soviet Republic and the White Terror see Bodó, "Memory Practices: The Red and White Terrors in Hungary as Remembered after 1990," *East Central Europe* 44, no. 2–3 (2017): 186–215; Bodó, "Violence Glorified or Denied? Collective Memory of the Red and White Terrors in Hungary, 1919–Present," *Hungarian Studies Review* 46–47, no. 1–2 (2019–2020): 44–54.

5. Reisz, "Trianon ismeretlen emléke"; Reisz, *A nemzet levéltára*, 454–455.

6. Zoltán Ólmosi and András Oross, "Meszeljünk vagy ne? A Magyar Országos Levéltár freskóinak sorsa az ötvenes években" [Whitewash or not? The fate of the frescoes of the Hungarian National Archives in the 1950s], *ArchivNet* 4, no. 6 (2004), https://www.archivnet.hu/kuriozumok/meszeljunk_vagy_ne.html; Reisz, *A nemzet levéltára*, 454–455.

7. Horvay, "Önéletrajz" [JH: Autobiography], in *Az Est Hármaskönyve 1923* (Budapest: Az Est Lapkiadó Rt., 1923), 328. See chapter 5.

8. "Horvay János: Kossuth-szoborcsoport" [JH: Kossuth sculptural group], *Dombopedia*, accessed 2 December 2024, http://dombopedia.hu/adatbazisok/kozteri -alkotasok-szobrok/horvay-janos-kossuth-szoborcsoport.html.

9. On Aba-Novák, see P. Szűcs, *A Római Iskola*; for a more recent monograph, see Molnos, *Aba-Novák*. On Dudits, T. Csaba Reisz has recently published a series of articles and is currently preparing a monograph.

10. On Derkovits's postwar reception, see Éva Standeisky, "Appropriations: Derkovits in Times of Change," and Büki, "The Past Is Still Present," in *Derkovits*, ed. Bakos and Zwickl, 122–135, 136–149.

11. Bakos and Zwickl, eds., *Derkovits*.

12. See, for example, an article in a prominent liberal weekly: [Tamás] Szőnyei, "Aba-Novák hagyatéka: Freskósors" [The heritage of Aba-Novák: The fate of a fresco], *Magyar Narancs*, 20 August 1998.

13. Tibor Hollauer, "Hova fészkel a turulmadár? Irredenta szobrok" [Where will the turul bird nest: Irredentist sculptures (interview with Ernő Raffay)], *168 Óra*, 4 September 1990, 10–11.

14. Tibor Kis, "Trianon-kuratórium: sztornó" [Trianon Board of Trustees: Abolished], *Népszabadság*, 11 September 1990, 1.

15. Péter Vajda, "A parancsnok marad" [The commander remains in place], *Népszabadság*, 3 April 1991, 1, 5.

16. On these events in the context of diaspora policy, see Waterbury, *Between State and Nation*, 60–65.

17. Nagy, "Trianon a magyar társadalom tudatában," 843–845; Waterbury, *Between State and Nation*, 42–49.

18. Thorstensen, "The Places of Memory in a Square of Monuments."

19. Feischmidt, "Memory-Politics and Neonationalism," 130.

20. Andrea Pető, "The Illiberal Memory Politics in Hungary," *Journal of Genocide Research* 24, no. 2 (2022): 243–244.

21. Waterbury, *Between State and Nation*, 6.

22. In August 2023, an article in the *Magyar Nemzet*, a daily newspaper close to the government, argued that when the Hungarian army entered Slovakia in 1968 as part of the Soviet suppression of the Prague Spring, this was a rightful step that should have led to the reannexation of parts of Slovakia to Hungary. See Balázs Ágoston, "Magyar remény 1968-ban" [Hungarian Hope in 1968], *Magyar Nemzet*, 18 August 2023.

23. Pető, "The Illiberal Memory Politics in Hungary," 241–249.

24. On Kossuth Square and its contextualization in current memory politics, see Fekete, "Unburied Bodies," 415–431.

25. András, *Határsértő képzelet*, 157.

26. On Turanism in Hungarian cultural diplomacy and scientific discourse today, see Katrin Kremmler, "Eurasian Magyars: The Making of a New Hegemonic National Prehistory in Illiberal Hungary," in *Digging Politics*, ed. Koranyi and Hanscam, 181–216. On the afterlife of Turanism from the interwar period to the present, see Ablonczy, *Go East!*

27. Péter Németh, "Ferenczy Noémi gobelinje Nyíregyházán" [NF's Gobelin in Nyíregyháza], in *Szent István emlékezete falikárpitokon 1938–2000* [The memory of St. Stephen in tapestries], ed. Zombori (Szeged: Móra Ferenc Museum, 2001), 32–33.

28. Pálosi, "Szent István kárpitok," 22–26; Bodonyi, *Teremtés*, 72–73, 162–163.

29. Anna Oelmacher, "Ferenczy Noémi művészete" [The art of NF], in *Ferenczy Noémi gyűjteményes kiállítása* [NF's retrospective exhibition] (Budapest: Nemzeti Szalon, 1956).

30. Pálosi, "Ferenczy Noémi művészi és tanári munkásságának eseménytörténete" [The history of NF's work as an artist and educator], *Ars Hungarica* 13, no. 2 (1985): 191–195; Bodonyi, *Teremtés*, 82–85.

31. For a more detailed investigation of this, see Veszprémi, "Sites of Memory and Forgetting."

32. Csaplár, *A Szegedi Fiatalok Művészeti Kollégiuma*.

33. See examples in Koranyi and Hanscam, eds., *Digging Politics*.

34. For examples, see e.g., Feischmidt, "Lehorgonyzott mítoszok," 382–387; Paul Stirton, "Public Sculpture in Cluj/Kolozsvár: Identity, Space and Politics," in *Heritage, Ideology, and Identity in Central and Eastern Europe: Contested Pasts, Contested Presents*, ed. Matthew Rampley (Woodbridge: Boydell & Brewer, 2012), 55–64; Koranyi, "The Thirteen Martyrs of Arad," 64–66; András, *Határsértő képzelet*, 125–128.

35. See, for example, Irene Götz, Klaus Roth, and Marketa Spiritova, eds, *Neuer Nationalismus im östlichen Europa: Kulturwissenschaftliche Perspektiven* (Bielefeld: transcript Verlag, 2017); Pető, "The Illiberal Memory Politics in Hungary."

36. See the works analyzed in András, *Határsértő képzelet*, 206–297.

37. Ottlik, *Iskola a határon.*

38. For an image, see "File:Kőszeg, Sgraffitós ház 2021 01.jpg," *Wikimedia Commons*, accessed 2 December 2024, https://commons.wikimedia.org/wiki/File:K%C5%91szeg,_Sgraffit%C3%B3s_h%C3%A1z_2021_01.jpg.

BIBLIOGRAPHY

Primary Sources

Archives

Archives of Political History and the Trade Unions, Budapest, fonds 878, series 1. Documents from the Hungarian Communist Party, Congress (c. 1928–1931).

Anonymous Sources

"II. Lajos: Szomory darabja a Magyar Színházban" [Louis II: Szomory's play at the Magyar Theatre]. *Színházi Élet* 11, no. 6 (1922): 3–12.

"The Admonitions of King Stephen," in Gergely Bisztray, ed., *Thousand Years of Hungarian Thought*, special issue, *Hungarian Studies Review* 27, nos 1–2 (2000): 31–33.

"A kormányzó, a kormány, a nemzetgyűlés, a hadsereg és az egész nemzet ünnepelte ma október 6. vértanúit" [The regent, the national assembly, the army, and the whole nation celebrated the martyrs of October 6 today]. *Magyarság*, October 7, 1926, 5.

"A kormányzó ünnepi külsőségek közt adta át a kitüntetetteknek a Corvin-Rend jelvényeit" [The regent has awarded the insignia of the Corvin Order to the recipients at a formal ceremony]. *Budapesti Hirlap*, February 24, 1931, 7.

"A láthatatlan emlékmű" [The invisible monument]. *Pesti Hirlap*, October 6, 1937, 1.

"A magyar kormány felhívta az osztrák kormány figyelmét a durva támadásokra" [The Hungarian government has made the Austrian government aware of the aggressive attacks]. *Nemzeti Ujság*, March 1, 1930, 5.

"A Magyar Történelmi Emlékbizottság felhívása" [A call of the Hungarian Historical Memorial Committee]. *Népszava*, March 1, 1942, 7.

"A mohácsi vész 400. évfordulójának ünnepe Mohácson" [Festivities on the 400th anniversary of the Mohács disaster in Mohács]. *Magyar Híradó*, August 1926, 132. Accessed September 20, 2024. https://filmhiradokonline.hu/watch.php?id=8531&fbclid=IwAR0AzBxq69BgFGg4BQQ8hVchtE_jVvkMu6nof392IIPZAduS8Adpqzygvw0.

"A négy szobor: Az irredenta emlékművek leleplezése" [The four sculptures: The unveiling of the irredentist monuments]. *Pesti Hirlap*, January 18, 1921, 2.

A Szent Imre év főünnepségeinek, nemzetközi gyűléseinek, kongresszusainak, értekezleteinek, kiállitásainak részletes sorrendje Budapest, 1930 augusztus 16–23 [Detailed schedule of the main celebrations, international congresses, meetings, and exhibitions of the Saint Emeric Year]. Budapest: Pallas, 1930.

"A Szent István Bazilika feltámadási körmenete az Irredenta szobrokhoz" [The resurrection procession of Saint Stephen's Basilica to the irredentist sculptures]. *Pesti Hírlap*, April 1, 1923, 8.

A Szent István Emlékév, kiadja a Szent István Emlékév Országos Bizottsága [The Saint Stephen Jubilee Year, published by the National Committee of the Saint Stephen Jubilee Year]. Budapest: National Committee of the Saint Stephen Jubilee Year, 1940.

"Az egyesség okmánya" [The document of accord]. *Pesti Napló*, October 10, 1929, 10.

"Az egyetemek ifjúsága az irredenta-szobrok előtt és a Vigadóban ünnepelte október 6-át" [University youth celebrated October 6 in front of the irredentist statues and in the Vigadó]. *Nemzeti Ujság*, October 7, 1926, 2.

"Az irredenta szobrok reprodukcióját szabaddá tették" [Reproduction rights for the irredentist sculptures have been waived]. *Nemzeti Ujság*, June 18, 1921, 5.

"Bevonultak a nemzet katonái: Horthy és hadserege Budapesten" [The soldiers of the nation have made their entrance: Horthy and his army in Budapest]. *Pesti Napló*, November 18, 1919, 3.

"Biró Mihály Horthy-albuma a biróság előtt" [MB's Horthy album in court]. *Jövő*, November 25, 1922, 4.

"Biró Mihály rajzai" [Drawings by MB]. *Előre*, February 10, 1921, 2.

[Caption on front page]. *Képes Krónika*, April 20, 1920, 411.

"Die Hüter der (Horthy-)Sittlichkeit." *Der Abend*, June 14, 1930, 1.

"Dudits Andor felajánlotta a kormányzónak a 'Vérmezei eskütétel' vázlatát" [AD has offered a study of the Oath in the Vérmező to the Regent]. *8 Órai Ujság*, May 26, 1923, 7.

"Elmaradt az irredenta szobrok leleplezése" [The unveiling of the irredentist sculptures has been postponed]. *Munkás*, December 10, 1920, 3.

"Eskü a Vérmezőn" [Oath in the Vérmező]. *Pesti Napló*, May 13, 1923, 8.

"Eskü a Vérmezőn képpályázat" [Oath in the Vérmező painting competition]. *Budapesti Hírlap*, August 1, 1920, 4.

"Esti levél: Vegyes ünnep" [Evening letter: A mixed holiday]. *Pesti Hirlap*, August 19, 1928, 4.

"Falitáblák, szemléltetőképek" [Wall tableaux, demonstrative images]. *Hivatalos Közlöny*, May 1, 1930, IV.

"Fényes felvonulás" [A dazzling procession]. *Budapesti Hirlap*, August 19, 1938, 4.

"Fényes pompával hordozták körül Nagy-Magyarország irredenta lobogóját Feltámadás napján" [The irredentist flag of Greater Hungary was carried in the procession with great pomp on Resurrection Day]. *Pesti Hirlap*, April 17, 1938, 15.

"Festessünk freskókat!" [Let's commission frescoes!]. *Népszava*, October 13, 1929, 14.

Hansard. Commons Chambers, vol. 126, March 2, 1920. https://hansard.parliament.uk/Commons/1920-03-02/debates/3b858272-559e-453f-ab49-7c905aec361c/Hungary.

"'Kossuth Lajost nem illik sarokba állítani': Rákosi Jenő és Horvay János a Kossuth-szobor helye körül támadt vitáról" ["It is improper to put Lajos Kossuth in the corner": Jenő Rákosi and JH on the debate around the location of the Kossuth statue]. *Pesti Napló*, April 1, 1926, 8.

"Közgyülés után" [After the assembly]. *Gyógyszerészi Hetilap*, June 23, 1929, 139.

"Leleplezték a megszállt területek szobrait" [The statues of the occupied territories have been unveiled]. *Új Barázda*, January 18, 1921, 1–2.

"Ma délben főpróbát tartottak a Horvay Kossuth-szobrának elhelyezéséről" [Today at noon a modelling of the location of Horvay's Kossuth statue took place]. *Uj Nemzedék*, July 4, 1926, 2.

"Márton Ferenc—a képrombolásáról" [FM—on his destruction of his painting]. *Nemzeti Ujság*, September 29, 1920, 5.

"Megelevenedik a magyar mult . . ." [The Hungarian past is brought to life]. *Pesti Hirlap*, August 22, 1928, 7.

"Meghívó" [Invitation]. *Világ*, May 16, 1920, 4.

"Mi ünnepélyesen esküszünk . . ." [We solemnly swear . . .]. *Pesti Napló*, April 13, 1920, 3.

"Mohács: Bemutató a Nemzeti Színházban" [Mohács: Premiere at the National Theatre]. *Szinházi Élet* 9, no. 5 (1922): 3.

Mohács és Pécs részletes útmutatója: a mohácsi kiállítás, ünnepségek, kongresszusok, pécsi dalosünnepségek részletes műsoraival [A detailed guide to Mohács and Pécs with detailed programs of the Mohács exhibition, festivities, congresses, and Pécs song festivals]. Budapest: Magyarság, 1926.

"Mohács." *Pesti Napló Képes Melléklete*, August 28, 1926, 36.

"Október hatodikán kigyulladt a Batthyány-örökmécses" [The Batthyány Sanctuary Lamp was lit on October 6]. *Nemzeti Ujság*, October 7, 1926, 2.

"Osztrák ítélet Horthy kormányzó megsértéséért" [Austrian verdict for offending Regent Horthy]. *Friss Ujság*, June 14, 1930, 4.

"Özv. Göttler Lászlóné Kioszk-vendéglője" [The Kiosk restaurant of the widowed Mrs. László Göttler]. In *Magyar városok és vármegyék monográfiája* [Monograph of Hungarian cities and counties], vol. 24, *Rákospalota és Rákosvidék*, edited by Oszkár Zsemley, 371. Budapest: Magyar Városok Monográfiája Kiadóhivatala, 1938.

Pesti Napló Képes Melléklete, September 5, 1926.

"Sajnos, muszáj takarékoskodni" [Alas, money is tight]. *Népszava*, October 17, 1931, 8.

"Több külföldi sajtótermék postai szállitási jogának megvonása tárgyában" [On banning the postal distribution of some foreign printed material]. *Pénzügyi Közlöny*, September 1, 1924, 532.

"Történelmi szemléltetőképek." *Nemzetnevelés*, August 17, 1937, 259.

"Trianon revíziója: A Szovjetunió elleni háború jelszava" [The revision of Trianon: Slogan of the war against the Soviet Union]. *Új Március* (July 1927): 326–330.

"Ultimátum a KB-hoz" [Ultimatum to the Central Committee], *Lukács Archívum Nemzetközi Alapítvány*, accessed 2 December 2024, https://www.lana.info .hu/lukacs-gyorgy/lukacs-gyorgy-muvei/lukacs-gyorgy-publicisztikaja -1920-22/ultimatum-a-kb-hoz/.

"Zehn Jahre Horthy." *Der Abend*, February 27, 1930, 8.

Attributed Sources

Ágoston, Balázs. "Magyar remény 1968-ban" [Hungarian hope in 1968]. *Magyar Nemzet*, August 18, 2023.

Bálint, György. "Derkovits Gyula." In *1514: 11 fametszet*, Gyula Derkovits. Budapest: Gondolat, 1936.

Balogh, Edgár. "Valóság és kultúra a csehszlovákiai magyarság életében" [Reality and culture in the life of the Hungarian minority in Czechoslovakia]. *Korunk* 10, no. 7–8 (1935): 505–515.

Barsi, Imre. "Nyugtalan ifjúság tükre" [Mirror of restless youth]. *A Hét*, April 30, 1961, 17.

Bíró, Béla. "Levél Madarász Viktor képeiről; Kossuth Lajos levele Madarász Viktorhoz" [Letter about VM's paintings; letter from Lajos Kossuth to VM]. *Szabad Művészet* 6, no. 2 (1952): 68–73.

Braun, Róbert. "A Dózsa-féle parasztfölkelés a legújabb magyar történetírás tükrében" [The Dózsa peasants' uprising in the mirror of recent Hungarian history writing]. *Századunk* 10, no. 4–5 (1935): 188–189.

British Joint Labour Delegation to Hungary. *The White Terror in Hungary*. London: Trade Union Congress and the Labour Party, 1920.

Brogyányi, Kálmán. "A Csehszlovákiai Magyar Tudományos, Irodalmi és Művészeti Társaság művészeti osztályának kiállítása" [Exhibition of the art section of the Czechoslovak Hungarian Association for Scholarship, Literature, and Art]. Originally published in *Forum 3* , no. 5 (1935), republished in Lajos Turczel, "Szemelvények Brogyányi Kálmán műkritikai és művészettörténeti munkásságából" [Excerpts from KB's art criticism and art history writing] *Limes* 9, no. 4 (1996): 33–60.

Buday, George. *George Buday's Fifth Little Book: Hungarian Folktales and Illustrations*. London: Westminster, 1949.

Buday, George. *George Buday's Little Book of Hungarian Folktales and Illustrations*. London: Favil, 1943.

Buday, George. *George Buday's New Little Book of Hungarian Folktales and Illustrations*. London: Westminster, 1945.

Buday, György. "Életemről, művészetemről" [On my life, on my art]. In *Buday György fametszetei* [György Buday's wood engravings], 13–28. Budapest: Magyar Helikon, 1970.

Buday, György. *Ifjúságunk népnevelési feladatai és az alföldi rádióleadó* [The tasks of our youth in community education and the radio channel in the plains]. Szeged: Bethlen Gábor Kör, 1929.

Dercsényi, Dezső. *A székesfehérvári királyi bazilika* [The royal basilica of Székesfehérvár], with an introduction by Tibor Gerevich. Budapest: Műemlékek Országos Bizottsága, 1943.

Dercsényi, Dezső. "XI. századi királyi kőfaragóműhely Budán" [An eleventh century royal stonemasons' workshop in Buda]. *Budapest Régiségei* 13 (1943): 257–293.

Derkovits, Gyula. *1514: 11 fametszet*. Budapest: Gondolat, 1936.

Derkovits, Gyuláné. *Mi ketten: Emlékezés Derkovits Gyulára* [Us two: Remembering Gy. D.]. Budapest: Képzőművészeti Alap, 1954.

Domanovszky, György. "A jobbágyság élete" [The life of serfs]. In *Magyar művelődéstörténet* [Hungarian cultural history], vol. 2, edited by Sándor Domanovszky. Budapest: Magyar Történelmi Társulat, 1939.

Duša, Ferdiš. *Dolu Váhom* I. diel, introduction by Rudolf Kratochvíl. Bratislava: K. Jaroň, 1934.

Duša, Ferdiš. *Dolu Váhom* / Viliam Ritter, *Roman slovenskej rieky*. [Down the Váh / Novel of a Slovak River]. Bratislava: K. Jaroň, 1933.

Elek, Artúr. "Az újabb magyar grafikai művészet" [Recent Hungarian graphic art]. *Magyar Művészet* 13 (1937): 201–228.

Engels, Friedrich. "The Peasant War in Germany." In *Collected Works*, vol. 10, Karl Marx and Friedrich Engels, 397–482. New York: International Publishers, 1978.

Erdei, Ferenc. "A magyar társadalom a két háború között" [Hungarian society between the wars], I and II. *Valóság* 19, no. 4 and 5 (1976): 22–53, 36–58.

Farkas, Imre. "Irredenta-szobrok" [Irredentist sculptures]. *Pesti Hirlap*, August 20, 1929, 7.

Farkas, Zoltán. "Gróf Klebelsberg Kunó képzőművészeti politikája" [The fine art policies of Count Kuno Klebelsberg]. *Nyugat* 26, no. 5 (1933): 321–324.

F. M. "Akik nem politizálnak. . . ." [Those who don't do politics]. *Magyarország*, November 20, 1921, 6.

Fülep, Lajos. "The Task of Hungarian Art History (1951)." Introduced and translated by Nóra Veszprémi. *Journal of Art Historiography* 6, no. 11 (2014). https://arthistoriography.wordpress.com/wp-content/uploads/2014/11/veszprc3a9mi-trans-fulep.pdf.

F. Z. "Derkovits Gyula emlékkiállítása" [The memorial exhibition of GyD]. *Magyarság*, October 28, 1934, 21.

Galsai, Pongrác. "'Nem a tárgyakban őrzöm . . .' Beszélgetés Derkovits Gyulánéval" ["I don't preserve it in objects" . . . conversation with Mrs. Gyula Derkovits] (originally published in *Nők Lapja*, November 17, 1962, 6–7). *Enigma* 20, no. 74 (2013): 56–59.

Gerevich, Tibor. "A legújabb magyarországi ásatások" [The newest Hungarian excavations]. *Magyar Szemle* 23, no. 1–4 (1935): 69–77.

Gerevich, Tibor. "Kolozsvári Tamás." *Az Országos Magyar Régészeti Társulat Évkönyve* 1 (1920–1922): 154–185.

Gerevich, Tibor. *Magyarország románkori emlékei* [Hungary's Romanesque monuments]. Budapest: Műemlékek Országos Bizottsága, 1938.

Gerevich, Tibor. "Római magyar művészek" [Hungarian artists in Rome]. *Magyar Szemle* (1932): 235–240.

Háy, Károly László. "Egy félbemaradt metszetsorozatról" [On an unfinished series of prints] (originally published *Művelt Nép*, April 17, 1955). In *Szabadság és a Nép: A Szocialista Képzőművészek Csoportjának dokumentumai* [Freedom and the people: Documents from the Group of Socialist Artists], edited by Nóra Aradi, 303–305. Budapest: Art History Research Group of the Hungarian Academy of Sciences, 1981.

Hegyi, Béla. "A Vigilia beszélgetése Derkovits Gyulánéval—két emlékeztetővel" [The periodical Vigilia interviews Mrs. Gyula Derkovits—with two reminders]. *Vigilia* 41, no. 1 (1976): 25–30.

Hollauer, Tibor. "Hova fészkel a turulmadár? Irredenta szobrok" [Where will the turul bird nest: Irredentist sculptures (interview with Ernő Raffay)]. *168 Óra*, September 4, 1990, 10–11.

Hóman, Bálint, and Gyula Szekfű. *Magyar történet* [Hungarian history], 8 vols. Budapest: Egyetemi Nyomda, 1928–1934.

Horvay, János. "Önéletrajz" [JH: Autobiography]. In *Az Est Hármaskönyve 1923*, 327–328. Budapest: Az Est Lapkiadó Rt., 1923.

Jajczay, János. "Képzőművészeti szemle" [A survey of fine arts]. *Magyar Kultúra* 21, no. 22 (1934): 482–484.

K. A. "Derkovits Gyula emlékkiállítása az Ernst-Múzeumban" [GyD's commemorative exhibition at the Ernst Museum]. *Pesti Napló*, October 28, 1934, 14.

Kállai, Emil. "Két Kossuth-szobor: Beszélgetés Horvay Jánossal—'Nem lehetett őt itt szónoknak ábrázolnom'" [Two Kossuth statues: Conversation with JH—"I could not depict him as an orator here"]. *Délmagyarország*, January 12, 1928, 4.

Kállai, Ernő. "A Dózsa-sorozat fametszetei" [The woodcuts of the Dózsa series]. In *1514: 11 fametszet*, Gyula Derkovits. Budapest: Gondolat, 1936.

Kállai, Ernő. "Tendencművészet és fotográfia" [Tendentious art and photography]. *Korunk* 2, no. 11 (1927): 766–771.

Kállai, Ernst. "Kunstgewerbe und Volkskunst in Székesfehérvár." *Pester Lloyd*, November 29, 1938, 3.

Kassák, Lajos. "A budapesti második nemzetközi fényképkiállítás" [The second Budapest international photography exhibition]. *Századunk* 2, no. 2 (1927): 526–528.

K-f. "Károlyi Mihály, Hock János és Kun Béla—nem szerepelnek az Országos Levéltár freskóján" [MK, JH, and BK are not depicted in the fresco of the National Archives]. *Az Est*, October 12, 1929, 5.

Kis, Tibor. "Trianon-kuratórium: sztornó" [Trianon Board of Trustees: Abolished]. *Népszabadság*, September 11, 1990, 1, 3.

Klebelsberg, Kuno. *Neonacionalizmus* [Neonationalism]. Budapest: Athenaeum, 1928.

Klebelsberg, Kuno. [Opening speech, May 14, 1920, General Assembly of the Hungarian Historical Society]. In *Beszédei, cikkei és törvényjavaslatai 1916–1926* [Speeches, articles, and legislative proposals], Kuno Klebelsberg, 20–39. Budapest: Athenaeum, 1927.

K. M. "Derkovits Gyula gyűjteményes kiállítása az Ernst Muzeumban" [GyD's retrospective exhibition at the Ernst Museum]. *Nemzeti Ujság*, October 28, 1934, 28.

Kosztolányi, Dezső, ed. *Vérző Magyarország: Magyar írók Magyarország területéért* [Bleeding Hungary: Hungarian authors for the territory of Hungary]. Budapest: Pallas Nyomda, 1921.

Kovács, Imre. "Két pogány közt egy hazáért. . . ." *Híd* (May 1938): 1.

Légrády, Ottó, ed. *Justice for Hungary: The Cruel Errors of Trianon*. Budapest: Légrády, 1930.

Lukács, György. *Megélt gondolkodás: Életrajz magnószalagon* [Lived thought: A biography on tape]. Budapest: Magvető, 1989.

Lukács, György. "Tézistervezet a magyar politikai és gazdasági helyzetről s a KMP feladatairól" [Draft theses on the Hungarian political and economic situation and the tasks of the Hungarian Communist Party], edited by Ágnes Szabó. *Párttörténeti Közlemények* 21, no. 4 (1975): 156–207.

Lyka, Károly. "Magyar művészet—magyar határok" [Hungarian art—Hungarian borders]. In *Vérző Magyarország: Magyar írók Magyarország területéért* [Bleeding Hungary: Hungarian authors for the territory of Hungary], edited by Dezső Kosztolányi, 87–92. Budapest: Pallas, 1921.

Madai, Pál. *Magyarország történelme gimnáziumok, reálgimnáziumok és reáliskolák III. osztálya számára* [The history of Hungary for secondary schools, grade 3]. Budapest: Franklin, 1926.

Mályusz, Elemér. "A népiség története" [The history of ethnicity]. In *A magyar történetírás új útjai* [New directions in Hungarian history writing], edited by Bálint Hóman. Budapest: Magyar Szemle Társaság, 1932 (2nd ed.).

Mednyánsky, Aloys Freyherr von. *Erzählungen, Sagen und Legenden aus Ungarns Vorzeit.* Pest: Hartleben, 1829.

Mednyánsky, Aloys Freyherr von. *Malerische Reise auf dem Waagflusse in Ungern.* Pest: Hartleben, 1826.

Megyery, Ella. "A kultuszminiszter római utja s a magyar-olasz kulturkapcsolatok: Beszélgetés Gerevich Tiborral az olaszországi magyar manifesztációkról" [The Roman trip of the minister of culture and Hungarian-Italian cultural relations: A conversation with TG about Hungarian manifestations in Italy]. *Magyarság*, 27 February, 1927, 5.

Mesenaki, George. "A megtréfált szobrok" [Sculptures pranked]. *Előre*, March 6, 1921, 6.

Nagy, Zoltán. "Varga Nándor Lajos." *Szépművészet* 2, no. 2 (1941): 90–94.

Oelmacher, Anna. "Ferenczy Noémi művészete" [The art of NF]. In *Ferenczy Noémi gyűjteményes kiállítása* [NF's retrospective exhibition]. Budapest: Nemzeti Szalon, 1956.

Ortutay, Gyula, and György Buday. *Bátorligeti mesék*, Ortutay Gyula gyűjtése, Buday György rajzaival [Tales from Bátorliget, collected by GyO, illustrated by GyB]. Budapest: Hungária, 1937.

Ortutay, Gyula, and György Buday. *Székely népballadák* [Sekler folk ballads], collected by Ortutay, ill. Buday Budapest: Egyetemi Nyomda, 1935.

Ottlik, Géza. *Iskola a határon* [School at the frontier]. Budapest: Magvető, 1999.

Pápay, Josef. "Im Lande der Nord-Ostjaken." *Abrégé du Bulletin de la Société Hongroise de Géographie*, supp. *Földrajzi Közlemények* 34 (1906): 4–5.

Pásztor, Árpád. "A cseh Dunán" [On the Czech Danube]. *Pesti Napló*, June 3, 1932, 4.

Péter, András. "Művészeti séták" [Walks through art]. *Tükör* 3, no. 7 (1935): 62–64.

Pethő, Sándor. "Két pogány közt egy hazáért" [Between two pagans for one homeland]. *Magyarság*, September 6 and 13, 1936, 1–2, 1–2.

P. Z. "Dudits Andor." *Magyarság*, supp. 2, March 1, 1931.

[Révai, József]. "A magyar munkásosztály és a revízió" [The Hungarian working class and revision]. *Új Március* (April/May/June 1929): 131–138.

[Révai, József]. Kemény. "Harcoljon-e a Kommunisták Magyarországi Pártja Trianon ellen?" [Should the Hungarian Communist Party fight against Trianon?]. *Új Március* (August–November 1929): 315–324. Republished in *Trianon*, edited by Miklós Zeidler. Budapest: Osiris, 2008, 398–406.

Rochowanski, Leopold Wolfgang, ed. *Columbus in der Slovakei.* Bratislava: Eos, 1936.

Róth, Miksa. *Egy üvegfestőművész emlékei* [Memories of a stained glass artist]. Budapest: Hungária, 1943.

Rothermere, Lord. "Hungary's Place in the Sun: Safety for Central Europe." *Daily Mail*, June 21, 1927.

R. Sz. I. "Az erdélyi művészek kiállitása" [The exhibition of Transylvanian artists]. *Uj Magyarság*, February 27, 1941, 6.

R. "Varga Nándor Lajos történelemkönyve fametszetekben" [NLV's history text-book in woodcuts]. *Magyar Nemzet*, June 5, 1941, 7.

Sós, Endre. "Dudits Andor tiltakozik az ellen, hogy megcsökönyösödött akadémikusnak tartsák" [AD protests against being regarded as a stuffy academician]. *Esti Kurir*, August 30, 1925, 6.

Szekfű, Gyula. "A barokk műveltség" [Baroque culture]. In *Magyar történet*, vol. 6: *A tizennyolcadik század* [The eighteenth century], Bálint Hóman and Gyula Szekfű, 130–173, 470–474. Budapest: Egyetemi Nyomda, n.d. [1932].

Szekfű, Gyula. "A politikai történetírás" [Political history writing]. In *A magyar történetírás új útjai* [New directions in Hungarian history writing], edited by Bálint Hóman. Budapest: Magyar Szemle Társaság, 1932.

Szekfű, Gyula. *Három nemzedék: Egy hanyatló kor története* [Three generations: The history of a declining age]. Budapest: Élet, 1920.

Szekfű, Gyula. *Három nemzedék és ami utána következik* [Three generations and what comes after]. Budapest: Egyetemi Nyomda, 1934.

Szirmay, István. "Ahol mindenki csak egy ujjal zongorázik" [Where everyone plays the piano with just one finger]. *Ujság*, September 18, 1927, 36.

Szomory, Emil. "Egy fiatal szobrásznő, aki boldog és egy hajdani istállóban alkotja remekműveit" [A young woman sculptor who is happy and creates her masterpieces in a former stable]. *Ujság*, April 8, 1928, 51.

Szőnyei, [Tamás]. "Aba-Novák hagyatéka: Freskósors" [The heritage of Aba-Novák: The fate of a fresco]. *Magyar Narancs*, August 20, 1998.

Tolnai, Károly [Charles de Tolnay]. *Ferenczy Noémi*. Budapest: Bisztrai Farkas Ferenc, 1934.

up. "Okmányokban, művészi és iparművészi remekekben fogja megőrizni a nemzeti múlt emlékeit az Országos Levéltár magyar Pantheonja" [The Hungarian Pantheon of the National Archives will preserve memories of the national past in documents, artworks, and works of artistic industry]. *8 Órai Ujság*, May 12, 1928, 4.

Urhegyi, Alajos. "A népiskolai történelmi szemléltető faliképek" [The historical demonstrative wall pictures for public schools]. *Magyar Tanítóképző* 30, no. 10 (1915): 356–360.

Vajda, Péter. "A parancsnok marad" [The commander remains in place]. *Népszabadság*, April 3, 1991, 1, 5.

Varga, Nándor Lajos. *A fametszet* [The woodcut]. Budapest: published by the author, 1940.

Varga, Nándor Lajos, and Gyula Rajk. *Magyar múlt*, Varga Nándor Lajos 40 fametszete Rajk Gyula szövegével [Hungarian past, 40 woodcuts by Nándor Lajos Varga, with text by Gyula Rajk]. Budapest: Globus, 1941.

Ybl, Ervin. "Az Országos Levéltár freskói" [The frescoes of the National Archives]. In *Az Országos Magyar Képzőművészeti Társulat Évkönyve az 1929. évre.* 81–98. Budapest: OMKT, 1930.

Secondary Sources

Ablonczy, Balázs. *Go East! A History of Hungarian Turanism*. Bloomington: Indiana University Press, 2022.

Ablonczy, Balázs. *Ismeretlen Trianon: Az összeomlás és a békeszerződés történetei, 1918–1921* [Unknown Trianon: Stories of the collapse and the peace treaty]. Budapest: Jaffa Kiadó, 2020.

Ablonczy, Balázs. *Trianon-legendák* [Trianon legends]. Budapest: Jaffa Kiadó, 2015.

Affron, Matthew, and Mark Antliff, eds. *Fascist Visions: Art and Ideology in France and Italy*. Princeton, NJ: Princeton University Press, 1997.

A Horthy-korszak vitatott kérdései [Debated issues of the Horthy era], conference proceedings. Budapest: Kossuth, 2020.

Albert, B. Gábor. "A református fiú-középiskolák történelemtankönyv-használata 1926-tól az 1930-as évek közepéig" [The textbook usage of Calvinist boys' secondary schools from 1926 to the mid-1930s]. *Magyar Pedagógia* 113, no. 2 (2013): 119–129.

Albert, B. Gábor. *Súlypontok és hangsúlyeltolódások: Középiskolai történelem tankönyvek a Horthy-korszakban* [Focal points and shifts in emphasis: Secondary school history textbooks in the Horthy era]. Pápa: Pedagogy Research Centre of the Faculty of Humanities of Pannon University, 2006.

András, Edit. *Határsértő képzelet: Kortárs művészet és kritikai elmélet Európa keleti felén* [Imaginary transgression: Contemporary art and critical theories in the eastern part of Europe]. Budapest: Humanities Research Centre Institute of Art History, 2023.

Andrási, Gábor, Gábor Pataki, György Szücs, and András Zwickl. *The History of Hungarian Art in the Twentieth Century*. Budapest: Corvina, 1999.

Antliff, Mark. "La Cité française: Georges Valois, Le Corbusier, and Fascist Theories of Urbanism." In *Fascist Visions*, edited by Matthew Affron and Mark Antliff, 134–170.

Babejová, Eleonóra. *Fin-de-siècle Pressburg: Conflict and Cultural Coexistence in Bratislava 1897–1914*. Boulder: East European Monographs and Columbia University Press, 2003.

Baioni, Massimo. "Interpretations of Garibaldi in Fascist Culture: A Contested Legacy." *Modern Italy* 15, no. 4 (2010): 451–465.

Bajkay, Éva. *Bíró Mihály*. Budapest: Reflektor, 1986.

Bajkay, Éva. "The Artist's Search for Identity in Vienna." In *Derkovits: The Artist and His Times*, edited by Katalin Bakos and András Zwickl, 62–75. Budapest: Hungarian National Gallery, 2014.

Bajkay, Éva. *Uitz Béla*. Budapest: Képzőművészeti Kiadó, 1987.

Bakhtin, Mikhail M. "Forms of Time and of the Chronotope in the Novel: Notes toward a Historical Poetics" (1981). In *The Dialogic Imagination: Four Essays*, Mikhail M. Bakhtin, edited by Michael Holquist, translated by Caryl Emerson and Michael Holquist. Austin: University of Texas Press, 1990.

Bakos, Katalin. "An Oeuvre with the Power to Engage." In *Derkovits: The Artist and His Times*, edited by Katalin Bakos and András Zwickl, 26–47. Budapest: Hungarian National Gallery, 2014.

Bakos, Katalin. "Fametszet és illusztráció: könyv, album, mappa, sorozat 1920–1940" [Wood engraving and illustration: Book, album, folder, series]. In *A modern magyar fa- és linóleummetszés (1890–1950)* [Modern Hungarian wood and linoleum engraving], edited by Enikő Róka, 71–103. Miskolc: Miskolci Galéria, 2005.

Bárdi, Sára. "Politikai ikonográfia a két világháború közötti magyar
     képzőművészetben: Esettanulmány: Háy Károly László Történelem jeli-
     géjű freskóterve (1942)" [Political iconography in interwar Hungarian art:
     Case study: KLH's fresco design submitted under the code-word *history*].
     In *Élő művek: Tanulmányok a Fiatal Művészettörténészek 7. Konferenciájának
     előadásaiból* [Living artworks: Papers from the 7th Conference of Young Art
     Historians], edited by Ilka Boér and Emese Pál, 185–203. Budapest: Martin
     Opitz Kiadó, 2022.

Baxa, Paul. *Roads and Ruins: The Symbolic Landscape of Fascist Rome*. Toronto: Uni-
     versity of Toronto Press, 2010.

Ben-Ghiat, Ruth. *Fascist Modernities: Italy, 1922–1945*. Berkeley: University of Cali-
     fornia Press, 2001.

Benjamin, Walter. "The Storyteller." In *Illuminations*, Walter Benjamin, translated
     by Harry Zohn. London: Fontana, 1992.

Benjamin, Walter. "The Work of Art in the Age of Mechanical Reproduction."
     In *Illuminations*, Walter Benjamin, edited by Hannah Arendt, translated by
     Harry Zohn. London: Jonathan Cape, 1970.

Berezin, Mabel. *Making the Fascist Self: The Political Culture of Interwar Italy*. Ithaca,
     NY: Cornell University Press, 1997.

Billig, Michael. *Banal Nationalism*. London: Sage, 1995.

Bíró-Balogh, Tamás. "A Vérző Magyarország második kiadása: Kosztolányi
     'jelentősen átdolgozott' irredenta antológiája" [The second edition of Bleed-
     ing Hungary: Kosztolányi's "significantly revised" irredentist anthology]. *Kal-
     ligram* 18, no. 11 (2009): 65–70.

Biskupski, M. B. B. *Independence Day: Myth, Symbol, and the Creation of Modern
     Poland*. Oxford: Oxford University Press, 2021.

Bizzer, István. "A Szent Imre-kultusz és a modern magyar szakrális művészet 1930–
     1950 között" [The cult of Saint Emeric and modern Hungarian sacral art].
     In *Szent Imre 1000 éve: Székesfehérvár 1007–2007: Tanulmányok Szent Imre tisz-
     teletére születésének ezredik évfordulója alkalmából* [1,000 years of Saint Emeric:
     Essays in honor of Saint Emeric on the thousandth anniversary of his birth],
     edited by Terézia Kerny, 158–175. Székesfehérvár: Székesfehérvár Diocesan
     Museum, 2007.

Bodó, Béla. "Memory Practices: The Red and White Terrors in Hungary as
     Remembered after 1990." *East Central Europe* 44, no. 2–3 (2017): 186–215.

Bodó, Béla. *The White Terror: Antisemitic and Political Violence in Hungary, 1919–1921*.
     London: Routledge, 2019.

Bodó, Béla. "Violence Glorified or Denied? Collective Memory of the Red and
     White Terrors in Hungary, 1919–Present." *Hungarian Studies Review* 46–47,
     no. 1–2 (2019–2020): 44–54.

Bodonyi, Emőke. *Jeges*. Szentendre: Pest Megyei Múzeumok Igazgatósága, 2008.

Bodonyi, Emőke. *Teremtés: Ferenczy Noémi művészete / Creation: The Art of Noémi
     Ferenczy*. Szentendre: Ferenczy Museum Center, 2020.

Boer, Pim den. "Loci memoriae–Lieux de mémoire." In *A Companion to Cultural
     Memory Studies*, edited by Astrid Erll and Ansgar Nünning, 19–26. Berlin:
     Walter DeGruyter, 2010.

Bogar, Karel. *Muž s beraní hlavou: Ferdiš Duša a Frýdlant nad Ostravicí* [Man with a ram's head: FD in Frýdlant nad Ostravicí]. Frýdlant nad Ostravicí: Montanex, 2008.

Borsa, Iván. "Az Országos Levéltár épületei 1874–1974" [The buildings of the National Archives]. *Levéltári Közlemények* 50, no. 1 (1979): 23–50.

Branczik, Márta, and Zsóka Leposa, eds. *Sonderwege: Karl-Heinz Adler und die ungarische Abstraktion.* Budapest: Kiscelli and Kassák Museums, 2017.

Brandenberger, David. *National Bolshevism: Stalinist Mass Culture and the Formation of Modern Russian Identity, 1931–1956.* Cambridge, MA: Harvard University Press, 2002.

Brennan, Sheila A. *Stamping American Memory: Collectors, Citizens, and the Post.* Ann Arbor: University of Michigan Press, 2018.

Bröker, Jan. *"Horthy Is a Nobody": Trials of Lèse-Régent in Hungary 1920–1944.* Master's diss., Central European University, Budapest, 2011. https://www.etd.ceu.edu/2011/broker_jan.pdf.

Brubaker, Rogers. "National Minorities, Nationalizing States, and External National Homelands in the New Europe." In *Nationalism Reframed: Nationhood and the National Question in the New Europe,* 55–76. Cambridge, UK: Cambridge University Press, 1996.

B. Szabó, János, ed. *Mohács.* Budapest: Osiris, 2006.

Bubryák, Orsolya. "'E meditullio basilicae erutum'? Megjegyzések a székesfehérvári Szent István szarkofág provenienciájához" ["Unearthed from the middle of the basilica?" Comments on the provenance of the Saint Stephen sarcophagus]. *Ars Hungarica* 35, no. 1 (2007): 5–28.

Bucur, Maria. *Heroes and Victims: Remembering War in Twentieth-Century Romania.* Bloomington: Indiana University Press, 2009.

Büki, Barbara. "The Past Is Still Present: A Painter in the Public Arena." In *Derkovits: The Artist and His Times,* edited by Katalin Bakos and András Zwickl, 136–149. Budapest: Hungarian National Gallery, 2014.

Burmeister, Ralf, et al., eds. *Magyar Modern: Hungarian Art in Berlin 1910–1933.* Berlin: Hirmer, 2022.

Bydžovská, Lenka. "'Heart in a Trance': William Ritter and Czech Modernism." *Centre Interdisciplinaire de Recherches Centre-Européennes,* accessed 1 December 2024, https://web.archive.org/web/20211008153727/http://www.circe.paris-sorbonne.fr/IMG/pdf/lenka_bydzovska_william_ritter_22_2_2011_fini.pdf.

Cabuk, Cornelia. *Otto Rudolf Schatz: Monografie und Werkverzeichnis,* edited by Stella Rollig and Christian Huemer. Vienna: Belvedere, 2018. https://werkverzeichnisse.belvedere.at/groups/otto-rudolf-schatz/results.

Case, Holly. "Revisionism in Regional Perspective." In *Territorial Revisionism and the Allies of Germany in the Second World War: Goals, Expectations, Practices,* edited by Marina Cattaruzza, Stefan Dyroff, and Dieter Langewiesche, 72–91. New York: Berghahn, 2012.

Cattaruzza, Marina, Stefan Dyroff, and Dieter Langewiesche, eds. *Territorial Revisionism and the Allies of Germany in the Second World War: Goals, Expectations, Practices.* New York: Berghahn, 2012.

Cesari, Chiara de, and Ann Rigney, eds. *Transnational Memory: Circulation, Articulation, Scales.* Berlin: De Gruyter, 2014.

Chamonikola, Kaliopi, Markéta Zácková, and Terezie Petisková. "New Content, New Images." In *Budování státu: Reprezentace Československa v umění, architektuře a designu*, edited by Milena Bartlová and Jindřich Vybíral, 8–17. Prague: UMPRUM, 2015.

Clark, Roland. *Holy Legionary Youth: Fascist Activism in Interwar Romania*. Ithaca, NY: Cornell University Press, 2015.

Csáki, Tamás. "Árkay Bertalan építészete 1925–1945" [The architectural work of BÁ]. In *Árkay: Egy magyar építész- és művészdinasztia* [A Hungarian architects' and artists' dynasty], edited by Tamás Csáki, 192–194. Budapest: Holnap, 2020.

Csákó, Beáta, and Dániel Samu Nagy. *Az Országház nevezetes termei* [Significant rooms of the Parliament]. Budapest: Országgyűlés Hivatala, 2019.

Csaplár, Ferenc. *A Szegedi Fiatalok Művészeti Kollégiuma* [The Art College of the Szeged Youth]. Budapest: Akadémiai Kiadó, 1967.

Csunderlik, Péter. *A "vörös farsangtól" a "vörös tatárjárásig": A Tanácsköztársaság a korai Horthy-korszak pamflet- és visszaemlékezés-irodalmában* [From "red fasching" to the "invasion of the red Tartars": The Soviet Republic in pamphlets and memoirs of the early Horthy era]. Budapest: Napvilág Kiadó, 2019.

Dabrowski, Patrice M. *The Carpathians: Discovering the Highlands of Poland and Ukraine*. Ithaca, NY: Cornell University Press, 2021.

Dénes, Iván Zoltán. *A történelmi Magyarország eszménye: Szekfű Gyula a történetíró és ideológus* [The ideal of historical Hungary: Gyula Szekfű the historian and ideologue]. Bratislava: Kalligram, 2015.

Dent, Bob. *Painting the Town Red: Politics and the Arts during the 1919 Hungarian Soviet Republic*. London: Pluto, 2018.

Diers, Michael. "Farbige Bilder des Grauens: Die Horthy-Mappe von Mihály Bíró." In *Mihály Bíró: Pathos in Rot*, edited by Peter Noever, 30–48. Vienna: MAK, 2010.

Dorsch, Michael. *French Sculpture Following the Franco-Prussian War, 1870–80: Realist Allegories and the Commemoration of Defeat*. Farnham, UK: Ashgate, 2010.

Dreidemy, Lucile. "'Denn ein Engel kann nicht sterben': Engelbert Dollfus 1934–2012—eine Biographie des Posthumen." PhD diss., University of Strasbourg and University of Vienna, 2012. https://theses.hal.science/tel-01249522/document.

Drobe, Christian. *Verdächtige Ambivalenz: Klassizismus in der Moderne 1920–1960*. Weimar: Arts and Science Weimar, 2022.

Éber, Márk Áron. "Melyik kettő? Miért kettős? A magyar szociológia kettőstársadalom-elméleteinek hasznáról és káráról" [Which two? Why dual? On the uses and disadvantages of theories of dual society in Hungarian sociology]. *Szociológiai Szemle* 21, no. 3 (2011): 4–22.

Egry, Gábor. "The Greatest Catastrophe of (Post-)colonial Central Europe? The 100th Years Anniversary of Trianon and Official Politics of Memory in Hungary." *Rocznik Instytutu Europy Środkowo-Wschodniej / Yearbook of the Institute of East-Central Europe* 18, no. 2 (2020): 123–142.

Erdősi, Péter. "Barokk és neobarokk: Két fogalom kölcsönhatása Magyarországon" [Baroque and neobaroque: The interaction of two concepts in Hungary]. *Korall* 23 (2006): 155–186.

Érszegi, Géza, ed. *Archivum Regni Regnum Archivi: A Magyar Országos Levéltár palotája* [The palace of the Hungarian National Archives]. Budapest: Hungarian National Archives, 2005.

Falasca-Zamponi, Simonetta. *Fascist Spectacle: The Aesthetics of Power in Mussolini's Italy*. Berkeley: University of California Press, 1997.

Feischmidt, Margit. "Die Verortung der Nation an den Peripherien: Ungarische Nationaldenkmäler in multiethnischen Gebieten der Monarchie." In *Grenzen und Räume in Österreich-Ungarn 1867–1918*, edited by Wladimir Fischer et al., 119–123. Tübingen: A. Francke, 2010.

Feischmidt, Margit. "Lehorgonyzott mítoszok. Kőbe vésett sztereotípiák? *A lokalizáció jelentõsége az aradi vértanúk emlékmûve és a millenniumi emlékoszlopok kapcsán*" [Anchored myths, stereotypes carved into stone? The significance of localization in the Arad Martyrs Memorial and the Millennium Monuments]. In *Mindennapi elõítéletek: Társadalmi távolságok és etnikai sztereotípiák* [Everyday prejudices: Social distances and ethnic stereotypes], edited by Boglárka Bakó et al., 370–391. Budapest: Balassi, 2006.

Feischmidt, Margit. "Memory-Politics and Neonationalism: Trianon as Mythomoteur." *Nationalities Papers* 48, no. 1 (2020): 130–143.

Fekete, Ilona. "Unburied Bodies: Hungarian National Identity 1989–2020." *Australian Journal of Politics and History* 66, no. 3 (2020): 415–431.

Filipová, Marta. "'Highly Civilized, yet Very Simple': Images of the Czechoslovak State and Nation at Interwar World's Fairs." *Nationalities Papers* 50, no. 1 (2022): 145–165.

Filipová, Marta. *Modernity, History and Politics in Czech Art*. New York: Routledge, 2019.

Fogu, Claudio. "Fascism and Historic Representation: The 1932 Garibaldian Celebrations." *Journal of Contemporary History* 31, no. 2 (1996): 317–345.

Fogu, Claudio. *The Historic Imaginary: Politics of History in Fascist Italy*. Toronto: University of Toronto Press, 2003.

Forgács, Éva. *Hungarian Art: Confrontation and Revival in the Modern Movement*. Los Angeles: Doppelhouse, 2016.

Gafijczuk, Dariusz, and Derek Sayer, eds. *The Inhabited Ruins of Central Europe: Reimagining Space, History, and Memory*. London: Palgrave Macmillan, 2013.

Gärtner, Petra. "Az idézet bűvöletében" [Under the spell of quotation]. In *Szent István király bazilikájának utóélete: A Középkori Romkert 1938-tól napjainkig* [The afterlife of King Saint Stephen's Basilica: The Medieval Ruin Garden from 1938 to the present day], edited by Petra Gärtner, 7–21. Székesfehérvár: Szent István Király Múzeum, 2016.

Gentile, Emilio. "The Myth of National Regeneration in Italy: From Modernist Avant-Garde to Fascism." In *Fascist Visions: Art and Ideology in France and Italy*, edited by Matthew Affron and Mark Antliff, 25–45. Princeton, NJ: Princeton University Press, 1997.

Geyer, Martin H. "'Die Gleichzeitigkeit der Ungleichzeitigkeit': Zeitsemantik und die Suche nach Gegenwart in der Weimarer Republik." In *Ordnungen in der Krise: Zur politischen Kulturgeschichte Deutschlands. 1900–1933*, edited by Wolfgang Hardtwig. Munich: R. Oldenbourg, 2007.

Gilkes, Oliver. "The Voyage of Aeneas: Myth, Archaeology and Identity in Interwar Albania." In *The Politics of Archaeology and Identity in a Global Context*, edited by Susan Kane, 31–49. Boston: Archaeological Institute of America, 2003.

Gioielli, Emily. "The Woman with No First Name." *fernetzt—Junges Forschungsnetzwerk Frauen- und Geschlechtergeschichte*. Accessed September 19, 2024. https://fernetzt.univie.ac.at/the-woman-with-no-first-name/.

Goebel, Stefan. "Cultural Memory and the Great War: Medievalism and Classicism in British and German War Memorials." In *Cultures of Commemoration: War Memorials, Ancient and Modern*, edited by Polly Low, Graham Oliver, and P. J. Rhodes, 135–158. Oxford: Oxford University Press, 2012.

Goebel, Stefan. "Re-membered and Re-mobilized: The 'Sleeping Dead' in Interwar Germany and Britain." *Journal of Contemporary History* 39, no. 4 (2004): 487–501

Gosztonyi, Ferenc. "'Cézanne után': Tolnai Károly 1934-es Ferenczy Noémi-monográfiájáról" [After Cézanne: On Károly Tolnai's 1934 Noémi Ferenczy monograph]. *Enigma* 26, no. 100 (2019/2020): 112–124.

Götz, Irene, Klaus Roth, and Marketa Spiritova, eds. *Neuer Nationalismus im östlichen Europa: Kulturwissenschaftliche Perspektiven*. Bielefeld: transcript Verlag, 2017.

Götz, Norbert, and Janne Holmén. "Introduction to the Theme Issue: Mental Maps: Geographical and Historical Perspectives." *Journal of Cultural Geography* 35, no. 2 (2018): 157–161.

Graziosi, Andrea. *The Great Soviet Peasant War: Bolsheviks and Peasants, 1917–1933*. Cambridge, MA: Harvard University Press and Harvard University Ukrainian Research Institute, 1996.

Griffin, Roger. *Modernism and Fascism: The Sense of a Beginning under Mussolini and Hitler*. Houndmills, UK: Palgrave Macmillan, 2007.

Guenée, Bernard. "From Feudal Boundaries to Political Borders." In *Rethinking France: Les Lieux de mémoire*, edited by Pierre Nora, vol. 1, *The State*, 81–103. Chicago: University of Chicago Press, 2001.

Gyáni, Gábor. "Érvek a kettős struktúra elmélete ellen" [Arguments against the dual structure theory]. *Korall* 2, no. 3–4 (2001): 221–231.

Hall, Murray G. "Anzengruber-Verlag Brüder Suschitzky (Wien-Leipzig)," in *Österreichische Verlagsgeschichte*, Murray G. Hall, vol. 2. Vienna: Böhlau, 1985/2016. http://verlagsgeschichte.murrayhall.com/?page_id=180.

Hamza, Imre, et al. *A magyar bélyegek monográfiája* [Monograph of Hungarian stamps], vol. IV. Budapest: Közlekedési Dokumentációs Vállalat, 1971.

Hanebrink, Paul. *In Defense of Christian Hungary: Religion, Nationalism and Antisemitism, 1890–1944*. Ithaca, NY: Cornell University Press, 2006.

Hanebrink, Paul. "Islam, Anti-Communism, and Christian Civilization: The Ottoman Menace in Interwar Hungary." *Austrian History Yearbook* 40 (2009): 114–124.

Hanscam, Emily, and James Koranyi. "Digging Politics: The Ancient Past and Contested Present." In *Digging Politics: The Ancient Past and Contested Present in East-Central Europe*, edited by James Koranyi and Emily Hanscam, 1–16. Berlin: Walter de Gruyter, 2023.

Harlov, Melinda. "A budapesti Hősök terén található Hősök Emlékkövének történeti áttekintése és lehetséges értelmezései" [Historical overview and possible interpretations of the Memorial Stone of Heroes in Heroes' Square, Budapest]. *A Nagy Háború* (blog). Accessed 2 December 2024. https://m.blog.hu/na/nagyhaboru/image/workshop/emlekko/harlovmelinda_hosok_emlekkove.pdf.

Harlov-Csortán, Melinda. "Roman Heritage in Hungary: The Case of the Fertőrákos Mithraeum on the Iron Curtain." In *Digging Politics: The Ancient Past and Contested Present in East-Central Europe*, edited by James Koranyi and Emily Hanscam, 157–179. Berlin: Walter de Gruyter, 2023.

Hatos, Pál. *Rosszfiúk világforradalma: Az 1919-es Magyarországi Tanácsköztársaság története* [A world revolution of bad boys: The history of the 1919 Hungarian Soviet Republic]. Budapest: Jaffa Kiadó, 2021.

Henschel, Frank. *"Das Fluidum der Stadt . . .": Urbane Lebenswelten in Kassa/Košice/ Kaschau zwischen Sprachenvielfalt und Magyarisierung 1867–1918*. Göttingen: Vanderhoeck und Ruprecht, 2017.

Holubec, Stanislav. "Between the Czech Krkonoše and the German Riesengebirge: Nationalism and Tourism in the Giant Mountains, 1880s–1930s." *Nationalities Papers* 52, no. 2 (2024): 337–359.

"Horvay János: Kossuth-szoborcsoport" [JH: Kossuth sculptural group]. In *Dombopedia*. Accessed 2 December 2024. http://dombopedia.hu/adatbazisok /kozteri-alkotasok-szobrok/horvay-janos-kossuth-szoborcsoport.html.

Judson, Pieter. "Marking National Space on the Habsburg Austrian Borderlands, 1880–1918." In *Shatterzone of Empires: Coexistence and Violence in the German, Habsburg, Russian, and Ottoman Borderlands*, edited by Omer Bartov and Eric D. Weitz, 122–235. Bloomington: Indiana University Press, 2013.

Judson, Pieter. "Reisebeschreibungen in der 'Südmark' und die Idee der deutschen Diaspora nach 1918." In *Zwischen Exotik und Vertrautem: Zum Tourismus in der Habsburgermonarchie und ihren Nachfolgestaaten*, edited by Peter Stachel and Martina Thomsen, 59–76. Bielefeld: transcript Verlag, 2014.

Kaenel, Philippe. "William Ritter (1867–1955): Un critique cosmopolite, böcklinien et anti-hodlérien." *Schweizerische Zeitschrift für Geschichte* 48, no. 1 (1998): 73–98.

Kallis, Aristotle A. "To Expand or Not to Expand? Territory, Generic Fascism and the Quest for an 'Ideal Fatherland.'" *Journal of Contemporary History* 38, no. 2 (2003): 237–260.

Kemp, Wolfgang. *Wir haben ja alle Deutschland nicht gekannt: Das Deutschlandbild der Deutschen in der Zeit der Weimarer Republik*. Heidelberg: Heidelberg University Publishing, 2016.

Kerepeszki, Róbert. "Nationalist Masculinity and Right-Wing Radical Student Movements in Interwar Hungary: The Case of the Turul Association." *Hungarian Studies Review* 41, no. 1–2 (2014): 61–88.

Kiliánová, Gabriela. "Ein Grenzmythos: Die Burg Devín." In *Heroen, Mythen, Identitäten: Die Slowakei und Österreich im Vergleich*, edited by Hannes Stekl and Helena Mannová, 49–80. Vienna: Facultas, 2003.

Kiliánová, Gabriela. *Identität und Gedächtnis in der Slowakei: Die Burg Devín als Erinnerungsort*. Frankfurt am Main: Peter Lang, 2011.

Kinchin, Juliet. "'Caught in the Ferris-wheel of History': Trianon Memorials in Hungary." In *Heritage, Ideology and Identity in Central and Eastern Europe: Contested Pasts, Contested Presents*, edited by Matthew Rampley, 21–40. Woodbridge: Boydell and Brewer, 2012.

Király, Erzsébet, Enikő Róka, and Nóra Veszprémi, eds. *XIX: Nemzet és művészet— Kép és önkép* [XIX: Nation and art—image and self-image]. Budapest: Hungarian National Gallery, 2010.

Klabjan, Borut. "Erecting Fascism: Nation, Identity, and Space in Trieste in the First Half of the Twentieth Century." *Nationalities Papers* 46, no. 6 (2018): 958–975.

Klimó, Árpád von. *Nation, Konfession, Geschichte: Zur nationalen Geschichtskultur Ungarns im europäischen Kontext (1860–1948)*. Munich: Oldenbourg, 2003.

Kollai, István. "Mátyás király és a szlovákok: Az emlékezet transznacionalizálódásának aktorai Szlovákiában" [King Matthias and the Slovaks: Actors of the transnationalization of memory in Slovakia]. *Regio* 25, no. 4 (2017): 140–154.

Kontha, Sándor, ed. *Magyar művészet 1919–1945* [Hungarian art 1919–1945], vol. 1. Budapest: Hungarian Academy of Sciences, 1985.

Kopócsy, Anna. "A jelen történelmi értelmezése fa- és linóleummetszet-sorozatokban a két világháború között" [The historical interpretation of the present in series of woodcuts and linocuts in the interwar period]. In *A modern magyar fa- és linóleummetszés 1890–1950* [Modern Hungarian wood- and linocuts], edited by Enikő Róka, 137–157. Miskolc: Miskolci Galéria, 2005.

Kopócsy, Anna. *Új Nyolcak: Festőnők a modern művészet sodrában* [The new eight: Women painters in the current of modern art]. Budapest: Holnap, 2021.

Koranyi, James. "The Thirteen Martyrs of Arad: A Monumental Hungarian History." In *Sites of Imperial Memory: Commemorating Colonial Rule in the Nineteenth and Twentieth Centuries*, edited by Dominik Geppert and Frank Lorenz Müller, 53–69. Manchester: Manchester University Press, 2015.

Koranyi, James, and Emily Hanscam, eds. *Digging Politics: The Ancient Past and Contested Present in East-Central Europe*. Berlin: Walter de Gruyter, 2023.

Kossowska, Irena, ed. *Reinterpreting the Past: Traditionalist Artistic Trends in Central and Eastern Europe of the 1920s and 1930s*. Warsaw: Institute of Art of the Polish Academy of Sciences, 2010.

Kostyál, László. "Trianon szobor-emlékezete" [Statue memory of Trianon]. Göcsej Museum, Zalaegerszeg. Accessed 29 November 2024, https://web .archive.org/web/20240715081057/https://gocsejimuzeum.hu/muzeum -iskola-szertar/trianon-szobor-emlekezete.

Kovács, Olivér and Gergely Buzás. "Szent István sírja" [The tomb of Saint Stephen]. *Altum Castrum*. Accessed 2 December 2024, https://archeologia.hu /szent-istvan-sirja.

Kővágó, László. "A kommunista párt és Trianon" [The Communist Party and Trianon]. *História* 3, no. 2 (1981): 7–9.

Kővágó, László. "A magyar kommunista párt nemzetiségpolitikája a Tanácsköztársaság megdöntésétől a felszabadulásig" [Nationality politics of the Hungarian Communist Party from the fall of the council republic to liberation]. *Párttörténeti Közlemények* 23, no. 2 (1977): 77–102.

Kremmler, Katrin. "Eurasian Magyars: The Making of a New Hegemonic National Prehistory in Illiberal Hungary." In *Digging Politics: The Ancient Past and Contested Present in East-Central Europe*, edited by James Koranyi and Emily Hanscam, 181–216. Berlin: Walter de Gruyter, 2023.

Kunt, Gergely. "Creating the New Hungarian Tatras: Symbolic Politics as a Means of Repositioning Tourism in Northern Hungary During the Interwar Period." *Journal of Tourism History* 15, no. 1 (2023): 20–42.

Lackó, Miklós. "A Blum-tézisek" [The Blum Theses]. *Történelmi Szemle* 17, no. 3 (1974): 360–371.

Lányi, Katalin, ed. *Történelmi szemléltetőanyag az első világháború korából* [Historical demonstrative material from the time of the First World War]. Budapest: Fekete Sas and Magyar Pedagógiai Társaság, 2003.

László, Szabolcs. "Memory Politics in an Illiberal Regime: Hungary's New Trianon Memorial." *ASEEES Blog.* Accessed 4 December 2024, http://www.web19b .aseees.pitt.edu/news-events/aseees-blog-feed/memory-politics-illiberal -regime%C2%A0hungary%E2%80%99s-new-trianon-memorial.

Lechner, Annette. *Die Wiener Verlagsbuchhandlung "Anzengruber-Verlag, Brüder Suschitzky" (1901–1938) im Spiegel der Zeit.* Master's diss., University of Vienna, 1994. https://www.wienbibliothek.at/sites/default/files/files/buchforsc hung/lechner-annette-anzengruberverlag.pdf.

Lengyel, András. "A 'Vérző Magyarország': Kosztolányi Dezső irredenta antológiájáról" [Bleeding Hungary: On the irredentist anthology edited by Dezső Kosztolányi]. *Literatura* 33, no. 4 (2007): 399–424.

Leposa, Zsóka. "The Statue of Hungarian Pain." In *War of Memories: A Guide to Hungarian Memory Politics*, edited by Dóra Hegyi, Zsuzsa László, and Zsóka Leposa, 63–75. Budapest: tranzit.hu, 2015.

Liber, Endre. *Budapest szobrai és emléktáblái* [Sculptures and plaques in Budapest]. Budapesti Statisztikai Közlemények 69/1. Budapest: Budapest Székesfőváros Statisztikai Hivatala, 1934.

L. Nagy, Zsuzsa. "Trianon a magyar társadalom tudatában" [Trianon in the consciousness of Hungarian society]. In *Trianon*, edited by Miklós Zeidler, 843–845. Budapest: Osiris, 2008.

Lorman, Thomas. *The Making of the Slovak People's Party: Religion, Nationalism and the Culture War in Early 20th-Century Europe.* London: Bloomsbury Academic, 2019.

Lővei, Pál. "Székesfehérvár, Romkert—1936–1938" [Székesfehérvár, Ruin Garden]. *Építés—Építészettudomány* 29, no. 3–4 (2001): 379–388.

Markója, Csilla. "'Vörös posztó': Városinstalláció 1919. május 1-én a források tükrében" [Seeing red: The urban installation on May 1, 1919, in the light of the sources]. *Enigma* 94, no. 25 (2018): 147–215.

McGlynn, Jade. *Memory Makers: The Politics of the Past in Putin's Russia.* London: Bloomsbury Academic, 2023.

Mevius, Martin. *Agents of Moscow: The Hungarian Communist Party and the Origins of Socialist Patriotism 1941–1953.* Oxford: Oxford University Press, 2005.

Mevius, Martin. "Reappraising Communism and Nationalism." *Nationalities Papers* 37, no. 4 (2009): 377–400.

Mikó, Árpád, and Katalin Sinkó, eds. *Történelem-kép: Szemelvények múlt és művészet kapcsolatából Magyarországon* [History–image: Examples of the relationship between past and art in Hungary]. Budapest: Hungarian National Gallery, 2000.

Molnos, Péter. *Aba-Novák.* Budapest: Kieselbach, 2006.

Molnos, Péter. "Aba-Novák Vilmos falképtervei a székesfehérvári Szent István-mauzóleumhoz" [VAN's designs for the murals of Saint Stephen's Mausoleum]. In *István a szent király: Tanulmánykötet és kiállítási katalógus Szent István tiszteletéről halálának 975. évfordulóján* [Stephen the Holy King: Essay collection and exhibition catalogue on the veneration of Saint Stephen on the

975th anniversary of his death], edited by Terézia Kerny and András Smohay, 221–230. Székesfehérvár: Diocesean Museum, 2013.

Molnos, Péter. *Derkovits: Szemben a világgal* [Derkovits: Facing the world]. Budapest: Népszabadság and Kieselbach, 2008.

Murádin, Jenő. *Az aradi Szabadság-szobor* [The Statue of Liberty in Arad]. Cluj-Napoca: Glória Kiadó, 2003.

Nagy, Zsolt. *Great Expectations and Interwar Realities: Hungarian Cultural Diplomacy 1918–1941*. Budapest: Central European University Press, 2017.

Németh, Péter. "Ferenczy Noémi gobelinje Nyíregyházán" [NF's Gobelin in Nyíregyháza]. In *Szent István emlékezete falikárpitokon 1938–2000* [The memory of St. Stephen in tapestries], edited by István Zombori, 29–33. Szeged: Móra Ferenc Museum, 2001.

Noever, Peter, ed. *Mihály Bíró: Pathos in Rot*. Vienna: MAK, 2010.

Nora, Pierre. "Between Memory and History: Les Lieux de Mémoire." *Representations* 26 (1989): 7–24.

Nora, Pierre. "Preface to English Language Edition: From *Lieux de memoire* to Realms of Memory." In *Realms of Memory: Rethinking the French Past*, edited by Pierre Nora, English edition edited by Lawrence D. Kritzman, translated by Arthur Goldhammer, vol. 1, xv–xxiv. New York: Columbia University Press, 1996.

Nordman, Daniel. "From the Boundaries of the State to National Borders." In *Rethinking France: Les Lieux de mémoire*, edited by Pierre Nora, vol. 1, *The State*, 105–132. Chicago: University of Chicago Press, 2001.

Olick, Jeffrey. "From Collective Memory to the Sociology of Mnemonic Practices and Products." In *A Companion to Cultural Memory Studies*, edited by Astrid Erll and Ansgar Nünning, 151–162. Berlin: Walter DeGruyter, 2010.

Ólmosi, Zoltán, and András Oross. "Meszeljünk vagy ne? A Magyar Országos Levéltár freskóinak sorsa az ötvenes években" [Whitewash or not? The fate of the frescoes of the Hungarian National Archives in the 1950s]. *ArchivNet* 4, no. 6 (2004). https://www.archivnet.hu/kuriozumok/meszeljunk_vagy_ne.html.

Orzoff, Andrea. "The Husbandman: Tomáš Masaryk's Leader Cult in Interwar Czechoslovakia." *Austrian History Yearbook* 39 (2008): 121–137.

Ostrowski, Florian-Jan. "Thracian Archaeology and National Identity in Communist Bulgaria: The Ideological Pattern of Museum Exhibitions." In *Digging Politics: The Ancient Past and Contested Present in East-Central Europe*, edited by James Koranyi and Emily Hanscam, 45–76. Berlin: Walter de Gruyter, 2023.

Paládi-Kovács, Attila. *Ortutay Gyula*. Budapest: Akadémiai Kiadó, 1991.

Pálosi, Judit. "Ferenczy Noémi művészi és tanári munkásságának eseménytörténete" [The history of NF's work as an artist and educator]. *Ars Hungarica* 13, no. 2 (1985): 181–198.

Pálosi, Judit. "Szent István kárpitok," [Saint Stephen tapestries]. In *Szent István emlékezete falikárpitokon 1938–2000* [The memory of St. Stephen in tapestries], edited by István Zombori, 9–27. Szeged: Móra Ferenc Museum, 2001.

P. Brestyánszky, Ilona. *Kovács Margit*. Budapest: Képzőművészeti Alap and Corvina, 1977.

Pelle, János. "Ortutay Gyula, a helyezkedés nagymestere" [GyO, great master of jockeying for positions]. *HVG online*, June 17, 2021. https://hvg.hu/velemeny/20100617_ortutay_naplo.

Pető, Andrea. "The Illiberal Memory Politics in Hungary." *Journal of Genocide Research* 24, no. 2 (2022): 241–249.

Pleskovics, Viola. "Additions to the History of Hungarian Medieval Royal Centre Rehabilitations in the Interwar Period." *Acta Historiae Artium* 63 (2022): 327–346.

Pleskovics, Viola. "Építőkövek az államalapító korából—Az 1938-as jubileum székesfehérvári romkertje" [Building stones from the time of the founder of the state—The Székesfehérvár Ruin Garden of the 1938 jubilee]. *Építészfórum*, August 20, 2021. Accessed 4 December 2024, https://epiteszforum.hu/kovek-az-allamalapito-korabol--az-1938-as-jubileum-szekesfehervari-romkertje.

Pótó, János. "A Neugebäude helyén: A Szabadság tér és emlékművei" [Replacing the Neugebäude: Freedom Square and its monuments]. *Mozgó Világ* 46, no. 1 (2020): 25–45.

P. Szűcs, Julianna. "A 'Modern' Official Art: The School of Rome." In *A Reader in East-Central-European Modernism 1918–1956*, edited by Beáta Hock, Klara Kemp-Welch, and Jonathan Owen. London: Courtauld Institute of Art, 2019. Accessed 11 November 2024, https://courtauld.ac.uk/research/research-resources/publications/courtauld-books-online/a-reader-in-east-central-european-modernism-1918-1956/20-a-modern-official-art-the-school-of-rome-julianna-p-szucs/.

P. Szűcs, Julianna. *A Római Iskola* [The School of Rome]. Budapest: Corvina, 1987.

Püski, Levente. *A Horthy-korszak parlamentje* [The parliament of the Horthy era]. Budapest: Országház Könyvkiadó, 2021.

Raento, Pauliina, and Stanley D. Brunn. "Picturing a Nation: Finland on Postage Stamps, 1917–2000." *National Identities* 10, no. 1 (2008): 49–75.

Rainer M., János. "Nagy Imre szovjet emigrációban, 1930–1939" [IN in emigration in the Soviet Union]. *Történelmi Szemle* 38, no. 3 (1995): 319–343.

Rákos, Kata. "Művészet és technika a modern életben—Magyar bemutatkozás az 1937-es párizsi világkiállításon" [Art and technology in modern life—Hungarian participation at the 1937 Paris World's Fair]. In *Opus Mixtum I*, edited by Miklós Székely, 104–111. Budapest: CentrArt, 2012.

Rapp, Christian. "Schnelle Neue Alpen. Schnappschüsse der Moderne aus Österreichs Bergen." In *Kampf um die Stadt: Politik, Kunst und Alltag um 1930*, edited by Wolfgang Kos, 122–130. Vienna: Czernin, 2010.

Rapson, Jessica, and Lucy Bond, eds. *The Transcultural Turn: Interrogating Memory Between and Beyond Borders*. Berlin: De Gruyter, 2014.

Reisz, T. Csaba. "Eskü a Vérmezőn" [Oath in the Vérmező]. Magyar Nemzeti Levéltár, May 17, 2013. Accessed 4 December 2024. https://mnl.gov.hu/a_het_dokumentuma/esku_a_vermezon.html.

Reisz, T. Csaba. "Trianon ismeretlen emléke az Országos Levéltár mennyezetén" [An unknown memorial to Trianon on the ceiling of the National Archives]. Magyar Nemzeti Levéltár, June 4, 2019. Accessed 4 December 2024, https://mnl.gov.hu/mnl/ol/hirek/trianon_ismeretlen_emleke_az_orszagos_leveltar_mennyezeten.

Reisz, T. Csaba, ed. *A nemzet levéltára: Fejezetek az Országos Levéltár történetéből* [The archive of the nation: Chapters from the history of the National Archive]. Budapest: Hungarian National Archives, 2023.

Reisz, T. Csaba. *Dudits Andor családja, élete és munkássága* [The family, life, and oeuvre of Andor Dudits], manuscript, sections on the *Oath in the Vérmező* accessed courtesy of the author.

Rigney, Ann. "Plenitude, Scarcity, and the Circulation of Cultural Memory." *Journal of European Studies* 35, no. 1 (2005): 11–28.

Rigney, Ann. "Remembrance as Remaking: Memories of the Nation Revisited." *Nations and Nationalism* 24, no. 2 (2018): 240–257.

Rigney, Ann. "The Dynamics of Remembrance: Texts Between Monumentality and Morphing." In *A Companion to Cultural Memory Studies*, edited by Astrid Erll and Ansgar Nünning, 345–356. Berlin: Walter DeGruyter, 2010.

Róka, Enikő. "A fametszet nagymesterei: Buday György, Gáborjáni Szabó Kálmán, Molnár-C. Pál" [The great masters of the woodcut: György Buday, Kálmán Gáborjáni Szabó, Pál Molnár-C.]. In *A modern magyar fa- és linóleummetszés 1890–1950* [The modern Hungarian wood- and linoleumcut], edited by Enikő Róka, 105–136. Miskolc: Miskolc Gallery, 2005.

Róka, Enikő. "Construction of Continuity: Nationalism and Art in Interwar Hungary." Manuscript. Keynote lecture at "In the Shadow of the Habsburg Empire." ERC CRAACE research group, Moravian Gallery, Brno, September 12–14, 2014.

Romsics, Gergely. *The Memory of the Habsburg Empire in German, Austrian, and Hungarian Right-wing Historiography and Political Thinking, 1918–1941*. Boulder, CO: East European Monographs, 2010.

Romsics, Ignác. *A Horthy-korszak* [The Horthy era]. Budapest: Helikon, 2018.

Romsics, Ignác. *Bethlen István: Politikai életrajz* [IB: Political biography]. Budapest: Helikon, 2019.

Romsics, Ignác. *Clio bűvöletében: Magyar történetírás a 19–20. században—nemzetközi kitekintéssel* [Under the spell of Clio: Hungarian historiography in the 19th and 20th centuries—with an international overview]. Budapest: Osiris, 2011.

Romsics, Ignác. "Hungarian Revisionism in Thought and Action, 1920–1941: Plans, Expectations, Reality." In *Territorial Revisionism and the Allies of Germany in the Second World War: Goals, Expectations, Practices*, edited by Marina Cattaruzza, Stefan Dyroff, and Dieter Langewiesche, 92–101. New York: Berghahn, 2012.

Romsics, Ignác. *István Bethlen: A Great Conservative Statesman of Hungary, 1874–1946*. Boulder, CO: Social Science Monographs, 1995.

Rubel, Alexander. "Dacian Blood: Autochtonous Discourse in Romania during the Interwar Period." In *Digging Politics: The Ancient Past and Contested Present in East-Central Europe*, edited by James Koranyi and Emily Hanscam, 257–286. Berlin: Walter de Gruyter, 2023.

Schenk, Frithjhof Benjamin. "Mental Maps: The Cognitive Mapping of the Continent as an Object of Research of European History." *European History Online* (EGO), July 8, 2013. http://www.ieg-ego.eu/schenkf-2013-en.

Sears, Małgorzata. *The Warsaw Group Rytm (1922–1933) and Modernist Classicism*. Kraków: Universitas, 2022.

Secklehner, Julia. "A New Austrian Regionalism: Alfons Walde and Austrian Identity in Painting after 1918." *Austrian History Yearbook* 52 (2021): 201–226.

Secklehner, Julia. "Artwork of the Month, December 2021: Židovská Street III (1935–36) by Imrich Weiner-Král'." *CRAACE blog*. Accessed 1 December 2024, https://doi.org/10.17605/OSF.IO/KGAZH.

Seegel, Steven. *Map Men: Transnational Lives and Deaths of Geographers in the Making of East Central Europe*. Chicago: Chicago University Press, 2018.

Seidl, Ambrus. "Szent Imre kultusza a budapesti Szentimrevárosban" [The cult of Saint Emeric in Saint Emeric's Town, Budapest]. In *Szent Imre 1000 éve: Tanulmányok Szent Imre tiszteletére születésének ezredik évfordulója alkalmából* [1,000 years of Saint Emeric: Essays in honor of Saint Emeric on the thousandth anniversary of his birth], edited by Terézia Kerny, 185–190. Székesfehérvár: Székesfehérvár Diocesan Museum, 2007.

Siklós, András. *Magyarország 1918/1919: Események/Képek/Dokumentumok* [Hungary 1918/1919: Events, images, documents]. Budapest: Kossuth, 1978.

Sinkó, Katalin. "A művészi siker anatómiája 1840–1900" [The anatomy of artistic success, 1840–1900]. In *Aranyérmek, ezüstkoszorúk: Művészkultusz és műpártolás Magyarországon a 19. században* [Gold medals, silver wreaths: The cult of artists and the patronage of art in nineteenth-century Hungary], edited by Katalin Sinkó, 15–47. Budapest: Hungarian National Gallery, 1995.

Sinkó, Katalin. "Árpád versus Saint István: Competing Heroes and Competing Interests in the Representation of Hungarian History." *Ethnologia Europeana* 19, no. 1 (1988): 67–84.

Sinkó, Katalin. "The Offended Hungária." In *War of Memories: A Guide to Hungarian Memory Politics*, edited by Dóra Hegyi, Zsuzsa László, and Zsóka Leposa, 13–38. Budapest: tranzit.hu, 2015.

Sinor, Denis. "Western Information on the Kitans and Some Related Questions." *Journal of the American Oriental Society* 115, no. 2 (1995): 262–269.

Sipos, Péter. *Legális és illegális munkásmozgalom (1919–1944)* [The legal and illegal workers' movement]. Budapest: Gondolat, 1988.

Smith, Jeremy. *The Bolsheviks and the National Question, 1917–23*. Houndmills, UK: Macmillan, 1999.

Srnenská, Dagmar, and Alma Münzová. *Imro Weiner-Král'*. Bratislava: Petrus, 2001.

Standeisky, Éva. "Appropriations: Derkovits in Times of Change." In *Derkovits: The Artist and His Times*, edited by Katalin Bakos and András Zwickl, 122–135. Budapest: Hungarian National Gallery, 2014.

Stirton, Paul. "Public Sculpture in Cluj/Kolozsvár: Identity, Space and Politics." In: *Heritage, Ideology, and Identity in Central and Eastern Europe: Contested Pasts, Contested Presents*, edited by Matthew Rampley, 41–66. Woodbridge: Boydell & Brewer, 2012.

Suny, Ronald Grigor. *The Revenge of the Past: Nationalism, Revolution, and the Collapse of the Soviet Union*. Stanford, CA: Stanford University Press, 1993.

S. Varga, Pál, Orsolya Száraz, and Miklós Takács, eds. *A magyar emlékezethelyek kutatásának elméleti és módszertani alapjai* [Researching sites of memory in Hungary: Theory and methodology]. Debrecen: Debrecen University Press, 2013.

Szabó, Ildikó. *Nemzet és szocializáció: A politika szerepe az identitások formálódásában Magyarországon, 1867–2006* [Nation and socialization: The role of politics in shaping identities in Hungary]. Budapest: L'Harmattan, 2009.

Szabó, Júlia. *A mitikus és a történeti táj* [The mythical and historical landscape]. Budapest: Balassi, 2000.

Szabó, Júlia. "Die Holzschnittfolge '1514' von Gyula Derkovits." *Acta Historiae Artium* 10, no. 1–2 (1964): 171–210.

Szabó, Miklós. "Politikai évfordulók a Horthy-rendszerben" [Political anniversaries in the Horthy regime]. *Világosság* 19, no. 8–9 (1978): 507–516.

Szakács, Béla Zsolt. "Gerevich Tibor (1882–1954)." *Enigma* 13, no. 47 (2006): 179–204.

Szarka, László. "Hungarian National Minority Organizations and the Role of Elites between the Two World Wars: Addenda to the History of Minority Nationalism in Central and Eastern Europe." *Hungarian Historical Review* 2, no. 3 (2013), 413–448.

Szarka, László. "Soknyelvű ország—egynyelvű álom és emlék(mű)." *Új Szó Online*, May 30, 2020. https://ujszo.com/panorama/soknyelvu-orszag-egynyelvu-alom-es-emlekmu.

Szegedy-Maszák, Mihály. "Vérző Magyarország." *Kalligram* 19, no. 4 (2010): 83–96.

Szentesi, Edit. "Birodalmi patriotizmus: Történelemszemlélet, történetírás, történeti publicisztika és történeti témák ábrázolása az Osztrák Császárságban 1828-ig [Imperial patriotism: History writing, historical journalism, and the visual representation of history in the Austrian Empire before 1828]." In *Történelem-kép: Szemelvények múlt és művészet kapcsolatából Magyarországon* [History–image: Examples of the relationship between past and art in Hungary], edited by Árpád Mikó and Katalin Sinkó, 73–91, summary in German: 779–781. Budapest: Hungarian National Gallery, 2000.

Szeredi, Merse Pál. "A 'Mácastílus irodalmi diktátora Lukács György sznob uszályában': Az Aktivisták a Tanácsköztársaságban" ["The literary dictator of Máca style in the snobbish entourage of György Lukács": The activists in the Soviet Republic]. *Enigma* 94, no. 25 (2018): 128–146.

Szücs, György. "'Pictura irredenta': Egy Csók István-kép elemzése" [Unredeemed painting: Analysis of a painting by István Csók]. In *A Magyar Nemzeti Galéria Évkönyve / Annales of the Hungarian National Gallery 1997–2001*, edited by Erzsébet Király and Anna Jávor, 297–305. Budapest: Hungarian National Gallery, 2002.

Tancer, Jozef. "Die Geburt Bratislavas auf den Seiten der lokalen Stadtführer 1918–1945." In *Zwischen Exotik und Vertrautem: Zum Tourismus in der Habsburgermonarchie und ihren Nachfolgestaaten*, edited by Peter Stachel and Martina Thomsen, 221–232. Bielefeld: transcript Verlag, 2014.

Thorstensen, Erik. "The Places of Memory in a Square of Monuments: Conceptions of Past, Freedom and History at Szabadság Tér." *AHEA* 5 (2012). http://ahea.net/e-journal/volume-5-2012.

Tomka, Béla. "A Horthy-korszak társadalom- és gazdaságtörténetének kutatása: Újabb eredmények és viták" [The study of the social and economic history of the Horthy era: New results and debates]. In *A Horthy-korszak vitatott kérdései* [Debated issues of the Horthy era], 17–32. Budapest: Kossuth Kiadó, 2020.

Tóth, Attila. "'Egy új, tisztultabb élet felé': A Hősök kapuja építészeti és helytörténeti jelentősége" ["Toward a new, purer life": The significance of the Gate of Heroes in architectural and local history]. *Szeged*, October 2000, 18–22.

Tóth, Attila. "Mit rejt a vakolat? A Hősök kapuja freskóiról" [What is hidden under the lime? On the frescoes of the Gate of Heroes]. *Szeged*, March 1993.

Tóth, Sándor. "A 11. századi magyarországi kőornamentika időrendjéhez" [On the chronology of eleventh-century stone ornament in Hungary].

In *Pannonia Regia: Művészet a Dunántúlon 1000–1541* [Art in Western Hungary], edited by Árpád Mikó and Imre Takács, 54–62. Budapest: Hungarian National Gallery, 1994.

Tóth, Sándor. "A székesfehérvári szarkofág és köre" [The Székesfehérvár sarcophagus and its circle]. In *Pannonia Regia: Művészet a Dunántúlon 1000–1541* [Art in Western Hungary], edited by Árpád Mikó and Imre Takács, 82–86. Budapest: Hungarian National Gallery, 1994.

Trigger, Bruce G. "Romanticism, Nationalism, and Archaeology." In *Nationalism, Politics, and the Practice of Archaeology*, edited by Philip L. Kohl and Clare Fawcett, 263–279. Cambridge, UK: Cambridge University Press, 1995.

Turbucz, Dávid. *A Horthy-kultusz 1919–1944* [The Horthy cult]. Budapest: Research Centre for the Humanities, 2016.

Turda, Marius. "From Craniology to Serology: Racial Anthropology in Interwar Hungary and Romania." *Journal of the History of the Behavioral Sciences* 43, no. 4 (2007): 361–377.

Ujváry, Gábor. *"Egy európai formátumú államférfi": Klebelsberg Kuno (1875–1932)* ["A statesman of European stature"]. Budapest: Kronosz Kiadó and Magyar Történelmi Társulat, 2014.

Ujváry, Gábor. "Nem a kard, hanem a kultúra: A Horthy-korszak kulturális politikája." In *A Horthy-korszak vitatott kérdései* [Debated issues of the Horthy regime], 97–112. Budapest: Kossuth, 2020.

Ungváry, Krisztián. *A Horthy-rendszer és antiszemitizmusának mérlege: Diszkrimináció és társadalompolitika Magyarországon 1919–1944* [The Horthy regime and an assessment of its antisemitism: Discrimination and social policy in Hungary]. Budapest: Jelenkor, 2017.

Varga, Bálint. *The Monumental Nation: Magyar Nationalism and Symbolic Politics in Fin-de-siècle Hungary*. New York: Berghahn, 2016.

Vari, Alexander. "Re-territorializing the 'Guilty City': Nationalist and Right-Wing Attempts to Nationalize Budapest during the Interwar Period." *Journal of Contemporary History* 47, no. 4 (2012): 709–733.

Váross, Marian. *Imro Weiner-Král'*. Bratislava: Slovak Fine Arts Fund, 1963.

Verovšek, Peter J. "Collective Memory, Politics, and the Influence of the Past: The Politics of Memory as a Research Paradigm." *Politics, Groups, and Identities* 4, no. 3 (2016): 529–543.

Veszprémi, Nóra. "An Introspective Pantheon: The Picture Gallery of the Hungarian National Museum in the Nineteenth Century." *Journal of the History of Collections* 30, no. 3 (2018): 453–469.

Veszprémi, Nóra. *Fölfújt pipere és költői mámor: Romantika és művészeti közízlés a reformkori Magyarországon* [Overblown makeup and poetic frenzy: Romanticism and popular taste in Hungary c. 1820–1850]. Budapest: L'Harmattan, 2015.

Veszprémi, Nóra. "Sites of Memory and Forgetting: Gyula Derkovits's Woodcuts of the 1514 Peasant War." *Oxford Art Journal* 46, no. 3 (2023): 379–405.

Veszprémi, Nóra. "Tales from Bátorliget." In *George Buday: Surreal Fairy Tales*, edited by Robert Waterhouse, 11–49. Manchester: Baquis, 2022.

Veszprémi, Nóra. "Whose Landscape Is It? Remapping Memory and History in Interwar Central Europe." *Austrian History Yearbook* 52 (2021): 227–252.

Vörös, Boldizsár. *"A múltat végképp eltörölni"? Történelmi személyiségek a magyarországi szociáldemokrata és kommunista propagandában 1890–1919* ["We'll change henceforth the old tradition"? Historical personalities in Hungarian Social Democratic and Communist propaganda]. Budapest: MTA History Research Institute, 2004.

Vörös, Boldizsár. "Károlyi Mihály tér, Marx-szobrok, fehér ló: Budapest szimbolikus elfoglalásai 1918–1919-ben" [Mihály Károlyi Square, statues of Marx, white horse: Symbolic occupations of Budapest in 1918–1919]. In Vörös, *Eszmék, eszközök, hatások: Tanulmányok a magyarországi propagandáról, 1914–1919* [Ideas, devices, influences: Studies on propaganda in Hungary], 139–161. Budapest: MTA Bölcsészettudományi Kutatóközpont, 2018.

Vörös, Boldizsár. "Térfoglalás Budapesten—térfoglalás a történelemben? A Nemzeti Hadsereg budapesti bevonulási ünnepsége 1919. november 16-án" [Occupying space in Budapest—occupying space in history? The celebrations of the Hungarian National Army's entrance into Budapest on November 16, 1919]. In *Ünnep–hétköznap–emlékezet: Társadalom és kultúrtörténet határmesgyéjén*, edited by Cecília Pásztor, 180–190. Salgótarján: Nógrád County Archives, 2002.

Vörös, Boldizsár. "Történelmi hősök, új rendszerek: Emlékszobrok Szovjet-Oroszországban és a Magyarországi Tanácsköztársaságban 1917–1918" [Historical heroes, new regimes: Memorial statues in Soviet Russia and the Hungarian Soviet Republic]. *Mozgó Világ* 24, no. 5 (1998): 85–105.

Waterbury, Myra A. *Between State and Nation: Diaspora Politics and Kin-State Nationalism in Hungary.* New York: Palgrave Macmillan, 2010.

Waterhouse, Robert, ed. *Their Safe Haven: Hungarian Artists in Britain from the 1930s.* Manchester: Baquis, 2018.

Waters, Leslie. *Borders on the Move: Territorial Change and Ethnic Cleansing in the Hungarian-Slovak Borderlands, 1938–1948.* Rochester, NY: University of Rochester Press, 2020.

Werth, Nicolas. "The Soviet State and Peasants." In *The Cambridge History of Communism*, vol. 1, edited by Silvio Pons and Stephen A. Smith, 399–423. Cambridge, UK: Cambridge University Press, 2017.

Williams, Raymond. "When Was Modernism." In *Art in Modern Culture: An Anthology of Critical Texts*, edited by Francis Frascina and Jonathan Harris, 23–27. London: Phaidon, 1992.

Wingfield, Nancy. *Flag Wars and Stone Saints: How the Bohemian Lands Became Czech.* Cambridge, MA: Harvard University Press, 2007.

Wingfield, Nancy M. "National Sacrifice and Regeneration: Commemorations of the Battle of Zborov in Multinational Czechoslovakia." In *Sacrifice and Rebirth: The Legacy of the Last Habsburg War*, edited by Mark Cornwall and John Paul Newman, 129–150. New York: Berghahn, 2016.

Winter, Jay. *Sites of Memory, Sites of Mourning: The Great War in European Cultural History.* Cambridge, UK: Cambridge University Press, 2014.

Wolff, Larry. *Woodrow Wilson and the Reimagining of Eastern Europe.* Stanford, CA: Stanford University Press, 2020.

Young, James E. "The Counter-Monument: Memory against Itself in Germany Today." *Critical Inquiry* 18, no. 2 (1992): 267–296.

Zahra, Tara. "Against the World: The Collapse of Empire and the Deglobalization of Interwar Austria." *Austrian History Yearbook* 52 (2021): 1–10.

Zeidler, Miklós. *A revíziós gondolat* [The revisionist idea]. Budapest: Osiris, 2001.

Zeidler, Miklós. *Ideas on Territorial Revision in Hungary: 1920–1945*. Boulder, CO: Social Science Monographs, 2007.

Zombory, Máté. *Maps of Remembrance: Space, Belonging and Politics of Memory in Eastern Europe*. Budapest: L'Harmattan, 2012.

Zwickl, András. "Between Conservatism and Modernism: Classicisms and Realisms of the 1920s in Central Europe." In *Local Strategies, International Ambitions: Modern Art and Central Europe 1918–1968*, edited by Vojtěch Lahoda, 77–83. Prague: Artefactum, 2006.

Zwickl, András. "Gyula Derkovits and European Art." In *Derkovits: The Artist and His Times*, edited by Katalin Bakos and András Zwickl, 48–61. Budapest: Hungarian National Gallery, 2014.

Zwickl, András, ed. *In the Land of Arcadia: István Szőnyi and His Circle 1918–1928 / Árkádia tájain: Szőnyi István és köre 1918–1928*. Budapest: Hungarian National Gallery, 2001.

Index

Page numbers in italics refer to illustrations.

Aba-Novák, Vilmos, 19, 24, 192, 207;
  Jászszentandrás murals, 153–54, 195;
  Szeged Gate of Heroes murals, 195–98,
  197, 206, 208; Székesfehérvár Medieval
  Ruin Garden murals, 27, 59, 137, 157–64,
  158, *159*, 167, 198, 206, 208
abstract art, 34–35, 161–62
allegories, 82–84, 151, 160
Alps, 105, 118
András, Edit, 211
Andrássy, Gyula, *33*, 44, 210–11
Andrew II (King of Hungary), 148
Antall, József, 209
antisemitism, 12, 47, 57, 86, 88, 115, 123,
  129, 139, 191, 214; anti-Jewish laws, 4,
  13–14, 21, 27, 58, 142
Apponyi, Albert, 44
April Laws of 1848, 41, 175
Arad, Michael, 100
Arad martyrs (6 October 1849), 75–77,
  80–81, 88, 98–99
archaeological research, 59, 136–37, 155–56,
  164–67, 208
Archduke Joseph Sanatorium Association,
  44–45, 173
Árkay, Aladár, 53
Árkay, Bertalan, 53, 157
Árpád, 15–16, 29, 36, 65, 84–85, 90, 91, 171,
  173, 197
Arrow Cross Party, 142, 234n2
art, official: cultural politics and, 136–68;
  dissent and, 23, 45–51, 200. *See also*
  abstract art; commemorative stamps;
  conservatism; cubism; ecclesiastical
  art; film; lithography; modernism;
  murals; photography; postcards;
  posters; printmaking; School of Rome;
  sculptures; surrealism; visual culture;
  woodcuts; *specific artists*
Art College of the Szeged Youth, 124
Artists' Welfare Committee (Hungarian
  Soviet Republic), 71

Association of Hungarian Sailors, 209
Attila, 84
Aulich, Lajos, 80
Austria, 9, 14, 46, 73, 104–5, 123
Austro-Hungarian Compromise (1867), 12,
  78, 174
Austro-Hungarian Monarchy, 34. *See also*
  Habsburg Empire
avant-gardes, artistic, 31, 42, 161–62. *See also*
  montage

Bakhtin, Mikhail, 111
Balaton, Lake, 112
Bálint, György, 181
Bangha, Béla, 191
Bárdi, Sára, 201
baroque, 56, 128, 141, 146, 149, 155
Barrias, Louis-Ernest, 83
Bartoniek, Anna, 23
Bartoniek, Emma, 23
Batthyány, Lajos, 78, 146, 176
Batthyány Sanctuary Lamp, 79–81
Béla III (King of Hungary), 148, 155
Benczúr, Gyula, 172–73
Benjamin, Walter, 5, 32, 152
Berezin, Mabel, 1, 39, 86
Bethlen, Gábor, 149, 206
Bethlen, István, 13–14, 22, 39, 44, 54, 57, 71,
  92, 138, 149, 152, 154, 206
Billig, Michael, 97
Bíró, Mihály, 23, 25; *Horthy* series
  (lithographs), 45–51, *48*, *49*, 67, 206; *Man
  with the Red Hammer*, 46
Bleeding Hungary (literary anthology),
  107–12, *108*, 135, 235n20, 235n22
Blühová, Irena (Irén Blüh), 129
Blum Theses, 183–86
Bohemia, 120
Bratislava, 74, 129–34
Bratislava Castle, 130, 133–34
Braun, Róbert, 179
British Parliament, 47

Brubaker, Rogers, 9
Bubryák, Orsolya, 166
Buda Castle, 114, 142, 157
Budaörs, Battle of, 43
Budapest: electric illumination of, *55*,
    55–56, 63–64, 67; Horthy's procession
    into (1919), 11, 13, 24, 29–32, 35–39, *37*,
    41, 56, 67, 103, *104*, 172–73; May Day
    celebrations (1919), 24, 29, 33–36, *35*, 38,
    41, 46, 179, 202; modernity of, 32, 64; as
    "sinful city," 25, 52, 56–57, 67, 89, 123,
    175, 191, 194; street names, 89, 99; as
    tourist destination, 56, 63–64
Buda Royal Palace, 88, 172, 211
Buday, Árpád, 124
Buday, György (George), 106, 124–28, *125*,
    191, 214–15; *Little Books*, 128; *Sekler Folk
    Ballads*, 125; *Tales from Bátorliget*, 124–26,
    125, 128
Bukharin, Nikolai Ivanovich, 150
Bulgaria, 76, 136
Bush, George, 99
Byzantine art, 59, 153, 166, 196

Calvinists, 16, 175
capitalism, 18, 21, 34, 88, 169, 187
Carpathians, 117–18
castles, 25–26, 102, *108*, 108–11, 116, *122*,
    122–23, 130–35, 145
Catholic Church, 15–16, 57–58, 62, 67, 175.
    See also Christian Hungary
censorship, 4, 14, 17, 98, 153, 215
Central Europe: change of borders at
    Paris Peace Conferences, 7–10, 70, 100;
    collective mental maps, 135; tourism and
    national space, 104–5. See also *specific
    countries*
Chalupka, Samo, 120
Charles IV (King of Hungary), 13, 43
Christian Hungary, 13, 15, 36, 41, 51, 54,
    57–58, 67, 86, 139, 149. *See also* Catholic
    Church
Church of Return (Budapest), 99
Clotilde Palaces (Budapest), 34
Codreanu, Corneliu, 31, 57
collective memory, 10. *See also* historical
    memory; memory politics
commemorative stamps, 59–62, *61*, 160;
    Freedom Square monuments, 94, *94*;
    Hungarian for Hungarian, 97, *97*
Communism, 4–5, 86, 127. *See also*
    Hungarian Communist Party; Hungarian
    Soviet Republic

Communist International (Comintern),
    184–90, 198–99
Communist Party of Germany, 189
conservatism, 20, 23, 45, 52, 75, 106, 112,
    120, 129, 139, 143, 151–53, 207, 211, 213
constructivism, 114–15
consumerism, 62–64
Country Flag Movement, 93–94, 100
Courbet, Gustave, 18
Craig, Edward Gordon, 52
crowds, 31–39. *See also* spectacles
Csaba, Prince, 84
Csánki, Dezső, 143–45
Csernoch, János, 44
cubism, 114, 118, 161–62
cultural diplomacy, 16, 22, 30–31, 138, 211
cultural heritage, 105, 107–12. *See also*
    castles; landscapes; vernacular culture
The Cultural History of Hungary, 178–79
cultural memory: art and, 199; convergence
    of, 79–80; persistent motifs as illusions,
    28; shifts in, 205–17; use of term, 10. *See
    also* historical memory; memory politics
Czakó, Elemér, 60–62
Czechoslovakia, 9, 78, 129; attacks on
    Hungary, 11, 33; battles against Habsburg
    Empire, 92–93; commemoration
    of First World War, 194; German
    partitioning of, 14; historical landscapes,
    25–26; Hungarian territory allocated
    to, 73; modernity, 130, 190; national
    identity, 5, 120, 130; national space, 105;
    regionalism, 132

Danube (Duna) River, 102, 116–18, 131
Darvas, Lili, 52
Daumier, Honoré, 49
Deák, Ferenc, 174
Dercsényi, Dezső, 156–57, 160–61, 164,
    166, 168
Derkovits, Gyula, 207–8; *1514* (woodcut
    series), 19, 27, 169–71, *170*, 179–93, *182*,
    185, 202, 213–15; placard for workers'
    demonstration (1930), *189*
Derkovits, Jenő, 180–81
Derkovits, Viktória, 179–81, 199
Dévény/Devín, 74, 94, 130–33
Dinarians, 118
Diósgyőr castle, 145
"Dismembered Hungary," 74–76, 79, 92,
    105, 116, 138
Dix, Otto, 46
Dollfuß, Engelbert, 174, 197

Domanovszky, György, 178
Domanovszky, Sándor, 175, 178
Donáth, Gyula, 88
Dorsch, Michael, 83
Dózsa, György, 169–70, 178–79, 191–92, 202
Dózsa-Farkas, András, 99
Dudits, Andor, 24, 27, 207; *Antal Grassalkovich with András Mayerhoffer, 147*; *The Collapse*, 150–52, 206; *The Golden Bull, 148*; National Archives murals, 137, 143–52, *147, 148,* 162; *Oath in the Vérmező, 40,* 40–45, 67, 143, 173, 197
Duša, Ferdiš, 106; *Down the Váh,* 119–23, *121, 122,* 135, 192

Easter, 87–88, 98–99
ecclesiastical art, 38, 41, 53, 56, 191–92
education, 146–48, 164, 171–75, 178–79, 209–11
Elek, Artúr, 192
Elizabeth Bridge (Budapest), 34
Előre (Forward), 98
Emeric, Saint, 54–57
émigré artists, 22–23, 45, 98
Engelbert, Saint, 174
Engels, Friedrich, 182, 188
Entente, 47, 78
Eötvös, József, 179
Erdei, Ferenc, 20–21, 215
Ernst Museum, 169, 181
Érsekújvár/Nové Zámky, 117
ethnic minorities, 9, 15, 25, 65, 109, 111–12, 141–42
ethnonationalism, 65, 74, 85, 93
expressionism, 112–13, 183, 192

Falguière, Jean-Alexandre-Joseph, 83
Falus, Elek, 34
Fascism: crowds and, 39; ideal fatherland, 231n43; modernity and, 19, 30–32, 56–57, 157. *See also* Italy; Nazi Germany
Fatra mountains, 118, 125
Fedics, Mihály, 126
Feischmidt, Margit, 209
Ferenczy, Károly, 64
Ferenczy, Noémi, 4, 23, 64; *Saint Stephen Tapestry,* 64–66, *65,* 212–13
Fidesz government, 209–10
Fifteen Years War (1591–1606), 102, 115
film, 41–42, 44, 46–47
Fischer, Joseph, 110–12, 119, 121, 128
Fogu, Claudio, 30, 177

For the Freedom of Art (exhibition), 200–201
France: monuments to defeat, 82–83, 85; Orphism, 162
Franz Joseph, Emperor, 171
Frederick I Barbarossa, 76, 93
Freedom Square (Budapest): commemoration of Trianon, 73, 80, 88, 93, 99–100; history of, 73, 77–79, 87–88; memory of 1848 and, 175; monuments of, 99, 105, 206, 209–11 (see also *Irredentist Sculpture Group; Reliquary Country Flag*); Monument to German Occupation, 211; rituals performed in, 86–89. *See also* spectacles
Friedrich, István, 38, 44
Fülek/Fil'akovo castle, 116
Fülep, Lajos, 24, 167
Fulla, Ľudovít, 190
Füredi, Richárd, 90
Futó, Tibor, 154

Garibaldi, Giuseppe, 177–78, 203
Gate of Heroes (Szeged), 154, *195,* 195–98
Geistesgeschichte, 140–41, 167
Gellért Hill (Budapest), *33, 36, 63*
Gentile, Emilio, 31
Gerard, Saint, *33,* 36
Gerevich, Tibor, 20, 56, 152–56, 160–61, 164, 166–68
German Peasants' War (1524–1525), 169, 182–83, 188
Germany: archaeology and, 137; historical irredentism, 76–77; historiography, 140; Holocaust memorials, 96; national space, 104. *See also* Nazi Germany
Geyer, Martin H., 77
Géza, Prince, 154
Giant Mountains, 104
Gödöllő mansion, 146, *147,* 149–50
Gömbös, Gyula, 14, 39, 44, 57, 154
Gönczi-Gebhardt, Tibor, *55,* 55–56
Göttler, Lászlóné, 96
Goya, Francisco, 48–49
Grassalkovich, Antal, 146, *147,* 149
Great Depression, 14, 54, 95, 154
Greater Hungary, 7–8, 15, 52–53, 75–76, 80; as organic whole, 77–81, 90–93, 107, 145, 158; tripartitioned in the sixteenth century, 17, 51, 116
Great Moravia, 120, 129–31
Greece, 76
Griffin, Roger, 3, 19, 30
Group of Socialist Artists, 198, 200

Guilleaume, Émile, 99
Gyáni, Gábor, 21

Habsburg, Joseph, 146
Habsburg, Rudolf, 171
Habsburg Empire: Catholic Church and,
175; collapse of, 10–11, 13, 134, 140,
171, 205; legitimism, 43; museums,
108; negative views of, 78, 146, 174–75;
positive views of, 16, 27, 139, 141–42,
174; rebellion against, 12–13, 198–99 (*see
also* Hungarian Revolution and War of
Independence)
Hadik, András, 146
Hadúr, 84, 88–89
Haller, István, 71
Hamburger, Mrs., 48, 226n66
Hampel, József, 165
Haranghy, Jenő, 117, *117*
Hargita (Harghita) Mountains, 89
Háy, Károly László, 198–203, *200*, *201*
Hegedűs, László, 172–73
Héjjas, Iván, 48
Henszlmann, Imre, 165
Herberstein, Sigismund von, 114–15
Hermann (Arminius), 77
heroes, 169–78, 193–98; pantheons of, 27,
170–71, 174–75, 178–79, 188, 193–94, 200,
202–3
Heroes' Square (Budapest), 16, 85, 194
Hevesi, Sándor, 52
historical landscape genre, 105–6, 109, 124,
134–135
historical memory, 1–3; political agency
and, 6; research and, 164 (*see also*
scholarship); use of term, 10. *See also*
memory politics
historicism: as artistic mode of
representation, 3, 19, 30, 33–34, 51–52,
54–56, *55*, 67, 142–43, 173, 210–11; as
historiographical methodology, 139–40
historiography, 136–42, 207
history: as linear narrative, 53; presentness
and, 42, 51, 53, 57, 67; as uncontested
truth, 152, 160
history painting. *See* painting
Hock, János, 150–51
Hofbauer, János (Johann), 131
Holocaust, 4, 58, 89, 96, 99, 210
Holubec, Stanislav, 104
Holy Crown Association, 208–9
Holy Right Hand, 157–58, *158*; procession,
58–59, 63

Holy Roman Empire, 76
Hóman, Bálint, 27, 59, 139, 141–42, 158, 164
Hormayr, Joseph, 110–11
Horthy, Miklós: as constitutional monarch,
13, 43, 197; cult of, 36–38, 154, 171,
173–75, 197–98, 202–3; Kossuth as
prefiguration of, 176–77, 200; oath
in Vérmező, 39–45, 67; procession
into Budapest (1919), 11, 13, 24,
29–32, 35–39, *37*, 41, 56, 67, 103, *104*,
172–73; as redeemer, 15, *36–38*, 196–97;
representations of, 17, 43–44, 97, 99, *159*,
160–61, 172, 201
Horthy regime, 2–3; antiliberalism, 13;
authoritarianism, 4, 27–28, 66, 216;
Christian nationalism, 13, 15, 58 (*see
also* Christian Hungary); conservatism
of, 2–4, 30, 36, 57; dissemination of
ideology, 25, 32, 44–46, 59–62, 67, 94;
ideology of, 5, 19, 24–27, 95, 137, 215;
masculine culture of, 23, 83–84, 97;
memory politics, 8–18, 21, 45, 66–68,
79, 144, 149, 171, 173, 175, 194, 198,
203; modernity and, 3, 32, 66–68; as
neobaroque, 30, 56, 67, 142, 173, 212;
opposition to, 17, 27, 45, 141 (*see also*
left-wing politics); political elite, 44; post-
1989 discussion of, 208–12; regeneration
ideology, 31, *36*, 56–57, 68; Second World
War and, 58; White Terror and, 45–51.
See also historicism
Horvay, János, 175–77, *176*, 207, 211
Hričov castle, 121–23, *122*
Hungarian Academy in Rome, 152, 153
Hungarian Academy of Sciences, 3, 145–46,
167
Hungarian Communist Party (HCP), 11,
14, 17, 21–22, 27, 127–28, 150–51, 169,
179–81, 183–92, 198–200, 202–3, 207,
213–14
Hungarian Cultural Institute (London), 127
Hungarian Democratic Forum (Magyar
Demokrata Fórum, MDF), 208–9
Hungarian Historical Association, 138
Hungarian Historical Memorial
Committee, 198–200
Hungarian History (Hóman and Szekfű), 141
Hungarian minorities (outside of
Hungary), 9, 129, 132, 209–10
Hungarian National Association, 94
Hungarian National Museum, 38–39, 44,
59, 141, 144, 158, 165, 167
Hungarian Pantheon, 143–44

Hungarian People's Republic, 11, 24, 29

Hungarian Red Army, *33*

Hungarian Revolution and War of Independence (1848–1849), 1, 12–13, 17, 41, 51, 75, 78–81, 174–77, 188, 198, 200, 207

Hungarian Royal Crown, 53, 58, 157–60

Hungarian Social Democratic Party, 5, 11, 14, 17, 46, 127, 150–52, 179, 181–83, 239n6

Hungarian Soviet Republic, 11–13; artists in, 71; counterrevolutionary activity during, 194; creation of, 150–51, 183; as destructive event, 103, *104*, 115; fall of, 38, 41, 47; Horthy regime's views on, 31–33, 35–39; left-wing émigré artists, 22–23. *See also* Hungarian Communist Party; Hungarian Social Democratic Party; May Day celebrations

Hungary: belief in cultural superiority of, 14, 109, 112, 138; coat of arms, 118, 125, 144–45, 150, 152; constitutionalism, 39, 51, 148–49, 175; hegemony of ethnic Hungarians, 16, 26, 74, 84, 88, 109, 112, 117–18, 139; national identity, 2–3, 5–8, 11–12, 60–62, 81, 85–89, 98, 100, 177, 190; national symbols, 78, 88, 97, 99, 118; territorial loss, 1–2, 5, 7–9, 11–12, 15, 17, 39, 96 (*see also* "Dismembered Hungary"; Greater Hungary; Hungarian Revolution and War of Independence; irredentism; Mohács, Battle of; Ottoman wars; revisionism; Trianon, Treaty of); tragic narrative of history, 8, 15, 17, 51, 80–82, 103, 177, 205, 216; tripartitioned in sixteenth century, 17, 51, 116. *See also* "Dismembered Hungary"; Greater Hungary

Hunor, 114

Huns, 84, 114

Hunyadi, János, 160, 173, 176, 197

Hus, Jan, 174

Huszár, Adolf, 80

Illuminated Chronicle, 114

Imrédy, Béla, 57

Independent Smallholders, Agrarian Workers, and Civic Party, 127, 214

International Eucharistic Congress, 54, 58, 63

irredentism, 69–70, 76, 103; cultural heritage and, 109, 111–12; as militant, 98, 100; as political religion, 86; resurrection and, 196–97; street names and, 184–85. *See also* irredentist spacetime

Irredentist Sculpture Group, 1–3, 6, 8, 25, 69–74, 76–89, 92–100, 107; imagery in, 82–85; location in Freedom Square, 1–3, 73, 87–89; miniature reproductions of, 94–95, *95*; photographs of, *2*, *72*, *94*

irredentist spacetime, 25, 70–101, 116–17, 145, 185, 202, 206, 209–10

Isabella, Archduchess, 56

Italy: archaeology, 137; ecclesiastical art, 56; Fascism, 1–4, 13–15, 30, 56–57, 86, 157 (*see also* Mussolini, Benito); Garibaldi and, 177–78; Hungary's relations with, 14, 24, 30–31, 54, 90, 92, 154–56; irredentism, 76–77; March on Rome, 30, 39; national identity, 15; regeneration and, 31; Risorgimento, 31, 70, 178; as source of Hungarian art, 155–57, 164–68; spectacles, 24, 30

Jacobins, 41

Jajczay, János, 154, 192

Jánošík, Juraj, 190

Jaroň, K., 119

Jászi, Oszkár, 139

Jászszentandrás, 153–54, 195

Jeges, Ernő, 107–9, 112; *The Castle of Beckó/ Beckov*, 108

Jewish-Christian dichotomy, 21. *See also* antisemitism

Justice for Hungary!, 86, *87*, 109–12, 115, 135

Kákay-Szabó, György, 56

Kállai, Ernő, 46–47, 49, 62, 181

Kallis, Aristotle A., 231n43

Kálti, Márk, 114

Károlyi, Mihály, 11, 14, 29, *37*, 107, 139, 150–51, 211

Kassák, Lajos, 42

Kassa/Košice, 96, 97, 117

Képes Krónika (Illustrated Chronicle), 37, 42

Kertész, K. Róbert, 71, 177, 194

Kiliánová, Gabriela, 239n85

Kingdom of Serbs, Croats, and Slovenes (later Yugoslavia), 9, 73, 184

Kisfaludi Strobl, Zsigmond, 56, 71; Kossuth monument, 207, 211; National Archives of Hungary and, 143–44; *North*, 71, *72*, 83, 84, 86, 97

Kiss, Ernő, 80

Klebelsberg, Kuno, 22, 27, 56, 137–47, 149, 152–54, 164, 174–75, 207

Kölcsey, Ferenc, 80

Kollwitz, Käthe, 169, 183

284   INDEX

Komárom/Komarno, 116
Kościuszko, Tadeusz, 92
Kossuth, Lajos, 17, 139, 146, 161, 175–77,
    176, 193, 200, 207
Kossuth Square (Budapest), 33, 175–77, *176*,
    207, 210–11
Kosztolányi, Dezső, 107
Kovács, Imre, 198–99
Kovács, Margit, 64
Kovács, Mihály, 173
Kralovánszky, Alán, 165–66
Kun, Béla, 11, 150–51, 183–84, 188
Kunfi, Zsigmond, 239n6

Ladislas I (King of Hungary), 158
Ladislas IV (King of Hungary), 114, 171
Landler, Jenő, 181, 183, 185
landscapes, 25–26, 102–35; modernity and,
    134; mountain ranges, 96, 105, 118, 125
    (*see also* Tatras); national territory and,
    103–35; peasantry and, 126–27; plains
    region, 105. *See also* historical landscape
    genre
László, Szabolcs, 100
League of Nations, 91
Le Bon, Gustave, 32, 34
Lechner, Jenő, 71, 90
Le Corbusier, 31
left-wing politics, 21, 35, 98, 127, 202; art
    and, 22–23, 45–51, 170, 192, 200, 208, 212
    (see also *specific artists*); historical heroes,
    179, 188, 193, 200, 202–3; nationalism
    and, 189; progressive, 20–21. *See also*
    Communism
Légrády, Sándor, 60–62, *63*
Légrády Brothers, 109, 112
Lenin, Vladimir, 33–34, *36*, 150, 207
Leopold I, 146
liberal nationalism, 12–13, *35*, 65, 88, 139,
    178
Liebknecht, Karl, *33*, *36*
Ligeti, Antal, 145
Lin, Maya, 100
lithography, 25, 45–51
Lithuania, 77
Lőcse/Levoča/Leutschau, 109
Lőrinc (Franciscan friar), 188
Lőte, Éva, 23, 195–96
Lotz, Károly, 144
Louis I (King of Hungary), 146, 149
Louis II (King of Hungary), 51
Luddites, 188
Lukács, György (Georg), 181, 183–87, 189
Lutz, Carl, *2*, 99

Lux, Géza, 156–57, 160
Lyka, Károly, 109

Madai, Pál, 173–75, 178–79
Madarassy, Walter, 157
Madarász, Adeline, 179
Madarász, Viktor, 179
Magor, 114
Magyarization, 12, 81
Magyars, ancient, 15–16, 74, 84, 144, 157
Mályusz, Elemér, 140, 145
Manderla, Rudolf, 134
Manderlák (Bratislava), 134
Manet, Édouard, 18
Marczali, Henrik, 139
Maria Theresa, Empress, 16, 146–47, 158
Márkus, László, 34, 52, 63
Márton, Ferenc, 39–40, 42–43, 201
Márton, Lajos, 94
Marx, Karl, *33*
Marxism, 182, 187, 190, 215
Masaryk, Tomáš Garrigue, 174
Masereel, Frans, 169, 183
mass production, 25
Matra mountains, 118, 125
Matthias Corvinus, 110, 114, 145, 146, 171,
    172–73, 197
Matthias Corvinus at the Gates of Vienna, *172*,
    172–73
May Day celebrations (1919), 24, 29, 33–36,
    35, 38, 41, 46, 179, 202
Mayerhoffer, András, *147*, 149
Medieval Ruin Garden at Székesfehérvár,
    26–27, 58–59, 137–38, 153, 155–67, *156*,
    158, *159*, *162*, *163*, 171, 206, 208
Mednyánszky, Baron Alajos, 110–11, 119,
    121, 128, 130
Memorial Site of Belonging Together (2020),
    100–101
Memorial Stone of Heroes (Budapest), 194
memory politics, 1–3, 10; aestheticization
    of, 32; development in interwar period,
    24; goals of, 21–22; interpretations of,
    216; memory as process, 10; post-1989
    shifts in, 205–17; scholarship and, 26–27;
    spatiality of memory, 1–2, 6–9, 25–26,
    74–77. *See also* heroes; Horthy regime;
    irredentist spacetime; landscapes;
    Medieval Ruin Garden at Székesfehérvár;
    National Archives of Hungary;
    revolutionaries; spectacles
mental maps, 7–9, 106, 217; transformation
    of, 134–35; Treaty of Trianon and, 7–9,
    81, 100–101

Mercié, Marius-Jean-Antonin, 83
Millennium Monument (Heroes' Square, Budapest), 16, *33*, 85, 194
millennium monuments (1896), 16, 74, 84–85, 88, 109–10, 131–32
Ministry of Religion and Education, 171, 173
modernism, 2–3; authoritarianism and, 66; defined, 18–20; regeneration and, 31; right-wing, 3–4; shifting reception of, 207–8; women artists, 23
modernity, 1–6; defined, 18–21; of Fascism, 19, 30–32, 56–57, 157; historical landscape and, 134 (*see also* landscapes); official politics of interwar Hungary and, 213–17; rupture and, 119
Mohács, Battle of (1526), 17, 51–53, 67, 76, 77, 204–5
Molnár-C., Pál, 191, 201
montage, 106–7, 114, 118–19, 180–81
Monument of the German Occupation (2014), 99
monuments: in meaningful locations, 78; soil used in, 92–93; space and, 8, 70–71. *See also* Gate of Heroes (Szeged); *Irredentist Sculpture Group;* sculptures; *specific monuments*
Moravia. *See* Great Moravia
Móricz, Zsigmond, 139
Munich, artists trained in, 71, *153*
Munich Agreement, 14
Munkács/Mukachevo, 74, 97
Munkás (Worker), 82
murals, 26–27; in Jászszentandrás, 153–54, 195; in National Archives, 26–27, 137–39, 143–50, 160, 167, 206, 208; in Ruin Garden, 27, 59, 137, 157–64, *158*, *159*, 167, 198, 206, 208; in Szeged Gate of Heroes, 195–98, *197*, 206, 208
museums, 108. *See also* Hungarian National Museum
Mussolini, Benito, 2, 4, 13–15, 24, 30–32, 39, 53, 56, 91, *137*, 156, 178, 203, 209

Nádasdy, Ferenc, 146
Nagy, Imre, 188, 211
Nagy, Vince, 151
Nagyvárad/Oradea, 116
National Archives of Hungary: history of, 141–43; murals in, 26–27, 137–39, 143–50, 160, 167, 206, 208
National Army, 13, 35–45, 196
national Bolshevism, 190
national borders: changes to (*see* Trianon, Treaty of; Versailles peace treaties); geographical features and, 116–17
National Commission for Monuments (Hungary), 60, 108, 155, 164
nationalism, Hungarian, 3–4; banal, 63, 73, 95, 97; Christian, 13, 15, 58 (*see also* Christian Hungary); ethnonationalism, 65, 74, 85, 93; left-wing politics and, 189; liberal, 12–13, *35*, 65, 88, 139, 178; neonationalism, 140–41; peasantry and, 106; romantic, 108; tourism and, 104–5
National Propaganda Committee, 107
National Széchényi Library (Budapest), 206
naturalism, 45, 50
nature, 119, 132; national territory and, 103–7. *See also* landscapes
Nazi Germany: "entartete Kunst" (degenerate art), 3–4; Hungarian alliance, 27, 127, 142, 154, 198–99, 201, 214; Japanese alliance, 14; memorial to Frederick Barbarossa, 93. *See also* Vienna Awards
neobaroque, 30, 56, 67, 142, 173, 212
Neumann, Béla, 48
New Building (at Freedom Square), 77–78
New Directions in Hungarian History Writing, 141
New Group of the Association of Hungarian Women Artists, 23
New Objectivity, 56
Nora, Pierre, 70
Nordman, Daniel, 116

Odilo, Father, 154
Oelmacher, Anna, 212–13
Olgyay, Viktor, 112
Opera House (Budapest), 146
Orbán, Viktor, 100, 210–11
Ortutay, Gyula, 124, 126, 214
Ottlik, Géza, *School at the Frontier*, 204–5, 216
Ottoman wars, 17, 51, 80, 102–5, 110, 116, 155, 176–77, 198. *See also* Mohács, Battle of (1526)

painting: history painting, 39–45, 152–54, 173; monumental, 153–54. *See also* murals; *specific artists*
Pálóczy, Antal, 78
Paris Peace Conference, 13. *See also* Trianon, Treaty of; Versailles peace treaties
Pásztor, Árpád, 132
Pásztor, János, *East*, 71, *72*, 83–84
Paul Eremite, Saint, 149
Pázmány, Péter, 146

peasantry, 22, 106, 120–28; 1514 uprising, 169, 178–87, 202; populist movement and, 214–15; working class and, 187–90
Pécs, 52–53
Pécs Socialist Party, 82
Pecz, Samu, 142–43
Pekár, Gyula, 79, 81
Peter I (King of Hungary), 166
Petőfi, Sándor, 146
Petten, Sándor, 97
photography, 46–47, 63; as documentation, 42; public rituals and, 38, 41–42
Piłsudski, József, 174
Pleskovics, Viola, 243n73
Pogány, Móric, 79, 195
Poland, 77, 92–93, 104
politics: crowds and, 31–39; relationship with scholarship and art, 136–68. *See also* Habsburg Empire; Horthy regime; Hungarian Soviet Republic; left-wing politics; memory politics; right-wing politics; Trianon, Treaty of
populist movement, 123–28, 164, 191, 202, 214–15
Pór, Bertalan, 129
positivism, 139, 148
postage stamps. *See* commemorative stamps
postcards, 50–51
posters, 54–56, *117*, 134–35
Pozsony/Prešporok/Pressburg, 96, 117, 129, 155. *See also* Bratislava
Pradier, James, 83
Prague, 120, 128–29; Prague Spring, 251n22
printmaking, 112, 134–35, 192; narrative series, 169, 190. *See also* lithography; woodcuts
Prohászka, Ottokár, 44
Pro Hungaria Women's World Association of the Hungarian National Association, 23, 94–95
Protestants, 16–17, 175
P. Szűcs, Julianna, 161
public rituals, *35. See also* spectacles

racial purity, 191, 214
racism, 27, 142
Raffay, Ernő, 209
Rajk, Endre, 234n2
Rajk, Gyula, 102, 234n2
Rajk, László, 234n2
Rákóczi, Francis II, 12, 17, 146, 160–61, 171, 200–201

Rákosi, Jenő, 44
Ranke, Leopold von, 139
Ratio Educationis (1777), 146–48
reality effect, 25, *32,* 42–43, 45, 50
rebellion, 27, 169–71, 193, 198–202, 216; peasant uprising (1514), 169, 178–87, 202. *See also* Hungarian Revolution and War of Independence (1848–1849)
Red Terror, 11
regeneration, 19–20; art world and, 153; Horthy regime and, 31, 36, 56–57, 68; landscape and, 106, 134; modernity and, 119; peasant culture and, 123–28; youth and, 56–57
Reliquary Country Flag, 90–93, *91, 96, 99,* 118, 208–9
Rembrandt, 112
renewal, 31, 56
resurrection, 19, 53, 97; irredentism and, 86–88, 98; as modernism, 31; Saint Stephen Jubilee and, 59
Révai, József, 181, 186, 198–99, 202
revisionism, 14, 54, 69–70, 76, 90, 96, 98, 138, 184, 186, 190, 194
revolutionaries, 146, 174–78. *See also* Hungarian Communist Party (HCP)
Revolution of 1848. *See* Hungarian Revolution and War of Independence (1848–1849)
Revolution of 1956, 205
right-wing politics, 21, 57–58, 88, 191–92, 202; countryside and, 123; modernity and, 27, 211–12; peasantry and, 106. *See also* Fascism; Horthy regime; irredentism
Rigney, Ann, 8, 79–80, 89
Říp Mountain, 105
Risorgimento, 31, 70, 178
Ritter, William, 119–20
rococo, 149
Roman Empire, 15, 137
Romanesque style, 59, 144, 155–57, 165
Romania, 9; Arad monument and, 75, 80–81; attacks on Hungary, 11, 33; commemoration of First World War, 194; Dacians and, 136; Hungarian territory allocated to, 73, 184; Legion of the Archangel Michael, 57; regeneration and, 31; traditionalism, 123
Rome Scholarship, 56, 59, 152–54, 157
Róth, Miksa, 143–44
Rothermere, Lord (Harold Sidney Harmsworth), 90–92

Saint Emeric Jubilee (1930), 54–58, 63, 67
Saint Martin's Cathedral (Bratislava), 134
Saint Stephen Jubilee (1938), 4, 15, 27, 57–68, 154–55, 160, 164–65, 198, 229n115. *See also* Medieval Ruin Garden at Székesfehérvár
Saint Stephen sarcophagus, *163*, 165–67
Saint Stephen's Cathedral (Budapest), 86
Saint Stephen's Day, 16, 63, 88
Saint Stephen's Mausoleum (Székesfehérvár), 155–57, *156*, *159*, 165, 167, 206
satire, 49–50, 130, 203
Schatz, Otto Rudolf, 190
Schedel, Hartmann, 114
scholarship: memory politics and, 26–27; relationship with politics and art, 136–68. *See also* archaeological research
Schönherz, Zoltán, 199–200, 202
School of Rome, 20, 22, 153–54, 157, 191, 207
sculptures: miniature reproductions of, 2, 25, 62, 94–96, 99–100, 206, 209. See also *Irredentist Sculpture Group*; monuments; *specific artists*
serfs. *See* peasantry
Sidló, Ferenc: National Archives of Hungary and, 143–44; *Saint Stephen*, 59, *60*, 62, 71, 161; *West*, 71, *72*, 83, 84, 88
Sipőcz, Jenő, 44, 79
Slovakia, 9; multiethnicity, 84, 112; nationalism and cultural heritage, 26, 96, 104–6, 110–11, 119–34; regionalism, 132; Soviet Union and, 251n22; territory reallocated to Hungary, 14, 58, 97
Social Democrats, 190. *See also* Hungarian Social Democratic Party
socialism, 31, 47, 170, 213
Socialist Realism, 207–8
social memory: use of term, 10. *See also* historical memory
Soviet Republic. *See* Hungarian Soviet Republic
Soviet Union, 14, 183, 186–87, 189, 198–99, 201, 251n22
spectacles, 29–32; crowds and, 32–39; Horthy's procession into Budapest (1919), 11, 13, 24, 29–32, 35–39, *37*, 41, 56, 67, 103, *104*, 172–73; May Day celebrations (1919), 24, 29, 33–36, *35*, 38, 41, 46, 179, 202; modernity and, 64–68; Mohács anniversary, 17, 51–53, 67, 76; oath in the Vérmező, 39–45, 51, 67; Saint

Stephen's Day festivities, *63. See also* Saint Emeric Jubilee (1930); Saint Stephen Jubilee (1938)
Stalin, Joseph, 187, 207
stamps. *See* commemorative stamps
Stephen I (Saint Stephen, King of Hungary), 15–16, 54, 58, 110, 144, 146, 148, 154–60, 164; *Admonitions*, 65; in Gate of Heroes mural, 196. *See also* Medieval Ruin Garden at Székesfehérvár; Saint Stephen Jubilee (1938); Saint Stephen's Mausoleum
Strasbourg, 82–83, 85
surrealism, 126, 129, 130, *135*
Suschitzky, Philipp, 46
Svatopluk, 120
Sylvester, Pope, 160
Szabó, Dezső, 123, 214
Szarka, Anita, 206
Szarka, László, 132
Széchenyi, István, 139, 146, 174
Szeged, 194–98
Szeged Youth, 124, 126–28, 214–15
Székesfehérvár, 58, 154–55, 165–66. *See also* Medieval Ruin Garden at Székesfehérvár; Saint Stephen's Mausoleum (Székesfehérvár)
Szekfű, Gyula, 17, 27, 30, 56, 140–41, 146, 149, 174–75; *The Exiled Rákóczi*, 12; *Three Generations*, 12–13, 139, 142
Szentgyörgyi, István, 143; *South*, 71, *72*, 84
Sziszek / Sisak, 116
Szomory, Dezső, *Louis II*, 51–52
Sztehlo, Lili, 23, 27, 137, 153; stained glass window at Ruin Garden, 157, 161–62, *162*, *163*, 167

Tamás of Kolozsvár, 161
Tatras, 104–5, 118, 120, 125
Teleki, Pál, 16
Temes / Timiş, 116
Temesvár / Timişoara, 116, 178
Than, Mór, 144, 145
theater, 51–52
Thurzó, Ferenc, 122
Tisza, István, 139, 211
Tomb of the Unknown Soldier (Bucharest), 194
Tormay, Cécile, 23, *36–38*
Tóth, Sándor, 166
tourism, 62–63; nationalism and, 104–5
Transylvania, 17, 51, 75, 96, 116, 124
Trencsén / Trenčín / Trentschin, 110–11

Trianon, Treaty of: acceptance of, 132, 185–
  86; anti-Trianon activism (*see* irredentism;
  revisionism); ban on official campaigning
  against, 79; blamed on liberal political
  elite, 10–11, 139; collective memory and
  mental maps, 7–9, 81, 100–101; historical
  context, 51; Horthy regime and, 19;
  Hungarian territorial loss, 1–2, 4–6, 11,
  69; landscape images and, 125–26; liberal
  nationalism and, 12–13; memories of
  1848–1849 and, 79–80, 88; Mohács and,
  51, 53; monuments to, 194; myths about,
  118; as national catastrophe, 5, 103;
  pain and suffering, 85, 177; post-1989
  discussion of, 208–10; prefiguration of,
  17; relocation caused by, 69; working
  class and, 186. *See also* "Dismembered
  Hungary"
Tripartitum manual of laws, 178–79, 192
Turanism, 16, 59, 62, 139, 155, 210, 211
Turan Society, 16
Turin Peace Treaty, 149
Turkish Wars, 129. *See also* Ottoman wars
turul (mythical Hungarian bird), 84, 88,
  90, 132
Turul Association, 88–89

Uitz, Béla, 188
Ukraine, 6, 187, 210
Union of Defensive Leagues, 39, 42, 44,
  69–71, 85, 94
United States, 46, 60
University of Kolozsvár/Cluj, 194–96
urban modernity, 18, 20, 22, 25, 32, 52, 64,
  86, 98–99, 123–24, 180
Urmánczy, Nándor, 44, 69, 82, 90
Ürményi, József, 146–47

Váh/Vág/Waag River, 110–11
Vajdahunyad/Hunedoara castle, 145
Varga, Nándor Lajos, 19; *Hungarian Past*, 26,
  102–6, *103, 104*, 112–19, *113*, 135, 191–92,
  193
Vari, Alexander, 64
Varjú, Elemér, 165–66
Vécsey, Károly, 80
vernacular culture, 20, 119, 126, 160–62,
  190, 215

Versailles peace treaties, 1, 4, 11, 70–71, 82,
  104, 118, 140, 185
Vienna, 12, 22–23, 46–50, 71, 114, 171–72,
  180–88
Vienna Awards, 27; First (1938), 14, 58, 97,
  197; Second, 208
Virgin Mary, 62, 86
visual culture, 1–6, 20. *See also* art;
  spectacles
Vítkov National Monument (Prague), 78
Voinovich, Géza, *Mohács*, 51–52

Wälder, Gyula, 56
War of Independence. *See* Hungarian
  Revolution and War of Independence
  (1848–1849)
Waterbury, Myra, 210
Wedgwood, Josiah (British Member of
  Parliament), 47
Weiner-Král', Imro/Imre, 26, 128–29;
  Bratislava, 129–35, *131, 133*
Werbőczy, István, 178, 182
White Mountain, Battle of, 93
White Terror, 13, 25, 45–51, 206
Wingfield, Nancy, 93
women: artists, 23, 64; imagery of, 82–84
woodcuts, 112–13, 134, 181–83, 192
working class, 186–90
World War, First: end of (*see* Trianon,
  Treaty of; Versailles peace treaties);
  heroes of, 194; modernization and, 5;
  monuments to, 93, 194
World War, Second, 14, 27, 198, 201–3;
  Horthy regime and, 58. *See also*
  Holocaust

You Have Taken Our Rivers (poster), 125, 135
Young, James E., 8, 70, 96
youth: and regeneration, 56–57. *See also*
  Szeged Youth

Zadravecz, István, 44, 69
Zakopane, 104
Zala, György, 33, 80
Zborov, Battle of, 92–93
Žižka, Jan, 78
Zrínyi, Miklós, 146, 171, 199–200, *200*, 202